ABOUT THE EDITORS

Quentin Beresford

Professor Quentin Beresford is the author/co-author of ten books including several on Aboriginal affairs. These include *Rites of Passage: Aboriginal Youth Crime and Justice* (1996); *Our State of Mind: Racial Planning and the Stolen Generations* (1998) and the multi-award winning biography of Aboriginal leader Rob Riley, *Rob Riley: An Aboriginal Leader's Quest for Justice* (2006).

Gary Partington

Professor Gary Partington has conducted extensive research in teaching practices in relation to Aboriginal students. He has edited, authored and co-authored numerous publications in the field, including many research reports and two previous books on Aboriginal education, *Ethnicity and Education* (1992) and *Perspectives on Aboriginal and Torres Strait Islander Education* (1998).

Graeme Gower

Graeme Gower is a descendant of the Yawuru people of Broome and has been involved in Indigenous education for thirty-two years. He is actively involved in the development and delivery of courses both in and outside the university sector to equip future Indigenous leaders and to develop the cultural competence of non-Indigenous undergraduates and professionals. He is also actively involved in research in Aboriginal education.

Reform and Resistance in Aboriginal Education

Fully Revised Edition

Edited by
Quentin Beresford
Gary Partington
& Graeme Gower

UWA PUBLISHING

First published in 2003 by UWA Press
Revised edition published in 2012 by UWA Publishing
Crawley, Western Australia 6009
www.uwap.uwa.edu.au

UWAP is an imprint of UWA Publishing
a division of The University of Western Australia

THE UNIVERSITY OF
WESTERN AUSTRALIA
Achieve International Excellence

National Library of Australia
Cataloguing-in-Publication data:

Reform and resistance in aboriginal education / Quentin Beresford, Gary Partington and Graeme Gower.
Revised ed.
ISBN: 9781742583891 (pbk.)
Includes bibliographical references and index.
371.8299915

Cover photograph by Sonja Porter
Typeset by J&M Typesetting
Printed by Griffin Press

CONTENTS

PREFACE

Since the first edition of *Reform and Resistance* was published in 2003, significant developments have impacted on the field of Indigenous education. The Howard government's introduction of Shared Responsibility Agreements and the Northern Territory Intervention embodied a focus on education as did the Rudd/Gillard Government's Closing the Gap commitment and the measures to enhance accountability for school performance. In fact, there is now a greater degree of bipartisanship in Indigenous affairs policy than has existed for the past few decades. However, this consensus has overseen a shift away from a so-called 'rights' agenda in Aboriginal affairs to one of focusing on socio-economic outcomes. Not all agree that such a shift will produce the desired outcomes.

Nevertheless, the shift has served to heighten the focus of state and federal governments on the state of education for Indigenous students. This renewed focus has highlighted that progress towards educational equality for Indigenous students continues to be painfully slow, although the new impetus in policy and funding may be a spur to faster progress.

This fully revised edition of *Reform and Resistance* brings together a range of experts from across Australia who draw on their research to examine and reflect on the progress and the challenges in Indigenous education. In setting out the issues, a balance has been struck between research/theory-based perspectives and practitioner-based ones. The combination of the two approaches will best serve the diverse audiences for whom this book is aimed: pre-service teachers, educational administrators and policy makers.

The structure of the book is mainly thematic. Each chapter highlights a critical issue and, as with the last edition, we have taken a broad scope of the historical, cultural, political and pedagogical influences on the education of Indigenous young people. While we have tried to avoid unnecessary duplication of issues, we have encouraged authors to provide whatever context is necessary on a particular topic. The result is a diversity of perspectives on some of the key issues.

We have been conscious, too, of placing as much emphasis as possible on the diversity of Indigenous voices on this important topic. Several of the authors (and one of the editors) are Indigenous and we value their input. But a large body of material exists that embodies Aboriginal perspectives on education and we have tried to give emphasis to this material.

Aboriginal educational disadvantage ranks as one of Australia's most pressing social issues, and it is our hope that this book will encourage debate and contribute to the development of best practice in the field.

Quentin Beresford
Gary Partington
Graeme Gower

ACKNOWLEDGMENTS

This second edition came about at the urging of colleagues at Edith Cowan University, notably Dr Bruce Campbell and our fellow editor, Graeme Gower. The realisation of the work is due to the contribution of the authors, some old, some new, who were willing to turn their extensive research experience in the field into this collection that encompasses the breadth of issues in Aboriginal education.

We thank Samantha Kenny at Edith Cowan University for her willingness to assist at moments of crisis, and Karen Anderson for her forbearance when pressing matters had to be delayed in order to complete the manuscript.

The staff at UWA Publishing have been very supportive from the inception of this second edition. To Kate Pickard and Anne Ryden, for their incisive suggestions regarding writing and content, Emma Smith for organising contracts, Anna Maley-Fadgyas and Sonja Porter for the graphics, and UWAP Director Terri-ann White, our grateful thanks for bringing this book to fruition.

1

BEGINNINGS...LIVING AND LEARNING IN REMOTE ABORIGINAL SCHOOLS

Helen McCarthy

Disclaimer: I wish to advise Aboriginal readers that while pseudonyms have been used, there are stories relating to deceased people in the following section.

I grew up on the wild southern coast of Western Australia where I had the freedom to surf the beaches and roam the open empty spaces, so having to move to Perth to attend university was truly a rude awakening. Clearly it was going to take something special to capture both my spirit and attention to hold me in the city. I studied primary teaching, majoring in Aboriginal Education which enabled me to complete my pre-service teaching practices in remote Aboriginal schools in the Pilbara and Kimberley regions in Western Australia. In addition, every year one of our enclave lecturers would organise awesome field trips to places of Aboriginal significance. Off we would go in the Aboriginal Teacher Education Program bus, all fifteen of us, out east beyond the city to the desert and the ancient ochre caves or down south to the kitchen midden mounds and rock art sites. As a graduate I believed my lecturers had inculcated me well and that my time spent in this rich context allowed me to grow even more deeply respectful of the multifarious Aboriginal ways of being and their attendant knowledge systems. I had steadily developed and gained what I thought was a pragmatic compilation of cultural competencies, but nothing prepared me for what I was bestowed.

William Pinar wrote that our lives and lived experiences are, 'not mere smudges on the mirror' (Pinar 1981, p. 184) but are, in fact, illuminating and the prerequisite for cultivating our capacity to know, explain and facilitate our capability towards transformation. Likewise, William Earle observed that when we write autobiographically, we write to ask, 'what it is for me to exist…Ontological autobiography…is a question of a form of consciousness' (cited in Pinar, 1981, p. 184). To authenticate my knowledge rather than write as an academic, I write this chapter autobiographically in an attempt to allow my consciousness a form to express what I have lived and learned. Doing it in this way has generated a reflexive awareness of better understanding my role as I participated firstly as a neophyte teacher, then as a student of life and then eventually as an educator. The first time I began to reconstruct my teaching experiences, I trawled around in my past, initially feeling shy to write about myself unabridged but was comforted to read, 'understanding of self is not narcissism; it is a precondition and a concomitant condition to the understanding of others. The process of education is not situated – and cannot be understood in the observer, but in we who undergo it' (Pinar 1981, p. 186). And undergo it I did. I got involved. I became what Giroux (1992) calls a 'border crosser'. I became transfixed and transformed: a single white face in a black world what seemed like galaxies away from my home. This is my journey…

My journey to the Other world

My first teaching placement in the 1980s was on an island deep in Arnhem Land in the Northern Territory, renowned for its fierce war-like clans and speakers of Anindilyakwa, considered by linguists one of the most complex languages spoken on earth. Flying onto the island I could see an extensive mine site with a gaping hole in the ground interspersed with a series of tailing dams. A multinational corporation had established the lucrative mine and a township characterised by lavish, spacious elevated homes, luxuriant tropical gardens and superb sporting and social facilities for their 2000 or so staff. Where I lived was diametrically opposed.

Nothing in my town seemed equivalent; not the dusty roads, the dilapidated houses with broken or missing louvers, the smells, the noises, the Aboriginal women brightly clad in their zipper front 'mission' style dresses, the naked children, the campfire lights, the unrelenting humidity of the steamy days and nights. Everything about the daily rhythm of life in my town reeked third world; it was as if I had actually left Australia. And in the midst of this extraordinary vibrant community, I was alone, completely reliant on my ability to learn to live amongst it and make a life of it.

After a sleepless sweltering night I walked to school grateful for the early morning coolness. The school was quaint: an older, double storey structure built from local timbers, with walls of louvres on all sides allowing for greater cross-ventilation to take advantage of the occasional breeze. I could see people chatting and preparing for the day and hear their conversations from inside the rooms as they wafted down to me. I really liked this notion that the community could also hear and observe what was going on in their children's classrooms.

My first day and the following month, however, were an unmitigated disaster. To my distress, during this time none of the students looked at me, much less talked to me. I knew I was white but this was weird, I felt as though I was actually invisible. The students' familiarity with having white teachers arrive and leave within a very short time was based on convincing longitudinal testimony: They simply made no effort to engage with me because as far as they were concerned, I would soon be gone.

...

I lived twelve years in Arnhem Land.

How life became a kaleidoscope: new ways of seeing my world

Living and learning with Aboriginal people carefully crafted my pedagogical practices leading me to want to know more. This desire afforded me an opportunity to merge praxis with theory, undertaking qualitative research in a doctorial study. I have written a critical auto/ethnographic investigation that explored the struggle for culturally-sensitive educational pathways for Aboriginal students incorporating the impact of this transformatory journey on me, documenting the 'outsider' who eventually, after learning the language and ways of living, becomes the 'insider', and I still did not get to tell half of it. So in this chapter I whittle that twelve year experience into a splinter of what I learnt, was taught, was allowed to know and was so generously bestowed during the time of my socio-cultural immersion in Arnhem Land. Following this, I returned home and spent another fifteen years in Wongutha country in the south east of Western Australia working and learning with Aboriginal peoples.

I present this commentary as my personal observations and acknowledge that they may not be the same experiences of what others in a similar setting may have encountered. My intent is to write with a profound hope that these few observations can be of some benefit, so that the same excruciating and costly mistakes I made perhaps will not be made by others. This list is by no means complete.

A few personal observations

Looking back, I wonder at the perpetually diverse events and episodes I was privileged to experience and I marvel how these have impacted on my conscious as well as unconscious behaviours.

Another space

The island seems like a technicolour dream I have awoken from, not sure whether to believe it or not.

Funny how it is the small things that give it away, like always using my hand in a questioning up turned motion or picking things up from the floor with my toes.

My dad laughed when I dropped a shirt which I was about to hang on the clothes line to the ground and immediately effortlessly flicked it back up with my foot. He asked 'Did those island girls teach you that?'

I know within me are learned sacred codes, ways of knowing that have been deeply etched in my psyche, as there are some things that linger in a space that I never totally understood, but only got to guess at its sanctity (December, 1984).

While my reflections are taken from a different time in a different space, the experiences contained in this chapter are still relevant. I suggest that they may possibly provide you with some familiar backgrounds that customarily seldom change in this amazing environment you are about to launch yourself into. I hope these few personal observations are pragmatic and usable and serve some purpose in your preparation for teaching and learning in remote and rural communities.

Normally I would write that 'reconnaissance is seldom wasted', but in this case simply nothing will prepare you for what you are about to undergo, so my greatest advise is just go with it. There are many reasons for this:

- Your previous 'trusty' knowledge and understanding of where you sat within your world and how things worked is now unreliable and suddenly seemingly useless. Your new daily practices move to a rhythm more akin to tides and seasons.
- The spoken language of your new community comes with an entire unique set of reverences, the tongue is intimately connected with the teeth and lips, phonemes pressed out retroflexed or interdentally. Get these right or you are sure to offend.
- Silence and sign languages are explicitly imperative and meaningful, learn to know when and how to use them.
- Getting a response to a question cannot be taken for granted and often an extended length of silence transpires. Be

mindful not to interject and repeat the question as, more than likely, you will never get a reply.

- Try not to make yourself acceptable by dropping the names of all your Aboriginal acquaintances to members of your new community. Let the Aboriginal person ask you questions about your possible Aboriginal contacts.

- For cultural propriety, back to back often replaces face to face. Due to avoidance protocols, certain relatives cannot communicate directly with each other; for example, a husband cannot speak to his mother-in-law and she must move quickly away to avoid eye contact .

- Understand and identify these relational connections because students in your class are obligated to sanction these avoidance protocols.

- Time seems luxuriously blurred and life happens at an exquisitely gracious pace until there is a fight, or the arrival of the mail plane.

- Relational obligations determine all events and hence all actions, carried out in a fitting manner, seldom for reasons relating to time, deadlines or money.

- Family/kinship/country connections are allied and concomitant. Therefore if there is a dispute and *you* need support, many Aboriginal people refrain from confrontation and have a 'mild record' of backing non-Aboriginal people. You may need to seek advocacy in other quarters.

- Social interaction transpires as functionally egalitarian, but if an elder says something that everyone knows is incorrect, all remain silent.

- The living present is preferred; it is the here and now that matters. Thinking about the long-term or being future-orientated implies ambition which can be viewed as 'incongruous'.

- The fundamental belief system is that every member of the community is beholden to their country and their clan.
- Going bush for many Aboriginal people is a way to gain privacy compared to living in town where they are forced to share public spaces.
- In Aboriginal culture, sorcery is real and ever present. You will see and hear things outside of your realm of comprehension. (Black) magic happens.
- Be authentic and be yourself. Aboriginal people have an uncanny skill in detecting when a person is being 'gammon' (false).

Certain school and community protocols are non-negotiable and must be observed regardless.

Some community protocols I have observed include:

- Never assume the right to take a person's photograph. Always ask permission and don't be offended if rebuked.
- Never show images or paintings of deceased people. Always forewarn that there may be images of people who have died and then once informed people can choose to view or look away.
- Never assume that people are known by one name. They may be referred to by their nickname or their ritual name, subsection name, moiety name, totemic name, position in their kinship name or called a name based on the individual's relationship to someone else.
- Never wander through a camp to look for someone without

an invitation. If no one approaches you, then it is clear no one wants to see you.

- Never walk straight up to the front door when you are permitted to do a house call. While there may not be a fence, there is an unseen boundary. It is wise to wait for the dogs to bark to draw attention to yourself.
- Never go to any ceremonial grounds without the appropriate people to accompany you.
- Never hit a camp dog; learn the vernacular for 'get away'. These canine assets traditionally play several vital roles including keeping people warm at night and scaring malignant spirits off through their barking.
- Never sell/offer/bring alcohol into a dry or alcohol-free community. Don't fall victim of people who will bribe you because they will not be there to defend you when the police escort you to court and then off the community.
- Never compromise yourself by being alone with an Aboriginal community member of the opposite gender. Always have a chaperone to serve as an alibi, preventing innuendo and gossip as this can have a maliciously detrimental effect on your position.
- Never underestimate the power of humour to defuse a faux pas or neutralise conflict. Aboriginal people see wittiness in all sorts of situations.

Some school protocols I have observed include:
- Never assume you can apply your ontological world view on to those you teach. Aboriginal child rearing strategies are different. Children are co-constructors of their own being and, as a consequence, enjoy significant independence

and experiential freedoms. They are raised with an expectation they will develop the capacity for self-regulation, self-motivation and self-efficacy.

- Never abruptly wake a sleeping student as they may not want to be suddenly taken out of their dreaming.

- Never use direct questioning as a pedagogical device to elicit what knowledge a student may possess. Rather put the question in the form of a proposition then you will get a clear yes or a no response.

- Never use complex explanations that describe more than one thing or idea. Rather demonstrate what you want achieved. You may need to repeat what you want modelled several times as often Aboriginal students are shy to 'have a go'.

- Never push a student for an answer or for a judgment, rather give them time to come to a decision and use terms like maybe, later, or after.

- Never focus singularly on an individual student – communal group paradigms work best.

- Never use corporal punishment or berate a student publicly.

- Never force a student to sit next to their 'poison cousin' – respect avoidance relationships.

- Never tease an uninitiated male adolescent about not having gone through the 'Law'.

- Never resort to sarcasm when you feel you are about to lose your temper. Try to divert your frustration towards self mockery to make light of the situation. If you don't, things will escalate which you will regret.

- Never expose the nether regions, dress suitably professionally, even if you are bare foot.

- Never invite a non-Aboriginal guest to the community school without first gaining permission or a permit from the Community Council.

Elaboration of key personal observations

While some things need to be experienced firsthand, there are some tricky situations that commonly occur. To help with your transition into your new community, I alert you to a few of them.

Housing

Pending the location of your placement, if you are recruited up north, the wet season will be in full blast and cyclones are synonymous with the start of the school calendar. The days are hot and humid and there are regular torrential downpours. Your skin is constantly clammy with sweat, your clothes are damp and your shoes are soggy. Anything you own made of leather will begin to spawn mould, a bit like the walls in your house which will become downy grey panels. This build up of mould is often exacerbated due to the poor quality of accommodation which may range from a donga or small transportable building to an older style environmentally inappropriate Anglo-centric house. You can expect the air-conditioning in your house to resolve this problem, and normally it would, if you are lucky enough to have a regular power source.

Another onerous housing issue, due to limited accommodation, is sharing with other single teachers. When I first arrived I had to share with a male teacher who went to the club most nights to play darts and socialise with the men. At first sharing a small house with someone who drank and smoked exasperated me, but I slowly warmed to him because he appeared to have a good relationship with his students, who seemed to like his casual manner. However, his lifestyle choices eventually emerged as unsustainable for the professional requirements demanded of a teacher. In my experience the school is usually the central heart beat of a community and when the siren goes for end of the school day, the reality is, that is when the next shift begins. For the majority of both the Aboriginal and non-Aboriginal staff, this involves running after school sporting programs, after school homework centres, making sandwiches for the next day's canteen, attending bilingual classes and working on inter-agency community projects. Teachers like my house mate who are not prepared to do ten or more hour days soon transfer out.

A further inevitable housing matter is that of 'visiting'. Students will come to your door and ask to 'visit'. Most teachers are worn down by the end of the school day and to have students visiting can be problematic. Essentially the children's objective is to innocently satisfy their curiosity as to what 'White Fella's' own and they will want to explore your house, experiment with your possessions and get something to eat or drink. When hoards of kids arrive they tend to swarm enthusiastically all over the place. Providing your voracious noisy visitors with a platter of fruit or a loaf of bread and a jug of juice may not seem much when you live in the city or a major town, but in remote communities perishable foodstuffs are not always easy to come by. As well, often these foods are very expensive. Consequently it is important to establish guidelines such as making sure the kids don't go to your refrigerator and help themselves. Other regulations may include not permitting them to go exploring in personal spaces like your bedroom, or only visiting certain days of the week for a certain period of time. These parameters send a message and the kids who do end up coming on a regular basis are the ones who like to sit down and share a yarn, fortuitously leading to the development of precious friendships. In the meantime the other kids, who don't like your rules, won't bother visiting and will save themselves for the next new white teacher, who predictably arrives very soon.

Modda car

An essential item to take to your new placement is a four wheel drive vehicle. A diesel vehicle would be advisable if petrol sniffing is a problem and you do not have access to Opal fuel, the low aromatic petrol with reduced intoxication producing solvents. Often having transportation becomes the catalyst for the formation of deep friendships with members of the community. In a strictly segregated manner, if you are a male teacher you will find yourself seeking companionship amongst the men and if you are female you will spend more and more time with the women. This grouping in most cases leads to being invited to go out bush for hunting and gathering expeditions and marks the start of your acculturation where you will learn astonishing things. You will gain knowledge about the land and how the topographic profile forged by metaphysical phenomena shapes the fundamental belief system of the community's socio-cultural existence, and their perceptual notion of the eternal role of their ancestors. Berndt and Berndt (1977) described a world view in which the 'primordial land was *given* (was *there*). The mythic beings shaped it and, so to speak, humanized it;...they were mythically substantiated and ritually validated' and 'They are associated with territories and mythical tracks and…were themselves transformed into sites where their spirits remain' (Berndt & Berndt 1977, p. 137). You will learn how.

Before birth, a person's foetus is animated by a spirit which breathes life into it and, so to speak, makes it human: that spirit is derived directly from a mythic being who continues to exist, spiritually, at a particular site. The very fact of this spiritual animation means that the child who is born is not only himself (herself) a manifestation of a sacred mythic character, but also has a very direct and significant linkage with the site (*and country*) associated with that mythic being (Berndt & Berndt, 1977, p. 138).

If you are female, you will discover this vital life affirming link, the connection of birth with country and learn a sacred attribute of women's business. After experiencing a dream or receiving a sign, the women will journey out to fertility water holes within their country to specifically swim in the water so the spirits can come into them and procreate new life. If you venture along, the women will be very stern, they will be constantly shooing you away from the water hole, prohibiting you from swimming in case a spirit accidently comes into you. White anthropologist Diane Bell experienced similar chastising when she began to document her acculturation living and learning with the women in the Great Western Desert as she wrote about her friend, the late Topsy Napurrula Nelson:

> Topsy led me by the hand (sometimes physically) through the maze of knowledge required of me as an adult woman in a desert community. It was she who either nodded approvingly at my response or moved

14

to protect me from dangers of which I was unaware when we found ourselves in unfamiliar situations. On reflection I now can see turning points when, having demonstrated competence at one level, I was permitted to proceed to another (Bell, 1985, p. 4).

The rate of this progression is determined by how well you behave and if you demonstrate a shared authentic affinity with the kids and the country. If you are found to be genuine, you will be allowed to experience simply unimaginable opportunities.

After your arrival

In my enthusiasm to share this life-affirming journey with you, I find myself jumping ahead a little. In reality often months will pass before you are really invited to participate in this intense collective community life. Firstly your initial experience may be quite exhausting as this vignette from my teaching journal implies:

> *I'm so tired of working long hours; researching, gathering and stratifying ideas to create motivating lessons so the kids can learn through their world by means of experiential real life performance and discovery not contrived authoritarian White Fella way.*
>
> *I am missing the love and security of my family so much that it physically hurts. I await their mail frantically. I feel as though I am losing grip without them. I am lonely and isolated and their mail is my lifeline.*
>
> *Nothing in my life seems predictable or comprehensible. The other day for no apparent reason, on no observable signal,*

the entire class got up and ran out of the classroom.

Puzzled I ran out after them calling them back. I stood there totally mystified, had there been a fire evacuation planned and I had not been informed? They ran on across the oval and stood among many others watching some event that was going on at a particular house.

Later some of them wandered back in, sat down, picked up their work from where they had left off and appeared totally nonchalant about the whole foray.

It took me days to find out what happened. No one had bothered to explain what occurred, because to them running to a fight is just what you do, it's the way it is, as natural as the air you breathe. Likewise, when you first arrive, no-one will tell you but it will be assumed that you will endure: loneliness, head lice, frustration, infected sand fly bites, significant communication misunderstandings, conjunctivitis, school lock down due to community fighting, large spider infestation, depression, scabies, witness unprecedented domestic violence, isolation, Giardia, power outages, tropical sores, lack of food due to store closure as a result of a cursing, unreliable internet service provision, student truancy, airport closure due to cyclonic weather, large visiting snakes and, at times, disgruntled parents from those students with behaviour problems whom you needed to discipline. The following vignette again taken from my teaching journal tells of my first disgruntled parent meeting.

I love big burly arms

Fighting persists in the camp. Two women have been evacuated from the island to Darwin Hospital with intensive head and body injuries. The kids who do come to school have been restless, fighting and teasing. Everyday fights end with kids throwing desks and chairs. God, no one listens, it is just bedlam.

A student was teased and became out-of-control throwing chairs around the room and to prevent injury to the other students I took hold of him, got him outside, calmed him down and told him to go home for a while. After some time the kids settled back into their work and all was fine until the busy hum of the classroom was silenced and the reason soon became evident.

Women began assembling outside my classroom door and it crossed my mind on seeing the Nulla-Nulla (women's fighting stick) that this wasn't a good sign. One of the women asked me to step outside and I could hear the kids whispering 'Awiyemba, Awiyemba' (fight, fight).

Once I was outside on the veranda one of the ladies asked me what had happened. I explained in English and she trans-lated my version of the event to her sister in Anindilyakwa.

The aunty (mother) of the child turned to me and fiercely denounced my story raising her fist towards my face and calling me 'rubbish one' and a liar. She circled me slowly, angrily welting me with profanities and derogatory remarks. I could feel my legs shaking and was so scared that she was going to flog me with her Nulla-Nulla that what happened next surprised me as much as everyone else.

Instead of withdrawing I stepped towards her and asked, 'What would you have done if it was your son who got his head split open by a chair?'

They conferred for a moment and then the posse of

supporters, as well as those just in it for idle curiosity, to my amazement just turned and left. I walked back into the classroom still shaking thinking, what just happened? Did I scare them? For the first time, I was really glad that I was a fairly tall basketball player with big strong arms.

Survival Skills 101

An invaluable skill that no one had mentioned that I would need working with children, was the art of self-defence. For reasons that were not clear to me there was one student, Cherry-Louise who had a penchant to inflict pain on me. She was the tallest of all the Year 5s, physically mature and very strong. Recently transferred into my group from the remedial class, she reacted violently to anyone who came within her personal space, lashing out at them as they moved past her. Whenever she spoke to any of her class mates, it was like she was barking at them and I often heard her growling to herself when she was not happy about something. One day without warning she attacked me with a large pair of scissors which, apart from taking me by complete surprise, really frightened me. I remember looking at her with an expression on my face of sheer terror as I asked her beseechingly, 'What have I done to upset you?'. After school I walked to her camp and spoke with her father and mother about what had happened. I found it difficult to believe that two calm parents could produce such a disgruntled daughter.

That year was my Cherry-Louise year. I consulted neurological journals, read psychology books, even pondered star signs in an effort to crack the Cherry-Louise code. I made a point to always tell her parents about her day and what was happening in her school life. I recorded this entry in my teaching journal:

How life can spin

Today Cherry-Louise said I could be a Wurra and I am ecstatic. Cherry-Louise who used to viciously defy me, menace me with scissors and throw desks at me has proclaimed that we are 'sisters'. On her instruction we are going for a ride to town and I am going to take her in my 'dirraka' (car) just the two of us.

A later journal entry documents what occurred as I drove to town with my former bête noire.

Cruising with Cherry-Louise

Went to Cherry-Louise's camp to speak to her mother to make sure it was 'Meningarba' (good) to take Cherry-Louise in to town today as we had previously arranged. Her parents were happy to see her so excited and I could see how proud she was as she sat up high in the car as we drove through the camp.

I remember thinking how refreshing it was that she wasn't embarrassed by me, not sliding down in the seat so no one could see her like the other kids did. This girl was impervious to shame and I loved her for that. At one stage she even waved!

We talked all the way to town and she had so much gossip to tell me. She is really maturing into a very special girl and is trying hard to manage her less-blatant angry behaviour.

Spending time hanging out with Cherry-Louise and the other kids swimming down the river and playing basketball after school has made a huge difference to my relationship with them and especially with her social skills.

After this excursion to town life with Cherry-Louise was very different. She adopted me as her sister and then self-appointed herself the role of assistant teacher. She was capable and gentle and I was grateful to have her in my class as she helped me interpret the way things were done. Teaching is all about first the building of trust and then establishing relationships.

Sometimes the outcomes are not forgettable

When you live in an Aboriginal community, you begin to move in motion with the cyclic pattern of its biorhythms. Some nights you achieve more sitting on the oval talking with the kids than you did in the daylight hours of your classroom. In the dark you see the reality of their lives and get what is really going on in their heads. Often you witness risk-taking behaviours such as excessive alcohol consumption, illegal drug usage, promiscuous sexual conduct, substance abuse (particularly petrol sniffing) and sometimes criminal activity. This risk-taking behaviour has a propensity to lead to fatal consequences. The following vignette tells of the fate of one of my students, Locky Mara.

No match

In between hearing the wonderful news that I was going to Milingimbi Bilingual Community School to teach, sad news arrived telling me Locky Mara has been killed.

He was trying to steal aviation gas to sniff, and one of the boys lit a match to see what they were doing, and the place exploded. The others panicked and took off leaving him.

Later someone returned and dragged him to the side of the road. He was flown to Darwin hospital with burns to

70 per cent of his body but died before they could evacuate him
to the Special Burns Unit in Adelaide.
   Locky was thirteen.

In the first four years teaching on the island, I attended forty-eight funerals. I never meant to count them but one day I was trying to find a note I had made about a student and was leafing through my teaching journal. Skimming the pages, I noted that many of the entries I had written were about feeling a sense of hopeless because I was unable to comfort families in their grief and loss. Likewise, my school roll was peppered with large sections of absenteeisms from kids away attending funerals. Where there had been a death in the classroom, I had put a small cross next to the deceased student's name. One such cross I still bear.

Benny-Benny Lara

For years I lived behind the Marba sisters' camp. Four sisters lived in several houses close together; one of the sisters, Missy, was not married but helped her eldest sister Loi, who was married to Kael Lara. Kael was Benny-Benny's dad, famous for surviving a crocodile kidnap but left with horrendous crocodile claw scars down his back. Kael was now suffering Machado Joseph disease, a neuro degenerative condition that has no known cure. The other two sisters, Diva and Florence, were married to Axel Lara, Kael's middle brother, in the house next door. Dadiwonga, the widowed mother of the sisters lived at the camp and sometimes Kael's younger brother Jack-Boy lived there too. Every morning from my kitchen window, I would see Benny-Benny's mothers and Dadiwonga making damper, washing down the kids, combing hairs and yelling instructions to ensure they got to school early. Loi and I worked as team teachers; at one stage we had two of her kids in our primary enrichment class. All her children were gifted and talented but, to me, Benny-Benny was extraordinary. He was always first to school. He constantly participated in all class activities and got the other students involved with his contagious cheerfulness and then helped them complete their work. Over the period he was in my class he performed as an exemplary scholar and athlete. I got the distinct impression that the aging elders were comforted to know that they had a future 'ceremony man' of such exceptional calibre. One rainy Friday night he removed the electrical cable from the external caravan power pole and suffered an electric shock. By the time the family got to him then raced to the health centre to get the ambulance…he was lifeless. While he lay on the ground unconscious no one knew how to do cardiopulmonary resuscitation. The sad irony of this inconsolable story is that Benny-Benny did. Losing a student leaves an unfillable, malingering sadness. It becomes apparent why many Aboriginal people suffer from a malaise of sorts, a melancholy brought on by great sadness due to the high number of deaths that continue to occur in their lives.

Forging friendships and connecting with community

The critical catalyst in terms of my acculturation was when one of the Aboriginal teachers at the school asked me to play basketball for the local community team in the white township. Playing basketball with the community girls made such a significant difference to my school life. Suddenly my students started to include me in their classroom activities. It felt awesome to finally fit in. Unexpectedly I was included in everything, and my little blue Suzuki would be seen roaring around the community full of girls heading to training or to basketball games. While all the girls were noteworthy, two in particular were deeply consequential, Jara Amarda and Mily Wurra.

Jara Amarda

Jara and I met at school. From the outset Jara talked long and passionately about education and how she felt learning needed to be reformed in the school recognising Aboriginal kids had to be taught 'both ways', in the Aboriginal and the non-Aboriginal way. Coming from a family of innovative artists and community leaders she had grown up surrounded by motivated revolution-ary thinkers. This was the ilk that Jara emanated from and her persistence to transform education in her community led her to continue with formal studies and take on complex senior leadership responsibilities.

Mily Wurra

I came to befriend Mily Wurra through basketball. She was an exceptional player and outmanoeuvred her opponents with her intelligence and speed. Mily and I spent a lot of time together. She was able to interpret and translate our two worlds and explain to me what was happening and why things in her culture were done the way they were. She always seemed to pull me out of tricky cross-cultural situations and protect me from possible harm, later elaborating on what could have happened and why I needed to be more alert. I remember the first time I ever saw Mily was at her younger sister's funeral. I had only just arrived on the island and it was the first funeral I had witnessed. She was devastated, seething with rage, throwing herself on the ground, wailing and smashing a bottle relentlessly against her head to draw blood. In the Aboriginal way, the more blood that is let, and flows, the easier it is for the spirit of the deceased person to return to their mythical place of being. Anthropologists Berndt and Berndt (1977) explain how the body is recycled back to the site of the spirit. The name of the deceased is no longer used and from then on is only referred to in their family or clan terms of their relational association. Some Aboriginal peoples use a generic noun to identify the name of the recently deceased. I recall being terrified as Mily ran towards where I was sitting smashing the bottle to her head and wailing. At first I thought she was angry at me and was offended by my presence but later I learnt this behaviour was what is expected. It is the Aboriginal way.

Aunty Jedda Barron

When I wasn't hanging out with the Jarra, Mily and the girls, I was at Auntie Jedda's camp. I'm not sure if the Barron family even wanted to adopt a homeless white girl but I was certainly happy to adopt them. Over time Aunty Jedda would take me fishing and show me the 'right way' to throw a line or she would sit on the beach with me under the Casuarina trees and tell me stories about her children and her life growing up on the cattle station. She talked about being taken from her mother and father: 'I cried for my mum, I grabbed hold of her skirt you know, I cried. But they said we had to go. So they took us away to the mission and there were hundreds of children already there' (J. Barron, personal communication, 1993). Aunty said once she got to the mission she just tried to make it a good place for herself and her siblings, 'we had clothes, one dress for walkabout, one dress for school and one dress for church' (J. Barron, personal communication, 1993).

Aunty Constance

Many Aboriginal children who were exposed to this regime suffered greatly from being forcibly separated from their parents. In Arnhem Land, Aboriginal children who had any white parentage were compulsorily taken from their families by Welfare Department personnel to a mission on the Roper River. As adults, many returned back home to the island. The following testimony from Aunty Constance tells of the long-term, emotional vulnerability that came from being taken from her mother as a child. Often without any provocation, the aunties would recount such stories of powerlessness. It seemed that in telling of their pasts they were trying to unburden themselves from their entrenched childhood sadness, since now as old ladies they had no strength left to lug their melancholy any further.

> **Aunty Constance**
>
> *I had brought my newborn baby daughter Billage-Billage, named after the red tail black cockatoo, to visit Aunty Constance and was sitting breast feeding her, sipping from a pannikin of tea, when Aunty started telling me about how she felt when she had watched the ABC television series called* Women of the Sun.
>
> *She said how she had watched as this white woman in the story comes up and takes this little Aboriginal girl by the hand and says, 'Come on, you are coming to live with me'.*

25

Aunty said 'You know Helen, all my life I've been living with this hard lump in my chest and I didn't realise I'd had it ever since I was separated from my mother.

When I saw that woman take this little black girl by the hand, it was just as if an explosion went off in my chest. I can't explain it to you Helen, but truly, it was as if it was me being taken into that house.

True God, I cried and cried when I was taken away because oh I loved my mother. I always felt that I had a place in my heart that was wholly and solely for my mother; the holy of holies.'

She talked about her life with the missionaries and the way she had been treated. She said that her anger was the thing that had pushed her to keep on going. She believed she had to keep busy, to prevent the insidious memories from that time taking over, or even taking, her life. Aunty Constance was awarded a Member of the British Empire Award (MBE) for her community service for helping her people.

The critical nexus–building relationships

Being around the Aunties presented me with the opportunity to get to know the women elders in the community. Three women immediately come to mind: Gulid, Imogene and Wudari. They were amazing artisans who continued to carve, paint, sing, dance, and walk for hours hunting and gathering, often carrying their grandchildren on their backs. These women also took time to guide me. They would show me things then say this is 'Aboriginal way' and share with me their stories about the events that had carved the composition of their lives.

Imogene would demurely cover her mouth when she laughed, like the missionaries had taught her to do as a child while Gulid was always tossing her head back laughing, with a mouth full of missing teeth. Likewise, the Aunties would patiently answer my questions, describing for me in scenario-type yarns the cultural setting in which many of my dilemmas were embedded, especially when I told them of the problems I was having with the students in my class and the fighting that was continuously happening. They suggested things I could do that would allevi-ate certain situations and essentially everything recommended seemed to make a difference.

As the years passed, I found myself documenting and emu-lating more and more Aboriginal ways of teaching suggested to me by the Aboriginal teachers and members of the wider Aboriginal communities. It seemed I could differentiate between the classroom behaviour of students whose white teachers used these ways of learning and those who did not. Likewise I could differentiate the relationships between white teachers who spent time in the community with the local people and those who did not.

Every weekend would see us out bush camping along the south side of the island. It was never planned; just in the moment. Families would fling everything including kids and dogs in the back of the Toyotas and off we would go, as the following vignette reveals.

Erriberriba-wa – (Going bush)
We left Friday night to drive south firstly along the jungle track then along the sandy beach. The full moon rose in total brilliance while we set up camp and drank steaming billy tea.

When the tides were right, we went crabbing while the Barron clan screamed and laughed and ordered others, especially the younger ones, to run errands, playing on the pecking order like only large families can.

I fell asleep to the sound of the incoming tide as it lapped upon the shoreline. Sunrise was spectacular, as was the smoked black toast and billy tea. After breakfast we went back over to Salt Creek to go shell fishing amongst the densely populated mangrove swamp, famous for crocodiles. The Barron clan with all their adopted white kids, me and Bluey and Bree-Boy, bent over like the number seven for hours, plucking and swearing and ripping and tearing our bodies and clothes to reap a pillow case of cockles.

Later we sat around the fire with Aunty and Uncle listening as they yarned and Uncle carved animal shapes into the soft wood he was working. They talked about what it meant to them to be a survivor of the stolen generation, to witness transformation of people and culture, progress not necessarily beneficial to the original islanders and the build-up of commercial ventures on the island, bringing with it money, machismo and hedonism.

I was suddenly conscious that this world of theirs was so fragile and how other outsiders, 'blowins' from the southern cities, obsessed in their global gluttony to exploit, made precarious decisions that impacted, often diabolically, on many local inhabitants' lives. I felt ashamed to be white.

Tonight the rising moon looked like a huge over-ripe orange leisurely ascending. I sat atop of the Toyota with a torch, crocodile spotting, straining to see 'red eye' while the others dragged the net across the creek.

This was the very place where years before Kael Lara
was snatched from out of his mother's arms by a crocodile. She
brazenly fought it off and legend has it she poked it in the eye,
grabbed her bleeding baby and ran.

I soon understood that what we did and when we did it was intricately connected to the tides and moon and seasons, and reading my new world seemed lusciously visceral and continual. I learnt how the Round Stingray or Yimaduwaya is ready to catch, when the Red Kurrajong or Miyarrawa flowers and the Wild Plum or Mangkarrkba turns green and how, when the Cocky Apple or Mukuwara flowers, it is time to catch turtle or Yimenda. The women showed me how to find the wild bee honey called Yilyakwa and how to treat the Zamia palm or Burrawang nuts to leach out the poison. I learnt to walk through the seasons reaping the lavish offerings by reading their signs.

Sensing the signs

Likewise reading body language became an equally important quest as an effective way to communicate over distances which accounts for much when it is too hot to walk or talk. Similarly reading the mood of the community was also an important skill to acquire as the following vignette suggests.

Awiyemba – (Fight)

Coming home from basketball training tonight I called into
Jamba's house to check tomorrow's excursion with him and,
just as I was getting out of the Suzuki, the most horrendous
fight broke out. I ducked for cover into the Lara's camp as a

throng of people came running and shouting up the centre of the road welding nulla nullas, spears and woomeras.

To the unskilled eye it could have seemed like a free for all. What was happening and who was challenging translated immediately into an unambiguous kinship obligation being played out.

Next minute, several women of the Amarda clan were set upon and a few were thrashed and forced down onto the road. Jamba leapt up, grabbed his woomera and spear and threw two hunting spears into the crowd clear in his intention to miss and interrupt the fighting.

Instantly the rattling of spears resonated loudly and what appeared to sound like multiple dramatical monologues added to the hectic deluge with people running everywhere.

Jamba's eldest daughter, Dendi, threw her baby into my arms and quickly followed her father and mothers into the fighting. Jamba's wives and daughters strode powerfully into the maelstrom; strong, fierce and protective of their clan as I sat surrounded by little children and nursing mothers.

I couldn't believe the intense antagonism, yet in a bizarre way, it seemed so healthy to spit it all out in the open and deal with it once and for all.

The fight was about a brother and a sister who were petrol sniffing and, since the community wanted to enforce a zero tolerance approach on sniffing, many members of the families wanted severe punishment for the sniffers and this was causing the dispute.

As people argued, Jamba sat by the fire listening to the dispute. Looking at his profile in the shadow cast by the fires I saw such a magnificent strength, a wise, competent and compassionate man who was always trying to establish a cultured future for his children and his clan.

When everyone had finished having their say and the sniffers were publically shamed, people walked back to their camps, chatting and laughing.

These acts are actually carefully orchestrated, judiciously co-ordinated, channelled retribution with the intent to reach a compromise rather than to draw blood. The intent of these frightening displays of shouting, detailed monologues full of mythical allusions and cursing along with the rattling of spears in a full frontal attack is amply terrifying as they are effective at saving 'loss of face', a seriously significant component of Aboriginal culture.

The journey ramps up

As the years passed, I no longer experienced those gut wrenching mornings as I had during my first year. Then I would walk to school and dread what was waiting ahead of me, especially the constant fighting and the incessant teasing. Now after significant time had passed and I had been suitably guided and preened, my journey was finally ramping up. Like Bell (1985) who had needed to demonstrate competence on one level before she was permitted to graduate to the next level of knowledge, I had finally graduated to the privileged position of being invited to the ceremonies.

The Ceremonies – sacred and sacrosanct

Each year during the dry season special mortuary ceremonies take place to commemorate the first year anniversary of the person who had died during the previous year. I always tried to write notes in my journal immediately after what had happened and the significance of the proceedings but my words failed dismally to accurately describe the rousing experience.

Amarda-langwa – (Ceremonies)

Each afternoon I have been going to the ceremonies. We sit and wait in the late afternoon sun as that wonderful, awe inspiring, indisputable sound of the didgeridoo and clapping stick music permeates its way through the jungle to our ears. The kids sit sucking on turtle egg while the women industriously pick and click nit eggs on each other's heads.

Then on a seemingly invisible command the women rise simultaneously and walk into the bush towards the clearing. We sit with our backs to the clearing until we hear the clapping sticks and the men moving nearer. We set off quickly to our moiety poles and stand huddled close together with our backs still to the men.

The moiety Morning Star pole is said to be like the dead person's body, so when we look at the post we remember the departed spirit. The men approach us, led by the ceremonial leaders of the appropriate clans and linguistic units.

Using the wooden clapping sticks to pulsate a guiding beat they direct the singing of the totem songs of the moieties, invoking the sacred names of the dead person's water hole and country with its mythical associations. Carefully we listen out for the signal before we step away from the poles and face the men and watch them dance in front of us.

There is this strangely powerful mix of tension and timelessness, that the celebration of death is, in fact, celebrating new life, new possibilities. Painted up, the men's bodies seem so much more impressive, even commanding. It is as if their cultural authority has been restored.

Then in ritual reciprocity, us women dance. This is all practice for the Mortuary ceremony which will be performed over several nights. It is exciting and frightening, cerebral and spiritual all at once.

After the practice is over we pile into vehicles and head back through the bush along the corrugated track, blanketed by dust as the sun sets on another day. It is funny when a vehicle overtakes. In the back are about twenty heads with their faces all coated in the traditional white clay or red ochre with intricate animal totems meticulously painted on their upper bodies.

We could be right back in the dream time. Living close to this mob has taught me that 'transition' is not easy. I feel an inner sadness that I can't quite put my finger on. I am learning the Aboriginal way, socialising in their world, using the appropriate symbols of an insider, but still it is their world... not mine. It is not my language, my colour, my dreaming... yet I am absorbed in something that I am totally committed to and don't want to be separated from.

Decades later, my total commitment to progressing the lives of the Aboriginal students with whom I work continues.

Summary

Whilst cognisant of trying to achieve the impossible, to compact thirty years in as many pages of this chapter section, I conclude my personal observations and yarn with one statement. I have been generously embraced and deeply enriched by sharing my life with Aboriginal peoples, learning to do things I never dreamed were even possible. One example of this is that after working and witnessing ongoing injustices directed against many Aboriginal students, parents and their communities, I was motivated to write a PhD dissertation, a demanding undertaking I would not normally have considered. What the people of Arnhem Land and Wongutha gave me was the reason to write, to craft their stories and tell of their struggle for culturally-sensitive educational pathways for their children. I continue to argue, it is akin to enmity to force another generation of young black people to endure an educational system that does little to venerate their epistemological traditions.

Some suggest that opposition to dominant Anglo-Australian hegemonic forces were reflected in 2008 with the first Welcome to Country ever staged at a parliamentary opening followed by 'the Apology' to Australia's Indigenous peoples. Some claim it was in 1998 with recognition of National Sorry Day while others suggest it was possibly due to the 1988 Barunga Statement and a few report it was the outcome of the 1972 Aboriginal Tent Embassy. A number believe it was the 1966 Gurindji walk off, if not the 1963 Yirrkala Bark Petition. Several testify it was the 1946 Pilbara Strike outcomes, others propose it was way earlier in the 1890s with Jandamarra, if not even earlier in the 1830s with Yagan and his father Midgegoroo. It's been recommended it was Musquito in the 1820s and various reputable sources say it was earlier with Pemulwuy in the 1790s. The one thing not in dispute is that the Aboriginal resistance to these prevailing forces started a long time ago and now, in the spirit of reconciliation, it is time for reform. Failure to do this is not an option.

2

THE CONTEXT OF ABORIGINAL EDUCATION

Gary Partington and Quentin Beresford

Over the past thirty years, there has been a significant improvement in the education of Aboriginal students. In the early 1980s, few achieved educational qualifications beyond the middle years of high school. Even fewer went on to complete post-school qualifications. At the time, the parents of many Aboriginal students had been denied an education. As outlined in the following chapter, until the end of the 1950s in most states it was government policy that Indigenous children were not permitted to enter state schools. If they received an education at all, it was provided by missionaries. Against this heritage, their children struggled to meet the demands of formal schooling in state schools, and teachers were ill equipped to meet their needs.

Thirty years on, there has been a generational change. Today, significant numbers of Aboriginal students are completing high school and gaining post-school qualifications in tertiary and Technical and Further Education (TAFE) institutions. Since the 1980s, federal and state governments have provided a range of supports that have improved outcomes for Aboriginal students. Despite these changes, however, a disproportionate number of Aboriginal students are not receiving a satisfactory education.

As Tom Calma, the Aboriginal and Torres Strait Islander Social Justice Commissioner and National Race Discrimination Commissioner at the Human Rights and Equal Opportunity Commission (HREOC) stated:

> The disparities between outcomes for Indigenous and non-Indigenous Australians in relation to all areas of the education system are documented and well known. And the statistics are not improving anywhere near the rate that they should be.
>
> Indigenous Australia has a population of over half a million people. We are the fastest growing population group in the country and have a significantly skewed age structure – with a majority of Indigenous Australians being young. Indigenous youth remain the most educationally disadvantaged group in Australia. As a direct consequence of this disadvantage many are not reaching the basic educational milestones.
>
> Education prepares us to make decent and proper choices. It is fundamental to the development of human potential and to full participation in a democratic society. It is also fundamental to the full enjoyment of most other human rights: most clearly the right to work but also the right to health.
>
> Many Indigenous children are fundamentally disengaged from education (Calma, 2008a).

Background

In the 2006 census, there were 517,000 Indigenous people in Australia. Nearly one third (32 per cent) live in cities, 43 per cent live in regional areas and 25 per cent in remote areas. The states with the largest populations of Indigenous people are New South Wales (30 per cent), Queensland (28 per cent) and Western Australia (14 per cent). Twelve per cent live in the Northern Territory, where they make up 30 per cent of the total population (Australian Bureau of Statistics 2010c).

The Indigenous population is increasing more rapidly than the rest of the population, at a rate of 2.2 per cent per annum (compared with 1.4 per cent per annum for the general population). This means that the Indigenous population of 517,000 in 2006 will increase to between 713,300 and 721,100 people in 2021 (Australian Bureau of Statistics 2010c). Most of this increase will occur through births (another source is through more people identifying as Indigenous), so there will be an impact on schooling, as approximately 200,000 more Indigenous students will enter the school system across Australia in the years to 2021.

In 2010, 162,831 Indigenous students were enrolled in schools across Australia. This was approximately 6,500 more students than in the previous year. Two thirds of these students are in primary school, and 85 per cent are in government schools (Australian Bureau of Statistics 2010d).

Employment

The level of employment of Aboriginal people is steadily increasing but is still well below the levels for non-Aboriginal people. In 2009, 58 per cent Indigenous people aged 15–64 years were reported as being in the workforce. This means they were either in work, were working for Community Development Employment Programs (CDEP) or were looking for work. In contrast, 76.7 per cent of non-Indigenous Australians were in the workforce.

The picture for unemployment was similar, with a much greater proportion of the Indigenous workforce unemployed. In 2009, the unemployment rate for the Indigenous population was 18 per cent, with an estimated 35,400 unemployed Indigenous people aged 15 years and over. (Australian Bureau of Statistics, 2010b). In the 2006 census, 14,700 Indigenous people indicated that they were working in Community Development Employment Projects (CDEP). This meant that they received unemployment benefits plus extra payments for community organised work or training. However, participants in this program were:

- twice as likely to work part time rather than full time (75 per cent compared to 39 per cent);
- more likely to report working in a low-skilled occupation (78 per cent compared to 60 per cent); and
- one third as likely to report having a non-school qualification (13 per cent compared to 37 per cent) (Human Rights and Equal Opportunity Commission, 2009, p. 18).

CDEP employment is less likely to provide a pathway to full time, skilled occupations and can be regarded as a stopgap measure to provide communities with a strategy for keeping their members occupied. Factors in the lower rates of employment for Indigenous people include the disappearance of work as industries become reliant on technology and mechanisation rather than unskilled labour; low levels of education, meaning they lack the skills to gain employment in industry; and an unwillingness of employers to employ them.

Income

Limited access to skilled work, high levels of unemployment and reliance on CDEP has resulted in lower income levels for Indigenous people compared with non-Indigenous people. This can be seen in Table 2.1 below.

Table 2.1 – Median gross individual weekly income (a) by Indigenous status and age, 2006

Age group (years)	Indigenous ($)	Non-Indigenous ($)
15–24	191	209
25–44	374	684
45–64	283	420
All	278	473

(a) Excludes persons whose income was unknown.
(Australian Bureau of Statistics, 2006d)

The weekly income of $278 for all age groups of Indigenous people is only 58 per cent of the weekly income of non-Indigenous people. Part of the reason for this is the large number of people who rely on government benefits.

Housing

As in other areas of their lives, Aboriginal people are disadvantaged in housing compared to non-Aboriginal people. In 2006, the proportion of Aboriginal people living in a home owned or being purchased by a member of the household was 29 per cent (for Torres Strait Islanders, it was 28 per cent). In contrast, the proportion of non-Indigenous people was much higher at 72.1 per cent (Steering Committee for the Review of Government Service Provision, 2009, p. 12.12). As a corollary of lower home ownership, a higher proportion of Aboriginal people than non-Indigenous people are renting their home (65 per cent compared to around 25 per cent).

A further indication of disadvantage in relation to housing was the much higher proportion of Aboriginal people living in overcrowded housing. In 2006, 25 per cent lived in overcrowded conditions, compared with 5.7 per cent of non-Indigenous people (Steering Committee for the Review of Government Service Provision, 2009, p. 12.15). The average Indigenous household (comprising data for both Aboriginal and Torres Strait Islanders) is larger than the average non-Indigenous household. In 2006, the average non-Indigenous Australian household comprised 2.6 people, whereas the average household with at least one Indigenous person was 3.4 people (Australian Bureau of Statistics, 2010a) and this contributes to overcrowding.

As well as overcrowding, Aboriginal people were more likely to experience homelessness. Figures for Aboriginal and Torres Strait Islander people show that the rate of homelessness was 3.5 times higher than for non-Indigenous people, with 176 homeless Indigenous people per 10,000 of population compared to fifty non-Indigenous people .

These figures clearly demonstrate a considerable disadvantage in housing that impacts on the quality of the home environment for study by Aboriginal students.

Health

The health of a community has important consequences for a range of other sectors of their lives. Education, employment, income and longevity are all affected by health and Indigenous people report lower levels of health than non-Indigenous people: in surveys, fewer state that their health is excellent or very good. Twice as many report fair or poor health compared to non-Indigenous people, and the gap between Indigenous and non-Indigenous people reporting fair or poor health increased significantly with age (Steering Committee for the Review of Government Service Provision 2009). Indigenous people's perceptions were confirmed by data on health outcomes: they are more likely to have poorer health than non-Indigenous people. This is the case with life expectancy, mental health, disease, maternal health, birth weight, young child mortality, hearing, disability and chronic disease (Steering Committee for the Review of Government Service Provision, 2009).

The poorer health of Indigenous people extends to mental health (Purdie, Dudgeon et al. 2010). The *National Aboriginal and Torres Strait Islander Health Survey* conducted in 2004–05 found that over one quarter of Indigenous adults reported high levels of psychological distress (Australian Bureau of Statistics, 2006c); double the rate for non-Indigenous adults. Mental health is an issue for children as well, for they experience high levels of stress associated with life events (Steering Committee for the Review of Government Service Provision, 2009). This is the case with the frequency of funeral attendance for many children who are often grieving (MindMatters, 2010) and this has the potential to impact on their schooling.

41

The quality of health was related to education, employment and income: those with high levels of education, who were employed and whose income was higher reported better health (Steering Committee for the Review of Government Service Provision, 2009). However, poor health impacts on students' potential to succeed at school.

Education

Information collected from the 2006 census indicated that Indigenous people's level of education was improving. For example, compared with data from the 2001 census, the proportion of Aboriginal people completing year 12 increased from 18.6 per cent to 21.9 per cent, while the proportion earning a degree increased from 4 per cent to 5.2 per cent. However, these figures were well below those for non-Indigenous people: 49 per cent completed Year 12, and 21.5 per cent had a degree in 2006.

The present educational status of students in the system reflects the lower level of education of Indigenous people. In academic achievement, retention, attendance and post school education, Indigenous students do not perform as well as non-Indigenous students.

Academic achievement

Across Australia, Indigenous students consistently achieve at lower levels in the NAPLAN assessments. This was the case with the 2010 NAPLAN results in all areas of assessment in all States. The disparity was worst in the Northern Territory, followed by Western Australia. In every year level assessed, Indigenous students' results were lower. In the review of NAPLAN for 2010, it is noted that the difference between Indigenous and non-Indigenous scores is decreasing for Reading, Spelling, Grammar and Punctuation but there has been no change in the results for Writing and Numeracy (Australian Curriculum Assessment and Reporting Authority, 2010b).

Attendance

The attendance rate is the percentage of enrolled students who go to school. Across Australia, the proportion of Indigenous students attending school is less than the proportion of non-Indigenous students. The table 2.2 illustrates this.

Table 2.2 – Attendance rates, Indigenous and non-Indigenous students

	Primary %	Secondary %
Indigenous attendance	87	78
Non-Indigenous attendance	93	89

(Department of Education, Employment, and Workplace Relations, 2008, p. 38)

Attendance rates vary with the year level of students and remoteness. In table 2.3, these two factors are clearly at work:

Table 2.3 – Secondary school attendance by remoteness area and by age, 2006

Age in Years	Major cities %	Inner regional %	Outer regional %	Remote %	Very remote %
Indigenous					
15	77	77	76	67	53
16	60	58	60	49	34
17	44	38	37	29	16
Non-Indigenous					
15	90	89	89	88	82
16	82	79	77	75	61
17	68	62	58	52	39

(Purdie and Buckley, 2010, p. 5)

Completions

In 2008, only 20 per cent of Indigenous people aged 15 years and over had completed Year 12 or equivalent (compared to 54 per cent of non-Indigenous people). This was up from 17 per cent in 2002 and marks a steady improvement in the completion rate for Indigenous people. This improvement is coming from the increasing number of young people completing their schooling compared to previous generations: by 2008, 31 per cent of Indigenous people aged 20–24 had completed Year 12 (Australian Bureau of Statistics, 2008).

Non-school qualifications

Non-school qualifications are awarded for educational attainments other than those gained in pre-primary, primary and secondary education. They include vocational education and university qualifications. Some of these can be completed concurrently with secondary schooling. In 2008, 32 per cent of Indigenous people aged 15 years and over had a non-school qualification. Of these, 42 per cent lived in major cities, 31 per cent lived in regional areas and 21 per cent lived in remote areas (Australian Bureau of Statistics, 2008).

In 2006, only 4 per cent of Indigenous people aged 20–64 possessed a degree from a university. This percentage is made up of 24,123 Aboriginal people and 1,556 Torres strait Islander people with a bachelor's degree or higher. In contrast, 21.5 per cent of non-Indigenous people possessed a bachelor's degree or higher.

It is clear that improvements in educational outcomes of Aboriginal students are occurring but there are still too many Aboriginal and Torres Strait Islander students who are disadvantaged by a host of factors that impact on their education.

Education is of vital importance in post-school life, yet far too many Indigenous students are not completing their schooling, or are achieving levels well below non-Indigenous students. The MCEEDYA Indigenous Education Action Plan reinforces the need for improvement:

> Significant gaps remain between the educational outcomes of Indigenous students and other students. This is clear on all indicators including participation in early childhood education, literacy and numeracy, attendance, retention, and post-school transitions. This gap limits the career prospects and life choices of Indigenous students and perpetuates intergenerational disadvantage (Ministerial Council on Education Early Childhood Development and Youth Affairs, 2010, p. 4).

Mutual obligation

When the Howard Government came to office in 1996, it set about changing the policy approach in Indigenous Affairs from one of 'symbolic' reconciliation towards a focus on 'practical' reconciliation. The shift was meant to signify that the previous federal Labor Government's emphasis on land rights, a formal process of reconciliation and self-determination was out of step with Liberal Party thinking about Indigenous affairs. The new Government wanted to focus on achieving improved outcomes for Aboriginal people in ways that did not conflict with their view that Aboriginal people should be accommodated into the mainstream of the nation and not be accorded 'special' rights. In formulating its approach, the Government appeared to draw on some of the ideas advanced by prominent Aboriginal intellectual and leader, Noel Pearson (Pearson, 2003) who had spoken about the urgency of getting Aboriginal people off passive welfare and of offering them the 'the right to take responsibility'.

A major plank in the policy shift was the application of the principle of mutual obligation; that is the act of giving something back in return for the assistance of government. This had been the Howard Government's approach to welfare reform. In Aboriginal communities the requirement of giving something back involved behavioural changes such as Indigenous youth on welfare being required to actively seek employment (Minister for Education Training and Youth Affairs, 2005). This process quickly became popularised as enforcing children's attendance at school and attention to their cleanliness, or, a policy of 'No school, no pool. Dirty faces. No petrol' (The Australian Associated Press, 25 December 2004).

The policy of mutual obligation was implemented in a more complex set of arrangements in 2005 as Shared Responsibility Agreements (SRAs) (see Implementation Review of Shared Responsibility Agreements, 2006). They were intended as whole-of-government approaches to improving the social, economic wellbeing of Indigenous people. Among the behavioural changes sought were:

- school attendance
- control of substance abuse
- engagement with training and work experience
- attendance at pre-natal, child safety and first-aid courses
- involvement in recreation courses
- development of diversion (from custody) programs.

They were the intended mechanisms for additional funding into Aboriginal communities and a mechanism to develop governance structures at the local level. A parallel process of Regional Partnerships was also introduced (Strakosch, 2009). Both were underpinned by enforceable contracts.

SRAs met with an initially hostile reception by many Aboriginal and non-Aboriginal people. Critics viewed the approach as patronising and forcing Aboriginal people to beg for basic services. However, this hostility dissipated as the underlying principles of the Agreements gained recognition. As Aboriginal intellectual and leader Pat Dodson explained when giving his belated support to the new approach (*The Age*, 7 December 2004): 'The resolution of the problems facing Aboriginal people in this country will require strong working partnerships between governments, industry and Aboriginal people'.

By 2007, nearly 200 SRAs had been signed (Strakosh, 2009), highlighting their role in forging a new relationship between government and Aboriginal people. In 2006 an extensive review (see Implementation Review of Shared Responsibility Agreements, 2006) was undertaken into SRAs which found broad support in Aboriginal communities for the approach and in ways that had made important contributions at the local level. Only a small proportion of the Agreements were judged to have experienced only minimal success. Yet, in 'every site the review team heard consistently, from both community and government stakeholders, that one of the improvements they would like to see was more realistic outcomes being negotiated' (Implementation Review of Shared Responsibility Agreements, 2006). This raises the persistent criticism about SRAs that the problems being address are interrelated and complex and that communities will differ in their ability to negotiate on their own behalf.

The Northern Territory Intervention

In 2007, the Federal Howard Government set in motion another of its far-reaching and dramatic policy changes in Indigenous Affairs when it announced a takeover of remote communities in the Northern Territory (NT). The Intervention, as the policy became known, affected 81 communities with an estimated population of 32,000 people. The justification for the policy was the release of the *Little Children are Sacred* report (Wild & Anderson, 2007), which documented widespread child abuse and family and community breakdown. The scale of the dysfunction in communities was widely seen to constitute an emergency. However, there was little acknowledgement that governments had been warned about a crisis in remote communities for many years. Not all remote communities are in a state of crisis; a number enforce bans on alcohol and function effectively.

Introduced with bi-partisan political support, the NT Intervention aimed to protect and better provide for children through a range of measures, including:

- provision of additional police
- compulsory health checks
- bans on X-rated pornography
- controls on substance abuse
- enforcement of school attendance through management of welfare payments
- improved housing and infrastructure.

48

However, the manner in which the Intervention occurred has attracted criticism. Firstly, the Federal Government had to suspend the 1975 Racial Discrimination Act to enable it to apply measures specifically to Aboriginal remote communities leading to claims that the legislation to implement the policy was discriminatory and lacked a constitutional basis (Aboriginal and Torres Strait Social Justice Commissioner, 2007). Secondly, no consultation was undertaken with affected Aboriginal communities (or Aboriginal leaders) beforehand. At the time of the Intervention, many Aboriginal people in the communities felt a strong sense of injustice that they had been blamed for the problems plaguing some of their communities rather than the failures of government policy. Aboriginal people had repeatedly complained to government that:

> services which most Australians take for granted are often not delivered to remote Indigenous communities, including adequately resourced schools, health services, child protection and family support services, as well as police who are trained to deal with domestic violence in the communities affected (cited in ibid., p. 222).

The release of the *Little Children are Sacred* report, together with the Intervention have served to further highlight the scale of Aboriginal educational disadvantage in remote communities. It has been estimated, for example, that 7,500 Indigenous children in the Northern Territory do not attend school and pre-school; in many instances, the staff and facilities simply do not exist for them (Australian Education Union, 2007). As will be examined throughout this book, the reasons for this are complex but, in the case of remote communities, the issues constitute failures on the part of families and communities to engage in education and the failure of education systems to fully engage the needs and expectations of young people living in remote communities (ibid).

The impact of the Intervention continues to elicit a range of positive and negative opinions, among both Aboriginal and non-Aboriginal people. Yet, a federal government appointed review into the Intervention, conducted in 2008, (Northern Territory Emergency Response Review Board, 2008) found that definite gains had been brought about by the Intervention and that it had achieved widespread, if qualified, support for its provisions. But debate persists on how long such a measure should be required; how it can be improved to better involve Aboriginal people; and whether it should be extended to other communities in the Northern Territory and to remote communities outside the Territory. On the latter point, many claim that the Intervention has simply shifted the problems of alcohol abuse from the more strictly controlled environments of remote communities to regional centres such as Alice Springs and Katherine.

However, the focus on education has not waned. In 2011, the federal Minister for Education wanted the NT Intervention to develop stronger efforts to get children to school.

The apology

The election to office of the Labor Government in December 2007 has provided both change and continuity in Aboriginal affairs policy. The starkest difference between it and its predecessor was the offering of an official Commonwealth apology to the Stolen Generations; children forcibly removed from their families in the era of assimilation which ran approximately from the 1930s until the 1970s. The call for an apology had emanated from the Human Rights and Equal Opportunity Commission's inquiry into the plight of this group, published as the *Bringing Them Home* report (Human Rights and Equal Opportunity Commission, 1997). The report called for Australian parliaments to offer official apologies and acknowledge their responsibility for the laws, policies and practices that led to the widespread removal of Aboriginal children from their families. In addition, it called for reparations and monetary compensation to those affected by the policy (Dow, 2008).

However, the release of the report coincided with the election in 1996 of the Howard Liberal Government and Prime Minister John Howard maintained a decade long opposition to offering an apology, claiming that the present generation 'should not be required to accept the blame and guilt for past actions and past policies'. In the intervening years all state and territory governments offered apologies, but the lack of an official Commonwealth apology continued to divide the community and acted as a spur to the reconciliation movement by encouraging hundreds of thousands of ordinary Australians to participate in 'Sorry Day' marches and other grass-roots activities.

Prime Minister Kevin Rudd's apology in federal parliament on 13 February 2008 was attended by hundreds of parliamentarians, former Prime Ministers (although John Howard chose not to attend) and representatives of the Stolen Generations. Thousands watched a live broadcast on the lawns of Parliament House. In his speech, Rudd acknowledged the need to 'remove a stain from the soul of the nation'. In his apology, the Prime Minister called for a new future for relations between Indigenous and non-Indigenous Australians:

> A future where we harness the determination of all Australians, Indigenous and non-Indigenous to close the gap that lies between us in life expectancy, educational achievement and economic opportunity...A future based on mutual respect, mutual resolve and mutual responsibility (Rudd, 2008).

The apology was widely seen as an important step to improved race relations in Australia even though it was criticised by some for failing to include a commitment to compensation as the apology offered by the Tasmanian Government had done and as had the Canadian Government for the policy of removal of Indigenous people which had operated in that country.

Closing the Gap

In 2008, a new initiative was agreed upon by the Council of Australian Governments, a body made up of all state and territory governments and the Australian Government. This approach, termed Closing the Gap, originated in the health needs of Indigenous people but the intermeshing of many issues has resulted in a policy that identified six primary targets:

- close the gap in life expectancy within a generation
- halve the gap in mortality rates for Indigenous children under five within a decade
- ensure all Indigenous four years olds in remote communities

have access to early-childhood education within five years

- halve the gap for Indigenous students in reading, writing and numeracy within a decade
- halve the gap for Indigenous students in year 12 attainment or equivalent attainment rates by 2020
- halve the gap in employment outcomes between Indigenous and non-Indigenous Australians within a decade (Council of Australian Governments, 2009b, p. 5).

The Council envisages a coordinated approach to change in each of the following areas:

- early childhood
- schooling
- health
- healthy homes
- safe communities
- economic participation
- governance and leadership.

However, the strategy has been criticised for its failure to include targets to reduce the over-representation of Aboriginal people in the justice system. Evidence to the House of Representatives inquiry into juvenile justice (2011, p. 24) indicated that it would not be possible to meet the health, education and employment targets without also addressing the high levels of Indigenous incarceration because imprisonment 'compounds individual and community disadvantage'.

Otherwise, Closing the Gap provides a strong focus on achieving outcomes through coordinated approaches, involving all governments and agreements with Indigenous communities. The policy is considered in more detail in chapter 13.

NAPLAN

The National Assessment Program – Literacy and Numeracy (NAPLAN) commenced in Australian schools in 2008. Each year since then, all students in Years 3, 5, 7 and 9 across Australia are expected to be assessed in reading, writing, language conventions (spelling, grammar and punctuation) and numeracy.

The purpose of the test is to determine if students have the appropriate skills needed as a foundation for further learning and for participation in society. The content of the test is based on a standard curriculum for each learning area and authorised by MCEETYA (Ministerial Council on Education Early Childhood Development and Youth Affairs, 2008). The Statements of Learning were developed collaboratively by the state, territory and Australian education authorities to provide a set of statements that describe the knowledge, skills, understandings and capacities that are considered essential learning for students (Australian Curriculum Assessment and Reporting Authority, 2011b). The results of the tests provide schools with comparative performance measures and parents are able to gain information on their children's performance. Masters (2010, p. 22) identified the following benefits of the assessment regime:

- identify individuals who are not meeting minimum literacy or numeracy expectations for their year level
- identify, at a school level, areas of the curriculum in need of further teaching and emphasis

- monitor the performance and progress of social inclusion priority groups, such as Indigenous students
- set targets for improvement at school, regional, state or national levels
- monitor changes in literacy and numeracy standards over time.

The tests are not designed to test content. They are designed to draw on knowledge and skills in literacy and numeracy that students develop through learning in the school curriculum. However, knowledge of the diverse test-taking skills that comprise the tests is essential if students are to perform at their best. Schools that provide preparation for such tests enable their students to experience reduced test anxiety (Gorman 2006). Teachers are advised that they should carry out such preparation by developing familiarity with test instructions and common forms of questions (Australian Curriculum Assessment and Reporting Authority, 2011b).

The NAPLAN tests are particularly relevant to the education of Indigenous students because their performance as a group in all tests is lower than the performance of non-Indigenous students at all levels of testing (Australian Curriculum Assessment and Reporting Authority, 2010b). This is the case across Australia and the gap is greatest in the Northern Territory, with Western Australian results also lower. These results are a strong confirmation of the well-known poor outcomes of education for Indigenous students. However, NAPLAN, in conjunction with components of Closing the Gap strategies, has the potential to provide a powerful tool for improvement in schooling for Indigenous students.

Indigenous languages policy

In August 2009, the federal government announced an Indigenous languages policy (Macklin and Garrett, 2009). This policy was developed in response to a report that stated that of the 145 Indigenous languages still spoken in Australia, 110 are at risk of disappearing (AIATSIS/FATSIL, 2005, cited in Purdie, Frigo et al., 2008).

The policy focuses on five key areas:

- bringing national attention to Indigenous languages
- encouraging the use of critically endangered languages to maintain and extend their everyday use as much as possible
- making sure that in areas where Indigenous languages are being spoken fully and passed on, government recognises these languages when it interacts with Indigenous communities
- helping restore the use of rarely spoken or unspoken Indigenous languages to the extent that the current language environment allows
- supporting the teaching and learning of Indigenous languages in Australian schools.

The policy has been introduced to prevent the decline in the use of endangered languages, strengthen pride in identity and culture, and support Indigenous language programs in schools.

In relation to the implementation of the policy in education, programs in Indigenous languages will be fostered in early childhood education but the federal government did not propose targeting funds towards providing additional Indigenous language tuition in other schools. This despite a recommendation from a federal government commissioned report that 'There must be practical national support and resourcing for school language programmes' (Purdie, Frigo, et al., 2008).

The policy leaves the task of implementing school based proposals for Indigenous language instruction to the state and territory governments. This is unfortunate given the limited support for such programs across Australia. For example, in the Northern Territory, where bilingual programs have been the strongest, a bilingual education strategy that had been operating since 1973 was effectively halted in 2008 when the Department of Education and Training announced that all schooling would be conducted in English for the first four hours of each day. If the implementation of Indigenous bilingual programs is not resourced and led by the federal government, it is unlikely that the policy will have a significant impact on Indigenous languages.

Aspirational students and industry partnerships

In the late 1990s and early this century, a number of states implemented programs designed specifically for Indigenous students who demonstrate aspirations to succeed at school (NSW Board of Studies, 1996; NT Education Department, 2000; Queensland Department of Education, 2000). One program that commenced at Karratha Senior High School in Western Australia in 1997, and is still continuing, demonstrated outstanding success and has been the model for numerous other programs in schools across Australia (Cunningham, Goddard et al., 2001; Partington, Galloway et al., 2009). The program is the Follow the Dream/ Partnerships for Success strategy that involves the selection of Aboriginal students with strong aspirations to succeed at school and provides support throughout high school.

The key strategy that enhances the success of students is the coalition of stakeholders in the students' success: industry partners join the Department of Education in supporting the program. Major mining companies such as Rio Tinto, BHP and Woodside Petroleum contribute resources including financial support to the program. This support, allied with the WA Department of Education's contribution, enables the operation of an after school enrichment centre with tutors to support the students. Also, a full-time coordinator manages the program at each centre, advocating for the students, coordinating tutoring and other resources and maintaining links with the partners.

The program is spreading across Australia as its success is observed. More recently, the Dare to Lead program has advocated the development of industry partnerships by schools to improve educational outcomes for Indigenous students (Dare to Lead, 2011b). A more detailed examination of the progam is included in chapter 13.

The above issues are currently influencing the direction of change in Aboriginal education and are significant elements in the diverse and complex changes that are occurring. In the next section, the theoretical underpinnings of Indigenous education will be outlined to provide the foundations for the following chapters in the book.

Theory and Aboriginal educational disadvantage

Poor educational outcomes can only be fully explained in the context of the wider society in which they occur. However, it is not always clear how this interaction takes place. Theory is a widely used tool in the social sciences to help explain complex social issues such as Aboriginal educational disadvantage. Theories can assist in identifying underlying patterns by unifying knowledge into general explanations. Such is the depth of educational disadvantage among Aboriginal young people that important insights can be gained from a range of theories. However, it is important to stress that theories are only a guide to social reality and that each of the theories discussed below are not mutually exclusive. In fact, a case can be made for the relevance of each of the theories discussed.

Neo-colonialism

From the time of the settlement of Australia, Aboriginal people had white control directly imposed upon them. Neither Australian colonial governments, nor the Commonwealth of Australia, when it was created in 1901, recognised the right of Aboriginal people to self-determination. This was in contrast to the process of white European settlement in New Zealand, Canada and the United States where official treaties recognised the sovereignty of Indigenous people. Even though such treaties were widely ignored and abused until the 1970s, they have enabled Indigenous people in other Western settler nations to gain some significant measures of control over their own affairs. This has not been the case in Australia where only limited forms of self-management and partnership with Government have ever been introduced. The exceptions are the power given to the Northern Territory Land Councils in the late 1970s and the greater autonomy given to some Indigenous groups following the granting of access to their land under the *Land Rights Act 1993*. But, in all other respects, policies are mainly developed for Aboriginal people by the non-Indigenous political system. This is often referred to as a system of neo-colonialism; that is governments continuing to act as if they were colonial powers.

The claim that governments retain a neo-colonial approach to Aboriginal affairs is generally seen to be manifest in the lack of recognition of the need to fully involve Indigenous people in policies and programs designed for them. Such an approach can become a normalised way of interacting with Indigenous people. As Maddison describes: 'Anyone who visits a remote Aboriginal community will see the multitude of white public servants – CEOs, teachers, nurses, police – who essentially run the place. In many communities there are multiple forms of "bureaucratic" and "technical dependency" that have developed' (2008, p. 49).

Concern over the long history of interventions in Aboriginal people's lives was renewed in 2007 when the Howard Government proclaimed its 'Northern Territory Intervention' as a response to a widely publicised report highlighting the problem of child sexual abuse in Aboriginal communities in the Territory, outlined earlier in this chapter. Underpinning the intervention was the deployment of police, army and volunteer doctors (Maddison, 2008). The scale and speed of the intervention polarised opinion in Australia. Critics (Stringer, 2007, np) called it a 'neocolonial moment' because remote communities were depicted as 'insufficiently colonised zones' needing greatly expanded government powers over Indigenous people who failed to be consulted in the process.

Racism

Even though today most non-Indigenous Australians are reluctant to acknowledge the existence of racism, discrimination
and prejudice that have been the dominant lived experiences
of most Aboriginal people. In common with other countries,
Australia has a troubled history of racism as official policy, not
just towards Aboriginal people but towards people of colour in
general as was manifest in the 1901 White Australia Policy.

During the era of official racism which lasted from settlement up until the early 1970s, legislation in the various colonies/
states denied citizenship rights to Aboriginal people; enabled
their confinement in reserves and settlements; enabled the
forcible removal of Aboriginal children from their parents; and
restricted and/or barred Aboriginal children from attending
state school.

These manifestations of racism are often referred to as 'old'
racism because they reflected beliefs in the biological inferiority
of Aboriginal people and the accompanying desire for the separation of the races. While such beliefs persist, 'old' style racist
thinking is widely thought to have declined and been replaced
by 'new' forms of racism which operate through stereotypes
manifesting as cultural intolerance such as the depiction of all
Aboriginal people as welfare dependent, drunks or incapable of
grasping opportunities. In turn, such stereotypes are thought to
reflect and reinforce non-Indigenous people's sense of superiority
and to bolster fears about supposed threats to 'national unity'
and 'social cohesion' (Dunne et al, 2004).

Thus, the shift from overt forms of racism to more covert
forms stifled discussion in Australia about its extent and impacts.
By the 1990s, racism was, as Pat Dodson maintained, 'like an

elephant in the room'; Aboriginals and informed whites were alive to its existence but there was little public discussion of it. Noel Pearson has written forcefully about the impacts of contemporary racism on Aboriginal people, describing it as a 'terrible burden' (Pearson, 2009a, p. 161):

> It attacks the spirit. It attacks self-esteem and the soul in ways that those who are not subject to it would not have an inkling. Racism is a major handicap; it results in Aboriginal people not having access to opportunities; in not recognising the opportunities when they arise, and in not being able to seize and hold onto opportunities when they recognise them.

White Australians, Pearson believes, do not understand the destructiveness of racism.

In the early 1990s, two significant developments brought racism to the fore. The first was the release of the Human Rights and Equal Opportunity Commission's *Report of the National Enquiry into Racist Violence* (1991). Established in 1988 as a result of concern from church and community leaders that the incidence of such violence was on the increase, the Commission held hearings in centres across Australia as well as calling for submissions from the public. Adopting a broad definition of racist violence to include physical attack, property damage, verbal and non-verbal intimidation and incitement to racial hatred, the Report painted a disturbing picture of a dark side of Australian life that political leaders had long preferred to ignore. The evidence gathered by the Inquiry was a telling insight into the nature of racism. It confirmed what people of colour the world over had for decades maintained; that there is far more racism than white people are prepared to admit (Delago & Stefancic, 2001). Racism, according to this view, had become institutionalized into the way in which wider society and its institutions interacted with Aboriginal people.

Described as an 'endemic problem' for Aboriginals, the report explained how the social construction of racial attitudes towards Aboriginals legitimised acts of racist violence. The continuities with the past remained striking; Aboriginal people were still portrayed as 'a law and order problem, as a group to be feared, or as a group outside assumed socially homogenous values'. Ignorance helped perpetuate such views. As the report commented: 'Aboriginal and Torres Strait Islander students still find that Australian history can be taught without acknowledging the status or rights of indigenous people, and that many teachers still hold inaccurate or derogatory stereotypes of Aboriginal people' (p. 348).

Few agencies were immune from criticism for either perpetrating, condoning or ignoring racist incidents: police, schools, media and shops. Part of the escalation in the rate of racist violence was explained in the report as a reaction to Aboriginal people campaigning for their rights; 'as a means of opposing legitimate political expression' (p. 72). Evidence to the report also explored the psychological impact of racist violence. Police forces around Australia came in for savage criticism in this regard. Police in the Northern Territory who dressed up in KKK garb; police in Perth who mocked and laughed at Aboriginals appearing in court; and police in just about every state who used racist language as a form of intimidation. The introduction of anti-racial vilification laws was part of the response to the report.

The second development which highlighted the underlying racism in Australia was the backlash to the 1992 High Court decision on native title (the Mabo decision) and the subsequent 1993 Native Title Act, which, together, granted Aboriginal people land rights – at least for those groups who could prove continuous occupation within their 'country'.

Conservative critics of the High Court decision and the government's legislative response revived what many saw as the racial backlash which stopped the Hawke Government from introducing national land rights legislation in the mid 1980s. The argument mounted then was that land rights would undermine the national interest by impeding mining. But research commissioned by the Hawke Government showed that community attitudes still harboured strongly prejudiced views about Aboriginal people (Beresford, 2006). Such views were in the forefront again during the heightened tension of the debate over native title in the early to mid-1990s. Prominent mining industry spokesperson Hugh Morgan was an active opponent of land rights in both the mid 1980s and the early 1990s. He believed that the Mabo decision encouraged Aborigines to 'think of themselves as separate and distinct from their fellow citizens. It promises racial tension. It guarantees economic stagnation'. Morgan decried 'the guilt industry' which could not accept that 'cultures are not equal, that some cultures will wither away' (Cited in Watson, 2002, p. 180). He accused those who stood by the Mabo decision as 'ashamed to be Australians' (*Sydney Morning Herald*, 28 July 1993).

Popular historian Geoffrey Blainey was also a forceful critic of granting Aboriginals access to native title. He argued that 'Guilt and reconciliation are becoming a sharp weapon for those who find it useful to deny the legitimacy of the nation'. It was these so-called threats to the integrity of the nation that worried Blainey. Commenting on the land presently held by Aboriginals, Blainey revived a long-standing fear among many non-Aboriginal people: 'In that long north-south corridor of Aboriginal lands there are only a couple of gaps of any size...If, in ten or fifty years' time, the Aborigines should move towards self-determination, this corridor could be the nucleus of a nation' (Blainey, 1993). Thus, land rights had 'gone far enough'. In other respects, Blainey articulated the traditional conservative view; land rights represented 'two Australias', one based on race (ibid.)

Debate about the contentious issue of racism and the way it had been experienced by Aboriginal people continued throughout the 1990s and into the early years of the twenty-first century. The release of the report on the removal of Aboriginal children from their families in the era of assimilation – the so-called Stolen Generations – complied by the Human Rights and Equal Opportunity Commission re-ignited the issue with the finding that racist attitudes motivated the officials who perpetrated the policy which, it was further claimed, could be described as genocide in its attempts to eradicate Aboriginal culture through assimilation. Such a finding was bitterly contested by many Australians who argued that the policy was motivated by the best wishes of earlier generations of people concerned about the effects of poverty and marginalisation on Aboriginal children. Such rationalisations were, in turn, seen as denialism by those who maintained that Australia had a racist past which it was reluctant to acknowledge (Manne, 2001).

Leadership to change community attitudes came from an unexpected quarter. In the winter of 1993, St Kilda's Nicky

Winmar, one of the Australian Football League's (AFL) most talented players, and one of a growing number of Aboriginal players, staged a lone protest over racism on the football field when he momentarily stayed on the ground after the siren ended play in the game against Collingwood, the League's most legendary working-class club. Standing in a warrior-like pose he lifted his jumper and pointed to his black skin in a defiant gesture to Collingwood fans whom, he later maintained, had issued a stream of racist abuse at him throughout the game. The image of Winmar standing alone on the ground in proud defiance, which was captured on camera, instantly become one of the iconic images of modern Australian popular culture.

Winmar's action set in motion sweeping changes to the rules governing the way in which the AFL dealt with racism and, in the process, the AFL embraced reconciliation as an integral part of the spirit of the game. Winmar's stance brought to light the ugly reality of racism in football; a culture of racist abuse that normalised its use as a legitimate tactic against Aboriginal players. In a mirror of the wider society, Aboriginal players were powerless to counter this culture: 'if you were abused you had to accept it, or if you retaliated then you had to accept the penalty' (McNamara, 2000). While the football authorities ignored Winmar's protest, it was impossible for them to do so two years later when Essendon's Michael Long, acknowledged as one of the most sublimely talented players in the competition, took the protest against racism in football to a new level. He alleged that a Collingwood opponent, Damien Monkhurst, had called him a 'black bastard'. On this occasion, mediation was arranged between the two players but no penalty was imposed on Monkhurst. Following the mediation, AFL officials confidently pronounced that the matter had been happily resolved. But Long had other ideas. He told the media that he was not happy with the way the matter had been dealt with. Another mediation session was arranged at which Monkhurst apologised. But Long was still not satisfied. He demanded that the AFL institute a system of fines and suspensions for players who engaged in racist abuse (McNamara, 2000). In June 1995 the AFL brought in 'Rule 30: A Rule to Combat Racial and Religious Vilification'; Long's actions, built on the initial stand by Winmar, had together changed the largest sporting code in Australia and, in so doing, set an example to the nation at large.

While the prevalence of racism in Australian society largely remained untested by the collection of data, anecdotal evidence confirmed its presence. In their study, Bourke et al., (2000, p. 20) found that many students spoke of racist experiences within the general Australian community. These students referred to a pervasive feeling that people looked upon them with suspicion just because they were Indigenous. In an earlier study, Beresford and Omaji (1996, p. 130) pointed out that today's Indigenous youth are highly sensitive to any racist overtones: 'Their explicit opposition to racism marks a break from past generations who were often passive in the face of racism in the sense that they frequently did not publicly challenge its perpetrators.'

The most recent research on racist attitudes in the community was collected in 2001 (Dunn, et al., 2004; Dunn, 2003) and involved a sample of over 5,000 people in New South Wales and Queensland. Among its key findings were that:

- 83 per cent of respondents agreed that racism was a societal problem
- 12 per cent of respondents believed that there was a natural hierarchy of races i.e. in 'old' racist values of white supremacy
- 12 per cent of respondents self-diagnosed their own racism
- 'new' racisms of cultural intolerance, denial of Anglo-privilege had a strong hold on popular opinion
- prejudice was strongest towards Muslims, but was also expressed against other groups including Aboriginals

How might such attitudes affect the education of Aboriginal students? While this question is difficult to determine with any accuracy and may well vary in different settings across Australia, the following might be generalised ways in which racism continues to impact on Aboriginal students:

- failure to recognise Aboriginal learning styles and needs
- the rigid enforcement of discipline policies that fail to take adequate account of the circumstances of Aboriginal life experiences
- failure to include an Aboriginal perspective in the teaching about Australian history and society
- normalisation of attitudes about Aboriginal students poor school outcomes.

In fact, 36 per cent of Indigenous Australians reported experiencing racism in the education system, higher than any other group. Some have argued that this is inevitable given the Western model of teaching. de Plevitz (2007) argues that this model embodies institutional racism in its failure to endorse

Indigenous core values and understandings and, hence, has as its unconscious aim the assimilation of Aboriginal people – a policy that was abandoned in the 1970s. Even though some would disagree with this view and strongly maintain that Aboriginal people must be given access to mainstream education and opportunities, it remains the case that those who succeed have to learn to live in two worlds.

Intergenerational transfer of disadvantage

Sociologists and criminologists have for decades recognised the strong tendency for disadvantage to reproduce itself within members of the same family over succeeding generations (Rutter & Madge, 1976). This notion of the intergenerational transfer of disadvantage is crucial to understanding the broad social position of Indigenous people in general but specifically the phenomenon of ongoing educational disadvantage. As discussed in chapter 3, the racial policy framework which guided Aboriginal affairs policy in Australia from the end of the nineteenth century until the 1970s has left a crippling legacy for many Indigenous communities. The combined impact of removal of land, segregated living, denial of citizenship rights, exclusion from state schools and forced removal of children created lifestyles and outlooks which became part of what was transmitted from generation to generation.

Although understanding among non-Indigenous people of the ways in which children are socialised in Aboriginal communities is limited, much greater attention has been given to this issue in the United States. As Boykin and Ellison (1995, p. 112) wrote, children learn minority roles from their families.

There is evidence that a similar pattern has been at work

in many Australian Indigenous families. Beresford and Omaji's (1996) book on juvenile crime among this group found the socialisation of children occurs within an intergenerational experience of racism. Parents who have been economically excluded are unable to express in their lives the bitterness they experienced and often pass it on to their children. Some Aboriginal parents' response to their children's education is shaped by their own experiences of school. The principal of Kununurra District High School in the Kimberley region of Western Australia has explained (Human Rights and Equal Opportunity Commission, 22 October 1999):

> Because school was such a negative experience for many parents it takes a very long time for that attitude to break down. We had a teacher who asked for teacher relief in order to go out and meet every one of the Aboriginal parents of the children he taught…and every parent that he approached went into hiding… The notion of a teacher coming out and meeting a family is still too threatening.

Teachers with experience understand this. It takes at least three years for them to secure good relationships so that they can visit without it being a threatening event for the parents. In many cases, however, the teacher has already moved on to another school before they have cemented firm relationships. As students' school experiences improve, their attitudes will change and this is clearly occurring for some. But it has not yet occurred for a critical mass of Indigenous students.

Intergenerational disadvantage has been linked to the

background causes of family violence within Aboriginal communities. Indeed there is a widespread view that current levels of dysfunctional behaviour are grounded in unresolved grief associated with multiple layers of trauma and disadvantage which have spanned many generations (House of Representatives, 2011). This realisation has helped highlight the impact of assimilation policies. Operating between the 1930s and 1970s, government officials removed large numbers of Indigenous children who were institutionalised and/or fostered out so that they could grow up within the dominant society. In reality, such practice fragmented many Aboriginal families. The children who were removed were often left with deep psychological scars which they carried into adulthood and which have been linked to mental health issues, substance abuse and poor parenting skills, with the latter paving the way for problems for the children of those who had been removed (Gordon, 2002; Human Rights and Equal Opportunity Commission, 1997).

The recent inquiry into child sexual abuse in the Northern Territory also linked its prevalence to wider intergenerational issues. The authors of the report note that the systematic maltreatment of Aboriginal children is a 'sensitive marker...of persistent economic decline and community disintegration' which, in turn, can only be explained in terms of the impact across generations of 'cultural disintegration, unresolved community trauma and racial abuse' (Wild and Anderson, 2007).

Welfare dependency
The socio-economic disadvantage that plagues many Aboriginal communities across Australia has long been regarded as a major handicap. Various explanations have been given for

the perpetuation of this often chronic disadvantage, including explanations consistent with intergenerational disadvantage: dispossession, racism and trauma. Noel Pearson has challenged the adequacy of traditional explanations for Aboriginal disadvantage. In line with new conservative thinking about the destructive impacts of passive welfare advanced in the United States in the 1980s, Pearson (2009a) presented a compelling case that Aboriginal access to welfare from the early 1970s had transformed many Aboriginal communities by encouraging Aboriginal withdrawal from the 'real' economy to a 'welfare' economy. This shift, he argued, resulted from two developments: the enforcement of equal wages for Aboriginals working in the pastoral industry from 1966 and the recognition of the citizenship rights of Aboriginal people following the 1967 referendum upholding Commonwealth responsibility in Aboriginal affairs.

Equal wages in rural industries commenced in the 1970s and resulted in a reduction of employment opportunities for Indigenous workers as employers turned to increased employment of non-Indigenous workers and increased mechanisation on the land. However, this did not apply to urban and regional districts where Indigenous unemployment was also high. Norris (2001) argued that lack of employment opportunities in rural and remote areas was not the case as non-Indigenous employment has remained high in these areas. Similarly, lack of access to skills and training is not a relevant argument for high unemployment because Indigenous unemployment is high in urban areas as well, where training is available. Although there is no definitive explanation for high Indigenous unemployment, it is likely that a combination of factors, including racism, lack of training, and the availability of welfare have contributed.

Citizenship rights paved the way for increased welfare provision by the Commonwealth. Decades later, Pearson maintains, passive welfare has become an entrenched system of governance over Aboriginal people by dominant whites; a means by which relatively powerless people have been converted into passive recipients or clients. In turn, this system of governance has become internalised by Aboriginal people as a 'welfare mentality' in which Aboriginal people see themselves 'as victimised or incapable and in need of assistance without reciprocation' (Pearson, 2009a, p. 151). Thus Pearson concludes that while dispossession, trauma and racism are 'ultimate' causes of the precarious position of Aboriginal people, they do not explain the 'recent, rapid and almost total social breakdown' of many Aboriginal communities (ibid., p. 165).

Critics of Pearson's views (see for example Martin, 2001; Maddison, 2008) on the causes of welfare in Aboriginal communities believe that a more complex set of issues must be taken into account to explain the social breakdown in many communities, including persistent neglect by governments and the pervasiveness of alcohol and other substance abuse. These critics have been concerned about the rise of a 'blame the victim' approach that has accompanied the arguments about passive welfare. Nevertheless, they share the same concern as Pearson about the deleterious impacts of welfare. Maddison (2008, p. 51) has argued that in many urban and remote communities, social security payments and income from CDEP 'make up the majority, if not the whole of the local economy', thereby leaving people dependent on welfare.

Nevertheless, Pearson's views have been given great prominence in the political discussion about changes to Aboriginal policy because they conformed to the wider ideological views about the limits to welfare held in government circles and especially during the long reign of the Howard Government (1996–2007). Pearson advocated the imposition of forms of reciprocity on Aboriginal people to end the destructiveness of Aboriginal people passively accepting welfare, whereas others called for more radical forms of Aboriginal self-determination and genuine partnership with government to address the problems created by welfare.

Resistance

The claim that some students actively resist – or undermine – school-based instruction has been widely applied to students from working class and ethnic minority backgrounds since the 1970s. Resistance theory helps define the relationship between the school and the dominant society by questioning the role of schools in sustaining dominant social practices and structures which are found in societies divided along class, race and gender lines (McLaren, 1998).

Resistance theory can be seen as a sub-set of broader conflict theory in which society is seen as composed of conflicting groups. Its intellectual origins can be traced to the nineteenth century writing of Karl Marx who attributed social conflict to the capitalist system of class distinctions. Thus, the ruling class possessed land and capital while the working class had only their own labour. Because the ruling class owned the means of production, Marx argued that they exploited and oppressed the workers; a situation that he believed would only be relieved through a revolution by the workers. Later writers such as Gramsci introduced the notion of hegemony, that is,

people's acceptance of the authority of the ruling class to domi-
nate them.

Within this broad intellectual tradition, resistance theory
views the school as representing a potentially oppressive institution of the dominant classes in society, whose power is resisted
by certain oppressed groups. It has been widely applied in
the United States to explain the poor educational outcomes
widely experienced by African-American youth. Howard and
Hammond (cited in Taylor, 1995), argue that 'blacks have a
propensity to avoid intellectual engagement and competition
since they view this activity as the preserve of dominant group
(white) behaviour'. Fordham and Ogbu (cited in Irvine & Irvine,
1995) further developed this theory by arguing that caste-like
minorities (that is, a minority group regarded as inferior by the
dominant society) develop, as a counter challenge, oppositional
social identities and oppositional frames of reference in which
intellectual activity is resisted as the domain of whites. This view
is maintained on the basis that minority groups internalise parts
of the dominant group mythology that blacks are intellectually
less competent than whites.

Ogbu's theory has been used by researchers examining
resistance among Navajo (Native American) youth. Deyhle's
(1995) extensive study of one Navajo community found that the
young are subject to racial discrimination in both the school and
the community to which many responded 'by withdrawing or
"resisting" education'.

Writers on Aboriginal youth have also employed a 'resistance'
perspective for several decades to explain anti-school attitudes.
In the early 1970s, one educator commented that: 'Schooling is
not an Aborigine [sic] procedure. They see schooling as a white

man's process. They leave schooling to the non-Aborigine [sic] because it is his. Where they have sought it, they have, almost totally, failed at it' (Grey, 1974, p. 47). More recently, Groome and Hamilton (1995, pp. 31, 47) have written:

> Teachers discussed with us the strong pressures which Aboriginal students placed on each other not to succeed. A climate can be created in which achievement is regarded as 'shame job'. We commonly heard of young students with ability who, under pressure from their peers, began to go backwards in achievement... When Aboriginal youth are unable to develop positive relations with teachers, they can develop identities which are oppositional to those desired by the school. These images tend to further structure the negative course of the relationships. They see themselves as losers who are processed, defined and recycled within the mechanisms of school. Their existence as persons is devalued and they become targets for reform or exclusion.

In their study of Indigenous students, researchers from the Queensland University of Technology (Purdie, et al., 2000, p. 8) found a similar response which they linked to intergenerational socialisation:

> There was a culture among many students of 'anti-intellectualism', of doing well in school as being of little value or something to be ashamed of. Even students whose teachers described them as very academically

able did not always feel good about themselves as students. This negative sense of self as a student was probably accentuated for many by the views of parents/ carers who do not think school is that important, and who openly tell their children that 'School never did me any good'.

The slow rates of improvement in educational outcomes for Indigenous students could be taken as confirmation that resistance may be weakening while still being a part of the response of many students. Indeed, James Comer, an American professor of psychiatry, maintained that three generations of continuous access to education are necessary if a family is to function successfully in the post-industrial economy (Comer, cited in Finnegan, 1998, p. 44). Such continuous access has eluded almost all Indigenous people.

Alienation

The theory of alienation is a further variation on the impact of power relationships between Indigenous youth and the wider society. Alienation is described as a state of oppression and a distressed psychological outlook. Although it is often ambiguous exactly what young people might be alienated from, the theory has attracted educationists concerned to explain both truancy and delinquency (Williamson & Cullingford, 1997). It, too, has its intellectual origins in the writings of Karl Marx who maintained that the working class was alienated from their true selves by the capitalist system. Two manifestations – often interrelated – are frequently identified in relation to Indigenous youth in nations which have been colonised: alienation from school and follow-on alienation from society. The aforementioned study on Navajo students, for example, found a widespread perception of discrimination among these youth; that they were up against a 'stacked deck'. Consequently, 'they have no reason to believe that their cooperation with the educational regime would bring advantages in either schools or in the workplace' (Deyhle, 1995, p. 409).

Alienation from school is often a result of a clash of cultures. In traditional orientated communities, for example, alienation is a consequence of a complex raft of differences that give rise to anxiety and frustration (Adermann & Campbell, 2008). Students may perceive that the system is stacked against them and they have little chance of succeeding in formal education and so their affiliation with school diminishes. Boon (2008) reported that the clearest predictor of dropping out of school for Indigenous students is the rate of suspensions. This may be a consequence of lack of affiliation with the purpose and processes of schooling. Other factors include perceptions by students that their language and culture are not valued and accepted by the school and they just 'fade out' of education (Bourke, et al., 2000, p. 28).

Alienation from broader society often follows alienation from school. A condition closely resembling a state of alienation among urban Indigenous youth was apparent by the early 1970s; that is, significant numbers of these young people were found to be aware of their socio-economic disadvantage and responded with absenteeism from school and aggression over their limited prospects for social advancement. During the 1990s, several researchers noted a rising incidence among Aboriginal youth of alienation from both black and white communities. Beresford and Omaji (1996) observed the difficulties of identity formation among marginalised urban Aboriginal youth. Cultural dispossession meant that such youth did not feel a legitimate connection to their Aboriginal heritage while also feeling excluded from mainstream European culture. Consequently, identity formation presented a real struggle for significant numbers of Aboriginal youth, many choosing to model themselves on African-American groups. Similarly, Jonas (cited in Aboriginal and Torres Strait Islander Social Justice Commissioner, 1999b, Summary, p. 7) has noted that young Indigenous people 'variously speak of being alienated from both black and white communities, of difficulty in coming to terms with the past, of living somewhere "between two worlds", and of being unable to find a point of balance'.

Other indicators of the relevance of alienation are discussed throughout this book highlighting that a significant number of especially urban Indigenous youth do exist in a subcultural lifestyle separate from mainstream values, their immediate families and their cultural heritage. This lifestyle does appear to be closely associated with a range of psychological conditions including low self-image and aggression. It is also associated with non-school attendance and a rejection of the value of education. A critical factor in this alienation from society appears to be the internalisation of experiences of racism.

Culturalism

Culturalism is a theory that rose to prominence in Indigenous education in the early 1980s. It provided an antidote to the dominant views of the 1970s that Indigenous students were unsuccessful at school because they had deficits in cognitive functioning or social environments that prevented them from performing well at school. The most important literature dealing with culturalism in relation to Indigenous education was produced in the 1980s and 1990s (Harris, 1980; Christie, 1985; Christie, 1986; Malin, 1989; Harris, 1990; Malin, 1990; Malin, 1998). Today, culturalism is one of a number of theories that contribute to understanding the school experiences of Indigenous students and, while still very relevant, its impact is accepted without the need to elaborate on the theory. Consequently, most of the seminal literature on the topic dates from the period 1980–2000.

The theory maintains that, in the realm of school, the cultural differences between Indigenous peoples and mainstream education are fundamentally at odds. In turn, this understanding is linked to interactionist theory which holds that through language and symbols, people develop a shared meaning about the world. Out of the evolution of these shared meanings, cultures have developed. However, from an interactionist perspective, people of different cultures can encounter problems in interaction because of the different assumptions about the meaning and purpose of interaction.

While not all Indigenous young people see themselves in the same way, it is clear that they do see themselves as belonging to a broad cultural group of Indigenous people with attachments to distinctive cultural 'markers', such as kinship group, history, language background and place. According to Purdie et al., (2000, p. 9):

> In general, it appears that if an Indigenous child thinks about his or her cultural identity, there is pride attached to saying 'I am black', or 'I am Aboriginal'

or 'I am a Torres Strait Islander' and this pride derives mostly from family and Indigenous community influences...it does not appear that most Indigenous young people dwell on their identities; in some respects they do not perceive themselves to be different from non-Indigenous people...but when pressed, many appear to think that other (non-Indigenous) people think they are different. This difference is often interpreted as being inferior.

However, the values of Indigenous people can be substantially different from those of Anglo-Saxon Australians, notably, traditional Aboriginal culture is 'preoccupied with the relatedness of land, kin and religious ceremony' (Harris, 1990, p. 27). Traditional Anglo notions of 'success' – school credentials, individual careers, and individual economic prosperity – do not necessarily reflect those of most Indigenous cultures (Boon, 2008) where success can be judged on intact extended familial relations, where individual jobs and educational success are used to enhance the family and the community, and aggressive individualism is suppressed for the cooperation of the group (Deyhle, 1995).

While it is inappropriate to generalise about Aboriginal people as a single group, the differences in cultural background between Indigenous and non-Indigenous people in Australia have important educational implications. Writing about remote Aboriginal communities, Christie (1984) commented that Aboriginal children perceive school very differently from non-Aboriginal children: its purpose, operation and the behaviours appropriate to it. Harris (1990, p. 8) noted the 'hidden values in the curriculum', which can inflict damage to Aboriginal society: 'The hidden curriculum includes what rubs off over time onto students during the school experience although it may not be deliberately taught. It includes such important elements as values, priorities and attitudes and what is viewed as normal'. In this way educational policies can be based on assumptions about the relevance of culture for Indigenous people; that they no longer live the 'traditional' way of life and are therefore more like mainstream Australians (de Plevitz, 2007).

However, there is nothing hidden about the difficulties Indigenous students have in accessing bilingual education. Not only are most Indigenous languages in Australia critically endangered, governments have been widely supportive of the need for the school curriculum to be based in English. Such a policy has overlooked evidence of a strong correlation between language and culture in the development of resilience among members of minority/ethnic cultures, but the corresponding loss of language and culture can have negative impacts on resilience and lead to stress and problems in socialisation and communication (Human Rights and Equal Opportunity Commission, 2009, see chapter 4).

In the inquiry into the protection of Aboriginal children from child abuse, the Northern Territory Board of Inquiry reported that schooling had to take into account the culture and language of Aboriginal students if it was to be effective. Two students aged 12 and 13 gave evidence of the failure of schooling (Wild & Anderson, 2007, p. 147):

We don't retain information – we hear teaching, especially in English and feel that we don't grasp what is being taught, and so it disappears. We go to school, hear something, go home, and the teaching is gone. We feel hopeless. Is there something wrong with our heads because this English just does not work for us? In the end, we smoke marijuana to make us feel better about ourselves. But that then has a bad effect on us. We want to learn English words but the teachers cannot communicate with us to teach us. It is like we are aliens to each other. We need radio programs in language that can also teach us English. That way we will understand what we learn.

The inquiry considered that 'a strong cohort of bilingual and trilingual teachers trained in cross cultural sensitivities is essential and of prime importance for the NT education system. To do anything less will see people in the Territory continuing to mis-communicate and result in further dislocation' (p. 147).

The different views around cultural needs and values – even at the unspoken level – can spill over into teacher responses to Aboriginal children. Teachers can have a tendency to treat Indigenous students differently from other students because of the ideas they have about the cultural characteristics of Aboriginal students (Groome & Hamilton, 1995). Some of these youth lack a positive identification with the culture of school because it is alien to their own cultural background. In relation to Aboriginal students, there is some evidence that, in remote communities, adolescents regard school as for children and they are therefore reluctant to attend. This view becomes more entrenched once social and cultural obligations increase during adolescence (Gordon, et al., 2002).

The introduction of the culturalist perspective on schooling for Indigenous students in the 1980s challenged prevailing dogmas. Today, it is widely accepted that schooling should take into account the languages and cultures of Indigenous students (Ministerial Council on Education Employment Training and Youth Affairs, 2006; 2010). Despite this, there is still a way to go to implement changes at the classroom level so that Indigenous students learn in a comfortable socio-cultural school environment. Throughout the chapters of this book, the importance of an understanding and utilisation of Indigenous cultures and languages will be expressed.

Although each of the above theories – internal colonialism, racism, intergenerational transfer of disadvantage, resistance, alienation and culturalism – offers particular insights into the problem of the on-going struggle to lift school outcomes among Indigenous youth, considerable overlap also exists between them. One way to understand these overlaps is the notion of intergroup power relations. Cummins (2001) explains that school failure does not widely occur in minority groups which are positively oriented towards their own and the dominant culture. However, where there are dominated groups, regarded as inferior by the dominant group, the conditions exist for school failure even before the children go to school.

3

SEPARATE AND UNEQUAL: AN OUTLINE OF ABORIGINAL EDUCATION 1900–1996

Quentin Beresford

The history of Aboriginal education in Australia has not received the attention it deserves. Educational policy makers, teachers and school communities have much to learn from the educational experiences of Aboriginal people. In particular, the poor provision for Aboriginal children has resulted in generations of uneducated, or partly educated, Aboriginal people. This legacy is now manifest in widespread intergenerational educational disadvantage which has proved difficult to overcome. Key manifestations of this intergenerational disadvantage are residual attitudes of suspicion within Aboriginal communities towards schools and ongoing resistance by many youth to the potential benefits of education.

The colonial period

The first school for Indigenous students was established in Sydney by Governor Macquarie in 1814. It was the first of repeated attempts to 'civilise' the Aboriginal population away from their tribal customs (and land) by inculcating Christian habits and the wider values of Europeans. Macquarie's unsuccessful attempt was followed nonetheless by Christian missionaries who tried to convert local Indigenous populations to Christianity. Children became a special focus. Some missionaries began the practice of forcibly removing children from their parents for this purpose, thus beginning the longstanding suspicion and hostility of many Indigenous parents towards schools as institutions of white oppression (Fletcher, 1989).

The early efforts to 'civilise' the Indigenous population petered out, succumbing to the twin ideas of biological determinism and the 'doomed race'. Throughout the nineteenth century officials were under the influence of prevailing racial theories which held that humans had natures which were linked to their biological race and that these were unchangeable. The parallel idea that Aboriginal people were innately inferior – childlike in their mental abilities and almost without initiative – led to the widely held idea that they were 'doomed' to die out completely in spite of the reality that they had survived for over 40,000 years (McGregor, 1997).

This idea, which was still prevalent in some parts of Australia in the 1950s, was sustained by the various attempts to link race to 'scientific' verification. Prominent among these theories was social Darwinism, an adaptation of biologist Charles Darwin's theories of natural selection through the survival of the fittest which he had developed on his voyages of natural discovery during the mid nineteenth century and widely published in *The Descent of Man* in the early 1870s. Developed into social theories by writers such as Herbert Spencer and Alfred Wallace Russell, survival of the fittest in the animal kingdom was transformed into the survival of races. Just as the animal kingdom was locked into a struggle for survival, so too, it was argued, were races. In the human struggle, some races 'had acquired a higher morality, a greater intellect and a superior sociability' such that those 'who had not progressed, could not progress' (McGregor, 1997, p. 24). They were condemned as belonging to this category as a consequence of the ignorance of European writers of their rich cultural heritage and life, and despite their capacity to survive and prosper in one of the harshest environments in the world. Even though they were thought to have been doomed in their traditional state, a special challenge came to be seen in the growing numbers of mixed descent and detribalised Aboriginal peoples. These were seen to require the 'care and protection' of white society.

The emergence of government policy

Between the 1880s and the 1930s a set of policies and practices for Aboriginal education slowly took shape. As state governments had the sole responsibility for Indigenous affairs until the late 1960s, policies and practices differed in timing and scope across the country. Yet, similar approaches emerged. In broad terms, Australian governments up until the 1960s held that Aboriginal children should be offered only minimal schooling consistent with the perceptions about the limitations inherent in their race and their expected station in life at the lowest rungs of white society. In states with large Aboriginal populations, this limited provision was greatly affected by policies which sought to separate Indigenous people from social contact with whites.

In shaping provision for Aboriginal education, governments responded to four forces:

- fears about Aboriginals as a race
- theories of racial inferiority which were widely used to justify limited provision of education

87

- community views on the need for segregation of Aboriginal people from whites, which underpinned the inadequacy of educational provision
- the official policy of assimilation of Aboriginal people within the broader Australian community, which governed the type of instruction offered to children.

The impact of each of these forces will be examined in greater detail below.

Fears about Aboriginals as a race

From the turn of the twentieth century, Australian state governments were increasingly pre-occupied with the 'problem' of a rising number of Aboriginal people of mixed descent, referred to by contemporaries in the racially coloured term of 'half-castes' (now regarded as an offensive term). Prevailing racial theory held that 'full-bloods' (another offensive term) would eventually die out due to their inability to withstand the impact of 'civilisation'. However, a rising number of Aboriginals of mixed descent caused contemporaries a great deal of concern.

When the first Commonwealth–State Conference on Aboriginal Affairs was held in Canberra in 1937, these concerns were given a full airing. Underpinning the discussions was anxiety about the future of race relations in Australia. Professor J. B. Cleland, Chairman of the South Australian Advisory Council of Aborigines, summarised the racial fears evident in states with a large Aboriginal population:

A very unfortunate situation would arise if a large half-caste population breeding within themselves eventually arose in any of the Australian states. It seems to me that there can only be one satisfactory solution to the half-caste problem, and that is the ultimate absorption of these persons in the white population. I think this would not necessarily lead in any way to a deterioration of type, inasmuch as racial inter-mixtures seem, in most cases, to lead to increased virility (Initial Conference of Commonwealth and State Aboriginal Authorities, 1937, p. 10).

As Professor Cleland's thinking illustrates, the ideal of racial har-mony was conceived by some to be biological absorption; that is, the eventual eradication of the so-called 'half-caste' population through intermarriage with whites. A resolution calling for this to be adopted as official policy was enthusiastically supported by delegates from South Australia, Western Australia and the Northern Territory and was carried by the conference.

The plan for biological absorption led to the forced removal of children from their families, and their institutionalisation in missions and government homes for the purposes of cultural assimilation and, eventually, intermarriage. The policy was most widely applied in Western Australia and the Northern Territory. In the former, authorities were given legal power of guardian-ship over all Aboriginal children up to the age of twenty-one and simultaneous control over the right of Indigenous people to marry (Haebich, 2000; Beresford & Omaji, 1998). Consistent with the idea of 'breeding out' the population, authorities rarely gave approval for institutionalised Aboriginals to marry a darker skinned partner; their preference being for whites or lighter skinned Aboriginals. In this way, it was possible for the advocates of biological absorption to imagine the eventual disappearance of the Aboriginal population in Australia.

Although the explicit racial overtones of biological absorption faded during the 1940s, the practice of forced removal continued. Tens of thousands of children were removed by authorities up until the 1970s because parents were judged to have failed to bring up their children according to white standards. By this, authorities meant that Indigenous children continued to be exposed to the cultural influences of their parents and were raised in conditions of poverty over which their parents had little control.

The Christian churches were at the forefront of institutionalising these children on behalf of the government. In the late 1940s, some fifty missions were scattered across Australia operated by all the major denominations (Beckenham, 1948, p. 12). Although some differences in approach were taken to providing for these children, some common patterns were evident. These can be summarised as:

- a primary focus on imparting Christian doctrine rather than formal education
- the prevalent abuse of children including physical, sexual and emotional such that mission life was a traumatic experience for many children
- the requirement for children to perform extensive manual labour as daily duties
- a poor standard of amenities, typified by dormitory-style accommodation
- low expectations held for children's vocational futures
- poorly-trained staff characterised by low levels of knowledge

and respect for Indigenous culture (Beckhenam, 1948; Haebich, 2000; Beresford & Omaji, 1998).

The combination of these characteristics had severe personal, as well as specifically educational, impacts on Aboriginal children. The broader impacts, especially on impaired psychosocial functioning, were detailed in the landmark inquiry into the Stolen Generations (Human Rights and Equal Opportunity Commission, 1997). It is important to recognise that the psychosocial impacts adversely affected the ability of many of these children to adequately fulfil their later role as parents, compounding even further intergenerational disadvantage.

Taken together, mission schools and segregated state schools were in the vanguard of the cultural assimilation of Aboriginal children. Beckenham in his 1948 study was critical of this underlying purpose. He claimed: 'The course given to Aborigines [sic] bears too much evidence of White conceptions of education.' Specifically, he claimed that there was 'little real adaptation of curricula, which are generally adopted from the White school for the Black school' (Beckenham, 1948, p. 37).

Racial theories and education

Just as the policy of biological absorption had been founded on racial ideology, so too was the prevailing attitude that Aboriginal children could not be educated beyond the early primary years. Racial prejudice towards Aboriginal people drove the idea that children needed only limited access to schooling because 'expert' opinion held that they lacked the intellectual capacity to be educated much beyond 3rd or 4th grade. In the late 1930s, the noted anthropologist E. P. Elkin described prevailing attitudes:

The education given depends on the goal to be reached, and this includes the social and economic position and opportunities which await the child when he [sic] reaches adult life. It is generally held that the only opportunity for employment available to aborigines [sic] is in labouring work and as shearers, stockmen and general hands on stations. In Queensland, for example, educational policy is guided by the conviction that 'because of racial and temperamental disabilities', the aborigines [sic] are handicapped in the fields of skilled labour beyond their own settlements (Elkin, 1937, p. 481).

Elkin went on to explain that this reasoning led authorities to limit 'native education to third standard, or at most, the fifth'.

In Western Australia, similar attitudes held sway. Police Magistrate Frank Bateman explained in the course of his 1948 inquiry into Aboriginal affairs in Western Australia that:

There are those who maintain that the half-caste child has equal ability to the white but this is not borne out by the facts. Practically every teacher I have discussed this matter with held the same view – until the 3rd or 4th standard they hold their place but from then on a gradual slipping occurs (Bateman, 1948, p. 24).

The potency of these racial views cannot be underestimated. Having condemned Aboriginal children as intellectual inferiors because of their race, it did not much matter what sort of education they received. A. O. Neville, longstanding administrator of

Aboriginal affairs before World War II, used this very argument in his book, *Australia's Coloured Minority*, to justify the widespread practice of segregated schooling, discussed in more detail below. 'The native child today,' Neville wrote, 'cannot keep up with his white competitors, and is normally a year or two behind them, which is an additional reason for his segregation during school years' (Neville, 1947, p. 158). Racial prejudice limited educational opportunity in another, equally pronounced, way. Up until the 1950s it was common throughout Australia for Aboriginal children to be excluded from state schools. Moves to formally exclude children surfaced in New South Wales in the 1880s and became formalised as government policy by 1902. In that year, the State Minister for Education, John Perry, ordered teachers in all 2,800 government schools to exclude Aboriginal children immediately when white parents objected. The practice became known as 'Exclusion on Demand'. In practice this meant that when Aboriginal parents sought relief or objected, they were told to send their children to the special Aboriginal schools on reserves (see discussion below). Such schools were typically not staffed by the Education Department and commonly not run by qualified teachers:

> On arrival there they were told that these special schools were for 'full bloods' only – since those of 'admixture' were to be assimilated...it is likely that 50,000 Aborigines were denied access [in NSW alone] to either white or the special Aboriginal schools in the first seventy years of this century (Tatz, 1999, p. 28).

Exclusion was frequently enforced on the grounds that children came to school from squalid camps and reserves where habits of hygiene were poor which, as discussed below, were caused by government underfunding of reserves and settlements. However, the justification based on poor hygiene masked deeper prejudices. In his book, Neville laid great stress on exclusion from state schools as the reason for the failure of Aboriginal children to obtain an education. He explained that, while it was theoretically possible for them to attend government schools, in practice, opposition from Parents and Citizens' Associations have 'seen to it that they shall not' (Neville, 1947, p. 149). Neville detailed instances in Western Australia, Queensland, and New South Wales where 'this sort of thing is very marked'. Finally, Neville offered the following justification for exclusion:

> The attitude of the Governments of the States is in effect, that State schools are provided for all children of any class or colour, but the Public says the coloured children shall not sit beside theirs at school. Why not face the facts squarely and admit that our own people have good reasons for their attitude, and, mainly because it presents a hopeless outlook for the coloured people themselves, that Governments are wrong to try and force the position (Neville, 1947, p. 149).

The 'good reasons' Neville attributes to whites were a combination of perceived uncleanliness and moral contamination. In 1935, H. P. Mosley, the Western Australian Royal Commissioner into Native Affairs, lifted the veil on the fears harboured by the wider community of association with Indigenous children living on reserves:

> All sleep together in one hut, no matter the age of the children, and intimate matters of sex relationship become in the minds of the young, details of such minor importance that one is not surprised to find girls at an early age having children of their own. It is no wonder that parents of white children objected to their boys and girls associating with the neglected half-caste at the State school (Royal Commission into the Treatment and Condition of Aborigines, 1934, p. 8).

Of course, the squalid conditions on most reserves, which led to the overcrowding, were a consequence of the government's policy on segregation and under funding of reserves. However, exclusion from state schools was widely enforced; in the late 1940s, Neville estimated only 1,500 Aboriginal children throughout Australia were attending state schools. Of the remaining approximately 20,000 Aboriginal children, only about 25 per cent were receiving any education at all, and most of these were in institutions, notably missions (see later in this chapter) (Neville, 1947, pp. 144–5).

Exclusion ended progressively during the 1940s and 1950s, depending on the timing at which various state education departments assumed full control for Aboriginal education from their respective Native Welfare departments. Yet, pockets of practice upholding *de facto* exclusion continued. In the early 1960s, a principal at Dubbo (New South Wales) was reported to have 'encouraged Aboriginal children reaching Sixth Class to remain on the reserve until they reached compulsory school leaving age' (Watts, 1978, p. 2.3).

While exclusion and confinement to primary grades were very specific manifestations of the application of racial prejudice to education, broader impacts also need to be taken into account. Prejudice towards Indigenous people remained a pervasive characteristic of race relations throughout post-World War II Australia. Its permeation into the very fabric of society constituted a form of institutionalised racism (Wieviorka, 1995, p. 62). Neville paints a compelling picture of this form of racism:

> ...representative opinion in town after town urges that the mixed bloods in or near it be put together further out on Government-run Settlements. A hostile reception meets any suggestion that these folk, including many with war service, should be freed from the prohibition on Aborigines entering hotel bars. In very many country towns, too, they must sit in a special part of the picture theatres, usually up in front, on pain of being asked to leave. In the metropolitan cities, they gravitate to the slum areas, where they can go their own way (Neville, 1947, p. 14).

Such outward expressions of racism were still common in many parts of Australia in the 1970s, and still exist in some quarters today. Although the impact of racism is difficult to fully estimate, Neville believed it was oppressive: 'in every aspect of life, the Coloured Folk are made to feel that they belong to a lower caste' (Neville, 1947, p. 14). Such a feeling was bound to affect the educational aspirations of many children. In fact, a study undertaken among Aboriginal students in Perth, Western Australia, in the early 1970s showed that most were aware of their socioeconomic disadvantages and that this was a cause of their leaving school early in their high school years (Makin & Ibbotson, 1973). Similar views were expressed in relation to Indigenous children in New South Wales. A 1974 conference was told about the intergenerational impact of racism: 'They [Indigenous people] have been made to feel inferior and the children have this inheritance of being born into a group of people who have been considered inferior, the children have started school with an inferiority complex' (Douglas, 1974, pp. 40–1).

Segregation

The necessity to segregate Aboriginal people from Europeans was widely discussed in the early decades of settlement. Initially, the policy of segregation was defined as 'protecting…an inferior and despised race' from 'advancing civilization' (Gale & Brookman, 1975, p. 56). However, as Neville explains, prejudice drove the longstanding policy of banishing Aboriginal people to reserves where they sensed 'and indeed are made to see, that they are not wanted within the compact residential areas of a town' (1947, p. 12). Frequently camps and reserves were located 'side by side with the rubbish dump, the cemetery, or the sanitary site' (Neville, 1947, p. 34). In all locations across the country, these places set aside for Aboriginal people were frequently condemned as 'dreadful', even as 'rural slum ghettos'. Neville provides a particularly graphic account. Generalising the conditions, he writes of 'flea-ridden' humpies; camp conditions characterised by 'fleas, germs and disease'; of unwashed clothing and bodies because of lack of running water and inadequate diets due to lack of cooking facilities (ibid., p. 136).

Such abysmal living conditions were widely reported by other observers. The following account given by a Queensland missionary of a camp at Ravenshoe in the late 1940s explains the connection between segregated living and the flow-on determination to enforce segregated education: 'The present hovels are dark, musty and unhealthy and their living conditions unsanitary in every way...the children are denied the right to an education being debarred from the local state school because of the disgraceful and unsavoury homes from which they came' (cited in Kidd, 1997, p. 181).

Such disgraceful living conditions were still widely evident in the 1970s. The effect on generations of children were understandably profound. Several observers believed that segregation stunted the physical, emotional and social development of Aboriginal children. Neville pointed out that camp conditions caused incorrect feeding of children, which was due to the lack of proper means of preserving foodstuffs. Pot-bellied children, their development arrested by rickets and malnutrition, were frequently the end result. Neville argued that the ill effects of segregated reserves extended beyond the physical. 'Children,' he said, acquired 'a warped outlook difficult to eradicate!' (Neville, 1947, p. 137). It was a fleeting attempt to identify the psychological impacts but few contemporaries were interested in pursuing the matter; during the 1940s and 1950s out of sight meant out of mind as far as most whites were concerned.

In the late 1960s, the impact of reserves started to attract sympathetic observers. One was Henry Schapper, a University of Western Australia academic. He described the conditions for

Indigenous communities on reserves as dependent poverty, a lifestyle that had become extreme by world standards. In turn, this dependency was manifest in a range of psychological conditions including apathy, depression, resentfulness, withdrawal and lack of ambition which, Schapper warned, were 'part of what is normally transmitted by parent to child from generation to generation' (Schapper, 1969, pp. 146, 147). A separate study undertaken at The University of Western Australia in 1975 expressed more direct concerns about the impact of reserves on children. Even though, by this time, exclusion from state schools had ended, reserve life blighted educational opportunity. 'Such children, in the last years of primary education or the first years of the secondary school, have almost no hope of success' (Education Department of The University of Western Australia, 1975, p. 107).

Yet the policy of segregation governed still other areas of education. By its very nature, segregation was borne of racial discrimination; one of the clearest expressions of the belief in the inferiority of Indigenous peoples. It reinforced the idea that no real commitment was needed towards the education of Aboriginal children. In Western Australia, for example, no attempt was made to provide schools on reserves in the populous south-west of the state. However, the state did establish and run two institutions for Aboriginal people where children were offered education, but one only aimed at educating them for servitude (Milnes, 1985, p. 155). The situation differed in other states, notably New South Wales and Queensland, where schools on reserves were established. Yet, such schools were poorly equipped and staffed. In the late 1940s, P. W. Beckenham, who wrote the first comprehensive history of Aboriginal education, criticised governments for failing to provide essential equipment and a comprehensive curriculum. 'The Black child's education is jeopardised by a colour consciousness that is unworthy of any democracy,' was his stern conclusion (Beckenham, 1948, p. 46). Of the quality of education on Queensland reserves, a national inquiry in the late 1960s found that 'schools were understaffed, class sizes were very large, and school buildings and equipment were often grossly inadequate' (Watts, 1978, p. 2.2). In other words, these inferior conditions were not calculated to encourage learning or, indeed, motivation.

The impact of segregation in education was felt long after its formal end during the 1950s. Decades of segregation, either by denying Aboriginal children a place in state schools, or by consigning them to a separate, but inferior, system, established intergenerational patterns of educational disadvantage. These patterns were observable to informed contemporaries by the early 1970s. Alex Grey (1974, p. 47), an experienced educator with Indigenous people, explained that Indigenous people typically saw education 'as a white man's process'. They knew little about school and its expectations:

Not only are the parents themselves often little schooled, they also have meagre understanding of the requirements for success in school. Therefore, they cannot help their children with academic content, skills for the conduct of or for kindling aspirations in continued schooling. Generally, parents are in the dark about the operational steps or means necessary for preparing a child to take advantage of the available learning opportunities. Boys especially do not experience what it means to live alongside and with a successful male. Consequently, Aboriginal children have no framework of experience that suggests to them that effort can result at least in the possibility of achievement.

Other studies confirmed these findings. Watts' (1978) survey of Aboriginal parents found that 61 per cent of mothers and 57 per cent of fathers reported that they did not help their children with their homework; the reason most frequently given was that they felt they could not help.

At the time of the above studies, the doors of state schools had been open to Aboriginal children for at least two decades. However, the damage had already been done. The high rates of non-attendance and early school drop-out, characteristic of the period following the end of segregation, were a tragic legacy of policies and attitudes which sought to deny generations of Aboriginal children a place in school. However, the formal end to segregation did not spell the beginning of a new hopeful era. If education was to be offered, it must serve white cultural and political ends.

Assimilation

The policy of assimilating Aboriginal people within mainstream Australia became official Commonwealth policy in 1951. In its various official manifestations, the idea was that Aboriginal people should adopt the outlook and habits of European Australians in return for similar opportunities. It was adopted without any consultation with Aboriginal people and was designed to replace discriminatory policies including segregation and the earlier policy of biological absorption.

Little has been recorded about the Aboriginal perspective on assimilation and its focus on the education of children. However, one study in the 1960s (Bell, cited in Taft et al., 1970) indicated that communities had little real understanding of the policy but they were aware of its impact on the break up of their local group life: 'Assimilation and education are seen as threats to the group's existence and as in the case of the deviant whose presence threatens the group, has to be opposed...the group is protected by rejecting assimilation and education.'

It is not possible to tell how widespread such a view was. Other evidence indicates Aboriginal parents valued the opportunities for their children to obtain an education (Bell, cited in Taft et al., 1970). Yet, the two positions are not necessarily contradictory. Many Aboriginal parents may have desired an education for their children, but one which respected key parts of their own culture. That some may have rejected education because it was offered on white terms only is hardly surprising; a sad testimony to the flawed aims behind the policy.

Such thinking, when applied to understanding the learning needs of Aboriginal children, resulted in the widespread adoption of a 'deficit' model; that is the poor performance of some groups (disadvantaged and minority students) was a problem with the student and not the school or with education system as a whole. Developed in overseas countries coming to terms with similar problems, the 'deficit' model complemented prevailing beliefs about Aboriginal people because it squarely placed the 'blame' for minority children's poor educational attainments on their socialisation, family patterns, cultural traditions and socio-economic situation' (Eckermann, 1998). Despite indications testifying to its adverse impact, assimilation through education remained official policy into the 1970s. By this time, its cumulative impact attracted critical attention. In 1974, a conference in New South Wales which attracted delegates from many states confirmed the following:

- curricula in all states included very few or no references to Indigenous culture
- offering the same curricula as white children was interpreted by teachers as providing equality of opportunity to Indigenous students
- most Indigenous children whose families had lost contact with their own languages came to school speaking an Indigenous version of English at home that was substantially different from 'school English'
- many Indigenous children had problems understanding the vocabulary of the school because it was outside their experience
- there was a widespread perception among Indigenous people that education was 'a white man's prerogative'
- even in long-established parts of the country, Aboriginal culture survived despite being highly truncated
- Indigenous children remained eager to learn and, to the extent that schools exhibited a feeling of a place of belonging, children would enter the spirit of school life energetically (Coppell, 1974).

By the early 1970s, the link between cognitive style and culture was receiving increasing attention and educational theorists began to challenge the view that culturally different children were incompetent. Overturning generations of educational thinking on this issue, the emerging view was that it was the child's performance, not their competence, which was deficient. Summarising this emerging new thinking, Watts and Henry (1978, p. 9) wrote that the 'gap between competence and performance is attributed to inappropriate situational cues – inappropriate because they fail to stimulate the child to action'. In other words, culturally different children have different cognitive styles which schools failed to understand and respond to, leading to under-utilisation of intellectual abilities.

In spite of this growing body of research and accumulated experience, belief in the positive good behind assimilation remained evident. A South Australian delegate to the 1974 New South Wales Conference summed up the residual commitment to the combined practices of removal of children and their location in mainstream culture:

> We identified a group of Aboriginal children adopted into South Australian families, some forty-three cases, of whom we were able to test thirty-five. Their performance was very nearly in some of the tests, and completely in others, equivalent to the performance of any European child you might like to test from a European middle class environment. These children had been adopted at the average age of 18 months and brought up in white families. I think we can say with complete confidence that had they been brought up in a mission settlement, they would not have been different from the other children in the mission settlement in performance. But when brought up in white families, they perform like white children (Seagrim, 1974, p. 60).

The author went on to explain that such differences in educational outcome were not just a matter of greater opportunities, much of the differences in outcome could be attributed to 'the attitude of the Aboriginal community'; in particular, the 'complete lack of white culture in homes'.

From the perspective of today, such views, even though sincerely held, appear insensitive and racially-based. They illustrate the depth to which assimilation had penetrated the broader community. Assimilation shaped several generations of Australians to believe that white society was superior and that, as a consequence, Aboriginals should be offered its 'benefits' so long as they renounced their 'inferior' culture. A minority of Aboriginal people gained from this policy by achieving in education and/or training (in spite of some onerous restrictions imposed on working permits) but the vast majority did not. Assimilation was a flawed experiment.

The emergence of the 'problem' of Aboriginal education

From the late 1960s, the poor state of Aboriginal education slowly came to be recognised as a major social and educational problem. The Commonwealth Government established an inquiry into the issue, while academics held conferences and published research examining the complex range of issues surrounding the failure of schools to engage most Aboriginal students.

The extent of the failure was confirmed in the 1971 Census. This data showed that while less than 1 per cent of the total Australian population had never attended school, this contrasted with almost one-quarter of the Indigenous population. Only 3.5 per cent of Aboriginal people had achieved senior secondary and post secondary education, compared with 29.6 per cent of the total Australian population (cited in Watts, 1978, p. 21).

Obviously such figures represented a crisis in the capacity of government education to meet the needs of Aboriginal communities. This failure was a key component in the on-going socio-economic disadvantage of the majority of Indigenous people. As one observer (McConnochie, 1982, p. 23) noted at the time: the inadequacy of the school system was 'seemingly designed to trap them [Indigenous people] in the lowest stratum of Australian society'. Flowing from these concerns was a more systematic attempt to explain the failings of the education system.

Shortcomings in the approach of schools

Research undertaken in the 1970s (Education Department of The University of Western Australia, 1975; Watts, 1978) highlighted the remoteness of schools from the Aboriginal students who came under their care. Most teachers and education policy makers had not questioned their approach to serving these children. Schools did not generally regard the problems of their Aboriginal students as an outcome of weaknesses in school organisation or policy; rather, they attributed them to the home backgrounds and general living environment of the children. Such justifications masked the deeper problems in the relationship between Aboriginal students and schools: the failure to develop relationships between the school and Aboriginal homes, the lack of culturally appropriate curricula, and the absence of appropriate training in cultural competency for staff.

During the late 1970s, many studies confirmed Aboriginal children's language difficulties within the European school setting. This had been an emerging area of research showing that the child's 'linguistic state' (that is, whether monolingual in an Indigenous language, bilingual in an Indigenous language and a non-standard form of English or monolingual in a non-standard form of English) created varying degrees of problems in communicating in 'standard' Australian English classrooms (Brumby & Vaszolyi, 1977).

In essence, schools had uncritically adopted their role within the broader policy goal of assimilation and, in this mode, they formed barriers to Aboriginal participation. One tertiary educator wrote of Australian schools in 1969:

> Our schools have an inbuilt value system that is essentially 'White Australian' in its orientation. Within the school we have provided a place for the Aboriginal child...[but] demands of him a cultural conformity to standards that he cannot meet, activities that are wholly out of context in his life, experiences to which he cannot respond (McMeekin, 1969, p. 24).

This value system permeated the approach adopted by most teachers. The evidence derived from studies showed a complex dynamic at work. Watts (1978, p 7.45) reported widespread prejudice:

> Teachers vary in their attitudes, but many hold unfavourable stereotypes about Aborigines [sic]. While some appear to have expectations based on a belief of a normal distribution of learning aptitude among their Aboriginal pupils, significant numbers, it would seem,

do not really expect a very high proportion of these pupils to achieve success at school.

From the perspective of some Aboriginal students, teachers were commonly racist. A Queensland study (cited in Watts, 1978, p. 7.59) reported a typical comment being: 'I don't like school 'cause the teachers don't like us dark kids, that might be only my idea, but I reckon they pick on the dark ones and make them feel small.' Such attitudes, however, revealed a large gulf in understanding between teachers and students. A Victorian study (ibid.) found that Aboriginal parents and their children believed teachers were racially prejudiced against Indigenous students. Teachers, on the other hand, were found to believe that these students lacked motivation, self-control and discipline at home.

Resolving these conflicting positions was clearly a difficult task. However, they were unlikely to be resolved while school authorities did little to encourage or equip teachers to understand the social lives of young Aboriginal people and to better appreciate the impact of wider discrimination on them. Yet, the research indicated the authorities needed to take up this challenge. During the 1970s, several studies (ibid., p. 7.90) indicated that many Aboriginal students suffered significant levels of psychological stress associated with feelings of marginality and conflict between traditional and modern lifestyles. In Bourke, New South Wales, one of these researchers found high levels of behaviour disorder in children aged five to fourteen during the early 1970s:

Few of the Aboriginal children in this area possessed the building blocks commonly regarded as desirable for the development of good mental health. They came from families in which quarrelling, alcoholism and physical violence were common, and in which the affective responses of their parents, especially their fathers, were unpredictable and often inconsistent... Poverty was chronic...separation from their parents was common...children also experienced racial discrimination at a very early age (cited in Watts, 1978, p. 7.91).

Failure to better understand and respond to the needs of Indigenous students created widespread resistance to school, both of an active and covert nature. Both forms were apparent to researchers from the late 1960s. Testifying to the presence of active resistance, one educator (McMeekin, 1969, p. 21) wrote that it affected the willingness of the child to respond to learning and to developing relations with teachers:

One unusually loquacious juvenile informant quite cheerfully admitted that she, in fact, had a profound respect and liking for one of her teachers but had determined in no way to demonstrate such feeling. She had quite deliberately set herself to making the teacher's task an impossibility by her refusal to conform in any way to the school situation. Her sole reason – he was white. Similar views were expressed by other pupils.

A sociologist (McKeich, 1969, p. 3) observed the reverse form of resistance: passive withdrawal. Indigenous high school students, he found,

...tend to withdraw from their teachers, so that it is sometimes impossible to 'get through' to them...They find regimentation irksome. They react to constant failure by giving up trying...Is it any wonder that they prefer the company of other part-Aboriginal children in the playground, and tend to segregate themselves?... The result of this self-segregation is the reinforcing of in-group sub-cultural habits, and lack of opportunity to validate cultural behaviour relevant to the wider group.

Lack of data continued to obscure the full extent of the education system's failure to meet the needs of its Aboriginal students. The first Commonwealth inquiry into Aboriginal education (Watts, 1978, p. 203) expressed criticism on this point, claiming there was little knowledge of Indigenous children's actual achievements, their attitudes and aspirations, nor of the extent of parental participation in schooling or even the degree to which Aboriginal communities felt that the school system had become more responsive: 'Indeed, we do not know whether the actual practices in classrooms and schools differ from those of a decade ago'.

Impact of wider socio-economic disadvantage

During the 1970s, researchers linked the continuing poor performance of Aboriginal students to health and housing issues. In rural New South Wales, for instance, many Aboriginal people lived in bush shelters or improvised dwellings, and in the north-west of the state, 20 per cent were found to be living in either a shed, tent, garage or humpy (cited in Watts, 1978, p. 20).

The situation was equally appalling in Western Australia. The reserve set aside for Aboriginals in the town of Moora, north of Perth, was 'an extremely depressing sight' (Tilbrook, 1977, p. 8). Located three kilometres out of town on land nobody wanted, it consisted of 'extremely dilapidated buildings' that created 'a run down and depressing atmosphere'. The communal amenities block contained only cold showers.

Although governments in Western Australia were committed to phasing out reserves, the transfer of people still living on them to towns and cities was a slow and degrading process. In the first instance, government policy dictated that residents were required to move into 'transitional' housing on the edge of town and when authorities were satisfied that these were being sufficiently looked after, and if their residence in these houses had stirred no complaints from neighbours, they could shift to a conventional town house (Tilbrook, 1977, p. 10). Thus marooned in reserve and transitional housing, many developed 'anti-government and anti-society reactions'.

By the 1970s, a reasonably detailed picture had been built up of the circumstances in which most Indigenous students came to regard school as an alien environment; a complex inter-play of intergenerational disadvantage, on-going poor housing and health, the imposition of assimilation and community racism. In particular, the policy of assimilation had damaging impacts on progress in Aboriginal education. In promoting an ethnocentric view of education, it undermined the ability and the willingness of Aboriginal young people to participate in learning.

The emergence of national policies on Aboriginal education

Until the 1967 referendum granting the Commonwealth the constitutional right to become involved in Aboriginal affairs, state governments had overseen the policies that led to the educational marginalisation of Aboriginal people. However, the Commonwealth was slow to act on the new powers given to it.

The Commonwealth's first major initiative in the area was the introduction in 1969 of the Aboriginal Study Grants Scheme. This was designed to assist Indigenous students to remain in school beyond the compulsory age and represented an understanding of the need to deal with the legacy of the past that had acted to dissuade most Aboriginal students from continuing education. The election of the Whitlam Labor Government in 1972 brought a new commitment to Aboriginal affairs and to education in particular. The creation of the Schools Commission, as an advisory body, provided a new focus on educational disadvantage, including that suffered by Indigenous people. The Commonwealth Government also created the Aboriginal Consultative Group as a specialist advisory body. The Group had as its mission the development of aspirations for education to complement moves towards self-determination for Aboriginals (Watts, 1978).

The Commonwealth also established the first major inquiry into Aboriginal affairs which reported to the Fraser Government in 1978. Among its recommendations were the need to improve teacher training and in-servicing; to train more Aboriginal teachers; to provide more culturally relevant programs; to improve school-work transition; and to raise the awareness of the broader community about Aboriginal issues (Watts, 1978).

Yet, the inquiry also highlighted some of the major barriers to achieving change: the marginalisation of Aboriginal education within state departments of education; insufficient commitment from teacher training institutions; insufficient commitment from schools to making their programs culturally relevant; and the lack of adequate data upon which to track students' progress. Such barriers had meant that most Aboriginal students left school with little opportunity to enter the workforce other than in unskilled or semi-skilled jobs. Most Aboriginal young people who stayed at school were placed into 'dumping classes' where it was a case of 'out of sight, out of mind' (Beazley, 1984, p. 20.4).

An inquiry set up in the mid 1980s in South Australia was equally scathing about inappropriate school practices for Indigenous students (Westley, 1984). 'Despite the rhetoric of recent years', the report noted, 'about catering for individual and cultural differences, there is still a very long way to go in these respects'. This was because teachers maintained inflexible learning processes which did not take into account the needs of Indigenous students and this resulted in widespread truancy.

Despite the growing body of knowledge about the problems hindering progress in Aboriginal education, little was done by way of redress. The Commonwealth Parliament reported on Aboriginal education in the mid 1980s (House of Representatives, 1985) and noted the continuing failure to address underlying social and economic factors that blighted the educational opportunities of most Aboriginal young people. The report highlighted that 'some Aboriginal children go to school tired and listless because their home circumstances prevent them from getting a good nights sleep and because many have no breakfast' (ibid., p. 8). Poor home circumstances also affected the ability of students to do homework, while others went to school without the required books and equipment.

The Commonwealth re-visited Aboriginal education again in 1988 when a taskforce undertook a three-month inquiry (Aboriginal Education Policy Taskforce, 1988). While covering similar ground to previous reports, the distinguishing feature of this inquiry was the call for a coordinated national policy. In the following year, the States and the Commonwealth agreed to establish the first National Aboriginal and Torres Strait Islander Education Policy out of which came the first National Aboriginal Education Policy the following year. The policy embodied five objectives. These were:

- to achieve equity in the provision of education to all Aboriginal children, young people and adults by the year 2000
- to assist Aboriginal parents and communities to be fully involved in the planning and provision of education for themselves and their children
- to achieve parity in participation rates by Aboriginal people with those of other Australians in all stages of education
- to achieve positive educational outcomes for Aboriginal people in school and tertiary education
- to improve the provision of education services across the nation at the local level.

The policy was accompanied by an enormous increase in funding from both state and Commonwealth governments – 250 per cent between 1990 and 1998 (Eckermann, 1998). Recognition that the goal of equity by the year 2000 was unlikely to be met was apparent by the mid 1990s, despite the large injection of government policy support and funding. Aboriginal groups explained that the failings of the policy were due to a lack of negotiation with Aboriginal communities on the educational needs of their young people. In effect, they suggested that the policy reflected the continuation of the tradition of assimilation (ibid.). A review of the policy conducted by the Commonwealth (cited in ibid.) 're-emphasised the need for extended consultation, negotiation and real Indigenous decision-making related to educational programs, staffing, teacher training as well as strategies for access and equity'.

The history wars

The 1990s revealed an important development in the country's willingness to get beyond a white perspective and embrace an Indigenous perspective about education. This debate centred around whether the mainstream education system could embrace education *about* the history of Indigenous people in Australia; one that reflected their sentiments and experiences. However, as the debate progressed obstacles emerged in the way of embracing bi-cultural approaches to Indigenous education.

Disputes about how much emphasis should be given to Aboriginal issues of dispossession and disadvantage during the colonisation of Australia began in the 1960s but intensified during the preparations for the bi-centennial of white settlement in 1988. Prominent Australian historian, Geoffrey Blainey, led the complaints by conservatives that the organisers of the event were trying to write the contribution of the British out of the event in favour of a view of Australia's history as a story largely of 'violence, exploitation, repression, racism, sexism, capitalism, colonialism, and a few other isms' (cited in Abjorensen, 2009, p. 143).

The debate was re-ignited in 1991 when then prime minister, Paul Keating, gave his controversial Redfern Address to mark the Year of Indigenous Peoples before a largely Indigenous audience in the inner-city Sydney suburb of Redfern. In his speech, Keating invoked a 'new' Australian identity, one that incorporated Aboriginality into the nation. This, he said, was a test of our self-knowledge, of how well we know 'what Aboriginal Australians know about Australia'. Linking this test to his vision of re-shaping Australia's standing in the world, Keating went on to say that 'the problem starts with us non-Australians'. Non-Aboriginal Australians, Keating declared, should engage with 'an act of recognition':

> Recognition that it was we who did the dispossessing. We took the traditional lands and smashed the traditional way of life. We brought the disasters. The alcohol. We committed the murders. We took the children from their mothers. We practiced discrimination and exclusion. It was our ignorance and our prejudice. And out failure to imagine these things being done to us.

Keating implored whites to imagine the Aboriginal experience of colonisation. In so doing it created the case for a new dialogue and a new relationship based around imagining the opposite: justice.

Keating's speech inflamed conservative Australians who drew on the British tradition as a key component of their identity as Australians. They felt Keating's anti-British rhetoric politicised history. A key component of the debate, which came to be depicted as the 'history wars', was how the nation should interpret the origins of European settlement – as a story of invasion or one of peaceful settlement. The former sought to embrace an Aboriginal perspective while the latter minimised and/or falsified the Aboriginal experience. Deep divisions opened up over this issue.

Chief protagonist of the 'invasion' view was prominent historian Henry Reynolds whose publications on the history of Aboriginal dispossession had been instrumental in informing Australians of their 'hidden' black history. In a 1994 feature article for *The Weekend Australian*, Reynolds stated that: 'white Australian resistance to change has focused on the crucial question of whether the country was settled or invaded. This has become the chosen battleground between the old story and the new'. Reynolds raised evidence indicating that, at the time of first contact, Aboriginals regarded the settlers as invaders. He based his claim on the observations of a range of contemporary early settlers including David Collins in New South Wales and G. A. Robinson in Tasmania, who used words like 'dispossessed', 'martyrs' and 'invaded' to describe their understanding of the Aboriginal viewpoint. Reynolds went on to to ask rhetorically: 'Why is it so difficult to accept today an interpretation of events which fair-minded colonists were comfortable with 150 years ago?'

Defenders of the 'settlement' thesis had their own answer to this question. An editorial in *The Weekend Australian* (cited in Reynolds, 1994) put the case:

Most Australians do not accept and will never accept
the denial of the legitimacy of their civilization which

the term invasion implies. It is wrong to rewrite our history so that it reflects an Aboriginal interpretation to the exclusion of a European interpretation.

Some saw this defence as an attempt to avoid an admission of guilt and to maintain a moral superiority about European settlement (Seth, 1994). Reynolds argued that the 'settlement' interpretation maintained a false premise: 'the test of an invasion has never been the justification or the rhetoric used by the perpetrator. Invaders rarely admit what they are about'.

The 'settlement/invasion' debate gained traction in the community as schools faced the dilemma about how to represent European foundations in Australia. School communities quickly became divided along philosophical/political lines. As Craven (1999, p. 56) highlighted:

Some teachers feel compelled either to strongly advocate the use of the word 'invasion' or adamantly refuse to refer to such a word in the classroom. Others will use the word 'invasion' when referring to Indigenous perspectives and 'settlement' when referring to non-Indigenous perspectives.

Queensland Labor Premier, Wayne Goss chastised the authors of a 1994 Grade 5 text who suggested that teachers use 'invasion' rather than 'settlement' as political correctness having gone too far (cited in Clark, 2002). In the same year a ruckus broke out in New South Wales over the same issue. Victoria Chadwick, the Liberal Education Minister, was forced to tone down references to 'invasion' in a new social studies syllabus whereupon the NSW Teachers' Federation threatened to ban the syllabus. John Howard weighed into the debate with some vigorous comments. He accused the Federation of 'ideologically driven intellectual thuggery' and argued that the reference to invasion should never have been in the syllabus in the first place (Clark, 2002). The shared views of Goss and Howard on the issue highlighted the challenge facing Australia in developing a shared history. As Indigenous educator Boni Robertson asked: 'How can Aboriginal and Torres Strait Islander peoples trust the government if it continually vetoes any attempt to share...[their] perspectives with all Australians' (cited in Pearson, 2007).

Conclusion

History has left a tragic legacy to the educational outcomes and opportunities for Aboriginal young people. Generations of racist-inspired policies produced intergenerational underachievement and alienation. Yet, the early attempts by Commonwealth and state governments to address this legacy were not met with sustained success. Lack of meaningful engagement with Indigenous people about their educational needs has been cited as a common reason for the slow progress during the 1990s. Yet, the continuation of high levels of socio-economic disadvantage, family dysfunction and the attending government neglect of these issues exacerbated the failings of government policy in education. New approaches were clearly called for and these slowly came forth in the first decade of the twenty-first century.

4

MODELS OF POLICY DEVELOPMENT IN ABORIGINAL EDUCATION[1]

Quentin Beresford and Jan Gray

Over the past two decades there has been a multiplicity of approaches and policies to improve the education of Indigenous young people. As other chapters in this book have shown, reducing the educational disadvantage experienced by this group represents a complex social-policy problem. Rigney (2010) suggests that a key part in closing the gap in educational outcomes necessitates closing the gaps in the strategies currently being used to address the problem. As will be seen in this chapter, there are a wide range of approaches currently under discussion with little consensus on what approaches work best and in which situations. While diversity might be a key component of success, fragmentation of approach is not likely to be effective.

Policy as an issue for educators

The need for teachers and related professionals working in the area to better understand policy development in Indigenous education is underpinned by the following issues:

---

[1] An earlier version of this chapter was published in *The Australian Journal of Education* (vol. 50, no. 3, 2006). We thank the Board and the Editor to re-produce it here in a revised and updated version.

- The complexity of the continuation of educational disadvantage among this group: teachers and schools are the 'street level' agency through which government policies are implemented. The more that teachers are informed about how policies have been developed, and their appropriateness at the local level, the more effective they will be in discharging their role.

- The development of policy approaches based on partnership:
    - the introduction of Shared Responsibility Agreements and Regional Agreements, outlined in chapter 2, are based on the assumption that those working in Aboriginal communities will be active in assisting communities implement approaches consistent with this policy framework.

- The development of national policy approaches:
    - Indigenous education has been governed by an on-going cycle of national targets and policy aspirations such as Closing the Gap and national literacy and numeracy testing, as outlined in chapter 2.

- Policy is an on-going and frequently fraught process:
    - policy in Indigenous education has changed continuously over the past thirty years and more. New approaches are devised as data is gathered and as ideas change. Teachers need to be active participants in this dynamic process given their closeness to the lives of Indigenous youth and their professional expertise in the classroom.

- Closing the gap between Indigenous and non-Indigenous student outcomes conforms very closely to a particular class of policy problem defined as 'wicked problems'. This concept assists in bringing together the various strands of complexity into a single classification. The notion of wicked problems was first formulated in the 1970s by Rittle and Webber (1973) as an alternative to the limitations of linear thinking as the prevailing form of problem solving. They identified a group of problems that are ill-formed, embedded, confusing and consisting of many clients and decision-makers. Some of the particular features of wicked problems identified by Rittle and Webber include:

- They can be described in different ways and have different solutions
- There is always more than one plausible explanation for them
- They involve a multiplicity of factors embedded in a dynamic social context
- There is no one way to solve them; no right or true test for a solution
- Each is unique.

Tackling issues as challenging and as 'wicked' as Indigenous educational disadvantage requires holistic approaches comprising both vertical and horizontal policy processes (Gray & Beresford, 2008, p. 201):

Vertical policy making captures the power vested in central government to set agendas for schools and other agencies. The notion of wicked problems assumes that the executive government needs to become an active player in solving them. However, on its own, vertical policy making has limits to its effectiveness because of its remoteness from clients and their actual needs. However, policies allowing schools greater autonomy in decision-making, risk leaving complex educational issues unaddressed. Therefore, the optimum governance strategy is a combination of centralised political authority to provide the necessary governance structures with flexible local and Indigenous implementation and input.

Horizontal policy making captures recent trends in developing partnership models to address social and community issues. To date, many of the partnerships struck between education departments, other government agencies and Indigenous communities have lacked ongoing commitment to sustain any durable support structures. In part, the Shared Responsibility Agreements were intended to address this deficiency.

Peach (2004, p. 30) describes the success of using a horizontal structure in tackling formidable social problems in Canada:

> While major policy initiatives designed to make significant changes in serious multi-faceted social problems generally take years to demonstrate progress, those jurisdictions that have had horizontal policy initiatives in place for some time and have seriously implemented the public administrative changes necessary to make them effective have started to see some improvement in social outcomes.

Policy models

Seven discrete program delivery models can be identified out of current practice in Aboriginal education in Australia:

1. the social justice model
2. the community development model

3. the enhanced coordination model
4. the cultural recognition model
5. the school responsiveness model
6. the elitist model
7. the compensatory skills model[2].

1 – Social justice model

A social justice model of Aboriginal education refers to the need to address structural disadvantages acting to impede the progression of students at school. It draws upon a range of complementary theoretical perspectives including the relationship between education and social differentiation (Welch, 1996) and the over-representation of Aboriginals as an underclass in Australian society. The latter is especially prevalent among many urban Aboriginal youth (Purdie & Buckley, 2010; Ross & Gray, 2005; Munns & McFadden, 2000; Gray & Beresford, 2008).

The theoretical base of the social justice model is further exemplified by the application of parallel theories of resistance and alienation; that is, because of their marginalised status in Australian society, Aboriginal youth have, for generations, felt that education is 'white fellas' business and consequently actively and/or passively resist participation in its processes (Beresford & Partington, 2003). The relevance of a social justice perspective to Aboriginal education needs little reminder. Various studies have highlighted that Aboriginal people experience lower

---

2   These models were devised through a critical understanding of the literature in Indigenous education (for a summary of this literature see Beresford and Partington, 2003) and through an interaction between this literature and extensive research undertaken by the authors in the area (Beresford, 2001, 2004; Beresford and Partington, 2003; Gray and this literature see Beresford and Partington, 2003) and through an interaction between this literature and extensive research undertaken by the authors in the area (Beresford, 2001, 2004; Beresford and Partington, 2003; Gray and Beresford, 2001, 2002; 2006; 2008; Gray, 2000; Gray and Partington, 2003; Partington and Gray, 2003; Gray and Sibbel, 2009).

incomes, higher rates of unemployment, lower rates of home-ownership and more overcrowded living conditions than do non-Aboriginal people (see Gordon, 2002; Zubric, et al., 2006; Purdie & Buckley, 2010). Despite this level of disadvantage, a growing number of Aboriginal parents have voiced the request to provide a good education for their children. At times this is reinforced by Aboriginal and Islander Education Officers (AIEOs) who work at the school (Partington, et al., 2009). In other words, rapid improvement in educational outcomes is likely to be dependent on addressing the underlying structural issues of poverty and low income.

The official discourse on Aboriginal education policy acknowledges the importance of a social justice approach but it has struggled to develop a coherent framework because of: (a) the complex causes of Aboriginal socioeconomic disadvantage, (b) its links to Aboriginal youth alienation, (c) the range of school-based programs needed to alleviate its impacts on Aboriginal young people, and (d) the links needed between school-based and wider community programs. It is important to note that good policies will not necessarily bring about change. The impact of policies is influenced by informed support of school leadership and teachers (see the FTD/PFS report: Partington, et al., 2009).

That current polices addressing social economic disadvantage are not effective was acknowledged in the national framework for Indigenous youth (Department of Education, Science & Training, 2004), which stated that the current inequity in education and employment 'shows that existing support structures and programs are often not providing the impetus for substantial and sustained improvements'. Investigations initiated by state education departments have paid little attention to the social justice model. The on-going nature of this challenge is confirmed in more recent research and policies (Purdie & Buckley, 2010; Commonwealth of Australia, 2011; Partington, et al., 2009). The review of Aboriginal education conducted by the Queensland Education Department sought firstly to marginalise the utility of the model and secondly to reconceptualise it within the department's own preferred community development model. While noting that 'it is tempting for teachers, who, in the main, are people of goodwill, to try to deal with the many social issues that affect students, such practices tend to shift the focus of schools from education and "enabling" to welfare provision'. This task, the department's report further asserted, was 'rightly the province of other agencies' (Senate Employment, Workplace Relations, Small Business and Educational References Committee, 2000, p. 7). Later reports continue to acknowledge that this task 'will require significant effort and collaboration by governments, their agencies, communities and the non-government, corporate and philanthropic sectors' (Ministerial Council for Education, Early Childhood Development and Youth Affairs, 2010, p. 3).

Moreover, these agencies are likely to be far more effective in their task by linking with industry and education to help families and communities escape poverty and welfare traps. Nevertheless, many schools have found it necessary to develop their own practical approaches such as breakfast and lunch programs; bus pick-ups for students; the appointment of school/community health workers and the integration of health into the curriculum (see Department of Education WA Annual Report, 2010a; and Partington, et al., 2009).

A long-standing component of the social justice model has been the availability of the Aboriginal and Torres Strait Islander Study Assistance Scheme (ABSTUDY) for secondary and tertiary students. It provided a means-tested income support for Aboriginal youth over sixteen years of age covering school and tertiary study. This form of direct financial support to families was introduced in 1969. The Commonwealth Government commissioned a review into ABSTUDY in 1998 and, amid concerns that the program offered more generous payments to Aboriginal students than was available under the Youth Allowance and Newstart schemes, adjusted the payments to complement the later programs.

An altogether separate strand of the justice model relates to the ongoing impact of dispossession and racial policies on Aboriginal communities, otherwise identified as trans-generational disadvantage and trauma (Beresford, 2006). Policies such as forced removal of children from families, segregation onto reserves, exclusion from state schools and limited access to mainstream employment have had profound intergenerational effects. Such policies have often impeded the process of parenting and the socialisation of Aboriginal children across the generations. In recent years, there has been growing understanding of trans-generational disadvantage and trauma in both academic literature and official reports (Beresford & Omaji, 1996, 1998; Human Rights & Equal Opportunity Commission, 1997; Tatz, 1999; Zubric, et al., 2006) yet there is very limited acknowledgment in the official Aboriginal educational discourse about the extent of these problems.

Past policies of segregation, protection and assimilation formed the context for the relationship between Aboriginal people and education. Schools and the churches were institutions for assimilation and, as a result, the relationship was troubled from both sides (Education Queensland, 2000, p. 13). It is in this context that the term 'intergenerational disadvantage' is relevant to the lives of many Aboriginal people. The Human Rights and Equal Opportunity Commission's Report (1997) into the Stolen Generations highlights that this policy alone has had widespread impact across the generations including on-going trauma, loss of cultural identity and impaired parenting abilities. In turn, these impacts have deterred some Aboriginal parents from accessing mainstream services: 'Many Indigenous parents experience anxiety in rearing their children' (p. 224). The extent to which these responses will continue to be passed down the generations is difficult to determine, but it is likely that some Aboriginal people will continue to harbour suspicions about mainstream institutions, and, for some, this will include schools. The Education Queensland report briefly acknowledged that this is an ongoing issue: 'A minority of schools have been successful in increasing the participation of Aboriginal and Torres Strait Islander parents in school life, but most Education Queensland staff report that this is difficult' (Education Queensland, 2000, p. 13).

The provision of education for Aboriginal students living in remote communities can be conceptualised within a social justice approach. As the Social Justice Commissioner noted in the 2008 annual report (Chapter 2, p. 3):

There are some very large gaps in the provision of education services in remote Australia...many remote Indigenous students receive a part-time education in sub-standard school facilities. If students across the country are assessed using the same test and are deemed to be educationally competent or otherwise using the same measures, then governments must provide consistent levels of education resources across the country. It is not possible or practical or desirable to move all remote students into urban areas, so quality education must move to them (Aboriginal and Torres Strait Social Justice Commissioner, 2008).

The Building the Educational Revolution program (BER) introduced by the Government in 2009 (DEEWR, 2009) provided significant financial support for schools across Australia to upgrade educational facilities. This included a focus on rural and remote schools. So far there is no evidence to suggest that the improved school facilities have had a positive impact on any measures of academic improvement for Aboriginal students.

An additional element a social justice model of Aboriginal education needs to take account of is the over-representation of Aboriginal youth in the criminal justice systems of each state, and the role of schools in both preventing anti-social behaviour among this group and responding to the needs of those Aboriginal young people returning to school under various community program orders. The lack of available community-based programs, especially in rural and remote regions impedes the ability of Aboriginal offenders to re-integrate back into their communities.

2 – Community development model

There is an emerging consensus among those investigating Aboriginal education (and also among a number of people interviewed by investigators, that partnerships with the community are crucial to effecting improvements. This model contains two main components: the need for partnerships between schools and Aboriginal communities and the need for schools to link with the broader community to develop solutions tailored to local circumstances. While all states operate programs to link schools with Aboriginal communities (see MCEECDYA Education Action plan, 2010; DOEWA Annual Report 2009; Purdie & Buckley, 2010), Education Queensland has provided an articulation of the importance of this approach:

> The challenge is to ensure that an effective framework exists that enables local communities to work with schools, community agencies and state government agencies locally. While interagency approaches are already apparent in some areas, these are often developed without input from the community...The local community is supported by agencies to become involved in and take responsibility for the services used by that community. In the process, community members are empowered to participate in building community infrastructure and community capacity. Such approaches allow social institutions, industry and education to play a role in helping families and communities to escape poverty and welfare traps (Education Queensland, 2000, p. 7).

But just what constitutes proper community development is frequently contested. As Iffe (2002, p. 10) notes, the terms 'community' and 'community-based' are highly problematic with the potential for both progressive and regressive change. Among the potential problems, Iffe highlights the possibility for a reduced commitment by government to welfare, an increased burden on women, and the rise in inequality based upon the varying capacities of communities. These are the very problems that have been raised by the introduction of Shared Responsibility and Regional Agreements, outlined in chapter two. They were also articulated a decade ago in a Commonwealth parliamentary inquiry into urban Aboriginal communities which found that partnerships 'presupposes that the individuals, families and organisations of a community have the capacity and inclination to seek solutions to problems, take advantage of opportunities and enter into effective partnerships with governments. However, not all Indigenous communities have that capacity' (House of Representatives Standing Committee on Aboriginal and Torres Strait Islander Affairs, 2001, p. 53).

Not surprisingly, success in utilising a community development model has been patchy. State ministers for education acknowledged as much in 2006:

> Past practices of community consultation have had very limited success and a more formalised partnership is required between schools and their local Indigenous communities. Subject to the consent of the parties, a formal agreement should be negotiated between the local school and the local community that clearly articulates, for example, arrangements relating to community participation in school governance, expectations of student attendance and performance, and curriculum focus (MCEETYA, 2006, p. 21).

Of continued concern is the need to develop a community response to improve social norms characteristic of many
Aboriginal youth. As the federal inquiry into Aboriginal juvenile
crime (House of Representatives, 2011, p. 49) noted:

> The social norms for many young indigenous people
> include negative values and beliefs that do not lead to
> wellbeing or positive social engagement. Therefore...
> [there is a need] to rebuild positive social norms in
> communities and to achieve this it is essential to
> engage local communities and their leaders in the
> design of local diversion programs.

Aboriginal leaders agree that a community development
approach is vital to building the capacity of Aboriginal communities to better deal with their youth. Shane Phillips from the
program Tribal Warriors told the inquiry that: 'we are asking for
a bottom-up approach here. We are asking for the strengths of
our own community to be the guiding light' (p. 50).

3 – Enhanced coordination model
The need to improve coordination between government and
non-government services and schools has been widely recognised as a major challenge facing Aboriginal education. In 2000,
the Ministerial Council on Education, Employment, Training
and Youth Affairs (MCEETYA) highlighted the need for better
coordination of government services:

> The lack of an integrated long-term plan for the pro-
> vision of cross-portfolio services to the Aboriginal

and Torres Strait Islander community at urban, rural, and remote levels has resulted in services not being provided in a cohesive manner. There is a close relationship between low levels of educational outcomes and issues in other portfolio areas such as poor health, overcrowded housing and poor access to government services and infrastructure...Any improvement in these other portfolio areas is likely to generate better educational outcomes (MCEETYA, 2000, p. 51).

The basis of this model lies in the policy theory that modern governments 'are networks of loosely linked organisations rather than a single hierarchy to command and control' (Bridgeman & Davis, 2004, p. 94). Departments have their own goals, statutory responsibilities and organisational cultures. Nevertheless, governments require overarching policy frameworks as the needs of most target groups straddle the artificial divisions of government departmental structures.

The Ministerial Council developed a 'partnership cube' as a published model for better coordination. This focussed on developing stronger partnerships between government, communities and education systems to overcome the deficiencies in the delivery of cohesive services to Aboriginal communities both urban and remote. Better coordination was a central point in the implementation of the National Indigenous English Literacy and Numeracy Strategy, the Howard Government's major initiative in Aboriginal education. Released in 2000, implementation of the strategy was identified as requiring 'a cooperative effort between the Commonwealth, states and territories, as well as non-government education providers and

Indigenous communities, families and parents' (Department of Education, Science and Training, 2000).

Despite these efforts, problems in coordination persist. The reasons have been summed up by Bridgeman and Davis (2004, p. 93):

> The complexity and scale of government, and the need for specialisation, make it impossible for any one person – or even a committee such as cabinet – to keep all the relevant variables in play. The considerable costs of perfectly meshing policies and programs can outweigh the benefits. Coordination may be necessary, but it is an ideal that can be realised only with many compromises.

Nevertheless, there is now widespread recognition among both Aboriginal and non-Aboriginal experts, that the often complex problems in Aboriginal affairs cannot be fully resolved without partnerships between communities and government and without better coordination of government services (see Zubric, et al., 2006).

4 – Cultural recognition model

The need for Aboriginal students to have access to their own language, learning styles and cultural identity has long been regarded as essential to improving their educational outcomes. In turn, this understanding is based on interactionist theory, which holds that through language and symbols people develop a shared meaning about the world (see chapter one).

The official discourse on Aboriginal education has a strong

focus on this issue. The 2000 Senate review went to the heart of the matter: 'The central curriculum issue in Aboriginal education over the past decade has been how to provide a curriculum that is both academically rigorous and culturally relevant to Indigenous peoples'. The review further noted the benefits of addressing this core issue: 'Teaching a culturally appropriate curriculum, which recognises and builds upon the cultural and linguistic background of Aboriginal students, could also aid learning across the curriculum.' The review concluded, however, that 'many teachers and curricula have still not moved far in these directions' (Senate Employment, Workplace Relations, Small Business and Educational References Committee, 2000, pp. 60–74).

The Queensland Education Department's review of Aboriginal education is scathing about the lack of progress in cultural recognition. The review found that there is little acknowledgment of or support for cross-cultural pedagogy; that teachers lack cultural awareness; that the distribution of education advisers is inequitable and that some of these advisers have questionable knowledge; and that teachers' pre-service education in cross-cultural pedagogy is inadequate (Education Queensland, 2000).

Similar criticisms were made by the independent review of Indigenous education in the Northern Territory (Collins, 1999). Collins began his investigations at the very time the Territory government announced a phasing-out of funding for bilingual education programs. In his report, Collins argued strongly for the retention of the program on the basis of 'its value in reinforcing and strengthening Aboriginal identity in all its forms'. He went on to say that Aboriginal parents, teachers, and students 'all put to the review the importance of English acquisition, but not at the expense of their own culture and language' (1999, p. 120).

Steps to rectify this situation have been recently taken by the federal government with the introduction in 2009 of the nation's first national Indigenous languages policy. This step represents an important official recognition of the link between language acquisition and culture and the flow-on effects between cultural identity and the development of resilience in young people and improved cognitive functioning (Social Justice Commissioner, 2009). Therefore, the ability of Aboriginal students to learn in their primary language is seen to be critical to their success as learners. Two students from North East Arnhem Land said the following about the use of English in their classrooms:

> We don't retain information – we hear teaching, especially in English and we feel we don't grasp what is being taught, and so it disappears. We go to school, hear something, go home and the teaching is gone. We feel hopeless. Is there anything wrong with our heads because this English just does not work for us? (cited in Social Justice Commissioner, 2009, chapter 3, p. 5).

In terms of education policy, the research strongly demonstrates that:

> bilingual education approaches are more effective than English-only approaches in assisting students transfer mother tongue literacies to second language literacies. The evidence shows that bilingual approaches work

> in any language environment where indigenous stu-
> dents or minority language students are attempting to
> transfer their first literacies to the dominant language
> (ibid., p. 37).

Yet, a bilingual approach is not well represented in policy approaches in Australia. In 2006, only nine government schools and three Catholic schools were bilingual schools instructing students in indigenous languages and all were in the Northern Territory. In October 2008, the Northern Territory Minister for Employment, Education and Training announced the dismantling of bilingual education in the handful of schools where it was operating. Henceforth, the first four hours of instruction were to be conducted in English with only the last hour and a half in Indigenous languages.

Culturally appropriate language is also important to urban-based Aboriginal youth most of whom are speakers of Aboriginal English (a non-standard dialect of English). The failure of schools to recognise this form of language 'will be to invite resistance, whether active or passive, on the part of Indigenous students' (Ministerial Council on Education, Employment, Training and Youth Affairs, 2006, p. 17).

More broadly, a cultural recognition model will foster the acquisition among teachers of appropriate levels of cultural competence. There is a wide range of evidence discussed in various chapters of this book that many teachers have been given inadequate preparation in this regard and struggle to demonstrate competency principles in their dealings with Aboriginal students. But, as the *Little Children are Sacred Report* (Wild & Anderson, 2007, p. 203) highlights:

teachers who are more culturally aware and tuned into Aboriginal children's cultural needs have more successful educational outcomes than those who don't. This is because the teacher is better able to engage the children and the children feel more comfortable.

Pearson (2009b) further articulates this need for culturally aware teachers in his view that quality teaching for remote communities involves teachers committed to the No Excuses approach and to an agenda of effective instruction rather than trying to attract high achievers who are unlikely to stay for the long term.

Thus, while strong on arguing for cross-cultural education, the policy has been poorly applied in this area. The recent House of Representatives inquiry into juvenile crime (2011) considered the matter of cultural recognition in schools and maintained that there were a minimum set of activities that all schools should follow, including:

- hanging the Aboriginal flag alongside the Australian flag in the school grounds
- learning about local Indigenous sites of significance
- incorporating an acknowledgement of country at significant school events
- commissioning a local Indigenous artist to paint a mural within the school grounds
- using local Indigenous names for classrooms and house teams
- celebrating Indigenous cultural days.

5 – School responsiveness model

The importance of developing positive relationships between Aboriginal students and schools hardly needs much elaboration. The Senior Secondary Assessment Board of South Australia's study of the 46 Aboriginal students in that state who completed the Certificate of Education in 1999 found that the extremely low figure highlighted the crisis factor in Aboriginal education and confirmed that support from school was crucial to success (Senior Secondary Assessment Board of South Australia, 2001, p. 24). Partington, et al., (2009) found the influence of supportive school structures, learning environments and policies were critical to maximising the opportunity for Aboriginal students to complete twelve years of schooling.

The significant challenges schools face in responding to the needs of Indigenous and minority youth has attracted the attention of researchers for several decades. Ogbu (1978) questioned the capacity of schools in the United States to respond to the reform agendas of governments and so improve minority education. He claimed that implementation of compensatory programs was impeded by inadequate understanding of the problems of minority failure in education, lack of clear goals and strategies and lack of prior preparation of local school officials. Similar problems have been noted by the reviews considered in this chapter.

The 2002 New South Wales Public Education Inquiry argued that the strategic problem 'is how to change the social relations around teaching and learning within mainstream schooling to engage Aboriginal students, strengthen their identity and increase their level of success' (Vinson, 2002, p. 21). The inquiry noted that three factors were crucial to the ability of schools to improve outcomes for Aboriginal people: a committed principal, well trained Aboriginal education workers, and schools adapted to the needs of Aboriginal learners. Broadly similar findings were made in the 1999 Northern Territory report (Collins, 1999).

These findings may well have every appearance of rationality, but do they go far enough in highlighting the challenges facing schools? The 2000 Senate inquiry into Aboriginal education stated that there are deeper forces at work: 'Although education systems no longer take a deliberately oppressive role,' the report noted, 'they retain elements of assimilation and internalised racism that can make them alienating environments for many Indigenous people.' (Senate Employment, Workplace Relations, Small Business and Educational References Committee, 2000, p. 61).

It is relatively clear what a model of school responsiveness needs to take into account: the socioeconomic context of Aboriginal students, the importance of recognising culture, adapting curricula to Aboriginal learning needs, dealing with racism, and meeting the opportunities and the requirements of community participation. These issues are widely represented as key challenges for Indigenous education in all the literature and official reports produced over recent years.

6 – Elitist model

Western Australia has focused much of its recent policy development in Aboriginal education in recent years pursuing merit selection of Aboriginal students to complete Year 12. Established as an elite model in education, the Follow the Dream/Partnerships for Success (FTD/PFS) scheme is designed to support those students who are reaching literacy and numeracy benchmarks and who have aspirations to enter university (see Partington, et al., 2009). The program is designed to lift the number of Aboriginal students entering university straight from school by offering additional support and resources to students and families. For several years, the program has been the largest single Aboriginal education program in the state and, as such, represents a significant new departure in the national debate about Aboriginal education policy.

Partington, et al., (2009, p. 7) suggested that the FTD/PFS strategy was novel in that it focused resources on students who had the greatest potential for success and, as such, was open to claims of elitism and privilege. The underlying assumption was that Aboriginal students were more likely to achieve high school graduation through this strategy than the previous egalitarian approaches that attempted to raise the achievement levels of all students, or alternatively, programs that focused on those least likely to succeed. The research quoted an executive director in DET who noted:

> It was a challenging bit to actually maintain a sense that this was not a program for everyone, part of its strength had to do with the fact that you had to get selected into the program, that...you had to make commitments alongside not being too precious about what elite meant because...these kids aren't these schools' high flyers, they are good kids who want to work well, whose parents have signed up and who produce an environment of something special at the school level, that it sort of has a ripple effect (K. O'Keefe, personal communication, 24 August, 2004).

Partington, et al., (2009, p. 7) found that the achievement of a group of students with the best attributes to succeed would create a blueprint for the success of other Aboriginal students and set in train a new perception of potential futures.

The theoretical foundations of such a model create complex linkages to the political and sociological writings on elitism and especially the commonly understood notion of rule by elites; however, elitism conjures a wide variety of meanings, including the idea of a select group of people. Nyquist (n.d., p. 6) has more specifically defined elitism as 'any attempt to impose rules governing the selective process in certain areas of endeavour... which puts at a disadvantage some group (or groups) who would do better with a different set of rules'.

Constructing a significant component on Aboriginal education policy around the differential rewarding of Aboriginal young people challenges widespread egalitarian ideas in education that schools should strive for equality of opportunity for all. As Walker (1992) comments, elitism 'seems at least formally compatible with an unequal schooling system, for example a system which includes elite fee-charging schools whose graduates enter the professions or have the wealth to join or influence political elites.'

The Department of Education and Training of Western Australia claims that its program 'instils community pride by enhancing the capacity of partners and students to change existing mindsets to a culture of excellence and achievement of aspirations' (Department of Education and Training Western Australia 2003, p. 51). Participating students are offered extra work outside school hours and individual education plans. It is expected that older students will become role models for the younger aspirants on the program.

Can such a policy thrust be defended in Aboriginal education? Nyquist (n.d.) argues that elitism is unavoidable in society due to the problem of limited access. In the case of Aboriginal education, it could be argued that there is limited access to the kinds of resources that are needed to achieve success for all Aboriginal students and there is limited access to tertiary places. Secondly, the concept of elitism being applied to Aboriginal people does not necessarily carry the same negative connotations as it does for the broader community because of the presence of extreme disadvantage among the former. In other words, disproportionately rewarding some Aboriginal students may be necessary so that the Aboriginal community can begin to enjoy the same opportunities as the broader community. The FTD/PFS program is discussed in more detail in chapter 13.

7 – Compensatory skills model

The poor performance of Aboriginal students in basic literacy and numeracy has worried educationalists and policy makers for decades. While the Closing the Gap, Prime Minister's Report (Commonwealth of Australia, 2011, p. 14) concluded that:

> Education is a key factor for improving wellbeing and life outcomes; it is an important determinant of health and employment. Literacy and numeracy skills are fundamental to reducing inequality in education. The gap in reading, writing and numeracy is influenced by a range of factors including school attendance, teacher quality and parental engagement.

So far, public officials have not been able to resolve the central issue: can improved outcomes in literacy and numeracy be achieved through better classroom practice, or are improvements inextricably linked to the broader resolution of the sociocultural barriers Aboriginal students commonly face at school?

There are sharp differences in the official discourse on this matter. MCEETYA (2000, p. 43) argued against the utility of compensatory programs. For decades, education systems have been conducting compensatory programs for Aboriginal and Torres Strait Islander students to provide additional support. While these programs have been responsible for the considerable progress made in Indigenous education, they have often had two unintended side-effects: first, they marginalise the target group and the personnel who implement the programs, and second, they become the focus of perceptions about unfair access to additional resources. The 2000 Senate review adopted an opposing viewpoint:

> The Committee is concerned that a pre-occupation with teaching strategies, culturally relevant curricula and other elements of classroom practice – important as they are – should not be allowed to outweigh a consideration of the principal goal of school, which is the inculcation of life skills, including proficiency in literacy and numeracy (Senate Employment, Workplace Relations, Small Business and Educational References Committee, 2000, p. 93).

Then there is the view expressed in the Queensland Education Department's review; namely, that classroom teachers and administrators needed a sufficient understanding of cross-cultural and

144

language pedagogy to advance literacy (Education Queensland, 2000, p. 29). This supports Pearson's (2009b) call for a focus on culturally committed teachers to work with remote Indigenous students.

The Closing the Gap strategy (Commonwealth of Australia, 2011; Purdie & Buckley, 2010) to improve education, health and educational opportunities and outcomes for Aboriginal people took the widest possible course through this debate. In striving to achieve comparability between Aboriginal and non-Aboriginal students, it identified six key targets (p. 2):

- Close the gap in life expectancy between Indigenous and non-Indigenous Australians by 2031.
- Halve the gap in mortality rates for Indigenous children under five by 2018.
- Ensure access to early childhood education for all Indigenous four year olds in remote communities by 2013.
- Halve the gap in reading, writing and numeracy achievement for Indigenous children by 2018.
- Halve the gap in Year 12 or equivalent attainment rates for Indigenous young people by 2020.
- Halve the gap in employment outcomes between Indigenous and non-Indigenous Australians by 2018.

The Commonwealth Government has allocated over $8 billion for the period of the strategy (p. 2). Many of the programs funded by the Commonwealth under the strategy are directed at 'readiness for learning' initiatives (DEST, 2002, p. 84; MCEECDYA, 2010); in other words, addressing some of the structural disadvantages impeding the acquisition of literacy and numeracy. Although there have been some success with these targets, so far there has been no significant improvement in educational outcomes for Aboriginal children (Department of Education WA, 2010a; Purdie & Buckley, 2010). This being the case, the issue with the compensatory skills model is the extent to which it can exist in an effective form outside parallel linkages with all other models, and especially social justice and school responsiveness models.

Adoption of the compensatory skills approach has gone furthest in North Queensland through the advocacy of Aboriginal leader Noel Pearson for using 'direct instruction' or 'explicit instruction'. He has argued passionately for this traditional method:

> In Aboriginal communities, the approach to literacy must be qualitatively different because the majority of students are in the bottom quartile. It is not sufficient to modify the mainstream formula. Explicit, phonics-based reading instruction is imperative for Aboriginal students (Pearson, 2009b, p. 53).

Acknowledging that this approach remains controversial among educators, Pearson argues that:

> There is a class blindness in the insistence of opponents of explicit instruction: yes, if you're white and from a moderately advantaged background, then whole language may be fine. But if you're black and from the wrong side of the tracks, it is not (p. 54).

The compensatory skills discourse has taken a higher public national profile since the introduction in 2008 of the National Assessment Program – Literacy and Numeracy (NAPLAN) for all Australian students in years 3, 5, 7 and 9. This mandated annual testing program reports on four areas: reading, writing, language conventions and numeracy. The accountability focus of the public reporting of all NAPLAN data through annual reports and the MySchool website exposes the gap in educational outcomes for Indigenous students at school, state and national levels. All data since the inception of this national testing in 2008 shows mean scores for Indigenous students are consistently and substantially lower than those for non-Indigenous students. The impact on pedagogy and curriculum has been a serious focus on compensatory skills development, with systems, schools and teachers mandating minimum curriculum time for literacy and numeracy, and specific skills-focused pedagogy, on a daily basis. This skills focus leaves little room in an already crowded curriculum for teachers to draw on culturally appropriate, engaging activities in the classroom, further increasing the potential alienation of Indigenous students already vulnerable through structural disadvantage. The public nature of this data has impacted on teachers' awareness and attitude to their Indigenous students, often evidenced through increased pressure for students to perform, limited expectations of achievement, and increased resistance to inclusion of Indigenous students in the testing program. Currently, nine per cent of Indigenous students across Australia do not undertake these tests. NAPLAN data is used at all levels to set targets for the improvement of Indigenous educational outcomes (Commonwealth of Australia, 2011).

Conclusion

Given the finding that the models are discrete but not mutually exclusive, it is important that a framework for their integration be developed. It is likely that an integrated approach is most likely to flow from planned interagency coordination that explicitly recognises the primacy and role of each model. In effect, an application of the models provides a functional blueprint for identifying the roles and responsibilities of each agency required to provide resources.

The models are applicable, too, for planning at the school level. The principles behind each of the models can be used to review school performance with its Indigenous students; to feedback to policy makers on the effectiveness of national/state approaches; and as food for thought on where each school needs to place its own particular emphasis.

5

TEACHERS AND FAMILIES WORKING TOGETHER TO BUILD STRONGER FUTURES FOR OUR CHILDREN IN SCHOOLS

Sharon Gollan and Merridy Malin

The following letter from an Aboriginal parent to the teacher of her child encapsulates the concerns felt by many Aboriginal parents when their child first enters the school.

> *Dear Teacher,*
>
> *As you navigate your way through your life-long learning, I write to help you understand that my son has fundamental human rights, mandating that his well-being and cultural identity is not denied. Along with his family, extended family and language group, I have placed my trust in you to 'grow him up culture strong'.*
>
> *So let me tell you how I perceive 'quality [schooling]'.*
>
> *Similar to our Dreaming, I see quality [education] as an evolving, holistic, healing, educative and spiritual process that provides meaningful opportunities for personal growth. It teaches us the rules for living, caring and understanding our environment, our social relationships, the importance of our land and animals, the history of our people, learning messages from our Ancestors and much more. It helps us to realise our potential.*

When you acknowledge the significance of our Dreaming to the centrality of our being, you might think more carefully about how and why you read a Dreaming story to all the children in your care and why you must ensure it doesn't become a token effort, something you need to 'demonstrate'.

I want you to challenge the reality of 'whiteness' in all that you say and do to ensure you don't just give lip-service to what working inclusively means. When was the last time you watched an Aboriginal specific TV show, read a book by an Aboriginal author, attended an Aboriginal community event, listened to an Aboriginal band or radio station, listened to an Aboriginal leader speak, learned some Aboriginal language words? If you can tick these off, does that mean your work is done in acquiring knowledge about Aboriginal peoples?

Together, we can work towards minimising this reality, to close the gap between the 'them and us' mentality. Ask yourself, how well has the [school] included Aboriginal perspectives in its practices, routines, environments, philosophies and policies? Have you sought advice from our local Aboriginal Elders? I can help you here, but you must be willing to do it. I don't remember being asked to be involved in the [school's] decision-making processes. I can only hope that assumptions were not made about my literacy, language capabilities and socio-economic status or that I don't understand or care about such things.

Of course I care — how you care for and teach my son will leave an indelible imprint on his sense of self.

Please involve me and my family in decision-making from the outset, not after the fact. We just have to find a way to understand each other's language. Tell me, how does making boomerangs, didgeridoos and dot paintings contribute to you relating to him, nurturing and affirming his cultural identity? How does this inform you of all there is to know about him, his strengths, abilities, heritage, family, community, language, interactions, kinship obligations and spirituality? Please do not classify my son as disadvantaged the minute he steps through the door. Rather, look to and build on his strengths and provide culturally relevant learning opportunities for him to work on any areas of need...the employment of Aboriginal [staff] is important to my family and me. We would like to drop him off one day and see Aboriginal [teachers] working alongside non-Aboriginal [teachers] as equals, [teaching] children in a mutually respectful way. How well you enact these things will determine how I recommend your [school] to others.

I want to thank you for...[teaching him to read and write; to understand and apply mathematical principles and other learnings from the school curriculum].

Please keep doing all these things you do so well, but most of all, I want you to embrace and celebrate his Aboriginality, as this celebrates him.

Yours faithfully,
An Aboriginal mother

Tina Quitadamo (nee Couzens) a Kirraewurrung/Gundjitmara woman, wrote this letter to her young son's child care workers (Quitadamo, 2009, reprinted with permission). Substituting the term 'carer' for 'teacher' and 'care' for 'teaching'; the message remains the same.

Introduction

Tina's letter presents concerns that many Aboriginal families have when their children enter the school system. Aboriginal parents send their children to school hoping that the teachers will see in them their strengths, their vitality and their love for learning. Parents hope that the teachers will get to know their children well, will listen to them to find out what they already know and what motivates them, and how to extend them to new learning. But, as Tina Quitadamo states, fundamental to all this is to 'embrace and celebrate' their Aboriginality, their values and beliefs. This entails going beyond the superficial and stereotypical aspects of culture to the living culture which is encountered through involving Aboriginal community members and family members in the everyday activities of school.

Aboriginal children gain their understanding of this world through their connections to country and the values and beliefs of the country that they are born into. As Sims, O'Connor and Forrest (2003, p. 69) state, 'We grow up immersed in our own culture, our own experiences and our own language. Through these we construct our understanding of the world.' Aboriginal families connected to these values and beliefs pass on Aboriginal ways of being through stories, taking children back to country and teaching cultural ways. In these ways, children learn their identity and who they are and how they should be. However, this sense of self gets interrupted on entering the schooling system where they are quickly introduced to another set of values and beliefs, another set of experiences, language, and processes that are so different from their own.

Aboriginal families have many stories of teaching practices that have been disrespectful and harmful to the well-being of their children and community. As we journey through this chapter, we will look at certain issues that we believe are important for teachers to gain an understanding of ways for assisting young Aboriginal students to experience a sense of belonging and respect as they and their families journey through the schooling system.

Through the stories of Aboriginal people reflecting on their own histories and cultures, and through discussion of research that we believe accurately reflects the experiences of some Aboriginal families in relation to historical events, culture, and childrearing, this chapter will address the experiences in the lives of Aboriginal children and families and move towards a more respectful and constructive teaching practice that will lead to building stronger futures for Aboriginal children in schools.

Past policies and legislation

The history of past policies and legislation in Australia 'brings with it particular experiences for Aboriginal Australians. Colonisation perpetrated injustices of genocide, stolen land, loss of languages, separation of communities and families' (Gollan & O'Leary, 2009, p. 709). As a result of these discriminatory policies and legislation, Aboriginal families and their communities still experience limited access and participation in many areas, such as education, health and employment.

Reflections of Sharon Gollan

My belief as a professional working and teaching in the field of Social Work has been that people who enter into the human services area whether as social workers, nurses, or teachers have a desire to respectfully assist individuals, families and communities, so that their clients are enabled to resolve issues in their lives in order that they can reach their full potential in an enriching way. However, in most circumstances, this has not been and continues not to be the case. Too often, Aboriginal students have been stereotyped as 'non-achievers' and their parents as not being interested in their children's schooling. The students' lack of educational success has been expected and attributed to the child's family background (Beresford, 2003). There is a widespread belief among Aboriginal people, as well as being supported by recent health research, that mainstream services have been, and continue to be, inadequate and inappropriate for meeting Aboriginal people's needs. Improved services will only occur if service providers evaluate and amend their practices in partnership with Aboriginal people (Aboriginal Health Council of South Australia, 1995, p. 25; WA Joint Planning Forum on Aboriginal Health, 2000; Australian Health Ministers' Advisory Council, 2006).

This belief has led to a relationship between various professions and Aboriginal people fraught with alienation and distrust. These feelings stem from the roles, function and actions of past policies and legislation that disrupted and disempowered Aboriginal families.

The forced removal of children from their families

As was stated in the *Bringing Them Home* report (Human Rights and Equal Opportunity Commission, 1997), Aboriginal and Torres Strait Islander children have been forcibly separated from their families since the first European fleet arrived in 1788. Children were taken to be used as cheap labour for European settlers. They were targeted by governments and missionaries aiming to remove them from what were considered to be the 'primitive customs' of their parents and communities and to assimilate them into European values and work habits. (HREOC, 1997, p. 27). The removal of children was achieved throughout Australia through various government policies, such as the protection, segregation, assimilation and child welfare policies of the nineteenth and twentieth centuries (HREOC, 1997).

In 2008, around 8 per cent of Aboriginal and Torres Strait Islander adults (26,900) had personally experienced removal from their natural family (Australian Bureau of Statistics, 2010a). An additional 38 per cent of people had had family members removed. People aged over forty-five were the most affected as a result of government policies during the 1900s. These recent survey statistics underestimate the actual proportion of people removed because many of those affected are now deceased (HREOC, 1997, p. 17).

Brian Butler, when Chairperson of the Secretariat of National Aboriginal and Torres Strait Islander Child Care (SNAICC), stated:

> Literally thousands of Aboriginal adults live with the trauma caused by these removal policies. Many of the mothers and fathers who had their children taken away are guilt and grief stricken. Their children are traumatised by the thought that they were unwanted. Identity conflicts rage in these children – now adults – who have lived most of their lives as non-Aboriginal people (Butler, 1990, cited in Walker, 1993, p. 4).

There would be few Aboriginal families in Australia who were not affected by the policies and informal practices of governments, churches and welfare bodies.

The different stories amounted to the same thing – the splitting up of families, fostering and adopting of light skinned children, institutionalisation, and, in many cases, abuse. Forced removals were highly traumatic for both children and their families. The National Inquiry concluded that:

> the policy broke important cultural, spiritual and family ties which crippled not only individuals, but whole families and even whole communities...Members of the Stolen Generations suffered higher rates of sexual abuse, maltreatment, dislocation of family life, poverty and hardship than other Aboriginal people (Reconciliation Network Fact Sheet, 2011).

Some of the long-term repercussions of child removal were also exposed by the national inquiry into the deaths of Aboriginal inmates in Australian prisons. Between October 1987 and November 1990, the Royal Commission into Aboriginal Deaths in Custody investigated the deaths of ninety-nine Aboriginal people in police and prison custody which occurred in the late 1970s and 1980s. Their final report concluded that:

> The cases heard by the Commission seem to indicate child separation had a profound impact on certain individuals' lives – almost half of those who died in custody had been removed from their parents. (http://www.austlii.edu.au/)

Jean Carter (Edwards & Read, 1989, p. 161) wrote of family members who were taken:

> The importance Aboriginal people place on family; it's the first and foremost thing. When you're stripped of that, I reckon you maybe don't care...It's sorta like a shame thing, eh. I guess (my brothers) went through a lot of that. And feeling really powerless, and what could they do. And they drank, and died really early. They all died in their forties.

The impact of the removal policies has been passed on to subsequent generations, as psychiatrist Dr Jane McKendrick reported:

> When (some Aboriginal people who were removed) come to have their own children they've really got no idea how to parent in either the conventional Aboriginal or non-Aboriginal way...so their children are very often removed from them (by welfare agencies) which sets up this terrible cycle which goes on for generations. (http://www.hreoc.gov.au/social_Justice/bth_report/report/ch25.html#Heading241)

We are seeing the impact of these policies in the lives of Aboriginal children, families and communities today. The psychological impact of the trauma of separation experienced by parents and grandparents is still apparent in some grandchildren today often resulting in behavioural and truancy issues in school.

Experiences of racism

Another stressful aspect of contemporary life for Aboriginal people is the high incidence of racism. Gallaher, Ziersch, Baum, Bentley, Palmer, Edmondson and Winslow (2009) in their investigation into the health and everyday life of Aboriginal and Torres Strait Islander people who live in urban areas, found that 93 per cent of those interviewed had experienced racism at least sometimes and two thirds reported experiencing it often.

Racism is an ongoing experience for Aboriginal families. In Malin's (1989) study, for example, one parent described how her four and six year old daughters were called derogatory names usually by white adult males in the supermarket or walking down the street. They also sometimes received racist taunts from children and their parents in their immediate neighbourhood.

Because of such experiences of racism, young Aboriginal children may be distrusting of non-Aboriginal people and feel intimidated, on entering school for the first time, to be sur-rounded by a majority of non-Aboriginal people. Furthermore, studies have found that racism is a common occurrence in schools (Groome, 1988; Walker, 1993; Mansouri, Jenkins, Morgan & Taouk, 2009). Walker (p. 51) stated:

> Our kids face racial problems from day one at school, and have to cope with growing up at home with such strong cultural values and being so proud of who they are and then going out and mixing with the wider society to be confronted with bigots who have few clues about the sensitivities of our people.

A recent example of what children may encounter is reported by a mother, (Mitchell, Graham, Hammond, et al., 2010):

> I got home from work one day and my daughter was sitting on the lounge and I could see she was sad and upset...something was on her mind. So I asked her what was wrong and she said to me. 'Mum what's niggers?' And I got a shock because I didn't think a young person would say 'nigger' these days, and I told her all about it and I asked why and she said that a little girl called 'me and Stacy[1] niggers'. Stacy was one of the Sudanese girls she was friends with. So I told her not to worry, that 'I'll sort it out'...I felt sick, disgusted. I also felt ashamed. Not for me and my daughter, but for the other little girl cause she is saying these words and probably don't know what they mean.

Mansouri, et al., (2009) in their study of 900 secondary school students across Australia found that 80 per cent of students from non-Anglo backgrounds had experienced racial vilification. The abuse was reported as being perpetrated by teachers, administrative staff and fellow students. Reported racist teacher behaviour included exclusion, unfair treatment or inaction in response to student racism. Fellow student racism included verbal insults through jokes, name-calling, and sarcasm, exclusion or physical attacks. Although only a small sample of Indigenous youth was included in the study, the authors reported that 'Indigenous youth may suffer more debilitating forms of racism than other Australian youth' (p. 6).

---

1   All names used in vignettes are pseudonyms.

Different parents offer various support and advice to their children in response to racism. The Adelaide parents in Malin's study said that they warn their children before they go to school that some white children may tease them because they are black. The parents repeatedly remind their children that they should not forget that they are Nunga (Aboriginal) but be proud, that being Nunga is special; that they are the original people of Australia. They tell them that part of being Nunga also means that they have a special relationship with the land, plants and animals and the ancestor spirits that occupy that land; that they feel things from the heart and 'see' things in ways that non-Aboriginal people cannot (1989, p. 194).

One parent also explained, 'Parents know that Aboriginal kids have to cope with lots of antagonistic situations. We bring our kids up to be somewhat tough so they can cope with this...' (p. 191) so they can learn to be strong and resilient. By navigating their way through all of these experiences, they then develop other strategies to manage racism. Walker (1993, p. 52) stated:

> Some families have faced racist attitudes head on, by
> educating themselves in an attempt to fight the white
> man's system on the white man's level; who then can
> help other families to stand up and deal with situations
> in the best way possible.

Sadly there are many families unable to manage the ongoing experiences of racism. They become so tired because of the many issues that they face and the many losses in their lives. They seem to be always managing grief, managing racism, visiting sick family members in hospitals. Sometimes it all becomes too overwhelming for families.

Maintenance of cultural values affecting family and identity

Aboriginal families are diverse in culture, history, size and appearance. They come from many different Aboriginal nations around Australia, and despite all being called Aboriginal are grounded in 'countries' and languages as diverse as the nations of Europe.

Aboriginal people are connected to one another through family. As Walker (1993, p. 51) says, 'Traditionally, the Aboriginal family was a collaboration of clans composed of mothers, fathers, uncles, aunties, brothers, sisters, cousins and so on. This size family was the norm but is recognised in today's terms as 'extended family'. The extended family is still part of rural, remote and urban life.

Children can live between parents, grandparents and other extended family members (Wilson, 1995). Sims, et al., (2003, p. 77) explain, 'the protection and teaching of children is a community responsibility...Children are a community resource and community responsibility' and not solely the responsibility of their biological parents. In many Aboriginal families, the grandparents, particularly grandmothers, bring up the children. This has been part of Aboriginal child-rearing practice that stems back in time. However, it can lead to difficulty at times for Aboriginal families, for example, when enrolling children into schooling or when picking children up from school. The school enrolment form requires a tick in a box about the legal guardianship of the child and whether there are any legal orders, and schools often have a list of adults permitted to pick children up after school. Both these issues require additional and sometime difficult negotiations and compromises between Indigenous families and the school.

One of the threads connecting the city with the bush is the connectedness of kin. Aboriginal people today, on meeting someone new, will work out how they are related and their country of origin and most people find connections very quickly. Understanding family connections begins early in life and many families explicitly explain to their children how they are connected to others through kinship. For example, children as young as three were able to explain how they were connected to cousins through their parents' siblings (Malin, Campbell and Agius, 1996).

Some groups also extend their kinship connections to animals, plants, land formations, the rain, or the wind, rivers, stars and seas (Turner, 2010).

Walker (1993, p. 51) wrote:

Our families are proud people, and our children grow up knowing that 'Black is beautiful' and learning to be 'Black and proud'. The home, the nurturing place of learning, teaches us a lot about ourselves, but unfortunately does not always prepare our children for the roller-coaster ride ahead of them.

Without exception, every Aboriginal participant in the Malin, Campbell and Agius (1996) study which drew upon and extended Malin's 1989 research in Adelaide, placed a great deal of importance on their Aboriginality, their family, its history and genealogy, what remained of the traditional language, and the region of origin. This is equally true for families today (SNAICC, in press).

Case study of parent-child relationships and values

The concepts of child-parent relationships amongst Aboriginal people can be very different from that of non-Aboriginal families (Altman & Hinkson, 2007). The following case study is drawn from the ethnographic study of Malin (1989) and Malin, Campbell and Agius (1996)[2]. It characterises the Aboriginal families of the study as living relatively resourceful and frugal lifestyles in metropolitan Adelaide. They spoke a dialect of Aboriginal English that was often misunderstood in the classroom. The parents valued independence, emotional strength and self-reliance in their children which was balanced by a nurturing and socially considerate orientation. By the time children were old enough for school, they were capable of shouldering considerable responsibility and had sophisticated social skills.

Collective responsibility

The world of Aboriginal children is a very social, collaborative one. At home, the children tended to play with other children rather than with toys. A particular kind of nurturing was encouraged by the mothers and performed by the children towards one another. 'Affiliative acts' entailed child behaviours, attitudes and knowledge characterised by altruistic expressions

---

2   All the generalisations presented here and referenced to Malin (1989) and Malin, Campbell and Agius (1996) are based upon numeracy counts of twelve hours of video-recorded activities in everyday life of two Aboriginal and two Anglo-Australian families where the Aboriginal actions are significantly more numerous than or qualitatively different from the Anglo-Australian actions.

of love and compassion, pride and pleasure in the other child's deeds or state of being or the promoting of the other's physical or emotional wellbeing. Specifically, this involved a child offering help, support, comfort, affection or information to another child; amusing a baby or toddler and the offering of food or objects of interest to the child; offers of protection or supervision; knowledge about the whereabouts of a younger child; explanations by a child to a third party on behalf of another child or to another child on behalf of a third party; and instances in which a child draws the attention of a third party to an aspect or action of a child in an altruistic way. For example, the Aboriginal children performed 'sharing and caring' deeds 97 times during six videotaped hours as compared with 23 times by the Anglo children (Malin, p. 349).

The sophisticated social skills of an Aboriginal ten year old are illustrated below during a visit by a mother and her children to the three-year-old sister, 'Kaiya', who was in hospital. The ten year old comforted her little sister when she began to cry because they were about to leave her there for another night. She said gently:

'And you come out tomorrow, unna? You see Daddy, Papa, Nanna.' Some time later she said, 'And when Mum go home, Mum'll tell Dad, unna? And Mum and Stella and Jason and Ruby and Wayne come up and see you tomorrow, unna?' and a few minutes later she added, 'Kaiya, Aunty Elsie (the school bus driver) love you!' (Malin, Campbell & Agius, 1996, p. 46).

Autonomy

In the Malin study, the Aboriginal families valued and worked to develop in their children independence and self-reliance in certain matters, provided that they still remained aware of their social responsibilities. The children were encouraged not to dwell on their own minor injuries or upsets, to be able to resolve their own disputes, and to not take themselves too seriously. Along with these strengths was the expectation that children could be relied upon to make certain decisions for themselves and that their judgements concerning such decisions were trustworthy. They were skilled observers and possessed a great deal of practical competence at a relatively early age. Around the house, on reaching school age, they were able to, for example, fry an egg, make toast, prepare their own breakfast cereal, cut an orange, change a baby's nappy, fill a baby's bottle, and perform other small tasks.

The Aboriginal children's 'invisible' talents in the classroom

In Malin's study, when the Aboriginal children went to school, the extensive talents and knowledge that they had were invisible to the teacher who was not familiar with their home culture. The teacher's strengths lay in teaching students more like herself and her expectations and the cultural orientations of the Aboriginal students clashed.

The teacher was unaware of the social knowledge that the five year old Aboriginal children had so rapidly acquired in the classroom. She was oblivious to the fact that the Aboriginal children were more likely than the non-Aboriginal students to know of the whereabouts of students not currently present and of the wellbeing, academic activity, personal appearance, friends, relatives and interests of their fellow students. The Aboriginal students were more likely to assist other students who were in difficulty either academically or practically. They perceived themselves as collaborating with others and of achieving collectively, even when the class task had not been organised in that way. They were more likely to send positive messages to other students during the course of the day, either through silent smiles, stroking of the hair or face or leaning on a neighbour in an unobtrusive way. They often expressed spontaneous joy at another student's achievement and, in their early days at school, they displayed little envy in response to the successes of others. In addition, they would perform as interpreters acting on behalf of students who had been misunderstood either by the teacher or other students. They offered explanations to students where misunderstanding had occurred. For example, in twenty-one videotaped hours in the classroom, 62 per cent of the 'sharing and caring' deeds were performed by the Aboriginal children who comprised only 21 per cent of the student population (Malin, p. 510). However, these kinds of behaviours, if seen by the teacher, were often considered to be distractions from the academic task and attracted reprimands.

In their first week of school, the five year old Aboriginal students' independent orientations were evident, for example, in their rapidly-acquired knowledge of the layout of the school yard, and of the locations of the classrooms of siblings and cousins. The non-Aboriginal children made use of the skills of their five-year-old Aboriginal peers, for example, by asking them to tie up their shoe laces, open their drink cartons, unwrap their cling-wrap sandwiches, and help them undo difficult clasps in the 'dressing-up corner'. The Aboriginal children were also more likely to help the teacher by tidying up piles of books and containers of pencils lying around the classroom. For example, in 21 videotaped hours in the classroom, 79 per cent of the 'displays of practical competence' were performed by the Aboriginal children who comprised only 21 per cent of the student population (Malin, p. 472).

These Aboriginal values of independence being balanced by collective responsibility are consistent with those highlighted in studies in other Aboriginal communities (for example, Hamilton, 1981; Coombs, Brandl & Snowdon, 1983; Waltja, 2001; Sims, et al., 2003; Shaw, 2008; Turner, 2010; and SNAICC, in press).

Teachers can become aware of these types of skills by unobtrusively observing the children's interactions with one another during free-play activities and also discussing with parents, students and Aboriginal school staff the children's out-of-school interests, activities and achievements.

Achieving cultural inclusiveness in the school and classroom

The national Closing the Gap strategy aims to reduce the gap between Aboriginal and non-Indigenous Australians in life expectancy, child mortality, access to early childhood education, educational achievement and employment outcomes. The strategy is being implemented through the Council of Australian Governments (COAG), which has agreed to three major priorities for schooling reform:

- raising the quality of teaching in our schools
- ensuring all students are benefiting from the schooling they receive, especially in disadvantaged communities

- improving the transparency and accountability of schools and school systems at all levels. (Department of Education, Employment and Workplace Relations, 2011a)

The focus on Aboriginal children in the schooling system is not just a recent discussion (Walker, 1969; Aboriginal Education Policy Task Force, 1988; Groome & Hamilton 1995). There has been much documentation of the importance of teachers having support and access to cultural training in order to help provide a safe environment for Aboriginal children both in the classroom and in the school grounds (Russell, 2007). Some ideas for improving the circumstances for Aboriginal students in schools follow below.

Addressing racism

Addressing racism is crucial to student safety as there have been many stories of how experiences of racism against Aboriginal children and their families has been a major factor for Aboriginal students' disengagement from the schooling system (Russell, 2007; Mansouri, et al., 2009).

Some departments of education have developed policies and guidelines in response to school-based racism. An example of this is the South Australian Department of Education and Children's Services (2007) approach. Their major recommendation is that a 'whole-school approach' be used, which includes the following principles:

- active support and involvement of the school's leadership team

- genuine, open and clear use of democratic and collaborative principles
- staff consensus and ownership over the change process
- the school identifying as an agent of change
- the development of a learning culture.

The success of this approach is also dependent upon an understanding by all school staff of the nature and processes of racism, including issues of power, and the development of strategies to address racism. Opening up a dialogue around the issue of racism in a school can help create a space for the voices of Aboriginal students and their families to be heard.

Knowing the student as a cultural being

It will be easier for a teacher to provide a culturally inclusive classroom if s/he comes to a greater understanding of:

- his or her own cultural background
- the student's family
- the child's cultural background.

Knowing the child as a cultural being involves understanding the complexity in that person's makeup and not only avoiding an automatic tendency to see all children as 'the same' but also not pigeonholing all Aboriginal students into the same 'difference' category. Aboriginal children come from diverse backgrounds and enter school with a diverse range of skills. Nevertheless, it is likely that many Aboriginal students will share some common cultural traits. Some possible values and cultural traits were described earlier. In understanding these, teachers will be better able to recognise some of the skills that Aboriginal children bring to school.

Acquiring this background knowledge could also be achieved through asking advice from the Aboriginal Education Officers, inviting family members into the school to talk about 'culture' and by attending community events.

Knowing the student as a learner

Teachers need cultural knowledge but they also need to know how to teach. Good teachers have an understanding of how children learn and they know how to tap into children's natural abilities to learn and to convince them that they have some control over their own learning (Christie, 1985).

Knowing the child as a learner acknowledges the universal human potential to learn but also allows the teacher to facilitate each student's learning so he or she is being continuously extended step by step towards his or her potential.

Teachers can also ensure that what they do in their daily teaching is working for the Aboriginal students and, if it is not, then they need to change it until it does work.

Improving the relations between families and schools

Aboriginal parents, in interviews with Hayes, Johnston, Morris, Power and Roberts (2009, p. 62), stated that they were optimistic that relations between families and schools could be improved in the following ways:

- by modifying the physical layout of the front office so it was more welcoming to Aboriginal parents

- by ensuring parents are treated in more culturally sensitive ways through:
  - cultural competency training for non-Aboriginal workers
  - the appointment of more Aboriginal staff
- through regular newsletters to parents with information about future events
- by informing parents about due dates for major assignments
- through information about school procedures
- through visits by the 'Year Adviser' to the homes of parents who have not attended formal parent-teacher evenings to discuss the progress of the student and any concerns of the students, parents and teachers
- through regular informal gatherings such as barbeques where teachers and parents can meet and talk in a relaxed, non-threatening setting.

Other resources

Some schools already have programs in place to provide support for students and their families and to assist teachers to develop strategies for helping Aboriginal students to feel as if school and the classroom are places where they belong. A first step would be for new teachers to enquire within their schools to find out what is already in place. The next step would be to search the various education departments' websites to see what resources are already developed. Some examples are:

- http://www.decs.sa.gov.au
- http://www.whatworks.edu.au
- http://www.strongersmarter.qut.edu.au
- http://www.snaicc.asn.au

Conclusion

All students have the right to a quality education. All schools and school systems need to be held accountable to Aboriginal students and their families. Individual teachers, principals, schools and teacher-education programs can all contribute to the provision of an exemplary education for Aboriginal children by working in partnership with Aboriginal families.

It is time for teachers to evaluate the appropriateness of their teaching programs rather than looking for deficits in the Aboriginal child or their family. Malcolm Gollan, Aboriginal singer and songwriter, wrote in his song called 'The Program':

Something wrong with the program; there's nothing wrong with me!

There's something wrong with the program; there's nothing wrong with me

In hearing this song, Aboriginal parents might wonder whether their little ones will be provided with a safe schooling and not be left questioning that there's 'something wrong' with them.

History provides an explanation as to why many Aboriginal parents are intimidated by schools and teachers, and are reluctant to enter the school grounds. Schools need to come to the parents in whatever ways the Aboriginal staff and parents groups indicate are the most appropriate.

Future teaching graduates, whether they are specialising in early childhood, junior primary, middle primary, or secondary schooling, need to understand the history and experiences of Aboriginal families and communities. They need to graduate with a commitment to work in a way that creates opportunities for Aboriginal young people's experiences in the classroom, creating a place that is culturally safe and inclusive.

The challenge for us as practitioners is to take individual responsibility for creating a classroom or program that is culturally respectful, safe and inclusive. Where will Aboriginal children be in ten years time? And how will you be remembered as a teacher?

Acknowledgements

We would like to thank the many people who contributed to this chapter including South Australian teachers Malcolm Gollan, Nicole Gollan and Tina Quitadamo, Sharon Gollan's grandchildren, Katho Campbell, Laura Agius and Stephen Meredith, and the South Australian community people who shared their stories and experiences with us.

6

LANGUAGE AND THE CLASSROOM SETTING

Ellen Grote and Judith Rochecouste

Language is the means through which education is delivered in the classroom. It is the medium through which teachers interact with students and through which content is presented in learning resources. Language facilitates the acquisition of knowledge, the improvement of skills and the nurturing of social and emotional well-being that enables students to advance through the education system.

For many Aboriginal students, however, the language of the classroom, i.e., Standard Australian English (SAE), is a variety of English that is strikingly different from the language used at home and in their communities. This means that Aboriginal children are expected to learn to read and write in an unfamiliar dialect. Moreover, many Aboriginal children have a history of chronic ear disease which can result in conductive hearing loss (CHL). This condition impinges on their ability to hear the new dialect/language they are learning, making it difficult to fully engage in the classroom and to achieve academically.

This chapter focuses on two of the most common sources of communication difficulties for Aboriginal learners: (1) the mismatch between Aboriginal students' home language(s) and the

SAE dialect used at school; and (2) CHL commonly resulting from otitis media or middle-ear infection. Both can undermine the ability of Aboriginal students to acquire SAE and the SAE literacy skills required for academic success.

In order to illuminate the language and communication issues experienced by many Aboriginal students, the chapter presents an overview of how the differences between SAE and Aboriginal English (AE), the home language of the majority of Aboriginal people living in urban, rural and remote regions[1] (Eades, 2010), can obstruct communication and learning if not accommodated. It then considers the interconnectedness of language, identity and power and how this can affect the acquisition of SAE language and literacy practices. The difficulties of acquiring SAE as an additional dialect as opposed to learning SAE as an additional language are then outlined. This is followed by a discussion of the incidence of CHL among Aboriginal children and the damaging effects it has on a young child's initial language development and later their acquisition of SAE as an additional dialect/language. The discussion then turns to consider how the communication practices of AE speakers may differ from those of SAE speakers. Finally, a range of teaching and learning strategies are presented that can assist teachers to accommodate the language and literacy learning needs of Aboriginal students who speak AE as a home language as well as those who experience CHL.

---

1   According to a 2008 survey, approximately 8 per cent of children and youth aged four to fourteen living in rural regions and about 42 per cent living in remote settings speak a traditional Indigenous language as their home language ABS. (2009d). 4714.0 – National Aboriginal and Torres Strait Islander Social Survey, 2008 Retrieved 18 August, 2010, from http://www.abs.gov.au/ausstats/abs@.nsf/Latestproducts/4714.0Main%20Feature s52008?opendocument&tabname=Summary&prodno=4714.0&issue=2008&num=&v iew=. For most of these students, learning activities that promote the acquisition of SAE as an additional language are generally incorporated into the curriculum.

Language issues

SAE as the language of the school and of learning

Australian English has been described as the 'national and de-facto official language' (Lo Bianco, 2008, p. 343) of Australia. Its standardised form, SAE, is codified in dictionaries (e.g., Delbridge et al., 2009), grammar books and in style manuals (e.g., Peters, 2007). As a standardised language, SAE reflects the values and language practices of mainstream middle-class Australians, the most powerful segment of Australian society (Burridge & Mulder, 1998). For these reasons, SAE is the main language used in Australia's educational institutions as well as government and non-government economic, legal, justice, political, health, scientific, social and other organisations. Moreover, because 'many aspects of Australian life depend on effective communication in Standard Australian English' (Australian Curriculum Assessment & Reporting Authority, 2010a, p. 4), SAE language and literacy practices comprise the core of the English component of the Australian Curriculum.

Aboriginal English

While SAE is positioned as the 'official' language of the school, it co-exists alongside other fully functioning non-standard dialects of Australian English including Aboriginal English. However, Aboriginal English differs from the non-standard dialects spoken by non-Aboriginal people because it has developed in distinctively different ways and has been strongly influenced by Aboriginal languages and discourse practices (that is, ways of speaking/writing).

AE has been described as 'a range of varieties of English spoken by many Aboriginal and Torres Strait Islander people...

which differ in systematic ways from Standard Australian English at all levels of linguistic structure and which are used for distinctive speech acts, speech events and genres' (Malcolm, 1995, p. 19). These varieties comprise a continuum, with 'heavier' varieties at one end (sharing many features with English-lexified creoles[2]) and 'lighter' varieties at the opposite end (sharing many features with SAE) (Malcolm & Grote, 2007; Sharifian, Rochecouste, & Malcolm, 2004). Since AE can vary regionally, it is sometimes referred to by local names, e.g. Koori English in Victoria (Department of Education and Early Childhood Development, State Government Victoria, 2010; McKenry, 1996).

AE and SAE language systems are considerably different in terms of their phonology (sounds), lexicon (vocabulary), morphology (word formations), semantics (meanings), syntax (grammar/sentence structures), genres (text structures and schemas), discourse practices, pragmatics ('rules' guiding how language is used), metaphors, cultural conceptualisations and world views (Haig, Konigsberg, & Collard, 2005; Malcolm & Grote, 2007; Malcolm et al., 1999b; Malcolm & Rochecouste, 2000; Sharifian, 2005). It is the disparities between the two systems and cultural worldviews that make it more difficult for Aboriginal children to acquire SAE than it is for their non-Aboriginal peers who speak other non-standard dialects of English. Another complication making it difficult for Aboriginal children to learn SAE concerns the links between language, cultural identity and power.

---

2 Because Australian creoles such as Kriol (spoken in northern Australia) and Torres Strait Creole share many features with 'heavier' varieties of AE, many of the teaching/learning strategies discussed in this chapter apply to creole speakers.

Language, identity and power

SAE language and discourse practices are generally viewed as neutral and free of cultural values because they are not associated with any particular region in Australia and because most Australians encounter them on a daily basis and are accustomed to them (Malcolm & Konigsberg, 2007). For many Aboriginal students, however, SAE is the language of 'white fellas' who belong to a different speech community, which neither shares the same language variety nor adheres to the same rules for using or interpreting it (Hymes, 1972).

Membership in a particular speech community is usually, though not always, indexed by the dialect a speaker uses. Speaking AE enables Aboriginal students to communicate their alignment with their own speech community and therefore their Aboriginal identity (Malcolm, 1998; Malcolm & Koscielecki, 1997). So students may resist adopting the dialect of the non-Aboriginal speech community, viewing it as a challenge to their own Aboriginal identity, their affiliation with the Aboriginal community and indeed as acquiescence to assimilation.

Although some Aboriginal students may avoid learning and using SAE in the classroom, most Aboriginal parents, community members and government agencies are aware that SAE is the language of power in Australia. So they understand how learning SAE can provide advantages for Aboriginal students and their communities (AESOC Senior Officials Working Party on Indigenous Education, 2006; Department of Education, Western Australia, 2010b; Department of Employment Education and Training, 1994; Luke, Land, Christie, Kolatsis, & Noblett, 2002; MCEETYA, 2008). Aboriginal people view acquiring competency in SAE as a way to improve their quality of life and to defend their rights (Clayton, 1996; Harkins, 1994). Nakata (1999) points out that this has been the case since colonisation began when learning English was seen as a way to access power within Australia and internationally.

While SAE may provide access to power in the broader community (Sharifian, 2008), AE remains the language of power within Aboriginal communities. AE has long served a variety of important functions in employment situations, communicating with other Aboriginal communities, as a carrier of Aboriginal identity, for the transmission of culture and for artistic expression (Malcolm & Grote, 2007). In fact, if Aboriginal people speak SAE within their communities, they can be criticised for talking 'flash' or 'posh' (Eagleson, Kaldor & Malcolm, 1982, p. 240–3). Moreover, it has been noted that the maintenance of home language(s), culture and cultural identity can positively influence health, wellbeing and resilience (Aboriginal and Torres Strait Islander Social Justice Commissioner, 2009). It is important therefore for educators to value and encourage learners to develop competency in both varieties and to teach SAE, not as a replacement for AE, but as an additional language in their linguistic repertoire (Cummins, 1992; Lambert, 1981).

The challenge of learning SAE as an additional dialect
Researchers tend to agree that learning an additional dialect is more difficult than acquiring a new language (Siegel, 2010). It is the similarity and mutual intelligibility of the two dialects that make it so challenging. Because the differences between the two varieties are relatively small, they often go unnoticed by dialect speakers. Research in second language acquisition demonstrates that learners must consciously *notice* the difference between the

input of the target language and their own output before they can attend to it by changing the feature in their speech or writing (Gass, 1997; Oliver, 2009; Schmidt, 1990). So if learners do not take note of such discrepancies, they are unlikely to modify their output.

Another reason why learning an additional dialect is more difficult is because dialect learners begin at a point significantly closer to the target language than second language learners (Siegel, 2010). Highly proficient second language speakers who have reached a similar point in their acquisition of the target language also have difficulty advancing beyond this point toward native-like proficiency (Long, 2007). Both are at the stage where they can communicate effectively in most situations and any further progress made may be imperceptible. Moreover, while 'native-like' proficiency is rarely the goal of second language learners (particularly regarding pronunciation), AE speaking students are expected to achieve the same level of proficiency as their non-Aboriginal SAE speaking peers (Australian Curriculum Assessment & Reporting Authority, 2010a; Siegel, 2010).

Despite the huge overlap between two dialects, international research on the experiences of non-standard dialect speakers underscores the challenges they face when educators assume proficiency in the standard language (Edwards, 2004; Nero, 2006). Non-standard dialect speakers have been shown to read more slowly, write shorter texts, use a more limited vocabulary, make more spelling errors and receive lower marks on tests (Siegel, 2010). Yet poor performance, particularly on standardised assessments, is often interpreted as a sign of intellectual deficiency, cognitive impairment, language pathology or carelessness (Gould, 2008; Siegel, 2010). In many cases, however, poor outcomes can be linked to the student's non-standard language background (Garcia & Menken, 2006). For example, a Western Australian survey (Zubrick, et al., 2006) found that only one-fifth (20.5 per cent) of AE speaking students (age four to seventeen) were ranked as average or above in overall academic performance, compared with just under half of those who spoke Australian English (47.3 per cent).

In summary, poor academic performance can be attributed to the disadvantages faced by AE speakers, including:

- learning literacy skills in an unfamiliar dialect
- little or no explicit instruction on dialectal differences
- negative attitudes toward and lack of understanding of the linguistic features and discourse practices of the dialect
- constant correction on dialect features appearing in their speech and writing
- being reprimanded for using their home language in the classroom
- disparities in cultural conceptualisations (Baugh, 1999; Sharifian, 2005; Siegel, 2010).

Conductive hearing loss

Another major source of difficulty for Aboriginal children learning SAE language and literacy skills is ear disease. Otitis media usually results from a viral or bacterial infection brought on by a cold, influenza or respiratory infection (Burrow & Thomson, 2003). It is a phenomenon observed among indigenous peoples around the world, one that is linked to the poor living conditions of marginalised communities, particularly those in remote regions (Galloway, 2008). Otitis media is recognised as the most common source of CHL among Australian Aboriginal people (Burrow, Galloway & Weissofner, 2009).

CHL results when fluid from the infection accumulates in the ear canal, obstructing sound transmission. Pressure from the inflammation can cause severe pain, irritability and sometimes fever. When left untreated, pressure from the fluid may cause the tympanic membrane to rupture so that a discharge is released (Couzos, Metcalf, & Murray, 2001); hence, the condition is sometimes called 'glue ear' (Thomson, 2003, p. 117) or 'runny ears' (Zubrick, et al., 2004, p. 144). The chronic nature of the disease makes it difficult for the tympanic membrane to repair itself so many children experience fluctuating levels of CHL (Zubrick, et al., 2004). (See chapter seven for further details about this disease.)

Reported rates of CHL vary from 30 to 80 per cent of Aboriginal children with approximately 70 per cent of adults experiencing some hearing loss from exposure to the disease earlier in life (Burrow, et al., 2009; Couzos, et al., 2001; Galloway, 2008; Preston, 1994). Ear disease occurs more frequently in infants and very young children (Zubrick, et al., 2004) which is particularly concerning because the first two years of life are generally recognised as the critical period for language development (Higgins, 1997). Although CHL can change over time, it can have deleterious effects on first language development in young children and impair the ability of school-aged children to acquire SAE as an additional dialect in the classroom (Partington & Galloway, 2005).

Aboriginal children with CHL who are learning SAE are therefore doubly disadvantaged. They are challenged firstly by having to learn to discriminate between the unfamiliar sounds in SAE and secondly by an impaired ability to actually hear the sounds in the target language (Aithal, Yonovitz, & Aithal, 2008). CHL exacerbates the acquisition of SAE because it impacts upon the learner's capacity to:

- develop phonological awareness (or the ability to distinguish between and produce new sounds and sound segments)
- access a consistent language model due to fluctuations in hearing
- process auditory input
- develop short-term auditory memory
- extend their auditory memory of sequential sound patterns (Aithal, et al., 2008; Partington & Galloway, 2005; Walker & Wigglesworth, 2001).

Many AE and creole speakers with normal hearing struggle to discriminate between SAE sound pairs such as *t* and *d*, *t* and *th* (as in *thank*), *p* and *b*, *k* and *g*, *f* and *p*, *b* and *v*, *sh* and *ch*, among others. (See Berry & Hudson, 1997, for other potentially troublesome sounds.) The task becomes increasingly more challenging for learners with CHL, especially when the sound occurs in unstressed or final positions or when articulated softly (Galloway, 2008). Moreover, while developing graphophonic skills (or the ability to link sounds with corresponding letters) is difficult for AE speakers with normal hearing, it is all the more so for those with CHL. This skill is crucial for the development of reading and writing skills, which in turn impacts on academic achievement (Walker & Wigglesworth, 2001).

The inability to hear and understand the teacher can diminish the academic performance of Aboriginal children and their interest in school and learning. The effects of CHL are further exacerbated by the background cacophony of normal classrooms. These learners may fail to notice verbal cues which signal classroom routines and facilitate comprehension. The diminished capacity to follow along and participate in learning activities can lead to anti-social behaviours (Partington & Galloway, 2005). The condition can also compound other factors that put Aboriginal children at educational risk, such as irregular attendance, poor physical health as well as their social and emotional wellbeing (Burrow, et al., 2009). It is therefore critical for teachers to ensure that Aboriginal students undergo auditory screening to identify those who may be experiencing CHL. The strategies that can be implemented to address the needs of Aboriginal students with CHL are discussed below.

Communication practices of Aboriginal English speakers

Clearly languages and dialects differ in their range of sounds, words and grammatical structures, but languages also differ in the way that they are used. Referred to as pragmatics, these uses, which can be reflected in the choice of words and the allocation of meaning, are determined by cultural conceptualisations and experiences. 'Cultural conceptualisations are the ways in which people across different cultural groups construe various aspects of the world in their experience' (Sharifian, 2009, p. 163). Cultural conceptualisations 'are developed through interactions between the members of a cultural group and enable them to think, more or less, in one mind' (Sharifian, 2003, p. 190). The range of cultural and social experiences, and subsequent cultural conceptualisations, of speakers of AE are most often markedly different from those of an SAE speaker and this is reflected in their use of language.

Influence of family and familiarity on communication

Fundamental to understanding the communication practices of Aboriginal people is the acknowledgement of commitment to family which cannot be underestimated when teaching Aboriginal students. Firstly, the concept of family may be quite different from that held by the non-Aboriginal educator. Family, in the context of Aboriginal society, is the extended family rather than the nuclear family of most Anglo-Australians. Furthermore, relationships within the extended family are stronger than many educators will realise. This is demonstrated by the use of the term 'Mum' to refer not only to one's biological mother but also to the equivalent of one's aunt in Anglo cultures (Sharifian, 2006, p. 5). Another example of this closeness is evident in the term 'cousinbrother/sister' for a 'first cousin' or a cousin with whom one is particularly close (Sharifian, 2006, p. 16).

Evidence of strong familial relationships will be manifest in the speech and behaviour of Aboriginal students. They will readily acknowledge the kinship ties of those related to them and who may be in the same school or even the same classroom. Students' narratives will begin with mention of those present who are invariable family members, often before the establishment of the time and place of the event described. As Sharifian (2005, p. 15, after Eades, 1988, p. 98) notes, among Aboriginal people 'place of residence, travel, social networks, leisure activities and personal loyalties all revolve in some way around one's kin'. Indeed, Sharifian points out that in the south-west of Western Australia the word 'relation' appears to have formed a suffix '-lation' and is used to describe concepts such as one's own relations, e.g. 'ownlation'.

Aboriginal notions of family and the relationships therein demonstrate to us some of the cultural conceptualisations or schemas which may not be shared with non-Aboriginal educators and therefore can lead to significant misunderstanding in the classroom context.

Shared knowledge vs old/new systems

A major consequence of the familial closeness described here is the sharing of social and cultural knowledge in close-knit communities, where everyone will be aware of what is happening. This means that the level of detail required when speaking will differ from that used in SAE. There may not be a need to be specific about time, place and quantity. Where in SAE we have quite strict rules for distinguishing between 'new' and 'old' information both in our sentence structure and in our system of cohesive ties, no such prescriptive need occurs in AE. This has been referred to as 'minimal verbal processing' by Sharifian (2001, p. 130) which 'may stem from the assumption of shared cultural schemas made by a speaker about the audience. In such cases the speaker may find complex or detailed verbal processing unnecessary' (Sharifian, 2001, p. 131).

In the educational context, oral and written texts by Aboriginal students may require considerable interpretation to be understood by a non-Aboriginal educator thus demonstrating the need for teachers to work closely with their Aboriginal Islander Education Officer (AIEO). Misunderstanding and linguistic exclusion can occur if the educator dismisses an

Aboriginal student's oral or written text as lacking vital information, coherence and cohesion.

A further consequence of shared knowledge systems is evident when Aboriginal students willingly share their story-telling with others who may have also contributed to, or be familiar with, the events of the story which involved family members.

Broadcast vs dyadic speech

Walsh (1991, p. 2) reports on observing, among Aboriginal speakers, a manner of broadcasting information which contrasts with the Anglo-Australian style of dyadic or two-way interaction. In dyadic speech situations people generally face each other, focus (look at each other) and take turns in speaking. This style may even be used when talking to more than one person whereby the speaker looks directly at each person or group expecting their attention and feedback whether by eye-contact, nodding or articulating agreement (e.g., *Mmm*) etc. In an Aboriginal non-dyadic communication style, however, eye-contact may sometimes be avoided because it is considered disrespectful. Moreover, the audience is free to listen or not – to tune in and out as they see fit (see Walsh, 1991; Liberman, 1985).

Clearly a lack of understanding of this communication style can lead to considerable difficulties in a classroom. Aboriginal students may avoid eye-contact with the teacher, leading the latter to the assumption that they are not paying attention. Aboriginal students may be unfamiliar with the relatively strict turn-taking structures that are followed in SAE and where what is interpreted as interruption by the educator may be considered shared story-telling by the students.

Questioning – focus of attention, shame

The use of questioning, and in particular direct questioning, has become a subject of some controversy in studies of Aboriginal languages and A.E. Eades (1982), for example, reports the absence of direct questions, particularly 'why' questions in South East Queensland AE, yet Harris (1984) recounts a classroom incident where questioning by Yolngu children was likened to the habit of non-Aboriginal students. Additionally, Christie (1985) claims that Yolngu children were confused by questioning in the classroom because the teachers obviously knew the answer already. Much subsequent literature and advice to educators and health and legal professionals has, as a result, continued to advise against the direct questioning of Aboriginal people. More recently, however, Moses and Yallop (2008) have refuted these claims and have presented extensive data showing Kriol speaking children from Yakanarra in the Kimberley region of Western Australia asking numerous questions of the non-Aboriginal researchers. The authors conclude that 'the numerous and varied questions asked by the children are more likely to be prompted by the arrival of a "new" person, an infrequent visitor about whom relatively little is known and of whom new information can be gleaned, rather than the fact that that person happens to be non-Aboriginal' (p. 52). They note, moreover, that the children displayed 'an ability to use a wide repertoire of questions and to ask them without inhibition in certain circumstances' (p. 52). The children's behaviour in the classroom, however, could be quite different, showing a reluctance to ask or answer questions. This Moses and Yallop attribute to the use of Standard English and the pragmatics of the classroom:

[i]t is far more likely that these children often find the Standard English spoken by their teachers is incomprehensible and the situation in which they are asked to perform (individually, in front of their peers and uncertain of the correctness of their response) one that is liable to expose them to shame[3] (p. 52).

Reeders (2008) offers a further explanation for differences in questioning and answering between Aboriginal and non-Aboriginal people. She suggests that, with the cultural limitations on eye-contact and the manner of broadcast rather than dyadic speech, an Aboriginal speaker is less likely to select an interlocutor to take the next turn. Therefore, 'any member of the audience may respond...and so the responsibility for answering is dispersed among the group. This weakens the predication strength of the question.' (p. 119).

The conceptualisation of ownership, space, time

In modern western society considerable emphasis is given to exactness in the quantification of time and amount. Even in the educational context, classes and free time extend for specified periods of time marked off with sirens or bells, assignments are due on particular dates (e.g., Friday week, in a fortnight) and readings are of a specified length (e.g., a chapter or a section). The educational environment therefore is highly structured and contained within abstract boundaries which may not exist in the cultural conceptualisation of Aboriginal learners.

Speakers of AE may, however, have quite different concepts

---

3   The Aboriginal concept of 'shame' refers to feelings of embarrassment or shyness in the face of being singled out from the group for a range of reasons. See further discussion page 21 (xxx, double check once typeset).

of time which lack the precision which governs life in an educational context. This vagueness is evident in AE expressions of *lots of (lotsa)*, *big mobs/bi-ig mobs*, *drekly*, *one time*, etc., which are adequate in Aboriginal culture but may not be so in a school environment. Consequences for the classroom are reflected in oral and written texts and also in assignment submissions.

Differing conceptual understandings of space and ownership can also have an impact in the classroom. Students from an Aboriginal background where sharing within the family is the norm may find the notion of one's own desk, pens/pencils, books, etc., new. The fact that the classroom and the school grounds 'contain' students during specific hours of the day may also be a new concept. Cultural cognition, however, 'is an emergent system in that it results from the interactions between members of a cultural group across time and space' (Sharifian, 2009, p. 162) and is subject to adjustment with new information and experiences. Aboriginal students, therefore, will soon adjust to the educational environment. However, as with much of what humans learn, its relevance to their needs governs any willingness to learn.

Connections, respect, reciprocity, responsibilities

Families and related cultural responsibilities are of the utmost importance to Aboriginal people and will most likely take precedence over educational commitments. School-aged children are expected to meet their obligations[4], such as caring for siblings or other family members, participating in community

---

4   The word 'obligation' is perhaps the best translation in English. Note, however, that it does not include any connotation of 'chore'. People are not necessarily 'obliged' to fulfil certain roles, they actually want to be there for each other (see further Department of Education WA (in Press) *Tracks to Two-Way Learning*).

events such as funerals, and moving with family to other towns or communities in the face of crises.

The concept of reciprocity underpins most aspects of Aboriginal community life. This is realised in the sharing of food and other valued items:

> Each person shares with those persons from whom he or she has received benefits in the past, and from who benefits will be received in the future. Reciprocity also governs the cultural norm of avenging wrong-doing: this is the notion of 'payback' or 'squaring it up' (Fryer-Smith, 2002, p. 2:15).

Silence, body language, non-verbal communication

In spite of our use of a complex range of sounds and con-structions to make meaning in our languages, meaning is also frequently conveyed non-verbally through body language and silence. As a result we have metaphors such as 'reading' one's body language. Many languages incorporate extensive sign languages. Although English is not rich in sign language, we do have, for example, the 'thumbs up' sign, and other gestures such as shoulder shrugs, eye and hand movements, etc. Similarly, sign systems have developed in factories where noise is a factor and in monasteries where silence is the rule (Kendon, 2008, p. 359). By contrast, Australian Aboriginal languages, and consequently AE, are rich in 'manual-coding', sign languages or gestural systems 'where they have been highly elaborated in relation to prolonged taboos on the use of speech' (Kendon, 2008, p. 359).

Of further relevance to the educational context is the use of silence. Silence in western English speaking communities is generally avoided. In fact, English speakers feel uncomfortable with periods of silence, hence the expressions, 'deadly silence' or 'pregnant silence'. However, long periods of 'comfortable' silence have been observed in Aboriginal interaction by Walsh (1991). Mushin and Gardner (2009, p. 2036) link silence in Aboriginal interaction to the non-dyadic style of speech proposed by Walsh where there is no obligation to maintain talk. Mushin and Gardner conclude further that the absence of any 'particular orientation of the clock time...[means] time to interact is much less limited than those who live with appointment times...and so whose interaction must always be punctuated by needing to be elsewhere' (Mushin & Gardner, 2009, p. 2049).

Teaching and learning strategies when working with Aboriginal learners

Establishing relationships and trust

The most important strategy for working with Aboriginal learners is the establishment of trust. Aboriginal learners come to our educational contexts with considerable knowledge which has been learned from people with whom they are familiar and whom they trust. Therefore getting to know your learners and letting them get to know you are strategies fundamental to educational success.

The strategies that you use will depend on your students' educational level. Clearly, early childhood learners can be engaged in play and talk about home and family, and by the freedom to use their home language or dialect if they are not familiar with or comfortable in SAE. This learning process should be two-way, enabling the young students to learn about you and your family through photographs, videos, etc. These strategies are also applicable to other educational levels. For older students you might also exchange likes and dislikes. This enables you to find common areas of interest which can promote conversation. Students' areas of interest can also be found by setting tasks which allow free writing or discussion – activities which also show their current skill level. Older learners can also contribute to the curriculum and to their assessment preferences, and provide information on their preferred learning styles.

Prescriptive vs descriptive approaches

There are two major perspectives on language that are important for education. The first is the prescriptive view which holds to the teaching of grammatical rules (prescriptive rules) which must be obeyed: it is a 'right or wrong' view of language. However, language cannot be fully explained in terms of set rules because it is continually changing and we do not think about rules when we speak. Also, when we write we use the language of the protagonists in the text to represent them authentically, or the language that our reader audience will expect to make sure that they understand.

Beginning writers will write as they speak and this is an important part of their development as writers. Teachers need to be careful not to 'put students off' writing by being too prescriptive and wanting the rules obeyed. Scaffolding and modelling with explanations of the rules used in SAE will provide access to SAE literacy in a more positive way than explicit correction according the rules.

Recognising and avoiding miscommunication

Miscommunication between AE speaking students and the SAE speaking teachers is common. This can be attributed to differences in worldview, differences in the way language is used and its functions in the two cultures. Educators will come to the classroom with their own assumptions of what happens in a classroom, developed from both their own experiences and their training. Students, however, will not necessarily share these same assumptions.

There may be assumptions about what is new and what is shared knowledge. An Aboriginal student might refer to something that he/she assumes is general knowledge, while an SAE speaker will expect to be told more detail. In the research report entitled *Two-Way English,* Malcolm et al., illustrate shared knowledge in an example where a student introduced 'the rock' into a story without having referred to it previously. The assumption was that 'everyone knows that there will be a rock on the side of the road' (1999a, p. 86). The need for more detail in SAE speech gives AE speakers the opinion that SAE speakers always want to know more (see also Malcolm, et al., 1999, p. 3). Explicit teaching of SAE text cohesion through a range of language activities can be implemented to assist the student to bridge from AE to SAE.

SAE speakers also have assumptions about time that they expect their students to share. In English-speaking western culture, the concept of time is all-pervasive. We have metaphors that reflect its value, e.g., *Time is money, to spend time,* etc. These same assumptions will not be shared by AE speakers and the notion of time is quite different in their worldview. In the Aboriginal world, time is very different. It is often linked to events which the listener will be familiar with, e.g., *When did it happen? After Neighbours, When Gary got his new ute*, etc. Moreover, family and family events are often used to provide a temporal reference, e.g., *When did it happen? When cousin Billy was here.* The implications of these differing approaches to the description of time are important in an educational context. For example, students' spoken or written narratives may be digressive and circular rather than following a linear structure and students may not initially understand deadlines for homework or subject content, so time frames such as weeks, fortnights, terms, decades etc., might need to be explicitly taught.

Differing assumptions about space can also result in miscommunication. The Aboriginal learner may not have had the reinforcement of boundaries that non-Aboriginal learners have had (e.g. *Don't go out of the yard, Keep off the garden, Don't cross the road, Don't go too far, Stay out the neighbour's garden, Don't go into the shed* – see *Tracks to Two-Way Learning*, in press). In fact, Aboriginal children will have experienced considerably more freedom than their non-Aboriginal peers and will most likely have developed the concomitant responsibilities. Spatial assumptions also connect to concepts of ownership: *in Jenny's bedroom, inside the teacher's house, in our yard, in her desk*, etc., which may not be familiar to a student from a communal society.

Closely related to spatial assumptions are those relating to direction. AE speakers place more focus on the getting to and from a place than on the measurement of the distance travelled. General expressions such as *dat-a-way, this-a-way* may suffice for a speaker of AE, whereas in the modern western world direction is often grounded in the individual, e.g., *turn left, turn right, it will be on your right*. (Harris, 1991, p. 28). In terms of educational implications, tasks requiring explicit directions and measurements (such as logical arithmetical problems) may be difficult because of different conceptualisations of direction, time and space and may require the student to develop an understanding of measurement systems before being introduced to such problems.

Size and number can also be measured very differently in AE where there is a tendency to be more general than precise: *mob, big mobs, plenty*, or even *1 2 3 mob*. Educators might find that their students have difficulty with numbers and the specific measurement of quantity. As a result, students may use explicit numbers (10, 100, etc.) in a general sense rather than as representing any exact number leading to miscommunication between the teacher and the student. The SAE convention of exactness and detail may therefore need to be introduced.

A further important assumption that can have considerable impact in a classroom context is the behaviour of listeners and speakers. Different languages have different responsibilities for speakers and listeners. In non-Aboriginal society, listeners are obliged to provide feedback to the speaker and this indicates that they are concentrating and understanding, agreeing or disagreeing with what is being said. This feedback comes with the expectation that the listener look directly at the speaker. Such feedback and eye contact is not always required in AE interactions, nor is it always necessary to nod, or make polite noises to indicate attention. As Harris (1980, p. 137) claims, in Aboriginal society 'everyone has the right to be heard and to speak...but no-one guarantees to listen'. Subsequently, an educator may assume that a student is not listening because he/

she does not behave according to the SAE conventions of paying attention, particularly to an older person.

From an educational point of view, especially in classrooms where strict turn-taking and the verbal display of knowledge is the norm, silence can be misinterpreted. The following extract from the NSW Department of Education Board of Studies provides advice regarding silence among Aboriginal students:

> The use of silence should not be misunderstood. It may mean that people do not want to express an opinion at that point in time, or that they are listening and reflecting about what has been said. It is important that this silence is respected and not interrupted unnecessarily. Silence is not a chance to take a break or leave the room, but rather an opportunity to contemplate what is being spoken about (Board of Studies NSW, 2008, p. 11).

The use of silence and eye contact by Aboriginal learners needs to be understood and accommodated by non-Aboriginal educators; otherwise these differences from non-Aboriginal interaction can influence attitudes towards speakers of AE and subsequent stereotyping. Indeed, both Eades (1982) and Malcolm (1993) found that Aboriginal students' absence of verbal contributions in class generated negative attitudes towards the students' abilities more generally.

Questions and answers

In spite of the on-going debate about the appropriateness of direct questioning, educators need to reflect on how much classroom discourse is manifest as questions and answers. Questions and answers in the classroom context enable the teacher to ascertain what has or has not been understood of the content. However, there are many other ways of establishing this. For example, relaxed one-to-one conversations with students, collating portfolios of students' work over time, and designing activities whereby students can demonstrate their understanding in other ways (e.g., role-play, posters, drawings).

Most importantly, educators need to avoid situations which cause *shame* for Aboriginal students. Harkins (1990) describes *shame* as feelings of embarrassment or shyness which, according to Eagleson, Kaldor and Malcolm (1982) are brought about by being made the focus of attention whether for positive or negative purposes. Such situations cause the person to lose 'the security and anonymity provided by the group' (p. 99). *Shame* might be demonstrated, for example, by a failure to respond to a question because this would draw attention to the individual, or because the question is inappropriate and cultural restrictions forbid the respondent to answer. Hence, silence can be a consequence of *shame*. *Shame* might also be experienced in the face of persons of authority and has therefore been linked to the concept of respect. Educators therefore should be advised to invite volunteers to respond, rather than select individuals.

Strategies for students with CHL

Students with CHL have difficulty in distinguishing sounds so will benefit from explicit teaching and frequent practice of problematic sounds. This means demonstrating the difference between sounds. A typical example is between voiced and voiceless sounds (e.g., *p* vs *b*; *d* vs *t* and *k* vs *g*). In this case students need to understand the physical features of voicing (vibration of the vocal chords) and how voicing can be heard as a buzzing sound when the ears are covered, or felt as vibration of the larynx when voiced sounds are contrasted with unvoiced sounds. Similarly, students will need to know the difference in articulation of stop consonants and fricative consonants (*b* and *v*; *p* and *f*; *d* and *th*). The students need to observe and practise differences in lip movement (see further Berry & Hudson, 1997, Chapter 6.4) while uttering minimal pairs (e.g., *vat* vs *bat*; *pin* vs *bin*; *pin* vs *fin*, etc). Instructions such as 'Watch my lips' or 'Put your tongue just behind your top teeth' will help students become sensitised to differences in articulation. Ideally one sound should be the focus of observation and practice until it is mastered and then it is time to move on to another. Success in the recognition of sounds will be enhanced if the ambient noise in the classroom is controlled. This includes external noises such as traffic and internal noise such as shuffling and the movement of chairs.

These strategies can be further enhanced through the use of a classroom-wide sound-field amplification system or individual sound assistance devices (e.g., FM devices to receive signals from a microphone used by the teacher or personal air or bone conduction hearing devices). These devices can be used during language and literacy lessons to make it easier for children to hear and discriminate between sounds (Galloway, 2008). (For a comprehensive review of strategies for teaching students with CHL see Burrows, Galloway & Weissofner, 2009).

Code-switching

We all change the way that we speak depending on who we are speaking to. If we change our words to sound more formal (e.g.

when talking to our boss) or more casual (e.g. when talking to friends at the football), we are changing our *register*. If we change our language or dialect, however, we are said to be *code-switching*. Code-switching, therefore, is a linguistic term to describe the ways that speakers of one or more languages or dialects can switch from one to the other. This is a positive and advantageous skill for speakers of AE and its perfection should be encouraged. To be able to switch from AE to SAE in appropriate contexts enables the Aboriginal student to maintain his/her identity or Aboriginality as well as gaining access to opportunities in mainstream education and employment.

Code-switching can be promoted in the classroom by providing opportunities for the use of the first language or dialect, e.g., free writing, role-play, discussions, etc. (see further Berry & Hudson, 1997). Indeed, much research in second language acquisition has identified the importance of maintaining and valuing the first language for successful acquisition of the second language (e.g., Cummins, 1992). For speakers of AE, code-switching means bidialectalism and biculturalism or enabling AE speaking students to embrace two dialects of English and two cultures:

> A key outcome of two-way bidialectal education is that non-standard dialect speakers will be equipped with the capacity to switch from one code to another and back again: that they will learn to code-switch (Department of Education and Training, Catholic Education Office and the Association of Independent Schools of WA 2000).

Conclusion

This chapter has explored the language and communication issues faced by many Aboriginal students stemming from a mismatch between their home language and the language of the classroom. When learning SAE as an additional dialect or language, concurrently with educational content, a large proportion of Aboriginal learners are further disadvantaged by CHL. A range of strategies have been presented to help teachers address both issues. Explicit teaching of the differences between the features of AE and SAE, and fostering the development of code-switching skills are critical to the acquisition of SAE language and literacy skills and academic success. Moreover, ensuring that children's ear health is checked and that adequate strategies are put into place to address the needs of those with CHL is also essential. However, effective teaching also depends on nurturing positive relationships with Aboriginal students and communicating respect for their home language.

7

THE IMPACT OF HEALTH ON THE EDUCATION OF INDIGENOUS CHILDREN

Neil Thomson, Jane Burns and Naoibh McLoughlin

Introduction

There is growing recognition of the impact of the health of Aboriginal and Torres Strait Islander students on their education. The association of health with education has lifelong implications for many Indigenous people who are caught in a vicious cycle of poor education and poor health. The health status of Indigenous people needs to be viewed within the context of economic opportunity, physical infrastructure and social conditions, which influence the health of individuals and communities. These factors are specifically manifest in measures such as education, employment, income, housing, access to services, social networks, connection with land, racism, and incarceration. On all these measures, Indigenous people suffer substantial disadvantage.

Australia's Indigenous population is relatively young: in 2006, one-half of all Indigenous people were aged twenty-one or under compared with one-half of all non-Indigenous people being aged 37 or younger (Australian Government, 2010). Nearly 40 per cent of the Indigenous population are children aged less than fifteen years compared with 19 per cent in the non-Indigenous population. For Indigenous young people, many aspects of health impact on their educational capacity, participation and outcomes. Two factors that have major consequences for education are intellectual disability and poor hearing. Other factors include ill health or social and emotional wellbeing concerns, which may cause Indigenous students to be absent from school or may reduce their capacity to learn.

The early years in life influence lifelong learning, behaviour and health (Steering Committee for the Review of Government Service Provision, 2009). Early childhood education can provide an opportunity for early detection and treatment of hearing, language, visual and behavioural problems, which are particularly important for children from disadvantaged backgrounds. The relationship between nutritional status and educational performance has been the subject of some research, as has the role of psycho-social stimulation, particularly for young children. Many students are susceptible to infections, including respiratory, gastrointestinal, ear, eye and skin infections. Of particular concern in relation to education are ear infections, as they can affect a student's hearing with long-term effects on learning. Bullying and racism affect the social and emotional wellbeing of students, as do problems like family violence and the students' and their families' use of alcohol and drugs. Lower socio-economic background and circumstances have also been shown to have a link with leaving school early (Wilkinson & Marmot, 2003).

The aims of this chapter are to increase the awareness of teachers about: (1) the great health disadvantages experienced by many Indigenous people; and (2) the many physical and psychosocial health aspects that must be taken into account when considering the educational requirements of Indigenous children. After providing a brief summary of some key indicators of Indigenous health status, the chapter considers a variety of health issues impacting on education. Physical health aspects are grouped according to whether they arise prenatally or occur after birth. Various important aspects of social and emotional wellbeing are summarised, but it should be borne in mind that these and the physical health aspects interact in their impacts on education.

Key indicators of Indigenous health status[1]
Mortality
Expectation of life at birth
Life expectancy for Indigenous people is generally less than for non-Indigenous people (Australian Bureau of Statistics, 2009c). Indigenous males born in 2005–2007 could expect to live to 67.2 years, about 11.5 years less than the 78.7 years expected for non-Indigenous males. The expectation of life at birth of 72.9 years for Indigenous females in 2005–2007 was almost ten years less than the expectation of 82.6 years for non-Indigenous females. For those jurisdictions with reasonable information about Indigenous deaths, the median age at death (i.e. the age below which 50 per cent of people die) in 2008 for Indigenous males ranged from 49 years for those living in South Australia (SA) to 59.9 years for those living in New South Wales (NSW) (Australian Bureau of Statistics, 2009b). These levels are around 20 years less than those for non-Indigenous males, which ranged from 66.3 to 79.2 years. The median age at death for Indigenous

---

1   Attention is restricted here to measures of mortality and reproductive health.

females in 2008 ranged from 53.5 years for SA to 63.8 years for NSW. These levels are also more than 20 years less than those for non-Indigenous females, which ranged between 75.7 and 84.6 years. In 2006–2008, age-specific death rates were higher for Indigenous people than for non-Indigenous people across all age groups, but the rate ratios were particularly high in the young and middle-adult years (Australian Bureau of Statistics, 2009b).[2]

Infant mortality

Another commonly used measure of the health of a population is the infant mortality rate, which is the number of deaths of children under one year of age in a calendar year per 1,000 live births in the same calendar year.[3] For those jurisdictions with reasonable information about Indigenous deaths in 2006–2008, the highest Indigenous infant mortality rate was in the Northern Territory (NT) (13.6) and the lowest in SA (6.4) (Australian Bureau of Statistics, 2009b). These rates are considerably higher than those for the total population in these jurisdictions, which range from 7.8 in NT to 3.5 for both WA and SA.

Causes of death

For deaths identified as Indigenous in 2001–2005, cardiovascular disease (also known as 'diseases of the circulatory system', which

---

2 Age-specific death rates relate the number of deaths in a particular age group to the population size at that age group. In this chapter, rate ratios are generally the rate for Indigenous people divided by the rate for non- Indigenous people.

3 This measure has been used widely to compare health internationally or the changes in health over time within countries. It has also been used to compare the health of a country's sub-populations. However, international comparisons of a country's sub-population (such as Indigenous Australians) with populations and/or sub-populations in other countries are of doubtful validity.

includes heart disease and stroke) was the leading cause of death for Indigenous males and females living in Qld, WA, SA and the NT (Australian Bureau of Statistics & Australian Institute of Health and Welfare, 2008). The number of deaths recorded for Indigenous males was 3.2 times the number expected from the age–cause-specific rates for non-Indigenous males, and the number recorded for Indigenous females was 2.7 times the number expected from the age-cause-specific rates for non-Indigenous females.[4]

For Indigenous males, the next most frequent causes of death were injuries (including transport accidents, intentional self-harm and assault) (SMR[5] 2.9), malignant neoplasms (cancers) (SMR 1.5), diseases of the respiratory system (SMR 4.3), and endocrine, nutritional and metabolic disorders (mainly diabetes) (SMR 7.5) (Australian Bureau of Statistics & Australian Institute of Health and Welfare, 2008). For Indigenous females, the most frequent causes of death were malignant neoplasms (SMR 1.6), endocrine, nutritional and metabolic disorders (SMR 10.1), external causes (SMR 3.5), and diseases of the respiratory system (SMR 3.6).

In the period 2003–2007, the most common cause of death for Indigenous infants was the set of conditions originating in the perinatal period (such as birth trauma, disorders related to foetal growth, and respiratory and cardiovascular disorders specific to that period) (Australian Institute of Health and Welfare, 2010). Sudden infant death syndrome (SIDS) was around four times as

---

4   The estimates quoted here have not been adjusted for the overall under-identification of Indigenous people in death registration systems, so true ratios are likely to be slightly higher.

5   The standardised mortality ratio (SMR) is one measure for comparing death rates in two populations. The SMR is the observed number of deaths in a study population divided by the number expected if the study population had the same age-specific rates as the comparison population.

common among Indigenous infants as among non-Indigenous infants.

For the period 2002–2006, the leading cause of death for Indigenous children aged 1–14 years was injury (including poisoning), accounting for almost one-half of the deaths, followed by diseases of the nervous system and diseases of the circulatory system (Australian Institute of Health and Welfare, 2009).

Indigenous mothers and babies

In 2008, there were 15,000 births registered in Australia with one or both parents identified as Indigenous (5 per cent of all births registered) (Australian Bureau of Statistics, 2009a), but this figure probably underestimates the true number slightly as Indigenous status is not always identified, and there may be a lag in birth registrations. In 2008, Indigenous women had more babies and had them at younger ages than did non-Indigenous women – teenagers had 20 per cent of the babies born to Indigenous women, compared with only 4 per cent of those born to non-Indigenous mothers (Australian Bureau of Statistics, 2009a). The median age of Indigenous mothers was 24.7 years, compared with 30.9 years for non-Indigenous women. The highest birth rates (known technically as fertility rates) were for the 20–24 years age group for Indigenous women and in the 30–34 years age group for non-Indigenous women. The fertility of teenage Indigenous women (75 babies per 1,000 women) was more than four times that of all teenage women (17 babies per 1,000). Teenage births, which are associated with lower incomes and poorer educational attainment and employment prospects of the mother, have higher levels of complications during pregnancy and delivery (Steering Committee for the Review of

Government Service Provision, 2009). In 2008, total fertility rates were 2,515 births per 1,000 Indigenous women and 1,969 per 1,000 for all women (Australian Bureau of Statistics, 2009a). The highest total fertility rate for Indigenous women was for WA (3,160 babies per 1,000), followed by SA (2,936 per 1,000) and Qld (2,728 per 1,000).

Health aspects of importance to education
Prenatal health

Good maternal health is beneficial for mothers and their babies and contributes to reduced perinatal and infant mortality and smaller proportions of babies of low birthweight (Steering Committee for the Review of Government Service Provision, 2009).[6] Risk factors that can be addressed through antenatal care include anaemia, poor nutrition, hypertension, diabetes and glucose intolerance, genital and urinary tract infections and smoking (Australian Health Ministers' Advisory Council, 2008). The intra-uterine environment is generally seen as protective, but adverse exposures in foetal life can have lifelong impact on a person's health and, hence, their education.

Maternal nutrition

Healthy nutrition in pregnancy is vital for mothers and their babies; foods recommended include those rich in iron, protein and calcium (Hunt, 2007). Pregnant women are advised to take folate (a B group vitamin) during pregnancy, as it reduces the risk of neural tube defects in a baby (Bower, 2006). These defects include anencephaly (absence of portions of the brain,

---

6 Low birthweight, defined as a birthweight of less than 2,500 grams, is associated with higher levels of illness and disability around birth and beyond. It may also be associated with illnesses, such as heart and kidney disease, later in life.

skull and scalp), spina bifida (malformations of the vertebrae and spinal cord) and encephalocoele (protrusions of the brain though openings in the skull), which result when the neural tube (a structure that develops into the brain and spinal cord) fails to close properly in the first weeks of pregnancy. Closure requires folate, which cannot be stored in the body, so should be taken in pregnancy (Australian Institute of Health and Welfare, 2010).

In 2008, less than one-half (49 per cent) of Indigenous children aged 0–3 years had mothers who had taken folate prior to, or during, pregnancy (Australian Bureau of Statistics, 2009d). More generally, babies born to women who are either below or above normal weight may experience more health problems than do other babies (Hunt, 2007). Access to healthy food is an issue for many Indigenous women, particularly those living in remote locations.

The effects of smoking tobacco and drinking alcohol during pregnancy

Smoking tobacco during pregnancy can lead to health issues for a baby (Graham, et al., 2007; Wills & Coory, 2008). In 2007, more than one-half of Indigenous mothers (51 per cent) were reported to have smoked tobacco during pregnancy, compared with 15 per cent of non-Indigenous mothers (Australian Institute of Health and Welfare, 2011b). If one or both parents smoke, the negative health effects of tobacco smoking may continue after birth (Steering Committee for the Review of Government Service Provision, 2009). Passive smoking has been associated with sudden infant death syndrome (SIDS) and higher rates of respiratory illness, asthma and ear infections in children (Jacoby, et al., 2008).

Alcohol consumption during pregnancy is a risk factor for foetal alcohol spectrum disorders, heart defects and low birthweight (Australian Institute of Health and Welfare, 2011b; Gray, Saggers, Atkinson & Wilkes, 2007) and it appears that the problem has been under-diagnosed among Aboriginal people (Gray, et al., 2007). Foetal alcohol spectrum disorder may lead to physical, behavioural and cognitive effects (Steering Committee for the Review of Government Service Provision, 2009). According to the 2008 National Aboriginal and Torres Strait Islander Social Survey (NATSISS), 20 per cent of Indigenous mothers reported consuming alcohol during pregnancy, but the majority (83 per cent) reported drinking less than usual during pregnancy (Australian Institute of Health and Welfare, 2011b).

The physical health of Indigenous young people
Low birth weight

The low birthweight (LBW – defined as a birthweight of less than 2,500 grams) of babies, resulting from intra-uterine growth retardation or a short gestation period (or both), may lead to ill-health throughout infancy and childhood (National Health and Medical Research Council, 2000). Low birthweight babies are at greater risk of dying in the first year of life (Steering Committee for the Review of Government Service Provision, 2009); and low birthweight can also lead to health issues later in life (examples are coronary heart disease and type 2 diabetes).

The average birthweight of babies born to Indigenous mothers in 2007 was 3,182 grams, almost 200 grams less than the average for babies born to non-Indigenous mothers (3,381 grams) (derived from Laws & Sullivan, 2009). Babies born to Indigenous women in 2007 were twice as likely to be of LBW

(12.5 per cent) than were those born to non-Indigenous women (5.9 per cent). The low-birthweight proportions for babies born to Indigenous women were highest for WA and SA (both 16.2 per cent).

Malnutrition in infancy and early childhood

For many Indigenous children, poor nutrition affects their health and hinders their growth (Brewster, Nelson, & Couzos, 2007). The effects of maternal malnutrition are exacerbated for many Indigenous children with poor nutrition in their early years of life (National Health and Medical Research Council, 2000; Brewster, et al., 2007). Mothers can assist in promoting healthy growth and development in their baby by breastfeeding, which also provides some protection against many conditions (including diarrhoea and respiratory infections). According to the 2004–2005 National Aboriginal and Torres Strait Islander Health Survey (NATSIHS), the breastfeeding rate of infants aged one to three years living in non-remote areas was 79 per cent, compared with a rate of 88 per cent for non-Indigenous infants (Australian Bureau of Statistics, 2006c). The growth of most Indigenous infants is satisfactory until breast milk becomes insufficient alone, after which time infants become more directly exposed to the relatively poor physical environmental conditions in which many Indigenous people live (National Health and Medical Research Council, 2000). Unhygienic living conditions, high levels of environmental bacteriological contamination, and sub-optimal nutrition mean that some Indigenous infants and young children enter the vicious synergistic cycle of infection– malnutrition. They can experience growth faltering, which is a reduction in the expected rate of growth along an infant's previously defined growth curve (McDonald, Bailie, Rumbold, Morris, & Paterson, 2008). In contexts of poverty, faltering growth typically occurs at about six months of age with the infant's transition to foods that are often inadequate in quantity and quality. This is a reason that many young Indigenous children are shorter and lighter than their non-Indigenous counterparts. The Northern Territory Emergency Response Child Health Checks found that more than one-in-eight Indigenous children (13 per cent) were underweight, and wasting was diagnosed in 13 per cent of those aged 0–4 years; 6 per cent of children aged 0–4 years had stunted growth (Indigenous Determinants and Outcomes Unit & Office for Aboriginal and Torres Strait Islander Health, 2009).

Anaemia

Iron deficiency anaemia may cause developmental (psychomotor and cognitive) delay in children. Indigenous preschool and school-aged children, particularly those living in remote communities, have a much higher prevalence of the condition than non-Indigenous children (National Aboriginal Community Controlled Health Organisation, 2005). In the Northern Territory Emergency Response Child Health Checks, the rate of anaemia in Indigenous children aged 0–15 years was 16 per cent (Indigenous Determinants and Outcomes Unit & Office for Aboriginal and Torres Strait Islander Health, 2009). One disease associated with iron-deficiency anaemia is hookworm disease (as the worms cause seepage of blood from the intestine), which is not uncommon in Indigenous communities in the north of Australia (McCarthy, 2009). It is quite a widespread disease in warm, tropical and sub-tropical places, such as the Kimberley and other parts of tropical northern Australia, especially where sewage disposal is inadequate (enHealth, 2010).

Ear disease and hearing loss

Indigenous babies and children are susceptible to ear infections, which can lead to hearing loss. Besides the impact on the general quality of life, loss of hearing has an enormous impact on educational achievement (Burrow, Galloway, & Weissofner, 2009). Conductive hearing loss is often caused by otitis media (OM), which is an inflammation of the middle ear occurring in various forms, both acute and chronic (Couzos, Metcalf, & Murray, 2007). It is caused by a bacterial or viral infection and is often the result of another illness (such as a cold). The early onset of chronic or recurrent OM, sometimes within weeks of birth, places Indigenous infants at increased risk of early conductive hearing loss. This is often greater in severity and duration than that observed among non-Indigenous children and may persist into childhood and adolescence. Chronic OM (persistent inflammation) can occur with or without perforation. If left untreated, both acute and chronic OM can cause hearing loss that may be mild to moderate in degree and intermittent or persistent – and more than one-half of all cases of OM will result in mild or moderate loss of hearing (World Health Organisation, 2004).

Exceptionally high rates of ear disease and hearing loss have been reported in many Indigenous communities, particularly in remote areas (Couzos & Murray, 2008; Senate Community Affairs References Committee, 2010).

Evidence of the extent of ear health problems is summarised below:

- The Western Australia Aboriginal Child Health Survey (WAACHS) in 2001–2002, found that 18 per cent of Indigenous children had recurring ear infections. Children aged 0–3 years (20 per cent) and children aged 4–11 years (20 per cent) were more likely to have recurring ear infections than older children aged 12–17 years (14 per cent) (Zubrick, et al., 2004).

- The 2004–2005 NATSIHS reported that 8 per cent of Indigenous young people aged 12–24 years had ear disease; this was more than twice the rate found among non-Indigenous young people (3 per cent) in the 2004–05 National Health Survey (Australian Institute of Health and Welfare, 2011b). OM was more prevalent among Indigenous young people (1.6 per cent) than among young people overall (0.4 per cent).

- In a survey of Indigenous children living in remote communities in northern and central Australia, nearly all children (91 per cent) aged 6–30 months were diagnosed with some form of OM (Morris et al., 2005).

- In the Northern Territory Emergency Response Child Health Checks, nearly 12 per cent of children who had audiology check had chronic suppurative otitis media – three times the rate the World Health Organisation classes as a massive problem (Indigenous Determinants and Outcomes Unit & Office for Aboriginal and Torres Strait Islander Health, 2009).

Prevalence of hearing loss

- The 2004–2005 NATSIHS found that Indigenous young people suffered from complete or partial deafness (5 per cent) at more than twice the rates of that among non-Indigenous young people (2 per cent) (Australian Institute of Health and Welfare, 2011b).

• The 2008 NATSISS found that an estimated 9 per cent of Indigenous children aged 0–14 years had ear or hearing problems. More than one-third (35 per cent) of the problems experienced were runny ears or glue ear (OM), and 28 per cent were hearing loss or partial deafness (Australian Bureau of Statistics, 2010a).

• In the Northern Territory Emergency Response Child Health Checks, 54 per cent of the 3,517 children who received an audiology check had some hearing loss (Indigenous Determinants and Outcomes Unit & Office for Aboriginal and Torres Strait Islander Health, 2009).

In 2007–2009, hospitalisation rates for ear and hearing problems were highest among children aged 0–4 years for both Indigenous and non-Indigenous people (Australian Institute of Health and Welfare, 2011a). More detailed data for the period 2004–2006 reveal that, for Indigenous children living in NSW, Vic, Qld, WA, SA and the NT, diseases of the middle ear (including otitis media) were the most common type of ear disease causing hospitalisation (Australian Institute of Health and Welfare, 2008a). Indigenous children aged 0–14 years were hospitalised for tympanoplasty (reconstructive surgery for a perforated eardrum due to middle ear infection) at almost four times the rate of other children. Diseases of the ear and mastoid process represented 3 per cent of hospitalisations among Indigenous children aged 0–4 years, and 7 per cent of hospitalisations among Indigenous children aged 5–14 years.

Otitis media–related hearing loss may persist throughout childhood and can have significant implications for the development of language and communication skills and subsequent school performance (Partington & Galloway, 2005). Children who cannot hear well are often angry and frustrated because they cannot communicate effectively (de Plevicz, 2007). They can be disruptive in class when they ask others sitting near them to 'translate'; this adds to Indigenous children's negative experience of school.

Respiratory infections

Respiratory disease represents a significant burden of ill-health and hospitalisation among Indigenous children (Chang & Torzillo, 2007; Kirov & Thomson, 2004). Acute respiratory infections (ARI) can be divided into upper respiratory tract infection (URTI) and lower respiratory tract infection (LRTI). URTIs, by far the more common, are caused generally by viruses, are usually self-limiting and mild in nature, and result in little or no mortality. In a proportion of cases, however, especially those caused by bacteria, URTIs can lead to serious complications. LRTIs, while less common than URTIs, account for most of the hospitalisations and mortality associated with ARI. LRTIs resulting in hospitalisations and/or death include pneumonia, bronchopneumonia, acute bronchitis and bronchiolitis. Viruses are responsible for many LRTIs, but the most serious forms are bacterial. The rate of LRTIs in Indigenous children is at least that of children in developing countries (O'Grady & Chang, 2010). There are good data on mortality and hospitalisation from ARI in Aboriginal children, but information on the incidence of ARI in Aboriginal children is scarce.

Evidence of the extent of respiratory infections is summarised below:

- In two remote Aboriginal communities in tropical northern Australia in 2002–2005, upper-respiratory-tract infections were the most common reason for clinic presentations of young children (0–4.75 years) for infectious conditions (Clucas, et al., 2008).

- The 2001–2002 WAACHS found that recurring chest infections affected 12 per cent of Indigenous young people aged 0–17 years, with infection rates highest for children 0–3 years (19 per cent) and lowest for children aged 12–17 years (8 per cent) (Zubrick, et al., 2004).

- In the Northern Territory Emergency Response Child Health Checks, 37 per cent of the 9,373 children who had a check had a history of recurrent chest infections (Indigenous Determinants and Outcomes Unit & Office for Aboriginal and Torres Strait Islander Health, 2009).

For Indigenous children aged less than five living in NSW, Vic, Qld, WA, SA and public hospitals in the NT, diseases of the respiratory system were among the most common cause of potentially preventable hospitalisations in 2006–2007 (Steering Committee for the Review of Government Service Provision, 2009). The rate for Indigenous children (86 per thousand) was twice as high as that for non-Indigenous children (44 per thousand). In 2006–2009, the hospitalisation rate for pneumonia for Indigenous children aged 0–4 years (15 per thousand) was more than three times the rate for other children (4.3 per thousand) (Australian Institute of Health and Welfare, 2011b).

In 2003–2007, respiratory diseases were the third leading cause of death of Indigenous children living in NSW, Qld, WA, SA and the NT – more than four times the rate for non-Indigenous children.

The great burden of respiratory infections among Indigenous infants and young children can cause significant disruptions to their lives and to their education. As well as absences from school, respiratory diseases can interfere with full participation in schoolroom activities.

Asthma

It is difficult to assess the extent of asthma among Indigenous children, but surveys suggest that levels are at least as high – if not higher than – as those for non-Indigenous children (Australian Centre for Asthma Monitoring, 2008). According to the 2004–2005 NATSIHS, asthma was the most commonly reported long-term condition (16 per cent) among young Indigenous people aged 12–24 years (Australian Institute of Health and Welfare, 2011b). The prevalence of asthma among Indigenous young people was not significantly different from that noted among non-Indigenous young people. In 2006–2007, Indigenous children aged 0–18 years had higher hospital admission rates for asthma (486 per 100,000) than did other children (436 per 100,000). For infants aged 0–1 year, the rate was slightly higher among Indigenous children (1,068 per 100,000) than among other children (895 per 100,000).

Gastroenteritis and intestinal parasites

Gastrointestinal disease is a significant problem for many Indigenous infants and very young children, the main conditions being predominantly intestinal infections (causing diarrhoea) and parasitic infestations. Diarrhoea remains a common cause of morbidity and hospitalisation – and occasionally mortality – among some groups of Indigenous children. Infectious diarrhoea can be caused by viruses, bacteria, and parasites. Diarrhoea is usually caused by the transmission of pathogenic microorganisms from faeces to the gastrointestinal tract via the mouth. Contaminated water and food are the major sources of diarrhoeal infection. Such contamination is facilitated by the overcrowding and unhygienic living conditions that prevail in some Indigenous communities. The most common causes of infectious gastroenteritis are norovirus (formerly Norwalk agent), rotavirus, giardia, cryptosporidium, pathogenic *Escherischia coli*, campylobacter, and salmonella (Hall, et al., 2006). Rotavirus is a common cause of paediatric gastroenteritis and Indigenous children are particularly susceptible; it is anticipated that rotavirus vaccination will be successful in reducing the impact of the disease (Bishop & Kirkwood, 2009).

The 2001–2002 WAACHS found that an estimated 5.6 per cent of Indigenous children suffered from recurring gastrointestinal infections and infection rates were twice as high for those living in extremely isolated areas compared to other areas. Infections decreased significantly after twelve years of age (Zubrick, et al., 2004).

Indigenous children experience more health problems from gastrointestinal infestations than do most non-Indigenous children. Of the various helminths (parasitic worms) infesting Indigenous people living in the northern parts of Australia, hookworm (McCarthy, 2009) and strongyloides (a type of parasitic roundworm) (Adams, Page, & Speare, 2003) are of particular significance. Strongyloides, if not adequately treated, can cause serious illness or death and it is most prevalent in rural and remote areas.

Skin infections and infestations

Skin infections, which tend to be more common among Indigenous than among non-Indigenous children, can be caused by poor living conditions (Green, 2001; McDonald, Bailie, Brewster, & Morris, 2008). They may lead to children being excluded from school as a 'quarantine' measure until the problem is sufficiently treated (Currie & Carapetis, 2000). The skin infections that most commonly affect Indigenous communities are scabies, pyoderma, fungal skin infections and a range of other skin infections caused by bacteria (Currie & Carapetis, 2000). Up to 70 per cent of children living in some Indigenous communities have skin sores, with group A streptococcus (GAS) the major pathogen. Indigenous people, particularly those living in the high-rainfall, humid areas of northern Australia, are also vulnerable to a variety of fungal and related organisms (Green, 2001).

The 2001–2002 WAACHS found that 8.5 per cent of Indigenous children had recurring skin infections (for example school sores or scabies), with children aged 4–11 years the most likely to have recurring skin infections (Zubrick, et al., 2004). The prevalence was 17.6 per cent in extremely isolated areas, more than twice the level of other areas. The Northern Territory Emergency Response Child Health Checks found that 30 per cent of the 9,373 children who had a check, had a skin problem; 10 per cent had four or more skin sores and 8 per cent had scabies (Indigenous Determinants and Outcomes Unit &

Office for Aboriginal and Torres Strait Islander Health, 2009). Scabies is endemic in many remote Indigenous communities, with levels sometimes around 50 per cent in children (Currie & Carapetis, 2000; Clucas, et al., 2008). The cycle of scabies transmission can result in pyoderma (includes impetigo, also called school sores), a bacterial infection of the skin that can lead to kidney disease and possibly heart disease.

Eye conditions

Indigenous children, particularly those living in remote areas, have better vision than their non-Indigenous peers (Taylor & National Indigenous Eye Health Survey Team, 2009). They are, however, more at risk of trachoma, an eye infection found almost exclusively among Indigenous people. The National Indigenous Eye Health Survey found that 2 per cent of Indigenous children aged 5–15 years had low vision, and 0.2 per cent were blind (Taylor & National Indigenous Eye Health Survey Team, 2009). The 2008 NATSISS found a higher prevalence of eye problems than the National Indigenous Eye Health Survey, with 7 per cent of Indigenous children aged 0–14 years experiencing eye or sight problems (Australian Bureau of Statistics, 2010a). More than one-third of the problems reported (37 per cent) were due to difficulty reading or seeing close up (long-sightedness), and 28 per cent were for difficulty seeing far away (short-sightedness). For those with eye or sight problems, 61 per cent wore glasses or contact lenses. The major cause of low vision was refractive error (56 per cent). The 2001–2002 WAACHS reported 8 per cent of Indigenous children aged 4–17 years did not have normal vision in both eyes (Zubrick, et al., 2004).

In Australia, trachoma is found either in its infectious

(follicular) form or as scarring (resulting from repeated infections over years) (Burns & Thomson, 2003; Taylor & National Indigenous Eye Health Survey Team, 2009). It has been difficult until recently to develop an accurate picture of infectious trachoma because of the lack of systematic screening. The National Indigenous Eye Health Survey reported 3.8 per cent of Indigenous children had active trachoma (Taylor & National Indigenous Eye Health Survey Team, 2009). Trachoma was less common in urban areas, but 50 per cent of very remote communities had endemic trachoma. The Northern Territory Emergency Response Child Health Checks found that 8 per cent of Indigenous children aged 6–15 years had trachoma in at least one eye (Australian Institute of Health and Welfare, 2008b).

Oral health

Two major threats to the oral health of Indigenous young people are dental caries and periodontal disease. Dental caries is caused by acid-producing bacteria living in the mouth, which proliferate on sweet and sticky food (Harford, Spencer, & Roberts-Thomson, 2003). Periodontal disease (affecting the gums) is caused by bacterial infection often associated with poor oral hygiene. Indigenous children experience more caries than non-Indigenous children in their deciduous teeth (Jamieson, Armfield, & Roberts-Thomson, 2007). The Child Dental Health Survey (CDHS) found that more Indigenous children aged 4–10 years living in NSW, SA and the NT had caries in their deciduous teeth than did their non-Indigenous counterparts. The largest difference between Indigenous and non-Indigenous children was for those aged six, for which age group nearly twice as many Indigenous children had caries

(72 per cent compared with 38 per cent respectively). Not only did more Indigenous children have caries, they also had a larger number of decayed teeth at all ages (4–10 years) than did their non-Indigenous counterparts. The biggest difference was seen among Indigenous four-year-olds, who had more than three times the number of decayed teeth than non-Indigenous children of the same age. Poorer oral health for Indigenous children continues when they get their permanent teeth (Jamieson, et al., 2007). More Indigenous children aged 6–17 years had caries than did their non-Indigenous counterparts. The largest difference was for Indigenous fifteen-year-olds, who had 2.7 times the level of decay than non-Indigenous children of the same age. In the Northern Territory Emergency Response, 54 per cent of 3,355 Indigenous children who had a dental check needed treatment for caries (Indigenous Determinants and Outcomes Unit & Office for Aboriginal and Torres Strait Islander Health, 2009).

Periodontal diseases, including gingivitis and periodontitis, are more common among Indigenous children than among their non-Indigenous counterparts (Jamieson, et al., 2007). Children rarely develop severe periodontal disease, but gingivitis is relatively common, particularly among older children.

Injuries

Injury can cause permanent physical disabilities, long term cognitive or psychological damage or death (Australian Institute of Health and Welfare, 2009). Indigenous young people have higher hospitalisation and death rates for injury than do non-Indigenous young people. In 2006–2007, the hospitalisation rate for injury among children aged 0–14 years was 40 per cent higher for Indigenous children than for other children. The leading cause of injury was falls, accounting for 35 per cent of all injury hospital admissions for Indigenous children. Land transport accidents were responsible for 12 per cent of injury hospital admissions of Indigenous children; the rate of 226 per 100,000 for Indigenous children was 20 per cent higher than the rate for other children. The hospital admission rate for assault for Indigenous children was seven times the rate for other children; for Indigenous boys (97 per 100,000) the rate was almost five times that for other boys (21 per 100,000). Indigenous girls (116 per 100,000) were fourteen times as likely as other girls (eight per 100,000) to be hospitalised for assault. Indigenous children are also over-represented among victims of sexual assault (Aboriginal Child Sexual Assault Taskforce, 2006).

For 2002–2006, the injury death rate for Indigenous children living in Qld, WA, SA and NT (21 per 100,000) was more than three times the rate for their non-Indigenous counterparts (seven per 100,000) (Australian Institute of Health and Welfare, 2009).

The emotional and social wellbeing of Indigenous young people

The emotional and social wellbeing of young Indigenous people can impact in a variety of ways on their education at different times of their lives. Lack of emotional and social wellbeing that may stem from an environment where there is little stimulation and significant unstable relationships during the formative years of infancy and early childhood can lead to impairments in cognitive function and readiness to attend school (Wilkinson & Marmot, 2003). It is becoming more widely acknowledged that successful schooling is largely dependent on the wellbeing of the child, and that school attendance itself (separate to performance) is reflective of a student's state of wellbeing and indicative of potential mental health issues (Ravichandran, 2008; Social Inclusion Board, 2007). The greater proportion of Indigenous than non-Indigenous young people experiencing emotional wellbeing issues contributes to disparities in school attendance and attentiveness, which are reflected in educational outcomes (Zubrick, et al., 2005). A factor affecting the social and emotional wellbeing of many Indigenous young people is their regular experience of bereavement. Each year, Indigenous people grieve for about twice as many deaths per head of population as do other Australians; many of the deaths involving infants, children, young adults and men and women are unexpected and preventable (Kelly, Dudgeon, Gee, & Glaskin, 2009). There is an obligation for most Indigenous people to attend funerals, not only of close family members but also those of community members; this can mean a considerable amount of time away from school for a student (de Plevicz, 2007).

Indigenous children often experience a range of stressors and are sometimes trying to cope with several at the same time (Australian Institute of Health and Welfare, 2011b). In the 2008 NATSISS, around two-thirds (65 per cent) of Indigenous children aged 4–14 years were reported as experiencing at least one stressor in the previous twelve months. The most common types of stressors reported were the death of a close family member/friend (22 per cent), problems keeping up with school work (20 per cent) and being scared/upset by an argument or someone's behaviour (19 per cent).

Of those who had been exposed to stressors, 40 per cent

had experienced just one stressor, 14 per cent had experienced at least three types of stressors, and 12 per cent had experienced five or more stressors. Similar rates of boys (66 per cent) and girls (63 per cent) had experienced at least one stressor, but boys were more likely than girls to report having problems keeping up with school work (24 per cent compared with 16 per cent). Overall, stressors were slightly more common among Indigenous children living in non-remote areas than those living in remote areas (66 per cent compared with 60 per cent). Children who experienced stressors reported slightly lower rates of excellent/ very good health than those who had not experienced stressors (73 per cent compared with 83 per cent). They were also more likely to have: problems sleeping (25 per cent compared with 15 per cent); stayed overnight somewhere else due to a family crisis (13 per cent compared with 5 per cent); and missed days at school in the preceding week (29 per cent compared with 21 per cent).

The 2008 NATSISS found that higher levels of schooling were positively associated with social and emotional wellbeing and health (Australian Institute of Health and Welfare, 2011b). Indigenous people aged 15–34 years who had completed Year 12 were less likely (29 per cent) to have reported high or very high psychological distress than those who had left school at Year 9 or below (35 per cent). Those who had completed Year 12 were more likely to rate their health as excellent/very good (59 per cent) than those who left school at Year 9 (49 per cent). They were also less likely to rate their health as fair or poor (9 per cent) than those who left school at Year 9 (16 per cent).

The bullying experienced by Indigenous students can also impact on their social and emotional wellbeing. In the 2001–2002

WAACHS, it was found that about one-third of high school students said they had been bullied at school (Zubrick, et al., 2005). A recent study conducted in regional WA found that bullying of Indigenous children and adolescents occurred frequently and often in response to violent episodes in the family and community. Some adults surveyed, stated that some children's bullying behaviour seemed modelled on the family violence they experienced (Coffin, Larson, & Cross, 2010). Family violence is a significant cause of morbidity and mortality in the Indigenous population (Al-Yaman, Van Doeland, & Wallis, 2006).

In the WAACHS, approximately 24 per cent of the Aboriginal children aged 4–17 years surveyed were assessed as being at high risk of clinically significant emotional or behavioural difficulties (this compares with 15 per cent of other children) (Zubrick, et al., 2005). Aboriginal boys were twice as likely as Aboriginal girls to be at high risk of clinically significant emotional or behavioural difficulties. A number of health-risk factors were also found to be associated with a high risk of clinically significant emotional and behavioural difficulties. For example, young people who did not participate in organised sport were twice as likely to be at high risk of emotional and behaviour difficulties than were young people who participated in sport (16 per cent and 8 per cent respectively).

In the WAACHS, an additional survey was administered to Aboriginal young people aged 12–17 years to measure rates of suicidal thoughts and suicide attempts (Zubrick, et al., 2005). Findings included the following:

- Suicidal thoughts were reported by around one-in-six (16 per cent) young people in the 12 months before the survey.

- Overall, a higher proportion of females than males reported they had seriously thought about ending their life (20 per cent compared with 12 per cent). This was true for all ages from 12 to 17 years, except for those aged 16 years where males were more likely than females to report having thought about ending their life.

- Of those who had had suicidal thoughts in the 12 months before the survey, 39 per cent reported that they had attempted suicide in that period.

- Aboriginal young people who had been exposed to family violence were more than twice as likely to have thought about ending their own life (22 per cent) than Aboriginal young people who had not been exposed to family violence (9 per cent).

- A higher proportion of Aboriginal males reported they had thought about ending their life if they had low self-esteem (21 per cent) than if they had high self-esteem (5 per cent).

- Suicidal thoughts were associated with a number of health risk behaviours. The proportion of Aboriginal young people who reported suicidal thoughts was significantly higher among those who smoked regularly, used marijuana, drank to excess in the six months before the survey, were exposed to some form of family violence or who had a friend who had attempted suicide.

In 2008–2009, Indigenous young people aged 12–24 years were hospitalised three times more commonly than their non-Indigenous counterparts for mental and behavioural disorders (the rate for Indigenous young people was 2,535 per 100,000) (Australian Institute of Health and Welfare, 2011b). The leading specific causes for Indigenous young people were schizophrenia (306 per 100,000), alcohol misuse (348 per 100,000) and reactions to severe stress (266 per 100,000).

Substance use

Tobacco smoking, alcohol consumption and other substance use are common health-risk behaviours during adolescence. These behaviours can also become lifelong habits causing serious health problems later in life. In addition to students' own health risk behaviours, their home situation also can place them at risk. For example, alcohol use in the household, as well as being a major contributor to family violence (Commonwealth Office of the Status of Women, 1999), has been found to negatively affect children's behaviour and wellbeing (Zubrick, et al., 2005).

In relation to substance use, the following details have been found in surveys for Indigenous young people:

Smoking tobacco

- The 2008 NATSISS and the 2007–2008 National Health Survey reported that four in ten Indigenous young people (aged 15–24 years) were daily smokers, more than twice the proportion among non-Indigenous young people (16 per cent) (Australian Institute of Health and Welfare, 2011b).
- Analysis of the 2004–2005 NATSIHS and the National Health Survey showed that Indigenous young people aged 12–17 years were nearly three times as likely to be exposed to environmental tobacco smoke than all young people of that age range (identified as a daily smoker smoking inside the home) (Australian Institute of Health and Welfare, 2011b).

- In the WAACHS, an estimated 18 per cent of Indigenous young people aged 12–17 years who smoked regularly were at high risk of emotional and behavioural difficulties compared with 7 per cent of non-smokers (Zubrick, et al., 2005).

Alcohol use

- In the 2008 NATSISS, over one-third of Indigenous young people fifteen years and over reported 'risky' use of alcohol in the previous two weeks (Australian Bureau of Statistics, 2009d).
- In the 2004–2005 NATSIHS, Indigenous young people aged 18–24 years were more likely than non-Indigenous young people to drink at least once a week at risky or high-risk levels for short-term harm, (23 per cent and 15 per cent respectively). Similar proportions of Indigenous and non–Indigenous young people drank at levels that were at risky or high-risk levels for long-term harm (16 per cent and 14 per cent respectively).

Young Indigenous people are also at increased risk of ill-health through the harmful use of substances such as marijuana, heroin, amphetamines and inhalants (Australian Bureau of Statistics, 2009d). In the 2008 NATSISS, almost one-fifth of Indigenous young people fifteen years or over reported use of an illicit substance in the previous year. More than one-third (39 per cent) reported using an illicit substance at least once in their lifetime. Marijuana was the substance most commonly used, followed by pain killers or analgesics used for non–medical purposes, and amphetamines or speed. In the WAACHS, approximately 29 per cent of Indigenous young people aged 12–17 years who used marijuana/cannabis daily were at risk of clinically significant emotional or behavioural difficulties compared with 9 per cent of those who had never used marijuana/cannabis (S. R. Zubrick, et al., 2005). Indigenous males were more likely to use marijuana than Indigenous females, particularly at age seventeen years (45 per cent compared with 21 per cent), but for young people who used marijuana/cannabis, Indigenous females were more likely to be at risk of clinically significant emotional or behavioural difficulties than were Indigenous males.

Another behavioural risk factor is volatile substance use (VSU) which occurs predominantly among young people (Parliament of Victoria & Drugs and Crime Prevention Committee, 2002). Petrol sniffing is the most prevalent form of VSU by Indigenous people living in remote communities (d'Abbs & Maclean, 2008; Parliament of Victoria & Drugs and Crime Prevention Committee, 2002). Indigenous petrol sniffers are usually aged between eight and thirty years, with most in the 12–19 years age range; there have been reports of sniffers as young as five years old (Community Affairs References Committee, 2006; Legislative Assembly of the Northern Territory, 2004). Chroming (inhaling spray paint) also occurs in many urban and some rural communities; this tends to be a more experimental and transitory use by younger adolescents (d'Abbs & Maclean, 2008; Parliament of Victoria & Drugs and Crime Prevention Committee, 2002). VSU is difficult to address because of the availability of products: approximately 250 household, medical and industrial products are estimated to contain potentially intoxicating substances (d'Abbs & Maclean, 2008).

Teachers should be aware that some students may be using drugs; they need to follow recommended school policies and actions, such as providing education about drug use and referring students for professional care.

Racism and discrimination

Direct racial discrimination occurs when circumstances are similar and a person is treated differently to another with the different treatment accounted for by their race (de Plevicz, 2007). Racism can have a major impact on the social and emotional wellbeing of many Indigenous children, resulting in poor self-esteem, anxiety and depression (Malin, 2003; Malin & Maidment, 2003). Discrimination and lower socio-economic status have been adversely linked to health, particularly mental health issues and behavioural problems (Human Rights and Equal Opportunity Commission, 2005). A study in Darwin found that 70 per cent of Indigenous people reported experiencing racism in their daily lives (Paradies & Cunningham, 2009). In the WAACHS, young people who had been subjected to racism in the preceding six months were more than twice as likely to be at high risk of emotional and behavioural difficulties as those who had not experienced racism. The WAACHS found that over one-in-five young people (22 per cent) had been refused service or treated badly because they were Aboriginal (Zubrick, et al., 2005). The historical treatment of Indigenous peoples – such as a lack of acknowledgement of human rights – compounds the loss of identity, and subsequently has an adverse impact on the social and emotional wellbeing of many Indigenous people (Zubrick, et al., 2005).

Recent developments

In terms of both health and educational outcomes, Indigenous people are Australia's most disadvantaged identifiable sub-population. To address these and other concerns, all Australian governments, through the Council of Australian Governments (COAG)[7] committed in December 2007 to actively lessen the gap in disadvantage between Indigenous and other Australians through the initiative Closing the Gap (Council of Australian Governments, 2009). As a part of its deliberations about closing the gap, COAG agreed on a number of specific targets for reducing Indigenous disadvantage in the areas of education, early childhood development, health and employment. The targets are to:

- Close the life expectancy gap within a generation.
- Halve the gap in mortality rates for Indigenous children under five within a decade.
- Ensure access to early childhood education for all Indigenous four year olds in remote communities within five years.
- Halve the gap in reading, writing and numeracy achievements for children within a decade.
- Halve the gap for Indigenous students in year 12 attainment rates by 2020.
- Halve the gap in employment outcomes between Indigenous and non-Indigenous Australians within a decade (Department of Families Housing Community Services and Indigenous Affairs (FaHCSIA), 2009).

Strategies proposed as part of this agreement include initiatives and programs to improve ear health and education, such as:

---

7   COAG is 'the peak intergovernmental forum in Australia, comprising the Prime Minister, State Premiers, Territory Chief Ministers and the President of the Australian Local Government Association (ALGA)'.

- audiological rehabilitation services
- the installation of sound-field amplification systems in the classroom
- training for teachers to adopt teaching techniques that accommodate hearing problems
- phonological awareness programs in the classroom.

This is the first time that such a high level of commitment has been made by the Australian, state and territory governments and others, raising the possibility of substantial reductions in the health and other disadvantages experienced by Indigenous people. Importantly, effective, integrated comprehensive strategies and policies will need to be sustained for a long time, as improvements to the extent set in the various targets will not occur in the short-term. The timeframes for the 'closing the gap' targets suggest there is some awareness by governments of the enormity of the challenge, but the real test will be to sustain the commitments through changing political and economic cycles.

Conclusion

By reviewing the great health disadvantages experienced by many Indigenous people, and the physical and psychosocial health aspects of importance to the education of Indigenous children, it is hoped that this chapter will enhance teachers' awareness of the close relationship between health and education. As noted in the introduction, this awareness is important if teachers are to contribute fully in enabling Indigenous people to escape the cycle of poor health and poor education.

8

CRIME, JUSTICE AND ABORIGINAL YOUTH

Quentin Beresford

Five years ago, at the age of ten, 'Niven', from Adelaide's Woodville Aboriginal community, began misbehaving at school: 'I started getting into fights, swearing and not listening and doing my own thing', he later told a local newspaper (Messenger Community News, 7 July 2009). He stood a very high likelihood of sliding into contact with the juvenile justice system and, potentially, an adolescent life of crime. However, intervention by a local youth outreach program helped change the course of Niven's life. Not only did he move on to secondary school, he became involved in mentoring other Aboriginal students to stay on in school.

While such intervention programs are a vital link in helping Aboriginal youth transit the difficult challenges of adolescence and young adulthood, there have been continuing high rates of Aboriginal youth crime and over-representation of this group in detention and community-based orders. Typical of this group is 'Malcolm', a 12-year-old Aboriginal boy who is part of the intergenerational revolving door of the justice system for Aboriginal people across Australia. Described as showing 'lively intelligence' but shy, he is from a low socio-economic suburb of Perth. When observed by a journalist in 2010 (Laurie, 2010), he was about to face court to give evidence against two of his cousins. He had been asleep in the back of the car when his two cousins held up two terrified girls at a bus stop and stole their money and mobile phones. Already a regular drug user and school refuser, his father, brother and step-sister were incarcerated as were several of his cousins. Malcolm appeared destined to join his family in prison.

Three generations of his family were barely literate and his mother was battling to find stable accommodation after being evicted from state housing. Aboriginal youth just like him face the juvenile court system each day in all regions of Australia and are from very similar backgrounds, although the rate at which they appear differs significantly between states. The system leaves few Aboriginal families untouched. In South Australia, which has among the lowest rates of Aboriginal juveniles in detention, a recent inquiry by the State's Commissioner for Social Inclusion (Cappo, 2007, p. 35) observed:

> Almost every Aboriginal person I spoke to through-out the consultation had a son, daughter, grandson, granddaughter, niece or nephew who has had some type of contact with the youth justice system, whether it had been formal cautioning by police, or detention in a youth justice facility. From what I heard, many of those...had previous contact with the police at a very young age, and once old enough to attract a response from the youth justice system, quickly escalated within it.

Such comments represent a profound challenge to Australia's human rights record. Marginalised Aboriginal young people are one of the most disadvantaged groups in Australian society. It is therefore not surprising that a disproportionate number become involved in crime. While the focus of this chapter is the plight of this group, it is important not to over-emphasise the problem and overlook the significant number of Aboriginal young people who are living constructive and successful lives. Often the media gravitates to the former, constructing stereotypes of Aboriginal youth as criminals and drug users. Clearly this is not the case even though the harsh reality is that a disproportionate number are leading such lives. The challenge is to understand the complex causes of this behaviour.

An issue for educators

In urban, rural and remote locations, teachers will come up against students such a Malcolm; Aboriginal children and youth who have become disillusioned with school and often engage in crime. Another group will have siblings caught up in the juvenile justice system who will be subjected to its norms as a kind of rite of passage. Many will be growing up in dysfunctional single-parent households because fathers are in prison. Another group, still, will attempt to re-integrate into the education system following release from detention. In these ways, many Aboriginal families are touched by the operations of the justice system. Therefore, educators need to be informed about the causes of Aboriginal juvenile crime; the role of school as both a contributing and a preventative factor; and the ways in which the justice system impacts upon Aboriginal youth and their families. With a sophisticated understanding of the complex social issues facing Aboriginal young people, teachers and policy makers can play a crucial role in helping construct a positive future for these young people.

Extent of the problem

Statistics on crime are widely regarded as only a partial indicator of crime committed. Much depends on how crimes are reported and the role police play as the gatekeepers of the 'system'. And states vary considerably in the over-representation of Aboriginal youth in the justice system. Nevertheless, several generalisations can be made about crime and justice among this group:

- Aboriginal young people commit a disproportionate amount of crime; that is, relative to their number, more are involved in this activity than are non-Aboriginal groups.
- This involvement reflects the greater incidence of socio-economic and intergenerational disadvantage in Aboriginal communities.
- The on-set of offending behaviour is lower for Aboriginal youth than non-Aboriginal youth and their recidivism rates are higher.
- Aboriginal youth are over-represented at every stage of the juvenile justice system (that is, relative to their overall population): arrest, bail, community-based corrections and detention.
- Rates of incarceration for Aboriginal youth are higher than for non-Aboriginals.

The rate at which Aboriginal youth are incarcerated has long worried criminologists and human rights activists.

Australia-wide, slightly more than half of all youth in detention are Indigenous. Two aspects of the data on Aboriginal juvenile crime worry criminologists and human rights advocates: the ratios of over-representation at each stage of the justice system and the upward trend in this over-representation. Currently, the rate of detention for Aboriginal juveniles is 28 times higher than for non-indigenous youth (House of Representatives, 2011). In some states including NSW, Queensland and WA, the ratio is even higher. In 2008, over 40 per cent of all Indigenous men in Australia reported being charged formally with an offence by police before they reached the age of 25 (ibid.). The recent House of Representatives inquiry into Indigenous juvenile crime, the first such inquiry in more than 20 years, described such figures as a 'national crisis' and called for a national approach to the issue.

Several explanations for this over-representation have been advanced. Some (Cuneen, 2006) see it as a manifestation of racial bias in the justice system; that is, police and courts discriminate against these young people. More are arrested, charged and jailed than non-Aboriginal offenders even given the nature of the offences. Other explanations include the higher proportion of serious and repeat offenders among Aboriginal offenders which militates against their diversion from the harsher aspects of the justice system. However, it is also the case that more Aboriginal youth commit crime than non-Aboriginal youth ensuring a high level of contact with the juvenile justice system.

By the early 1970s, there were clear signs that many Aboriginal young people were being driven to the margins of society by a combination of school drop-out, racism, alienation, unemployment and drugs. Little was done to address these underlying issues, and especially the overarching school-related issues: truancy; drop-out; and under-achievement. For many young Aboriginal boys, the already substantial challenges in growing up were exacerbated by the parallel substantial rise in the Aboriginal adult male prison population; which increased the likelihood that many boys were growing up without fathers. Sadly, this latter pattern has not changed. Indigenous males in the 25–29 year old age range are the most over-represented group in prisons in Australia with one in every 14 being imprisoned (Senate, 2010).

The juvenile justice system

Prior to the 1980s, juveniles involved in crime and other anti-social behaviour were handled by welfare departments in each state which made decisions about whether, and for how long, they would be detained. Decisions made by bureaucrats came to be seen as lacking due process of law and of failing to protect the rights of children. In all Australian states, governments established a 'justice' model to deal with young people involved in offending. This consists of a Children's Court presided over by a judge. While the intention was to give a legal foundation for the treatment of children, the reformed system is often criticised for artificially separating young people's welfare and criminal issues. In this way, the justice system has overseen a considerable increase in the number of contacts with Aboriginal children and youth. Consequently, questions have been raised about the appropriateness of the model particularly for Indigenous youth and the extent to which it operates in a discriminatory fashion. The debate is complex and on-going. On the one hand is the claim that a greater number of Indigenous young people commit crime and more are in the category of serious and repeat offenders. Conversely, others argue that key parts of the justice model vary in the way they treat Aboriginal youth and that this inconsistency is often structured along lines of jurisdiction. For example, why is WA the leading state for incarcerating young people? Is it because of variations in the offending behaviour of Indigenous youth in that state or because of the way its juvenile justice system operates? Despite the variations between states, a recent study of Indigenous young people and the juvenile justice system in NSW, SA and WA (Allard, et al., 2010) found that, in each of these states, Aboriginal people were less likely to be diverted from the court system even after accounting for the effects of age, offence type and prior history.

Over the past decade, efforts have been made in all Australian states to reduce the number of young people entering the court system by diverting them into alternative programs. Police have the power to routinely give caution notices for minor offences while more serious first time offenders can be offered alternatives to the formal court system. This usually involves attending a family group conference that brings together the young offender and their support persons, the victim and their supporters, police and youth workers. The aim of this process is to encourage the young offender to take responsibility for their actions by being able to better experience its impact on the range of people involved.

Despite these initiatives, figures compiled by the Australian Institute of Criminology (Richards, 2007) show that Aboriginal youth continue to be over-represented in the number of youth arrested and incarcerated, and under-represented among youth granted bail and diverted to family group conferences or similar alternatives to court. This matter has been considered at length by a number of agencies dealing with Aboriginal young people including the WA Aboriginal Legal Service (WAALS, 2009). Although the situation varies across states, the conclusions reached by the WAALS highlight the combination of institutional factors and the absence of relevant programs: over-policing, poor utilisation of diversionary schemes by police, punitive police practices with respect to bail, the absence of crisis-care accommodation, bail hostels and rehabilitation programs, the lack of an interpreter service in Aboriginal languages, limited access to legal advice, mandatory sentencing and other tough laws.

Over-zealous policing of Aboriginal youth is a continuing cause for concern to Aboriginal groups. The South Australian Aboriginal Legal Rights Movement Inc (2009, p. 4) recently told a federal parliamentary committee that:

> Police Officers continue to ask our youth to give them their names and addresses knowing that these youths are known to the officers. This is seen as being harassment and leads to Aboriginal youth reacting negatively, sometimes resulting in their being arrested.

The organisation gave the following example in the town of Port Lincoln (p. 5):

> An Aboriginal youth returning home from football training at Mallee Park...noticed police parked outside his house. When he approached his gate police stopped him and charged him with breach of bail. His response was that he still had half an hour to go but

he was told that daylight saving had ceased and he was
half an hour over his curfew. He has to appear in court
on the date of the next hearing in Pt Lincoln.

The recent parliamentary report into juvenile crime (House
of Representatives, 2011, p. 196) has recognised that effective
police–Indigenous relations remain a work in progress:

> Some Indigenous communities and local police
> have forged strong positive relationships and work
> collaboratively to build safe and strong communi-
> ties. Unfortunately, other examples...are marred by
> attitudes of distrust, suspicion and fear. This negatively
> influences the potential outcomes of young Indigenous
> people's contact with the police.

Anecdotal evidence from South Australia highlights that
over-policing is part of the dynamic of poor relationships
between the two groups. A member of the Australian Legal
Rights Movement told the House of Representatives inquiry
into juvenile crime (2011, p. 200) that up to four cases involving
Aboriginal youth coming before the youth court in Adelaide
'are deliberately sent back by the judges because the subject
matter of the charge is not worthy of the attention of the court'.

Contact between police and Indigenous youth is heightened through their greater use of public space, higher rates
of homelessness and increased cognitive and/or mental health
issues. This can be a volatile mix when police over-zealously
use their powers to ask for names and addresses or issue move-
on warnings. Reacting with defensive-aggression, Aboriginal

youth are at risk of a trifecta of offences: offensive behaviour and/or, offensive language, resisting arrest and assaulting a police officer (Aboriginal and Torres strait Islander Social Justice Commissioner, 2008). In this way, such youth can quickly find themselves brought into the juvenile justice system where many will enter a 'revolving door' because of past offences.

Such practices, together with what appears to be a slow decline in the use of diversionary programs for Aboriginal youth, raise important questions about the functioning of police services as gate-keepers to the justice system. In particular, the discriminatory practices highlighted by the WA and SA Aboriginal organisations indicate some level of on-going institutional racism in police services which were widespread up until a decade or so ago. Police services have put considerable effort into eliminating racism but, as analysts of race relations in Australia point out, such attitudes and behaviours persist.

Social causes

The literature on youth offending has for a long time recognised a number of risk factors. These include:

- individual characteristics (e.g. lack of impulse control, poor social skills, lack of self-esteem)
- family background (e.g. poor parental supervision, family violence, criminal behaviour by parents)
- school experience (e.g. weak attachment to school and/or school failure/drop out)
- community characteristics (e.g. socio economic disadvantage, neighbourhood violence and crime) (see Cappo, 2007 for a summary of this literature).

The stark reality is that many Aboriginal young people face multiple numbers of these risk factors; in fact, it is not uncommon for all four to be part of their lived experience.

Unfortunately it is the case that, for some Aboriginal youth, crime is a way of life; it is not behaviour that is sanctioned in families. As Tatz (1999, p. 90) pointed out in his study of Aboriginal suicide, 'Even allowing for a greater propensity by police to arrest Aboriginal youth, for whatever reasons, the fact is that many Aboriginal youth commit crimes'. In some cases, this results from younger children imitating the behaviour of older siblings. A recent Queensland inquiry was told:

> The majority of the time, it's the eldest one gets into trouble or the second eldest one, and then the younger ones are thinking 'I'm going to be like my brother and sister, you know, I'm going to follow in their footsteps'...I have seen a whole family in there [juvenile detention], you know, all four of them. All in at one time (Forde, 2000, p. 250).

The internalisation of incarceration as a normal part of many Aboriginal young people's experiences is a crucial factor leading to recidivism. Indeed, Indigenous Australians, including youth, are the fastest growing prison population in all states and territories (Aboriginal and Torres Strait Islander Social Justice Commissioner, 2008). More than 80 per cent of Aboriginal young people progress from juvenile detention to the adult prison system.

Crime as a lifestyle combined with a fatalistic acceptance of incarceration conforms to what criminologists have long identified as the existence of a 'deviant' sub-culture of crime among young males from socially disorganised and/or dysfunctional backgrounds. Such patterns of behaviour can be transmitted from one generation to the next in families from different ethnic and racial backgrounds. This sub-culture underpins high intergenerational rates of imprisonment for many Aboriginal families. A survey conducted of juveniles in detention in NSW found that 41 per cent had a parent who had been in prison at some time during their formative years; 11 per cent had a parent in custody at the same time (House of Representatives, 2011). Such children normalise their contact with the criminal justice system. Some of the young offenders are parents themselves (ibid).

Brief insights into this subculture within Aboriginal communities surfaced in the following comments made to the press by an Aboriginal mother whose powerlessness to prevent her sons sliding into crime also defies easy stereotypes about lack of parental concern. She told *The West Australian* (8 February 2000) that:

> She had suffered years of heartache trying to help her two sons break a cycle of crime and drugs that started when they were eleven. Her sons are now in their twenties. Although one son has stopped his involvement in crime, the other is still offending. Prisons taught young offenders nothing but how to commit more crime and it was almost impossible to get a job after being in jail. Most young offenders came from broken homes, but that did not mean that their parents did not care. Most parents did not know what to

do...Her sons had always been well provided for and had been well behaved until they started high school. Then drugs, high-speed chases, ram raids, and theft began to rule their lives.

The social environment in which many Aboriginal young people grow up exposes them to a range of risk factors known to be associated with youth offending. Some of these risk factors were identified in the WA Aboriginal Child Health Survey (De Maio, et al., 2005) which found that:

- 24 per cent of Indigenous children were rated by their parents as being at high risk of significant emotional or behavioural difficulties.
- 70 per cent of Indigenous children were living in families that had experienced three or more major life stress events (such as a death in the family, serious illness, family break-down, financial problems or arrest).

The complex interplay of factors causing the high proportion of Aboriginal youth to commit crime has been well understood for more than 20 years (see Beresford & Omaji, 1996) but constitute an enormous challenge for Aboriginal communities and governments to address. For policy makers, the range and intractability of the underlying causes that lead too many young Aboriginal children into crime constitute a 'wicked problem'; one that embodies a multiplicity of causes and defies single and/or simple solutions (see chapter 4, Models of Policy Development).

Underpinning its complexity, the over-representation of Aboriginal young people in crime and the justice system cannot be viewed as isolated, aberrant behaviour. It forms part of a wider pattern of anti-social behaviours including substance and alcohol abuse, school drop-out and, for some, involvement in sexual abuse and self-destructive behaviours including suicide. It is confronting for non-Aboriginal Australians to face up to the common origins of these behaviours and how many become entrenched into the lives of some (but by no means all) Aboriginal communities. Over the years, these have been explored in a number of well-publicised government reports and academic publications.

The historical experiences of Indigenous people are the starting point for understanding this complex range of behaviours. These historical factors include the segregation of Aboriginal people onto reserves; the denial of their citizenship rights; the denial of their wages; the forced removal of children from families; and the imposition of assimilation. In other words, the processes of colonisation that have lasted well into the twentieth century have left a terrible legacy of intergenerational disadvantage.

One of the clearest connections between past policies and intergenerational disadvantage can be seen in the impact of the policies sanctioning the removal of children from their families which was practised as official government policy between the 1930s and the 1970s. As explained in chapter 3, the predominant aim was to assimilate these children into wider society. The plight of these children-turned-adults was brought to light in the report of the 1997 Inquiry conducted by Human Rights and Equal Opportunity Commission. This report notes that, while many parents from the 'stolen generations' are very good parents, deep-seated problems in the process of parenting have been a tragic legacy of the policy. Those who grew up in missions and children's homes away from their culture and their communities sustained long-term damage in being able to form constructive relationships which, in turn, impaired their later ability to be parents. Many suffered from unresolved grief and trauma and had 'problem children' due to parenting styles that were 'disorganised, impatient and capricious'.

Authorities were aware of such children from at least the late 1980s (Beresford & Omaji, 1996) but little was done to address their issues. Such 'problem children' have in turn reached adulthood and have become parents themselves.

Removal of children from families together with the imposition of assimilation in many Aboriginal communities is part of a slow pattern of cultural disintegration which has also adversely impacted on many Aboriginal youth. Successive generations of Aboriginal youth, and especially those in urban areas, have experienced difficulties in the formation of their identities which contributes to a feeling of alienation from the wider society (Beresford & Omaji, 1996).

Compounding the problems associated with poor parenting has been the impact of violence in some communities, especially those in remote communities. Several reports have noted that the incidence of family violence rose during the 1970s and was often associated with access to alcohol. Children who have grown up exposed to heavy drinking and violence are prone to engage in anti-social and self-destructive behaviours (Board of Inquiry, 2007). Such children have spoken of being left unsupervised at a very young age and of siblings 'growing each other up'. Australia-wide, Indigenous youth are five times as likely to be the subjects of child protection orders than other children (Richards, 2007).

The upsurge in anti-social behaviours has led Noel Pearson, (Pearson, 2009a, pp. 163–4) prominent Aboriginal leader and commentator, to question the balance between issues of individual responsibility and the legacy of colonialism as explanations for the social problems facing Aboriginal people today. Of his own Cape York community in far north Queensland, he writes:

> The abuse and neglect of children today does not resemble the situation in the Peninsula communities of the 1960s or earlier. The number of people in prison and juvenile institutions today are unprecedented: the statistics started to emerge in the 1970s. There was not one Hope Vale person in prison in the early 1970s... Alcohol abuse in Peninsular communities became the huge problem that it now is only in these same recent decades. And these problems have bred new problems.

One of the tragic consequences for children born into those Aboriginal communities marked by alcohol abuse is the likelihood that they will suffer from Foetal Alcohol Spectrum Disorder (FASD), the term used to describe the range of effects that may occur in an individual who has been exposed prenatally to alcohol. In the worst-affected Indigenous communities it has been estimated as many as 30 per cent of newborn children have the disorder (The National Organisation for Fetal Alcohol Syndrome and Related Disorders, 2009). An equally alarming statistic is the number of FASD children who come into contact with the law; estimated at 60 per cent (Senate, 2010). A federal parliamentary committee (ibid., p, 144) was recently told that the impulsive behaviour associated with the disorder

> may lead to stealing things for immediate consumption or use, unplanned offending and offending behaviour precipitated by fright or noise...lack of memory or understanding of cause and effect may lead to breach of court orders; further enmeshing FASD sufferers in the justice system.

Indeed a similar pattern has been found for Indigenous youth suffering a variety of cognitive disabilities in addition to FASD, including intellectual disabilities, learning difficulties and autism. The Aboriginal and Torres Strait Islander Social Justice Commissioner (Calma, 2008b, p. 1) has recently written:

> An indigenous young person with either a cognitive disability or mental health problem slips through all the nets of early detection and assessment. They struggle at school and act up in class. Their presentation is simply attributed to bad behaviour. Rather than address the cause of the problem, the education system deals with the problem through punishment and exclusion. Not surprisingly, the young person drifts out of education and into poor peer relationships, boredom and offending behaviour. From there they are fast tracked into the juvenile justice system because they most likely lack the skills and support to succeed in early intervention or diversionary measures.

The impact of generations of discrimination, cultural assimilation and family dysfunction makes many Aboriginal youth feel alienated from society. Some respond by forming groups, often stereotyped in the popular press as 'gangs'. Among marginalised Aboriginal youth, groups are formed on family ties and around a collective sense of Aboriginal identity. Based on recent interviews with Aboriginal young people, sociologist Rob White (2009, p. 49) explains that these connections were central to the formation of one such group – the Barclay Murder squad in Darwin: 'Only family members could belong... [respondents] spoke about how they stayed in the gang because it was made up of family and friends who they had grown up with. The theme that local gangs are criminal gangs based on family emerged strongly'. Similarly, in Victoria, a group of Koori youth have formed the 'Koori Kripps', as a way of expressing their 'own identity, belonging and acceptance' (Aboriginal and Torres Strait Islander Social Justice Commissioner, 2008, p. 49). On-going encounters with racism exacerbate the sense of alienation for marginalised Aboriginal youth. Rob White (2009, p. 50) explains that in relation to the 'gangs' he studied:

> Racism was in many cases a unifying experience, if for no other reason than the fights and conflicts were based upon 'race' and ethnic background. One young Canberra man told us that 'Yeah, we're always fighting with most other people in the school 'cause we're just dark – outcastes compared to them'. This reinforces an outside identity, while at the same time forging stronger links internal to the group.

The extent to which this marginalised status – marked by school failure, poverty, racism, fractured family life and group identity – shapes the outlook of a section of Indigenous youth was revealed in a South Australian study by Dunne (1999). Surveying 60 youth (comprising equal numbers of Indigenous and non-Indigenous) who had had contact with the justice system in that state, one of the questions asked was 'where will you be in 10 years time?' Eighty per cent of non-Indigenous youth described themselves as belonging to the middle-class; that is house, car, married, children, employed. However, the answers given by the Aboriginal interviewees were very different – 75 per cent depicted themselves as being either dead, drunk or locked up. Dunn argues that such youth are subject to a form of confidence trick; they are exposed to trappings of a materialistic society while lacking access to the skills which enable them to participate equally. Such a prevailing sense of hopelessness manifests itself into high levels of drug and alcohol use. Indeed, in one NSW study (Gray, 2010), it was reported that almost 90 per cent of detained Indigenous youth had tested positive for drugs compared to 40 per cent for non-Indigenous.

The connection between poverty and juvenile crime has been explored by social researchers over many years. Non-Aboriginal youth caught up in the juvenile justice system are drawn disproportionately from poor backgrounds. It is not surprising, therefore, that the pervasive low incomes of most Aboriginal people act as a risk factor for young people's involvement in crime. Some of these children steal because they have insufficient food or other essentials or because they aspire to material goods that they feel they have no chance of ever obtaining (Beresford & Omaji, 1996). The Aboriginal and Torres Strait Islander Social

Justice Commissioner has recently reported (2008, p. 50) that they had 'many stories of Indigenous young people, especially in rural and remote areas stealing to survive'.

The common thread running through nearly all of the difficult life experiences of Aboriginal young people is the likelihood of them having poor parenting. As the NSW Government acknowledged in its 2010 submission to a federal parliamentary inquiry into Aboriginal Juvenile justice (NSW Government, 2010, p. 8).

The parenting skills of Aboriginal families are likely to have been impacted through removals in past generations, the effects of direct and indirect disadvantage and intergenerational involvement in the child protection and criminal justice systems. As a consequence, a significant proportion of Aboriginal parents have had little in the way of positive parenting role models and therefore have limited capacity for the inter-generational transmission of positive parenting skills.

School, teachers and Indigenous offending

Criminologists have long argued that school plays a role in the creation of patterns of offending behaviour among young people from all backgrounds. So-called strain theorists argue that schools are a major contributing factor to the on-set of delinquent behaviour. Gottfredson (2001, p. 2) explains why:

> Delinquent behaviour is a natural reaction to a system that judges all school students according to the same 'middle class measuring rod', despite differences in students' opportunities to achieve these standards. Youths whose behaviour does not conform with teachers'

expectations feel the strain associated with failure and rebel against middle-class norms.

However, this 'strain' effect may be more pronounced for Aboriginal youth because of the higher levels of risk factors they face and because of the cultural disconnect between their lives and the norms of school. Hence, there is a greater likelihood of them failing to thrive in the school system. Other criminologists (cited in Aboriginal and Torres Strait Islander Social Justice Commissioner, 2008) argue that school failure is directly linked to offending behaviour because of the child development principle of 'mastery'. This will propel many of those who fail at school to develop a compensatory skill at committing crime; in other words, young people are motivated to be good at some endeavour as part of developing self-esteem.

Operational aspects of the ways in which schools operate can also have a bearing on the likelihood of Indigenous children becoming offenders. As the Australian Law Commission (1997, p. 12) reported more than a decade ago, there is strong anecdotal evidence to suggest 'that a substantial portion of youth offending starts with exclusion from school'. As discussed in previous chapters, Aboriginal students are disproportionately excluded from schools; others exclude themselves by not attending. While teachers are often placed in difficult circumstances dealing with students who misbehave or are reluctant learners, they are best placed to identify and provide initial support to such students. Compounding the risk of exclusion are those Indigenous students suffering undiagnosed cognitive and mental health issues. Aboriginal workers close to this group believe the absence of early identification reflects an education system that does not always value Indigenous young people: 'nobody bothers with the Aboriginal kids sitting up the back of the class because there is an attitude that they don't do well and will just leave' (cited in Aboriginal and Torres Strait Islander Social Justice Commissioner, 2008, p. 58). Indifference to the plight of Indigenous students can reflect strains of broader Australian racism. Dr Chris Sara, Director of the Indigenous Education Leadership Institution, has argued (cited in ibid., p. 46) that:

> mainstream Australia has very negative perceptions of Indigenous people. This filters down to those involved with the education system. Some teachers have lower expectations of Indigenous children based on the 'complexity' of [them]...and perceptions that Indigenous families don't value education. Indigenous children and young people internalise these percep-tions and low expectations to the extent that there is collision between the school and children's mindsets which ultimately produce failure.

Like police, teachers can therefore be important gatekeepers to the criminal justice system. While it has not been common for teachers to be thought of in this way, the practical implications of their interactions with Aboriginal young people underscore this role. Whether through a lack of early intervention, negative attitudes, misplaced assessment, or lack of cultural competency, Indigenous young people who fail at school will likely mark a steady progression into offending behaviour and into the harsher ends of the justice system. As the Aboriginal and Torres Strait Islander Social Justice Commissioner (2008, p. 45) commented:

'We know that Indigenous young people who end up in the juvenile justice system have low educational outcomes, dropping out of school early'. One recently highlighted issue (House of Representatives, 2011, p. 103) was the failure of schools to recognise and respond to Indigenous young people suffering mental health problems. According to the NSW government:

> An Indigenous young person with...[a] mental health problem slips through all the nets of early detection and assessment. They struggle at school and act up in class. Their presentation is simply attributed to bad behaviour. Rather than address the cause of the problem, the education system deals with the young person through punishment and exclusion. Not surprisingly, the young person drifts out of education and into poor peer relationships, boredom and offending behaviour.

This reality raises the important issue of the ways in which educators and schools can play a role in preventing the onset of offending behaviour among Indigenous students. While a comprehensive consideration of the approaches to reduce the over-representation of Aboriginals in juvenile crime and the justice system is beyond the scope of this chapter, schools and education policy more generally are clearly important contributors to this process. Expert witnesses giving evidence to the federal parliamentary inquiry into Aboriginal juvenile justice (House of Representatives, 2011) called for a major shift in juvenile justice policy from an over-reliance on punitive approaches to one emphasising preventative measures. This shift has been conceptualised as a 're-investment strategy'; diverting some of the funds from detention to programs that address the underlying causes of crime which, of course, include a focus on the educational needs of this group. But any 're-investment' strategy will need to be undertaken in a holistic manner. As the Aboriginal and Torres Strait Islander Social Justice Commissioner (2008, p. 49) argued: 'if support and encouragement was given to these young [Indigenous] people to channel their strengths and energies into something more positive [than crime], they could also achieve a sense of mastery and increased self-esteem without offending and anti-social behaviour'. A similar message was delivered by the recent federal inquiry into juvenile crime (House of Representatives, 2011). It argued that there was a need for more holistic approaches to deal with the high likelihood of trauma, abuse or mental health issues among those Aboriginal youth who have come into contact with the criminal justice system.

Yet, the challenges of meeting the needs of these young people cannot be under-estimated. One of the most basic components of this challenge is inadvertently highlighted by the experience of Indigenous young people in custody. The Aboriginal and Torres Strait Islander Social Justice Commissioner (2008, p. 58) foregrounded this issue:

> Some young people were actually more functional when they were in custody. This was because they responded to the structure, routine and certainty of custody, compared to their chaotic lives outside. This is not a justification for custody but it does show that strategies and structure can work to support young people in the community.

Developing the capacity of schools – supported by state and federal government policies and funding – to play a role in the prevention of crime among Indigenous youth cannot be seen in isolation from their work to lift the participation rate among this group, the approaches for which are discussed throughout this book. Yet, it is worth highlighting the principles upon which crime prevention can be approached as part of this broader undertaking:

- Prevention programs cannot be developed in isolation from the communities in which young people live. They should involve consultation and genuine partnerships with Aboriginal people.
- Programs should be based around a whole-of-community approach that targets the full range of needs of local Aboriginal young people.
- Programs should aim to empower the Aboriginal community to develop and control their own solutions to the issues faced by their children.
- Schools in particular need to ensure that they are actively engaged in appropriate assessment and identification of behavioural and/or learning difficulties experienced by Aboriginal young people.
- Teachers, in particular, must ensure that they maintain positive attitudes towards, and encourage expectations for, Aboriginal young people.
- Schools must have a working policy of addressing racism.
- Schools must work towards having an understanding of the underlying issues of offending behaviour and a capacity to

work with relevant government agencies as part of a holistic approach.
- Schools must be actively engaged in whole-of-government' efforts to coordinate services to at-risk Aboriginal youth.

The over-representation of Indigenous children in both crime and the juvenile justice system is a continuing challenge for Australia's human rights reputation and to the quality of its democracy. The structural inequalities faced by Aboriginal people continue to have intergenerational effects that deny full participation of many Aboriginal youth in the life of the nation. The on-going high rates of imprisonment for both Aboriginal juveniles and adult males is a sad reflection of this reality. It is also a sad reality that the reasons underpinning these rates of incarceration are unlikely to be addressed quickly, but that schools, along with other agencies, have a vital role to play in bringing empowerment and hope in the search for ways to better link all Indigenous youth to social opportunities.

9

ATTENDANCE AND NON-ATTENDANCE AT SCHOOL

Jan Gray and Gary Partington

Encouraging positive school experiences is central to the process of lifting both achievement and retention rates among Aboriginal youth. While there is an emerging awareness that more Aboriginal children view school as rewarding and enjoyable than they previously did, this is not the experience of the majority. For most, school remains a place dominated by conflict and/or self-doubt. Explaining such responses is a complex matter, as the causes of non-attendance are constantly changing in accord with developments in modern life (Purdie & Buckley, 2010, p. 3). Chapter 1 explored the theoretical issues behind the often tenuous relationship between Aboriginal youth and school, while other chapters have dealt with the many underlying sociocultural factors.

The focus of this chapter is two-fold: to document and explain patterns of attendance and non-attendance; and to outline some of the specific school-based factors involved.

Participation of Indigenous young people in education

Current statistics indicate an increasing proportion of Aboriginal children enrolling in school (Australian Bureau of Statistics,

2006d). In fact, 25 per cent of Aboriginal children have excellent attendance patterns (Department of Education, Training and Youth Affairs, 2000a, p. 2; Australian Bureau of Statistics, 2006b). Australian Bureau of Statistics data and research studies show a continued pattern of increased engagement of Indigenous families with early childhood education, along with higher levels of retention and participation among Indigenous primary school students compared to Indigenous high school students.

Despite the social, economic and cultural factors impinging on Indigenous young people's potential to remain actively engaged in ongoing educational opportunities outlined in the previous chapters, there is clear evidence of improvement over the last decade in the participation of Indigenous young people in education. Some significant issues related to the rising profile of participation of Indigenous young people in education are highlighted in the 2006 Australian Bureau of Statistics information (Australian Bureau of Statistics, 2006b and 2010d, p. 27). For example:

- There has been a 33 per cent increase in Indigenous student participation in schooling since 1991.
- The school retention rates for students from Year 7/8 through to Year 12 have increased over the last decade from 36 per cent in 2000 to 47 per cent in 2010.
- The number of Indigenous students attending each level of school increased in every state and territory from 1996 to 2009, with a 45 per cent increase in Indigenous student enrolments in schooling (Years 1–12) since 2000.
- There has been a 27 per cent increase in attendance of 15–19 year-old Indigenous students in remote areas in the

last decade, with an 8 per cent increase in enrolments of this same age group of Indigenous students in metropolitan schools.

• There has been a 3 per cent increase in the completion rate of 12 years of schooling from 2001 (20 per cent per cent) to 2006 (23 per cent).

• Rates of Year 12 completion improved in all states and territories, with the largest increases recorded in Tasmania (up from 17 per cent to 22 per cent), the ACT (up from 42 per cent to 46 per cent) and Queensland (26 per cent to 30 per cent).

• Overall, there were similar rates of Year 12 completion for Indigenous males and females (22 per cent compared with 24 per cent).

• There has been an increase of 121 per cent in Indigenous Vocational Education and Training course enrolments since 1994, with a tenfold increase in enrolments in education courses designed to support the development of basic literacy and numeracy outcomes for Indigenous people.

The great appeal of TAFE and the funding available to support ongoing study for Aboriginal students who become disenchanted with school are illustrated by a comment made by a Year 9 Aboriginal boy: 'I don't want to get up and go to school for nothing. I can just wait and go to TAFE at 16' (Gray & Beresford, 2001). In contrast, both male and female Aboriginal students who re-engaged in their learning by taking up second chance opportunities saw entry to TAFE as the gateway to employment (Gray & Hackling, 2009; Ross & Gray, 2005).

It is important to note that participation of Indigenous

students in VET courses is characterised by high non-completion rates (42.16 per cent non-completion compared to 24.4 per cent non-completion for non-Indigenous students) and participation in lower level programs (42.3 per cent of students participating in Australian Qualifications Framework certificate levels I and II are Indigenous, compared to 24.3 per cent non-Indigenous students) (Australian Bureau of Statistics, 2006b).

However, despite the increasing participation and retention of Indigenous young people in education, the discrepancy between Indigenous and non-Indigenous participation and retention remains stark, as outlined in Table 1 summarising data from the 2006 Australian Bureau of Statistics data (Australian Bureau of Statistics, 2006b). Data from the 2006 census shows that little has changed since 2002 (Australian Bureau of Statistics, 2002). Although there is an overall increase in the number of children participating in primary school, the gap in average attendance between Aboriginal and non-Aboriginal students appears in primary school and widens in the early years of secondary school (Purdie & Buckley, 2010).

Table 9.1 – Apparent retention rates for Indigenous students, 2006

Retention	Apparent retention rate 2006	
	Indigenous	non-Indigenous
	%	%
to Year 9	98.4	100.0
to Year 10	91.4	98.9
to Year 11	67.7	88.8
to Year 12	40.1	75.9

Source: Australian Bureau of Statistics, 2006b.

The increasing disengagement of Indigenous students from schooling can be summarised in the 36 per cent difference in retention rate by Year 12 for Indigenous and non-Indigenous students (Table 9.1). Unfortunately, these ABS statistics show that the difference in retention has remained stable in the period 2001–06. On average, Indigenous students attend school less frequently than the rest of the student population, and spend at least two years fewer at school than non-Indigenous students (Gray, 2009a; Purdie & Buckley, 2010).

In their study of factors impacting on the alienation from school among Aboriginal students, Gray and Beresford (2001, p. 9) were able to provide an insight into the issues underlying the decreasing retention rate for Indigenous students entering secondary school in Western Australia. Aboriginal researchers working on the study described the growing student disillusionment with secondary school as a factor related to rejection:

> The enthusiasm for school dissipates after Year 8 and disillusion sets in when their expectations of school are not being met. As Noongar kids, they stick together. They get teased if they have white friends. When they are together there is cohesion and group attitudes are reinforced. Only the strong get through. Schools are not addressing the underlying issues and problems they face. TAFE is valued because that is the best they believe they as blacks can expect. The transition from high school to university doesn't happen very often so there are few role models. They don't see uni as an option (Gray & Beresford, 2001, p. 9).

In a study of the rejection of schooling of Koori students, Munns and McFadden (2000) found that Aboriginal parents in the Koori community saw their children's rejection of education as a natural progression, and less shameful than staying at school. These Aboriginal children eventually rejected education through their frustration with the schools' lack of capacity to support them in their unstable home lives, the inability of teachers to understand and address their emotional needs (Ross, 2009). Munns and McFadden (2000, p. 66) explained this rejection in the following way:

> As the students became increasingly aware that school was not for them, they also realised more and more that the community anticipated their failure. With this anticipation, there was cultural support for their opposition and resistance.

Ross (2009, p. 147) found in her study of early school leavers that for Aboriginal students whose parents had a history of failure at school, the pattern of school rejection was expected and often supported. The parents' lack of knowledge of schools and schooling left them unable to advocate for or support their children's continued education. One sixteen-year-old Koori student explained her decision to leave school in the following way:

> My dad just wanted me to continue education and my mum wanted me to be happy. My mum didn't mind…she just wanted me to get the education that I needed…it was sufficient to do TAFE (p. 147).

Respect for TAFE as a way forward in lifelong learning has been affirmed for some Aboriginal students engaged in second chance learning opportunities in schools where they feel respected (Gray, 2009b, p. 8). The acceptance of the role of TAFE in aspirations for qualifications is illustrated by the following comment from a 17-year-old Aboriginal student who was determined to complete his education and training: 'I want to be a plumber. I've already got my Cert II, in Building & Construction, so I'm pretty set (2009b, p. 8)'.

Forms of non-attendance

The diverse categories of school non-attendance frequently used in the literature and in data collection on a national, state and system level exacerbate the problem of defining, recording and eventually addressing students' absence from school. The definitions used in the 1996 House of Representatives inquiry into truancy were chronic truancy (includes school refusers and school phobics), truancy and fractional truancy (includes blanket or post-registration truancy). These categories are reflected in both local and international research surrounding issues associated with the 'truancy problem' for the past decade. These categories are still used in more recent research (Zubric, et.al., 2006; Ross & Gray, 2005; Purdie & Buckey, 2010).

From their research in Western Australia, Gray and Beresford (2002, p. 31) further refined the categories of non-attendance commonly identified in current literature. The following categories were found to represent patterns of non-attendance for Aboriginal students:

• Chronic non-attenders – that is, those enrolled in school but who are absent for more than 20 per cent of the time.

- Chronic fractional attenders – that is, those who attend school but who are persistently absent for part of many days.
- Non-enrolled students – students whose parents are transient and who condone their children dropping out of school altogether, usually at the age of eleven or twelve.
- Those suspended and excluded from school – these students constituted up to 17 per cent in one metropolitan school in Western Australia (Gray, 2000).
- Those high school students unable to integrate back into school after a period in detention and who drop out altogether.

A significant proportion of non-attendance among Aboriginal students begins as a result of out-of-school factors, with specific gender differences and impact, as identified by Gray and Beresford (2001, p. 21):

> The common attitude among parents is; the boys can leave school; they're running amok, you can't control them but they can go to TAFE when they've sorted themselves out. Girls have to be educated to stop them getting pregnant and having babies early. Boys also see themselves as men by around 14 and don't want to be treated like little kids. Many of them are being raised by women because their fathers are in prison and, consequently, they lack role models. Many of these boys see themselves as the man of the house and act in this role (Aboriginal interviewers).

However, non-attendance becomes a pattern that is hard to break, especially if triggered by school-based confrontation. Gray (2000, p. 156) found evidence to support the correlation between suspension and truancy, noting 25 per cent of students who were chronic truants in Year 8 and who eventually dropped out of school before the end of Year 9 were also suspended for ten or more days. An Aboriginal mother who had spent considerable time encouraging her adolescent son to continue with his schooling explained the link as follows (Gray, 2000, p. 237):

> The teacher picked on him for not wearing a white shirt to school. He didn't have a white shirt. And they suspended him from school. And, em, he just didn't go back (Aboriginal mother).

The extent of the non-attendance problem

The difficulties in collecting, collating and comparing data on non-attendance at a national level have been well documented (House of Representatives, 1996; Kilpatrick, 1998; Department of Education, Science and Training, 2000; Gray, 2000; Gray & Beresford, 2001, 2006; Kemmis, 1999; Purdie & Buckley, 2010).

The term 'truancy' is rarely used in recent research or policy documentation, with the discourse more explicitly reporting levels of attendance. There are several possible reasons why this change in discourse may have occurred:

- a shift to a more positive political discourse for the accountability of reporting outcomes

- national school reporting transparency through the 'Myschool website' needs a consistent level of reporting student attendance
- truancy has negative and dated connotations.

Whatever the term used to describe students' attendance at school, data from any research-based reports show that Aboriginal students are less likely in any school setting to attend as regularly as non-Aboriginal students. The rate of truancy quoted in most research for the United Kingdom, United States and each State of Australia, is 10 per cent. This does not necessarily refer to 'chronic truants', but is more likely to reflect nonattendance patterns. National data indicate that in 1998 almost 3 per cent of 14-year-olds were estimated to be absent from school on a long-term basis or not enrolled in school at all (Department of Education, Training & Youth Affairs, 2001, p. 4). This was a substantial rise from the 1988 data (1.5 per cent of 14-year-olds not engaged in schooling). For example, a common figure quoted for daily absenteeism in Western Australian government schools was 8,000 students per day (House of Representatives, 1996). Given that the total compulsory-aged government school student population of Western Australia in December 1998 was 199,643[1], this figure is approximately 4 per cent of the school population. Of course, most would be absent for legitimate reasons.

The research undertaken in WA by Zubric, et al., (2006) shows that the vast majority of Aboriginal young people under 15 years of age attended school fairly regularly. More specifically, the median number of days absent was twenty-six days (the

---

1   Education Department of Western Australia Statistics System, semester 2, 1998

median number of days absent for non-Aboriginal students was eight days). The problem of serious disengagement from school (truancy, rejection of schooling, non-attendance) is evident in data for Aboriginal young people aged 15 years and older A substantial proportion (47 per cent) of these young people of 15 years and more were no longer attending school nor engaged in work (32 per cent), and had seriously reduced their chances of academic and vocational success beyond their school years.

Cultural differences in patterns of attendance

Several key factors related to differences between patterns of Aboriginal and non-Aboriginal school attendance were identified in a Department of Education, Training and Youth Affairs project (Bourke, et al., 2000) and confirmed a decade later by Zubrick, et al., (2006) and Purdie & Buckley (2010):

- A much larger proportion of Indigenous students are absent from school for a comparatively large number of days (three times as many days absence per year than non-Indigenous students).
- Absences for Indigenous students are more likely to be reported as 'unexplained' and hence implied truancy.
- There are markedly higher rates of non-attendance in more isolated, traditionally-oriented communities. Census data show a general decline in school attendance for Indigenous students in terms of the distance of the school location from the metropolitan area.
- Mobility can result in extended periods of non-attendance for Indigenous students, particularly in remote communities.

- Indigenous students have a higher rate of suspension and exclusion from school.

Cultural differences in patterns of unexplained absences

The same report identified the disproportionate number of Indigenous students whose absence from school is described as 'unexplained'. By definition, truancy is 'unexplained absence', categorising all those students with legitimate absences – but no confirming parental note – as truants. For example, twice as many Indigenous girls had their school non-attendance categorised as 'unexplained' as non-Indigenous girls (64.7 per cent compared with 36 per cent).

In their large study of Aboriginal Child Health in Western Australia, Zubric, et al., (2006) found that almost half of all Aboriginal students (47.6 per cent) had more than ten days of unexplained absence from school. Further, the proportion of students who had more than ten unexplained absences was much higher among students who had been absent for at least twenty-six days in a school year. It was also noted that in many cases, carers were hampered by literacy problems in providing notes to cover these 'unexplained' absences.

Aboriginal truancy in Western Australia

Non-attendance studies in Western Australia by Gray (2000) and Gray & Beresford (2001) provide an opportunity to examine in more detail the non-attendance patterns of both Indigenous and non-Indigenous students in an education district of approximately 42,000 students. Overall, their studies confirmed the Department of Education, Training and Youth Affairs findings and provided new insight into the profound disadvantage faced by Indigenous students in Western Australia.

Table 9.2 – Percentages of absences by reason, Aboriginality and gender, 1997

Reason	non-Indigenous students		Indigenous students	
	Female %	Male %	Female %	Male %
Illness (Doctor*)	2.3	1.8	1.0	0.7
Illness (Parent*)	42.5	40.1	15.9	16.4
Family/social	19.2	19.2	18.4	18.3
Unexplained	36.0	38.9	64.7	64.6

Source: Bourke et al., 2000, p.15.

n=12,032 (Indigenous), n=189,236 (non-Indigenous)

* Note from doctor or parent to explain absence from school

An experienced school welfare officer in Western Australia interviewed by Gray (2000, p. 246) provided a context for the closer examination of differences in attendance patterns:

> If we didn't have the Aboriginal truancy problem, I would say we would hardly have an attendance problem. City and country. I think I can speak on behalf of every other school welfare officer in the State when I say the Aboriginal problem is getting worse (School Welfare Officer, 1999).

The Aboriginal truancy problem referred to by the school welfare officer was further explored by Gray & Beresford (2001) in the above education district (see Table 9.3 below). The extent of the Aboriginal truancy, suspension and exclusion problem faced by this district is clearly yet to be resolved. Aboriginal students represent 11 times the proportion of non-Aboriginal students defined as truant within the district (17.5 per cent Aboriginal students, compared with 1.6 per cent non-Aboriginal students, were referred as truant in 2000). Proportionately, twice as many Aboriginal students were suspended from school as were non-Aboriginal students (8.4 per cent compared with 3.7 per cent). The proportion of Aboriginal students confronted with school exclusion was 13 times the proportion of non-Aboriginal students (0.4 per cent Aboriginal students compared with 0.03 per cent non-Aboriginal students).

Table 9.3 – Referrals of Aboriginal students from schools in a WA Education District, 2000

Category	No. Aboriginal referrals	Proportion of group %	No. non-Aboriginal referrals	Proportion of group %
Truancy	380	17.5	631	1.6
Suspension	183	8.4	1446	3.7
Exclusion	9	0.4	10	0.03
School Psychologist	42	1.9	102	0.3
School Attendance Officer	76	3.5	93	0.2

Source: Gray and Beresford, 2001, p. 11. n=2,451(Aboriginal students), n=39,130 (non-Aboriginal)

Absentee rates in compulsory schooling

An earlier study by Gray (2000) similarly highlighted the extent to which Aboriginal students are rejecting regular school attendance from Year 1 through to Year 10. Data for the study were collected across four education districts and some 70,000 students over a three-year period. To confirm patterns evident in early data, a five-week snapshot was taken of attendance in one Education District in semester 1, 1999.

The significant difference between Aboriginal and non-Aboriginal attendance patterns is illustrated in the snapshot data, outlined in Table 9.4. Of great concern is the disproportionate number of Aboriginal children absent regularly in their early years of schooling (10 per cent of Aboriginal children in both Years 1 and 2 were absent for at least five days in the five-week period). Chronic absenteeism for Aboriginal students in Years 9 and 10 illustrated the growing proportion of alienated students (15 times as many Aboriginal students as non-Aboriginal students in Year 9 were absent for at least five days in the five-week period). The data illustrate the increasing number of Aboriginal students at educational risk during their high school years.

Table 9.4 – Unexplained absences in WA Education District in snapshot period in 1999

School Year level	% absent 5+ days	
	Aboriginal students	Non-Aboriginal students
1	9.6	0.3
2	10.7	0.3
3	7.3	0.1
4	6.3	0.4
5	4.8	0.2
6	4.9	0.2
7	10.1	0.2
8	9.8	0.8
9	23.1	1.5
10	17.2	2.6

Source: Gray, 2000. n=30,732

The same study reported that 10.05 per cent of Aboriginal students in Year 1 truanted for more than ten days in 1998, compared with 0.27 per cent of non-Aboriginal students.

Consistently through the remainder of the primary school year groups in 1998, Aboriginal students represented an average of 16 times the proportion of non-Aboriginal students reported as truanting in each year group from Year 2 to Year 7 (Gray, 2000).

The study showed the discrepancy to be even greater in secondary school, where 19.4 per cent of Aboriginal students were reported as truants in Year 9 (compared with 1.2 per cent of non-Aboriginal students) and 27.0 per cent in Year 10 (compared with 2.45 per cent of non-Aboriginal students). Given the simultaneous phenomena of Aboriginal students dropping out of school altogether and the high suspension rates for these students, almost all the Aboriginal boys in the district had disconnected from school by the end of Year 10 (Gray, 2000).

The stark differences between non-attendance patterns for Aboriginal and non-Aboriginal students at all levels of compulsory education are hard to ignore. Of great concern is the number of very young Aboriginal students with unexplained absences for more than ten days in the first five weeks of their school career; absences that drastically limit their opportunities to meet conventional age-related educational expectations.

Aboriginal truancy in the Northern Territory

A key review of Indigenous education in the Northern Territory undertaken in 1999 presented a similar picture of the disproportionate number of Aboriginal students becoming disengaged with their education at an early age (Collins, 1999). In particular, the review focused on the critical need to improve attendance in order to improve educational outcomes. The following response from a teacher interviewed in the review summarises this perspective:

If the kids aren't in school it doesn't really matter what we teach. Some of the kids have the equivalent of zero education because of their poor attendance (Collins, 1999, p. 142).

The view was taken that a minimum average attendance of four days a week was necessary for students to gain educational benefit, with evidence to demonstrate a clear correlation between regular attendance and student progress (Collins, 1999, p. 142). The review outlined the discrepancy between the increased proportion of Aboriginal student enrolments from 1983 to 1998 and the decreasing rates of attendance.

To provide more focused data related to school attendance of Aboriginal students, a series of case study schools were invited to provide a snapshot view of day-by-day attendance for a one-week period during 1998. The data in Table 9.5 illustrate the poor attendance rates for Aboriginal students in these East Arnhem Case Study schools. Of particular concern is the fact that at least 20 per cent of students were absent all week in each case study school. In case study schools 26 (50.8 per cent absent every day) and 28 (45 per cent absent every day), the majority of students did not attend at all.

Table 9.5 – 1998 attendance, East Arnhem case studies

Case study	% attended 5 days	% attended 3 days	% attended 2 days	% attended 1 day	% attended 0 days
25	37.3	13.5	11.8	8.5	22
26	14.1	8.4	12.4	7.1	50.8
27	29	11.3	13.6	4.5	34
28	14.4	7.9	9.4	12.8	45
29	33.8	14.2	10.9	9.4	24.9

Source: Collins, 1999, Table 16, p. 144

It is evident from the case study data that a significant proportion of students are at increasing educational risk through not attending school regularly. Only three of the five case study schools had a school attendance rate of more than 50 per cent for three or more days (case studies 25, 27, 29 had attendance rates of 62.5 per cent, 53.9 per cent and 58.9 per cent respectively). As was found in the truancy data from Western Australia (Gray, 2000), patterns of school attendance among Aboriginal students indicate a growing alienation from school as students reach puberty and high school. The impact of such a significant lack of engagement in schooling is an inevitable loss of educational opportunity. Clearly, the initial focus in developing strategies for maximising the potential educational opportunities for Aboriginal students is linked to engaging students in regular attendance.

Factors influencing attendance

Non-attendance at school remains perhaps the most severe manifestation of the dysfunctional relationship between school and Aboriginal students. Non-attendance has been a focus of research and policy development in Aboriginal education at least since the mid-1980s. The complex nature of the social problems hampering the successful engagement of Aboriginal young people in ongoing education is well documented, along with the realisation that there is no simple solution to the continuing disadvantage perpetuated by lack of equitable educational outcomes for these young people. Low rates of participation among Aboriginal children in primary and high school have been consistently noted in research and official inquiries, reflecting a broad understanding of the link between disadvantage, alienation, resistance to education, suspensions and exclusions (Legislative Assembly, 1991; Groome & Hamilton, 1995; House of Representatives, 1996; Beresford & Omaji, 1996, 1998; Collins, 1999; Gray & Beresford, 2006; Partington, 1998; Ross & Gray, 2005; Purdie & Buckley, 2010).

Aboriginal students are a minority group in almost all educational settings in Australia except remote community schools. Aboriginal children constitute 3.9 per cent of all Australian children aged between zero and 14 years, and 3 per cent of all Australian young people aged between 15 and 19 years in 2001 (Australian Bureau of Statistics, 2002). These proportions have increased by 11 per cent since 2001 (Australia Bureau of Statistics, 2006a). Across Australia, many metropolitan schools have no Aboriginal students enrolled, while others have small numbers. This invisibility in school settings perpetuates local school resistance to Commonwealth, state and system-level strategies for differentiated resourcing to begin to address the inequity of educational outcomes for Aboriginal students and encourage their regular school attendance (Gray, 2000).

Yet, given the significant problem it represents, there has been a lack of systematic analysis of the non-attendance issue and the full extent of the seriousness of the problem remains undocumented (House of Representatives, 1996, p. 50; Purdie & Buckley, 2010). Of equal importance is the lack of detailed understanding about the underlying causes of non-attendance as these relate specifically to structural disadvantage and life experiences of Aboriginal youth.

Identifying the specific factors that explain why some Aboriginal students are able to successfully negotiate school as a positive experience requires an understanding of the complex interplay of home and school. A combination of home, school and individual factors are involved in a student's decision to miss school (Purdie & Buckley, 2010, p. 2). The 2006 census data showed that Aboriginal attendance at school was influenced by a wide range of complex factors (Australian Bureau of Statistics, 2006a):

> A range of factors were associated with Indigenous students' attendance at school including their carer's education, risk of clinically significant emotional or behavioural difficulties, students in families with multiple life-stress events, whether a language other than English was the main language spoken at home (Aboriginal English or an Aboriginal language), difficulties sleeping, and whether the student attended day care.

The discrepancy between attendance data for Aboriginal and non-Aboriginal students remains an issue for educators. The reasons for the discrepancy are not entirely clear, but appear to involve a range of factors, including sense of self, school environment, literacy, family and community support.

Student factors
Sense of self
A Department of Education Training and Youth Affairs project examining the relationship between school outcomes and positive self-identity of Indigenous students (Purdie, et al., 2000) highlighted the need for Indigenous young people to have positive self-identities as students before improved participation and

retention could be achieved. This requires a school environment where students from a supportive home environment have a sense of belonging, where teachers have positive expectations of student success, where curriculum is perceived by the students to be relevant. Later studies confirm the continuation and impact of this need (Ross & Gray, 2005; Gray & Hackling, 2009; Purdie & Buckley, 2010)

School environment

Drawing on theories of cultural difference in education, Kickett-Tucker (1999) argued that Aboriginal sense of self comprises very different values and behaviours than is common in Anglo-Australians. These are characterised by Aboriginal children's preferred way of learning: working in groups, cooperation, sharing common group goals and learning by observation, an understanding of the real life significance of school-based learning, and jovial social interactions in the learning environment. While Kickett-Tucker argues that these values and behaviours are 'rarely encouraged in the mainstream academic context', they are more likely to be found in the primary school than in the high school setting.

Family support

For some students, parents provide positive motivation, often converting their own disappointment over missed educational opportunities into expectations for their children (Gray & Beresford, 2001). A Year 9 Aboriginal student described the parental encouragement to achieve at school in the following way: 'My Dad says I have to do what he didn't do' (Gray & Beresford, 2001).

A Year 11 Aboriginal girl expressed strong family support to remain at school and be the first in the family to complete 12 years of schooling and graduate from high school in the following way:

> My Mum and Dad were a bit surprised that I really wanted to keep going, but they're OK about it now. My Dad is passive about it, but says if I want to do it I can. If not – don't worry. Mum is a bit more positive. I think she feels as though I'm her 'last chance'. I want to be able to say that I passed Year 11 and 12 and I actually did it 'cause my mum and my dad dropped out in year 10 and my sister tried to do Year 11 and failed so I just want to be the one that goes 'yeah, that's right, I did it!' (Gray, 2009a, p. 649).

Community support

For some students, a sense of 'ownership' of the school is a central factor in attendance. The experience of the Barramundi School, in the Kimberley region of Western Australia, is instructive. In 1999, the school had two teachers, two Aboriginal and Islander Education Officers and 26 students (Partington, et al., 1999). The students' attendance was good – around 85 per cent attending daily. Nearly all the students had had contact with the justice system. The students clearly liked school, attended regularly and were acquiring skills that would enable them to get jobs in the local community or to go on to further education in Darwin or Perth. They no longer offended.

The reason for the transformation was the development of the school which was seen by the Aboriginal community as their school. While it was established by a largely non-Indigenous committee, this was done in consultation with the community. The school was set up on land the community regarded as theirs. The teachers were supportive of the community and were accepted by them. The curriculum was appropriate.

The men spoke highly of the school. They associated with the site which, for years, had been used for community activities. There was a community atmosphere with the women's group participating in the school. The boys were comfortable at the school. Their culture was acknowledged and embedded in the school's operation. For example, it was reported that in the other schools and at TAFE, teachers did not acknowledge cultural mores regarding the use of names. Barramundi did acknowledge these mores. Furthermore, the school was getting the boys educated; they were being kept off the streets and learning skills that would stand them in good stead in the future. The community was proud of their school and urged their children to attend.

Community approval did not extend to the district high school located just down the road, and which students used to attend before dropping out of school. A community leader said this of the school:

> Most kids try to go to school, but an invitation from the headmaster isn't there. The teachers must address them in a manner they understand. It is embarrassing for kids who haven't been to school for some time (Partington, Kickett-Tucker & Mack, 1999, p. 16).

The men were aware of the problems surrounding the provision of education for the students:

We trust the Europeans to give the education but it is
not happening (Partington, Kickett-Tucker & Mack,
1999, p. 17).

If the community is to become involved in the school, it must
do so as an equal partner. As with students in the classroom,
the discourse of principals and teachers clearly indicates their
attitudes and values to members of the Indigenous community.
If the school presents in an acceptable way and demonstrates
sincerity and persistence in their efforts to secure a sound relationship with the community, they are likely to achieve success.

The role of sport
Typically, Aboriginal students who enjoy school identify the
existence of strong, personal relationships with their teachers as
a significant factor. Kickett-Tucker (1999, p. 331) has explained
that the willingness of teachers

> to step back from their roles as teachers in order to
> socially interact with Aboriginal children in their world
> and on their terms was a crucial factor to establishing
> rapport and developing a good working relationship
> between teacher and child in the classroom.

Access to sport has been identified as an important link
for many Aboriginal students in the development of a positive outlook on school. Kickett-Tucker's (1999) research in this
area has highlighted the strength of this relationship. In the
first place, there is a widespread perception in the Aboriginal
community of the role that sport plays in fostering positive
feelings of Aboriginal identity and a sense of respect from the

wider society. In the school setting, playing sport conveys a range of benefits which can be a foundation for wider success. Kickett-Tucker identified these as including: producing social interaction between Aboriginal and non-Aboriginal students, enhancing the ability to demonstrate competence and leadership, and providing access to goal-setting. Feelings of being included as part of the school environment was a key benefit which flowed from involvement in sport:

> Praise and encouragement were constantly supplied by non-Aboriginal students to those Aboriginal students who displayed average to above average levels of sport skills and overall performances...When Aboriginal students displayed their competence in sport, non-Aboriginal students wanted to make friends and have them included in their teams.

Purdie & Buckley (2010, p. 9) noted that targeting of Indigenous students through programs with a strong sporting element to encourage continued engagement and re-engagement of these young people in their schooling. Of note are the programs run by the Clontarf Foundation, with the support of the Academy of Sport. The 2009 Annual Report (Clontarf Foundation) claimed 77 per cent attendance for students involved in the program, and 76 per cent of Year 12 students in the program achieving a fully recognised graduation (Purdie & Buckley, 2010, p. 10).

School-based explanations of non-attendance
Non-attendance through disengagement?

There remain a disproportionate number of Indigenous young people who continue to become disengaged from education in increasing proportion from their entry to school in Year 1 (Australian Bureau of Statistics, 2002; Australian Bureau of Statistics, 2006d). An increasing concern among educational institutions is the strong possibility that non-attendance is the outcome rather than the cause of poor literacy and numeracy amongst Indigenous students. Within the complex social dynamic surrounding the lives of Indigenous young people, non-attendance is considered an outcome of current school-based policies and practices. There is growing evidence to indicate that most school-based policies do not reflect the flexible, accessible and relevant curriculum needed to reconnect these young people into education (Collins, 1999; Gray, 2000; Gray & Beresford, 2001, 2006; Prime Minister's Youth Pathways Action Plan Task-force, 2001; Hickling-Hudson & Ahlquist, 2003; Ross & Gray, 2005).

A report commissioned by the Commonwealth Department of Education, Training and Youth Affairs (2000a) to examine ways to improve school attendance of Indigenous students identified a growing number of authors who contend that:

> the high rate of non-attendance of Indigenous students, the disproportionately high rates of school suspension and exclusion and low retention rates among Indigenous students are a reflection of the education system's failure to address the needs of Indigenous people (Department of Education, Training and Youth Affairs, 2000a, p. 19).

The strong link between regular school attendance and educational outcomes was highlighted in the Collins report of issues related to Indigenous youth and education in the Northern Territory:

> Attendance is important – kids who come every day do advance with literacy and numeracy more than those that don't because they don't learn those things anywhere else (Collins, 1999, p. 142).

The same study identified the impact on educational and behaviour management outcomes in school of the inability to engage Indigenous students into the learning community (Collins, 1999, p. 5).

Much of the difficulty that exists in some schools can be attributed to the lack of success enjoyed by Indigenous students. The inability to read and participate fully in academic activities, by a significant percentage of Indigenous students, is an inhibiting factor to Indigenous education participation, success and school attendance. Howard Groome (1995, as cited in Beresford & Omaji, 1998) pointed to the complexity of reasons for the high drop-out rate (including high truancy rates) of Aboriginal students, rarely related to intelligence or ability. He identified issues related to poor teacher/student relationships (often including racism) and no sense of belonging in a classroom as crucial to an Aboriginal student's perceptions of failure. He suggested that Aboriginal students feel that achievement at school implies pressure to relinquish their cultural identity and peer acceptance.

Ross (2009) showed the impact of these inter-related social, cultural, family and school factors on Aboriginal students' decision-making processes related to leaving school early and re-engaging in a second chance educational opportunity through TAFE.

As can be seen, the issue of Aboriginal non-attendance at school is complex, and needs to be considered in a social and cultural context. In a study of non-attendance in Western Australia (Gray, 2000), a female Aboriginal and Islander Education Officer described the complex home dynamic prioritising other needs than school attendance often faced by Indigenous families:

There is still a lot of truancy today at high school. Kids wag school. They take a day off, then a few more. But I think we have to look at the underlying issues of alcohol and the drugs that are around. In my job [in schools] I see it all the time. [The Aboriginal students] are not alcoholics yet, they may drink but a lot of them are on drugs. Drugs, alcohol and peer pressure and you are not going to keep many of them at school.

And they don't get the support from home. It's complicated. There's an anger and jealousy with stepfathers and mothers. All the usual family breakup stuff. Kids won't go home. It's hard. School is just not a priority. For some mums with all the alcohol problems and violence problems, they're only interested in survival. There's no way they can make education and learning a priority.

There is the need to get the kids out of your hair when things get really rough, but if mum's got an abusive partner who drinks with mates, then mum's trying to cope with cops and drunks and it's very, very difficult to get the kids to school. It's very hard to understand if you haven't been in the situation, but it's so difficult to keep the family household functioning, trying to support a couple of kids in a very small area. Everyone wants to talk and laugh and carry on.

As a kid, you can't fall asleep. Then you try and get up in the morning and find something to eat, something to wear. Alcoholic parents. No-one who really cares about you. No lunch money. Sometimes it's just easier for that child to be at home. Education at home is survival. Education at school won't fix that. It can be accessible later on, but survival and sorting these other issues is more important (Female Aboriginal Education worker, 1999).

There is little doubt that students who rarely attend school are at risk of becoming marginalised, not only at school but also within the community and on a long-term basis. Absence from school, unless supplemented with some other form of educational instruction, places students at risk of lower outcomes in numeracy and literacy and subsequent difficulties in gaining employment. This problem has been recognised at both national and state levels.

The label 'students at educational risk', of course, covers a broad range of students, with the risk factors well documented[2]. These risk factors are consistently identified as versions of homelessness, illiteracy, low socioeconomic status, abuse (as perpetrator and/or victim), dysfunctional family background,

2   There is now well-documented recognition, both internationally and within Australia, of the risk factors for those leaving school before the legal age (Beresford & Omaji, 1996, 1998; Devlin, 1996; Gewirtz, et al., 1995; Gray, 2000; Gray & Beresford, 2002; Batten & Russell, 1995; House of Representatives, 1996; Legislative Assembly, 1991; Nicholls, 1998; Munns & McFadden, 2001; Purdie & Buckley, 2010).

academic failure, substance abuse and physical, social and intellectual disability. As reported by staff and community members in the Collins Report: 'If you don't go to school, you don't get the outcomes' (Collins, 1999, p. 141).

Identified risk factors

As discussed in other chapters throughout this book, such high levels of non-attendance are a product of a range of sociocultural factors, including low socioeconomic background, low employment, single-parent and blended families, language other than English, student disabilities and student transience. These factors impact in a disproportionate way on Aboriginal children, placing them at extreme educational risk.

The nature and impact of these identified risk factors are, however, difficult to evidence in school and district data associated with Aboriginal students, because data used to create profiles of attendance, participation and retention are based on students who have engaged with educational institutions. Those Aboriginal students who have become totally alienated from education are not necessarily represented within this data. Participation rates do not necessarily reflect non-attendance issues (see Robinson & Bamblett, 1998; Ross & Gray, 2005).

Of the school-based issues relating to non-attendance, relationships with teachers and teachers' cultural understanding of Aboriginal pupils are crucial issues.

Literacy

The critical nature of the lower level of literacy achievement for Aboriginal students was highlighted by the findings of the 1999

Year 3 Reading National Benchmark results (Australian Bureau of Statistics, 2002). Although there is an increasing improvement in reading achievement in the last decade, in 2011 a third of the Aboriginal Year 5 and Year 9 students do not meet the national standard in reading. The data in Table 6 below shows the continued discrepancy between aboriginal children's literacy levels and those of non-Aboriginal children of the same age.

Table 9.6 – Students at or above national minimum standards for reading, 2009

Year Group	Aboriginal %	non-Aboriginal %
Year 3	75	95
Year 5	67	93
Year 7	73	95
Year 9	67	94

Informed by: MCEECDYA (2009) National Assessment Program, cited in the Closing the Gap Prime Minister's Report (2011)

The impact of the differing levels of literacy on student self-confidence and teachers' perceptions of Aboriginal student potential were key issues broached by Aboriginal students interviewed in a study of alienation from school (Gray & Beresford, 2001). Students expressed their disillusionment in the following ways:

I can't read the stuff. I feel stupid.

Some teachers told me I was too dumb to do TEE. They didn't think I'd finish it and get in. It made me feel dumb.

The critical impact of levels of literacy on an Indigenous student's decision-making processes related to returning to school and remaining at school was further evidenced in Gray & Hackling's (2009) study of senior students' rationale for remaining at school. Earlier, Gray (2000) found that literacy was a significant factor for chronic truancy and behaviour problems leading to suspension among Aboriginal students. For example, an Aboriginal educator involved in the study expressed her concern at the number of students who still could not read when they started secondary school: 'I don't know how many kids have got to Year 8 still reading at Year 3 to 5 level, if they're lucky. They just can't read' (Aboriginal Educator, 1999). Addressing the diverse literacy needs of illiterate adolescent Aboriginal students is a resource and pedagogical challenge for most secondary schools.

Teacher–student relationships

The absence of effective relationships between teachers and Aboriginal students can also be a crucial determining factor behind patterns of non-attendance. Yet, it is not a simple matter for teachers to establish effective relationships. Students may have had a range of unsuccessful relationships with white people, including teachers. Moreover: 'trust, understanding and support are linked in a complex manner over an extended period to accomplish sound relationships' (Harslett, et al., 1999, p. 5). These problems were demonstrated in the following unpublished transcript that was part of the data used to prepare a journal article (Partington and McCudden, 1990).

A Year 5 teacher arranged her class in groups. There was one group of six children at the front of the room, another of five children alongside them. At the back of the room was a group of four boys. Another three groups made up the class. When the teacher worked with the children in the front group, she was encouraging, supportive. When one girl had a problem, we observed the teacher kneeling down alongside her, taking her pen and demonstrating the answer:

> This is 5, should be here, 10 should be the second one. Yes I think you'd better make your amounts up there, Penny. Put the number right next to the dash so that you know. Otherwise it's going to be very hard to work out where the graph goes up to. OK so the first one is, 5 should be here, 10, 15, 20, 25, 30, 40. Keep going up like that.

This teacher was obviously helpful, pleasant, patient, nurturing. She explained clearly and demonstrated the results she wanted from the exercise. Later, the teacher went to the group at the back of the class, who, we observed, had been working quietly. Here, she stood hands on hips, a metre away from the boys. She glared at them and after briefly observing their work, said tersely, 'Quickly. Hurry up. 30, that's 32, so it's just 2 more. Alright?' and after observing them for a few seconds, stated, 'Next one', with no praise or comment.

The contrast in the teacher's treatment of the students in the two groups was startling. The child in the first group, an Anglo-Australian child with long blonde hair and blue eyes (all the students in the front group were Anglo-Australians) clearly had a good relationship with the teacher. The children in the back group didn't. They consisted of two Aboriginal and two Anglo-Australian children. Judging by the appearance of their clothing, the back children were much poorer than those in the front.

For students to want to come to school, they must feel a sense of belonging and empowerment. Skill development, particularly literacy and numeracy, are essential to this but also the social relationships they form within the school are important. In particular, they need to be able to work with their teachers. The teachers control students' access to positive relationships with them. Students are at a disadvantage in terms of status and knowledge when it comes to adjusting to school: they cannot force teachers to adopt ways with which they are familiar, and they lack the knowledge required to adjust to school without support.

It is a mistake to assume that Indigenous students will just fit into the social life of the school without some concessions to their particular individual, social, cultural and linguistic requirements. While some urban Indigenous students will fit in with few differences from the non-Indigenous students, others will experience considerable difficulties as a result of social processes embedded in schooling. For these students, the school is an alien and threatening environment and successful adjustment to the school requires understanding and support on the part of the teacher.

Teachers are often the first non-Indigenous people that Indigenous children come into close and regular contact with and, as such, they need to ensure painless access to school. Good relationships built from the first day the students come to school are essential and should extend to relationships with parents and the community as well if students are to feel comfortable in the classroom.

Aboriginal student perceptions of school

If we had observed the teacher only with the first group, we would have said she was a good teacher. If we had seen the teacher only with the second group, we would have said she was a bad teacher. So what sort of teacher is she? In fact, she is probably a pretty normal kind of teacher who, in working with the students in her class, develops reciprocal relationships (Partington & McCudden, 1990) so that with some students she is able to engage in mutually rewarding interactions while with other students she becomes antagonistic and remote.

If we are to explore the factors that contribute to the acquisition of learning among students, and especially Indigenous students, we need to take account of the diverse responses of the teacher. The discourse, or language of interaction, that took place in the two events clearly demonstrated to the students where they stood in the scheme of things.

Students do not operate in a social vacuum in the classroom. They hear what is going on around them. They know when they are being treated differently by the teacher. So what does Penny know about the teacher and herself? That the teacher likes her, that the teacher is helpful and puts her on the right track, and given the frequent praise she received, that she is a bright girl. The boys, however, learn that the teacher doesn't like them as much as she likes other students; that they are not very bright, that they are not very good at maths. Let us be quite clear that we are not just talking about relationships here.

We are talking about student self-image, perceptions of ability, teacher help, and the building of a positive attitude to school and subject matter. This latter group would hear and see what the teacher does with other students, and would resent the different way they are treated, seeing it as discriminatory and unfair. So they would form negative perceptions of the situation they are in and this would probably lead to the kind of resistance Geoff Munns reports from his research (Munns & McFadden, 2000). Older students often choose to leave school rather than put up with these kinds of conditions.

In an extensive study of Indigenous students' perceptions of schooling, Godfrey, et al., (2001, p. 10) reported that the students held low opinions of their teachers:

> Seventy three per cent of students believe that their 'teacher/s always help/s me' and report the same result for 'most of my teachers understand me'. This is clearly a positive result but other results are of deep concern. Alarmingly, 42 per cent of students report that they do not like their teacher, 37 per cent strongly disagree-disagree that 'my teacher cares what happens to me', and 39 per cent strongly disagree-disagree that 'most teachers at this school care about me'. Twenty per cent of the respondents strongly agree-agree that 'teacher(s) pick on me at school' and 12 per cent believe that 'the teachers gang up on me'.

These results are disappointing but indicate that many Indigenous students believe their teachers do not support them. In the same survey, Godfrey, et al., (2001) reported that 82 per cent of students indicated that they respected their teachers, even though many believed they receive poor treatment from their teachers.

Research by Partington, Godfrey and Richer (2001) supports the above observation. A student, whom we'll name 'Robyn', observed the following:

> I don't like Miss Cane. She gets on my nerves. She's always on you for something that [she says] you do. If someone throws a ball on the roof, she blames us. She jumps to conclusions. I don't like it. She gets on better with the Wadjilla [non-Indigenous] kids. She talks to them like they're her sisters and brothers. She talks to us really differently.

How do you get on with other teachers?
Miss Walton sometimes has pets. The student counsellors. They think they can put something over us. Can boss us around. They get it first. If you want to do something for the teacher they are there first.

What sort of students do teachers like most?
Students who dress and act intelligent. That's what teachers like most and if they're not like that they don't recognise them as much as the other students. Ms Walton gives jobs to them all the time. Mr Blair puts us in the picture. He is good with all students who don't get enough attention like Sandy and Andrew. He picks up bad things the student counsellors do, not like Ms Walton or Miss Cane. As soon as we

do something wrong they jump on us. (Partington, Godfrey & Richer, 2001).

The students were aware not only of their own position in the classroom but also that of other students, particularly the two weakest students, Sandy and Andrew, and they resented the neglect these students received at the hands of some of their teachers. They were able to construct theories to explain why they are unsuccessful in gaining the teachers' attention, and so Robyn built a theory based on social class and behaviour: students who dress and act intelligent. It is clear from her comments that she is not arguing a case for a merit-based system. Instead, she sees the favoured students receiving those favours because they know how to 'act intelligently', to dress appropriately, to speak to the teacher, to get in first.

This is not a hidden process that takes place without the awareness of the participants. Students like Robyn saw what was going on. Imagine the consequences for their academic self-esteem, for their relationship with the teacher, and their relationships with the other students. It is not surprising that Aboriginal retention rates are much less than non-Aboriginal rates. In Western Australia, for example, only 37.5 per cent of Aboriginal students in Year 8 in 2004 completed Year 12 five years later, in 2009 (Department of Education, 2010). In contrast, non-Aboriginal student retention for the period was 66 per cent.

If Indigenous students are to progress to higher levels of learning, they must acquire the skills and knowledge that the school has to offer. At present, for too many, the knowledge that is imparted is that they are second-class citizens in the school context. It is important that this message is changed and that the students achieve success so that they are empowered to succeed later in life and lose their reliance on state-controlled support services.

Improving attendance

Schools that demonstrate consistent improvements in Indigenous student attendance over time are likely to approach the issue as one part of a holistic change in school structures and processes. (Bourke, et al., 2000) identified a set of principles underlying such approaches, these included factors related to teacher professional learning on topics such as students' history, culture, contemporary lifestyle and diversity of languages; ensuring effective classroom discourse to minimise miscommunication; acquisition of literacy skills; Indigenous presence in the school so that Indigenous people are involved 'in all aspects of the schooling process from initial planning to implementation and delivery of programs to develop Indigenous ownership of educational programs' (p. 48); and empowerment of students.

Similar factors were evident in a study of a range of schools by the report on Indigenous education in New South Wales (New South Wales Aboriginal Education Consultative Group Incorporated and New South Wales Department of Education and Training, 2004). The report noted the importance of factors identified by Masters (2004):

- strong, effective school leaders whose primary focus is on establishing a culture of learning throughout the school
- learning being seen as the central purpose of school and taking precedence over everything else

- teachers with a thorough and up-to-date knowledge of their subjects and a deep understanding of how students learn particular subjects
- students with a sense of belonging and pride
- well-developed systems for evaluating and monitoring student performance
- high levels of parent and community involvement.

Additional factors were identified through a field trip to successful schools:

- a high priority for and whole school approach to Aboriginal education
- a principal and executive team committed to meeting the needs of students, teachers and parents
- Aboriginal community involvement in the planning and implementation of programs
- Aboriginal people employed as part of whole school literacy, numeracy, attendance or retention programs
- high expectations for Aboriginal student achievement
- teaching and learning programs and support programs that were well structured, highly organised and properly resourced
- teachers who knew their Aboriginal students and could make connections between school knowledge and the lived experiences of all their students
- explicit and rigorous teaching and learning programs that ensure engaged learning time for all Aboriginal students
- focused teaching that included a range of classroom practices and strategies in response to the needs of Aboriginal students

- positive whole school/whole community student welfare programs.

The report noted that:

> Schools that are making a difference for Aboriginal students identified their priority as student achievement by focusing on effective teaching and learning rather than student welfare programs and program funding. These schools typically demonstrated real partnerships with their local Aboriginal community based on shared responsibilities and positive relationships (2004, p. 87).

These principles were evident in prior work by Chris Sarra at Cherbourg School, where indicators of achievement, self-concept and attendance increased enormously as a result of the changes he instituted (Sarra, 2005). He addressed issues related to teacher effectiveness, parent and community support, student self-esteem and school curriculum. In consequence of this, within a short time attendance rates came to equal or better those of schools with predominantly non-Indigenous students. Utilising the strategies promoted by Sarra, Douglas (2009), working in a school similar to Cherbourg, improved student attendance from 30 per cent in 2002 to 87 per cent in 2004. The strategies employed in both cases involved the whole school and the community, and resulted in improvements not only to attendance but also student achievement and self-concept as well as teacher satisfaction.

In Western Australia, the Happy Kids program has utilised

similar strategies to engage Indigenous and non-Indigenous students at risk of dropping out of school. The goal of the program was to prepare Year 6 and 7 students for life in high school by building up their confidence and social skills. Key elements are the development of goal-setting skills, a sense of belonging and pride in their school, the involvement of Aboriginal people, particularly the school AIEOs, and a part-time coordinator who mentored and supported the students. Attendance of students in the most effective programs were above state attendance norms. Key features of successful programs include stability of coordinators, the commitment of teachers and school administration to the program, a clear focus on goals, effective implementation of the strategies and stability of coordinators and involvement of Aboriginal people (Partington, et al., forthcoming).

Conclusion

Despite increased enrolments in schools, Aboriginal retention and participation rates are falling (Australian Bureau of Statistics, 2006d, b). The long-term social consequences of alienation from schooling among Aboriginal young people cannot be ignored. Educational outcomes for Aboriginal students remain significantly different from non-Aboriginal students, particularly in literacy. Fewer than 20 per cent of Aboriginal students meet the reading standards and only 30 per cent meet the writing standards (Australian Bureau of Statistics, 2006b).

There are now clearly identified factors which assist children to remain engaged in regular schooling (Ross & Gray, 2005; Gray & Hackling, 2009; Purdie & Buckley, 2010). Relationships between children, their family, their community and their school are paramount to providing resilience and cultural understanding. Relevant and flexible curriculum and pedagogy constructed to respect the diverse learning needs of Aboriginal young people will increase the potential for students to remain linked to educational institutions.

The complexity of the barriers to achievement for these young people, however, is demonstrable. As outlined in earlier chapters, for many children, the nature of their extended family environment can compound the school-level misunderstanding of the cultural, social and environmental factors complicating regular patterns of school attendance and achievement. For many Aboriginal boys, the challenge of active participation in school expectations becomes a behaviour management hurdle with social exclusion consequences.

The wide range of 'outside' school factors impacting on Aboriginal alienation from school suggests the need for much stronger partnerships to be developed between service providers, to provide a safety net for early intervention to address underlying social issues inhibiting Aboriginal participation and achievement at school. To achieve such an equitable outcome for most Aboriginal students will take considerable rethinking of support mechanisms, school-based practice and coordination of existing services. Although there has been an enormous improvement in equitable access to, and participation in, education and training for Aboriginal students in the last decade (Robinson & Bamblett, 1998; Gray & Beresford, 2008), such opportunities are still not within the experience of most Aboriginal students.

10

FROM THE BIG PICTURE TO THE INDIVIDUAL STUDENT: THE IMPORTANCE OF THE CLASSROOM RELATIONSHIP

Matt Byrne and Geoff Munns

Introduction

If you could give one piece of advice to someone who was going to teach Aboriginal students, what would it be?

This question was posed to a group of teachers working in an urban school with a majority Aboriginal student population (Byrne, 2009). In each of their responses it was not long until the word 'relationship' was used. Teachers who have worked effectively with Aboriginal children know how important the development of positive relationships is to their learning (Doyle & Hill, 2008). Building a strong relationship with Aboriginal learners is arguably one of the most fundamental responsibilities a teacher has in the classroom (Docket, Perry & Kearney, 2010). In this chapter we propose that productive relationships between teachers and Aboriginal learners need to operate at two interrelated levels. The first is a 'big picture' socio-cultural curriculum relationship. In this chapter this level of relationship is outlined and illustrated in the REAP (respect, ears, attitude, personalise) framework. The second picture is the pedagogical relationship, produced in the verbal, written and symbolic classroom interactions between teachers and students. The second section of the chapter picks up this relationship through pedagogical case studies of two teachers utilising the Fair Go project's student engagement framework. In presenting these illustrative frameworks, we want to suggest that both these relationships need to operate productively and synergistically to maximise the learning outcomes for Aboriginal students.

The REAP framework

The REAP framework has been developed from a culmination of professional and personal experiences in the classroom over a number of years. Graeme Gower (Kurongkurl Katitjin, Centre for Indigenous Australian Education and Research, Edith Cowan University) was consulted in the development of the REAP framework and acknowledgement needs to be given to his role in helping to refine it. The REAP framework has been used extensively in the professional development of teachers and with a range of professionals from other sectors. It will be illustrated by research data from three research studies, namely *The Challenges Teachers Face When Working in a Low-Socio-economic Primary School* (Byrne, 2009), the *Keeping Kids on Track* (forthcoming) and the *Review of the Aboriginal and Islander Education Officer Program* (Gower, Partington, Byrne, Galloway, Weissofner, Ferguson & Kirov, 2010).

REAP (Figure 10.1) has four interrelated key elements: respect, ears, attitude and personalise. Each element provides insights into the complexity of the socio-cultural relationships of Aboriginal students and their teachers. It is important to acknowledge that a classroom does not operate in isolation from the wider political and educational systems, the school as a structural institution and the daily happenings in the local community.

Figure 10.1 – The REAP framework

What follows are explanations and illustrations of the four key elements of REAP.

Respect

Respect and reconciliation are interdependent components of relationships between Aboriginal and non-Aboriginal Australians. According to Reconciliation Australia, reconciliation 'involves building mutually respectful relationships between Indigenous and other Australians that allow us to work together to solve problems and generate success that is in everyone's best interests' (Reconciliation Australia, 2011). For teachers, it is imperative to build mutually respectful relationships in the classroom. A key question for teachers to ask themselves when making important decisions about classroom practice is, 'Will this build respect?'

Some suggested ways to build respect in the classroom are:

Show genuine care for students as people and learners
A supportive learning environment where students have a voice and feel they are active contributors to classroom learning helps to build respect and foster positive relationships in the classroom (Purdie & Buckley, 2010). Showing genuine care for students can often be seen as the common ground that links the classroom to the community and parents. Caring for students can be the bridge that facilitates the development of positive relationships and strong ties between the home and the classroom that are essential to Aboriginal students' achievement.

Try to understand before reacting
Teachers can often make the mistake of jumping to conclusions and making negative judgements about Aboriginal students and their families, without first taking the time to explore any background information that may be relevant. The following account by a new teacher in a remote Aboriginal community highlights the importance of trying to understand a situation in the classroom before reacting.

I had been in the school for nearly six months and was slowly finding my feet. Next week was my first ever parent teacher night and I had lots of good ideas and was going to wow my parents with the students' work. I spent hours with my students and the Aboriginal support teacher putting up work around the class, finishing off their portfolios and making sure everything was in its place. As the big night drew closer I was extremely proud of my students and the work they had done, and with myself for organising it all. All that was left now was for their parents to come and enjoy it! This was going to be huge!

The big night arrived. All was ready and I was still nervous but really excited to see what the parents would think. I had been down to the community to personally invite the parents with the principal, as had the Aboriginal teacher. A whole hour passed and still no sign of any parents. My excitement was turning to disappointment. After a couple of hours it was all over and not one parent had come. My disappointment turned into sadness and then frustration and anger. The principal walked into the room and I proceeded to vent my frustration after he enquired how I was. I remember saying things such as. 'What is the point of being here? The parents don't care about their children's learning so why should I? What a waste of everyone's time!' But as it turned out, I had a lot to learn.

The next day I was making my preparations for the day and the principal wandered in for a chat. I had felt pretty bad about some of the things I had said so I thought I would get in early and apologise. Lucky for me I had an understanding principal who knew he was dealing with a very enthusiastic and passionate young teacher, but one who was also very green. He started to talk to me about the reasons why my parents may not have come, other than the ones I had expressed the night before. I remember trying to think of some, but couldn't. As it turned out, there had been some urgent cultural business the community had to attend to which explained their absence. Suddenly everything made sense and from that moment on I always tried to understand a situation before reacting (Byrne, personal experience).

Value student experiences, background and culture

Aboriginal students' life experiences, background and culture may be very different to that of their classroom teacher. It is important that teachers do not perceive this difference as a deficit. A common response to difference is to withdraw. Misunderstandings that can evolve from these differences can block the establishment of positive relationships in the classroom. By building on students' experience and background and by incorporating Aboriginal culture into classroom life, teachers can demonstrate that they really value their students and build respect. There is a great diversity of Aboriginal culture across Australia. Many teachers make the mistake of thinking all Aboriginal people are the same and thus do not take the time to understand the local Aboriginal community context of the classroom and school in which they work. An understanding of this local cultural context and local area can help to inform effective practice in the classroom.

Acknowledge mistakes and encourage risk-taking

Research shows that the teacher being able to model risk taking can have a powerful impact on students' willingness and ability to engage with the learning experiences in the classroom. In the *Keeping Kids on Track* research (forthcoming) significant numbers of students mentioned teachers who encouraged risk-taking (having a go) as an important aspect of classroom learning. As one student commented, '*It's good for other people who haven't done these things. Before, some people were too scared. But now we say come on everyone's doing it. We encourage each other to take risks.*' Teachers confirmed the importance of encouraging risk-taking:

> *A key component was to encourage students to take risks and explore concepts outside their comfort zone...access to appropriate role models from a variety of different fields who have promoted self-esteem and risk taking behaviours...allow students to develop their self-confidence and complete activities outside their comfort zone.*

A key element of many important professional learning experiences is taking the time as the teacher to listen to and learn from other people in a number of ways.

Use your ears! Do a lot of listening and learning

The importance of listening is illustrated in the sequel to the earlier narrative about the parent teacher night.

After talking to the principal some more in the coming days I packed up my students' portfolios and headed down to the community for my parent meetings. It was like no parent teacher meeting I had ever heard about. I sat in a circle with about fifteen parents and a couple of the local elders and chairman (head elder) of the community on the grass under a tree. My moment had come, and I didn't waste any time in letting them know about how their children were going and what they needed to do and know about their children's education, because I was the teacher. I must have rattled on for over half an hour when the chairman of the community started to play with his ear. I noticed it out of the corner of my eye but was on a roll so tried not to notice. But after a while it really began to bug me. Why is he doing that? Then it suddenly dawned on me. Maybe it is time to stop? So I wound up and then looked at the chairman. I will never forget what he said next. 'Mr Byrne, you are listening to us, but you are not hearing us.' For the next three and a half hours he and the rest of the group began to share their experiences of schooling and what they wanted for their children at school and at home. It was my turn to be educated. My approach to education was never the same after that. I now had a chance of doing a good job because I heard what they were saying and was determined to do something about it (Byrne, personal experience).

Ask questions and be prepared to listen and to act

Many Aboriginal students are used to teachers promising the world and delivering nothing. Consistency of teacher actions and following through on promises are important ingredients to a successful classroom. Depending on the cultural context, asking direct questions of individual students in the classroom can be problematic until a positive relationship has been built with students. Often teachers are better off asking questions to the class in general and 'yarning' with the students as individuals and groups of students can then choose to respond as they wish. Valuable social and academic information can be gained from such conversations and can be used to inform future classroom practice.

You don't know it all

As seen in the story above, for early career teachers it is a fine line between having confidence in what you are doing, 'backing yourself', and obstinately sticking to 'my way is the best way' as there couldn't possibly be any other way of doing it. Learning on the job is an integral skill for successful classroom practice. The two examples below highlight how insights into working with Aboriginal students in the classroom can often be subtle and take time to develop.

Try to understand cultural responses to classrooms

There are many challenges teachers face when working in low socio-economic status (SES) schools and it is important for teachers to view these challenges as positive ways to develop themselves professionally. The following research data offers insights into the subtle differences that can arise between the learning and engagement of Aboriginal and non-Aboriginal students (Byrne, 2009).

Journal Entry 1

A number of the students were again going on walk about from their chairs and wandering around the classroom. It is mainly the Aboriginal students who are constantly up and out of their chairs.

(For the first time in this session the realisation came that it was predominantly Aboriginal students who were constantly out of their chairs and walking around the room interacting with their peers. This behaviour may be the result of work avoidance or could be more strongly related to the students' culture and be a sign of learning in community).

Journal Entry 2

Danny, Ralph, Felix, Lucelle and Lavinia were all constantly either out of their chairs or turning around talking to other students behind them. Danny and Heath would walk up to Bill to ask their questions rather than putting their hand up at their desk which Bill reminded them they needed to do.

(Observing a number of the Aboriginal students in this session again highlighted for me the notion of 'affirmation learning' and the need of peer and teacher affirmation in what they were doing. From these journal entries the term 'affirmation learning' was coined to describe the behaviour of Aboriginal students who constantly got out of their chairs to wander around the room and interact with other students and the teacher).

There was a strong indication that what was described as affirmation learning was tied to many Aboriginal students' apparent need for teacher, peer and student affirmation and a sense that this was linked to Aboriginal students learning better in community rather than isolation. Many of the teachers made the comment about how many of their Aboriginal students were often found out of their desks, wandering around the room, or out of class. Students who are constantly out of their chairs were described as being harder to manage, as they seemed to pose a distraction to other students and the class, and could interrupt the teacher's instructional time. Another way to view this behaviour is to see the cultural implications that may be tied to the students' behaviour and a lack of awareness on the teacher's part to pick up on these implications. Rather than blame students, teachers might have greater success developing strategies to harness Aboriginal students' cultural ways of learning by adapting their classroom practice to incorporate and affirm students' desire to learn within a community rather than in isolation.

Eliminate racism and discrimination in the classroom

The same research identified instances where Aboriginal students had experienced racism and racial discrimination in the wider community. Systemic racism experienced by Aboriginal students both in school and the wider community can act as a barrier to their educational success (Plevitz, 2007) and has been identified as a major factor contributing to Aboriginal students leaving school (Malin & Maidment, 2003; Beresford & Partington, 2003; Gray & Beresford, 2008). The following interview with a principal captures the impact of racism on students:

> When they [Aboriginal students] go to the shops, they're certainly viewed very differently. Yeah, they tell me stories where they're certainly racially vilified outside of school. I know that some of the kids are told that they can't take their bags inside and they've noticed that other kids are allowed to get away with it and they sort of pick up that being Aboriginal is viewed very differently, like you're going to steal stuff, like you're going to hurt someone. Some of the bigger boys, they tell me that they're looked at quite suspiciously when they're

walking around like they're going to cause some trouble like they're in a gang.

The principal went on to relay a conversation he had with a female Aboriginal student. The principal inquired into how she was feeling, as he had noticed she was a 'bit down'. The student responded questioning why she had to leave her bag at the front of the local deli and the other kids didn't have to. She went on to say that she wasn't going to steal anything, and that it wasn't fair that she had to leave her bag at the front just because she was Aboriginal. The school principal explained how he was initially lost for words before talking with Crystal about the injustice of the situation. The principal wondered how to respond. The incident highlights how important it is for teachers to consider how to respond to such questions. Furthermore, it is critical to ensure that racism in the classroom is constructively addressed so that it is not a barrier to Aboriginal students learning and engaging in the classroom. There is also an imperative for teachers to develop strong relationships with their students so they too can cue in to when students are a 'bit down' and then be in a better position to support their Aboriginal students' learning.

Attitude

The importance of having positive attitudes to all aspects of classroom life cannot be understated.

Attitude is everything

The attitude of the teacher often makes the most lasting impression on students, and first impressions are often what count. When remembering positive teachers, many people put it down to their positive attitude, their smile, their encouragement and how they always tried to help and support learners in the classroom.

Remain positive and monitor your emotional well-being

Teaching is invariably seen as an emotional process in which teachers need to 'manage, monitor and regulate their emotions to achieve teaching effectiveness and create a positive learning environment' (Zang & Zhu, 2008, p. 106). Research into teachers' challenges in schools with Aboriginal students (Byrne, 2009), found that the welfare roles often appeared more pronounced, and positive student and teacher relationships required a lot more time and effort to establish. Consequently, there can be significant social-emotional implications for teachers when working with Aboriginal students in the classroom. It is really important that teachers, especially early-career teachers, develop strategies to handle their emotional pressures. Talking with trusted colleagues, friends and family and having outlets and interests outside of the school were found to be good strategies in contributing to positive teacher, social and emotional well being in the classroom. Note that we also strongly recognise that there are tremendous emotional 'highs' that many teachers experience when they develop positive relationships with Aboriginal students.

Get and keep a sense of humour

Humour is often used by Aboriginal students and families as a way of connecting. Having a sense of humour in the classroom can help to make positive connections with students and their families. An important lesson for teachers is not to take themselves too seriously and to be prepared to have a laugh and be made fun of.

An attitude of reflective practice

The following recommendations came from research conducted by Byrne (2009) that recognised the importance of reflective practice for teachers who work with Aboriginal students:

- Teachers who primarily work with students from disadvantaged and diverse cultural backgrounds should engage in a process of reflection that considers the unique challenges this context presents. Where possible these challenges should be viewed as positive opportunities for professional development.
- To facilitate this process, schools need to find creative ways to build time for reflection into the school timetable, so as not to add to the already burdensome workload of teachers.

Reflection among research participants was seen to be a critical tool for identifying and monitoring challenges and helped to identify ways in dealing with them effectively. A teacher illustrated this point in the comment below:

> *Well basically having the journal's been good 'cause I can look back and see the steps. Like just before I handed it to you I looked back at week one and went wow, that was a challenge for me and now it's not quite so a challenge so it's been good for that.* (Byrne, 2009, p. 332).

Personalise

The last element of the REAP frame is Personalise. Central to this element is the notion of matching learning and teaching in the classroom to the needs of the students. The following ideas further explain this element.

Know your students and community

Knowing the students in the classroom enables teachers to be in an informed position to foster their learning in the classroom. Aboriginal students are very aware of the nature of the learning experiences offered them (Munns, Martin & Craven, 2008). Learning experiences in the classroom need to be well planned and take into consideration students' academic levels (foster higher-order thinking and be challenging), learning styles and rate of learning. Learning needs to be multi-model, meaning-ful and relevant to real life and incorporate group as well as individual work. These approaches are consistent with research into what makes a difference in classrooms, such as *authentic instruction* (Newmann, 1996) and *productive pedagogies* (Hayes, Mills, Christie & Lingard, 2006).

Importance of own space

For many Aboriginal students (especially older students) having a 'place' in the classroom that they can call their own and where they can store their school and personal things is very important. This helps to facilitate a sense of belonging in the classroom. Students who have a space (e.g. big drawer, cupboard space, shelf, storage box) in the class are more easily settled back into classroom life when they have been away as is sometimes the case with community business.

Working effectively with Aboriginal support workers

When resources are available to fund them, Aboriginal support staff can be an integral part of the classroom. Recent reviews in Australia (Gower, Partington, Byrne, Galloway, Weissofner, Ferguson & Kirov, 2010) identified four main ways to work effectively with students. These are:

1. They provide encouragement by:
   - building the students' confidence by working alongside them and encouraging them
   - ensuring a balanced view is held of students in the class.
2. They are strong supporters of education through:
   - being a strong advocate for education and encouraging students to attend regularly and strive for success
   - supporting student attendance
3. They mentor students
4. They provide classroom support.

The importance of their contribution to Aboriginal Education in Australia cannot be overstated and a focus on their work is a fitting place to finalise the discussion of the socio-cultural relationship.

Summary

We have presented the REAP framework as a way of highlighting the importance of the socio-cultural relationship between Aboriginal students and their teachers. As mentioned in the introduction, we see this 'big picture' view as one part of the overall relationship that is critical for engaged and enhanced academic outcomes. This chapter now turns to the pedagogical view to complete the picture.

Understanding the pedagogical relationship: teacher case studies

The previous section highlighted the importance of the relationship between teachers and Aboriginal students in the development of productive classroom practices. Using the REAP framework, it was suggested that teachers need to understand that classrooms are strongly impacted by the intersecting social, cultural and historical experiences of the adults and children within their communities. It is also worth remembering that what happens in schools and classrooms almost always affects the lives of local people, and this is particularly the case among Aboriginal people. The framework also pointed to a number of salient ways that teachers could strengthen their relationships with Aboriginal students. These are important principles underpinning a 'big picture' view of curriculum, often described as 'the dynamic relationship between teachers and pupils which reflects the social context in which the curriculum is constructed' (Grundy, 1994, pp. 27–39). In this section we invite you to hold these principles, and this view of curriculum together, as we get closer to the classroom practices of teachers. It is to the pedagogical relationship that this chapter now turns.

There are two main parts to this section. The first is the introduction of a research framework that has been developed to explain the pedagogical relationship between teachers and their students, particularly those from low SES backgrounds. The second is to use this framework to present case studies of two teachers who demonstrate 'exemplary' classroom practices for learners.

320

The *Fair Go Project* student engagement framework

The framework used to describe and analyse the pedagogical relationship has been developed in the *Fair Go Project*. This project has a particular focus on student engagement and low SES students and, in some of the schools where the research has been conducted, Aboriginal learners have been a significant part of the school population. There are good reasons to consider ways that teachers can enhance student engagement among Aboriginal students. First, there are strong correlations between engaged students and enhanced academic outcomes (Fredricks, Blumenfeld & Paris, 2004). Second, to generalise across Aboriginal students, they have historically not had the same emotional attachment and commitment to Western forms of education as students from other social and cultural backgrounds. In short, as a group, they have not gone the same educational distances physically (retention to higher levels), academically (results leading to further studies and/or opportunity) or emotionally (seeing schools as places that work for them).

The student engagement framework has a number of key ideas that can be examined in greater detail in Fair Go Team (2006) and Munns (2007). For the purposes of this chapter, there is a focus on the ways that engagement is influenced by the messages students receive in their classrooms. The work of Bernstein (1996) is used here. Bernstein argued that classrooms deliver powerful messages to students through their curriculum, pedagogy and assessment practices. These messages help shape individuals' perceptions of what they might do now and in the future, and what they might become when they leave school. In this way schools and classrooms operate to structure the consciousness of students (McFadden & Munns, 2002). Educators familiar with schools serving low SES and Aboriginal communities will no doubt recognise that students have historically received disengaging messages and that classroom practices are strongly implicated in this. Research has shown when classrooms are characterised by a conservative and controlling pedagogy that delivers low levels of de-contextualised learning (Johnston, 1990; Rowe, 2003; Hayes, et al., 2006), students soon learn that they are lacking in ability (Mills & Gale, 2002; Hayes, 2003), have no voice (McFadden & Munns, 2002), are not valued (Knight, 2002) and are compelled either to accept or to struggle over the classroom spaces (Comber & Thomson, 2001). On the other hand, the research of the *Fair Go Project* has shown that classroom messages can be engaging for students when the experiences and processes are shaped in particular directions. Put simply, when teachers design intellectually stimulating and interesting learning experiences and develop processes that build strong learning communities, then classrooms can be places where students are challenged and engaged, and are given opportunities to become more successful learners. The Fair Go pedagogy directly targets the messages that students receive in their classrooms. The following table (Table 10.1) shows that these messages are organised into five interrelated 'discourses of power' (knowledge, ability, control, place and voice).

Table 10.1 – Engaging messages for low SES students

knowledge	'We can see the connection and the meaning' – reflectively constructed access to contextualised and powerful knowledge
ability	'I am capable' – feelings of being able to achieve and a spiral of high expectations and aspirations

control	'We do this together' – sharing of classroom time and space: interdependence, mutuality and power
place	'It's great to be a kid from' – valued as individual and learner and feelings of belonging and ownership over learning
voice	'We share' – environment of discussion and reflection about learning with students and teachers playing reciprocal meaningful roles

Using the *Fair Go Project* student engagement framework to understand classrooms

The student engagement framework was most recently employed as an observation and analytical instrument in extensive case study research of thirty 'exemplary' teachers of students in poverty. The teachers were selected because they engaged their students in learning and so opened up increased possibilities for future educational success. In short, the project wanted to document and analyse the pedagogies of teachers whose students got up every school day and couldn't wait to get into their classrooms. Data were collected through observations and interviews with teachers and students. What follows are the classroom stories of two of these teachers. Sonia teaches Years 2/3/4 in a central school (Kindergarten to Year 12) in far western rural NSW, with a majority population of Aboriginal students. Nicole is an Aboriginal woman who teaches a 3/4/5 class in a primary school in Sydney's outer urban suburbs. This school has a 10 per cent Aboriginal student population.

Sonia

I talked with the kids about how they wanted to learn, and gave the kids a sense of ownership and safety in their classroom environment and they thrived, loved it. It was important for the classroom to be a fun place with laughter.'

Sonia's classroom makes learning a priority business. While it is characterised by strong intellectual quality, student choice and self-regulation, it is also a place for humour, fun and enjoyment. Student engagement is promoted in a number of ways. Learning is negotiated and is frequently the focus of classroom discussions. Goal setting, reflection and self-assessment are advanced so that students can feel good about themselves as learners and 'think hard'. There are high expectations and students are continually inspired to extend themselves. Authentic tasks help students connect the classroom with their own lives.

The student engagement framework shows how Sonia's pedagogy works across productively across the five discourses of power.

Knowledge

Sonia draws on students' funds of knowledge, relating familiar terms and words to the students' experiences and knowledge as a means of explanation and extended learning. In this way, students are helped to see the connections between what they know and what they are learning. This is developed in the classroom as a communal responsibility and students are expected to share and help each other out. Strong connections are established with Aboriginal ways of learning and it is continually reinforced in classroom conversations about learning: *'Isaac, this is Mr Shay* (fellow student), *he's going to be your new teacher. He's going to show you how to use this.'* Regular mathematics workshops are a good example of these processes. The focus is on practical hands-on activities that help refine understandings while providing students with opportunities to think and reflect on new learning. There is a tenor that invites responsibility in and maturity for learning. '*If you are in Year 2, I'm running a workshop out front. It will help you with ordering and estimating. It's the only time I'm offering this workshop. You'll need this as a prerequisite…*' As a student notes, '*We had workshop after workshop. We got it after that.*

Ability

Observations in Sonia's class clearly indicate that this is a consciously crafted learning community. Conversations about her approaches to teaching show a complete lack of deficit thinking, and you could almost be forgiven for thinking that this was a classroom in a more privileged area. All students' strengths and contributions are identified and accepted. Engagement is strengthened in processes that emphasise mastery, resilience and perseverance: '*I liked the way you stopped and thought about it, you just didn't stop.*' Combinations of workshops and whole class sessions work through negotiated, collaborative and problem-based learning. Workshop groups are fluid with students able to elect which one they need in consideration of their own learning needs. Students are able to self evaluate their tasks on completion using individual rubrics. Sonia connects with their culture by reminding them they are elders in the school. '*You shouldn't be shamed, but feel proud. Feel deadly.*' The pedagogy is both explicit and student-centred: explicit teaching and clear demonstration of core knowledge and meta-language for each lesson opens up opportunities for students to think, review and evaluate the central ideas. Visual learning journeys help students reflect on what they know and what are the next learning steps.

Control

This has been a long project in the class but one focused on learning and enjoyment. From the outset Sonia was determined not to just survive but to make a difference, and this meant changing the classroom culture: '...*seeing the students laughing and wanting to come to school.*' At first she found the students difficult and disengaged and she had to work hard to show students that their classroom was a safe and supportive environment. This means establishing learning as the core business. Praise and feedback is focused on learning, and persistence is rewarded: '*You guys are awesome...you finished in record time.*' When behaviour issues arise, they are rephrased around learning over compliance. Much time is allocated to addressing learning issues with individual students to build their confidence. At the same time, all students are provided with opportunities to self regulate their behaviour. When issues arise they are addressed individually and appropriate behaviour is negotiated. A student explains how this works: '*Last week I had a big skit! Most of us were off task. I had to think about what I was doing wrong. Now I know I was wrong, should be on task after I talked with Ms.*'

Place

Messages around place operate on a number of levels. The classroom connects with students as individuals and as Aboriginal learners and then to the local and wider community. At the immediate classroom level, Sonia plans hard to provide students with positive experiences along side expectations and guidelines for student autonomy. Students feel safe, secure and believe that learning can be fun. There is a real view among the students that they 'own' their classroom and make decisions about how it looks and what happens. '*You get to make your own choices about the class...*' '*We make the decisions.*' At a cultural level, dance groups are not just 'extras' but offer awareness and inclusiveness of Aboriginal culture and heritage. A student talks about this. '*We learn our lessons from nature. The emu dance teaches us to take care of and never neglect our families.*' Sonia provides genuine validation of, and displays affection for, the local community. As she explains, '*I love it here. Coming back...is coming home. Happy making a difference here.*' Links with ideas from the REAP frame are obvious here. The importance of community seeing teachers beyond the professional role through social interactions is paramount.

Voice

It should be obvious that encouraging and utilising student voice is a defining feature of Sonia's classroom. Students share information and assist each other, often explaining new concepts to other class members. In this way meaning and understanding are negotiated: '*I am confused. How do you do this? Now can you explain it to someone else?*' Rationales and purposes for completing tasks are established ('*the "what and the why" of what they are doing*'), and Sonia continually encourages reflection and student self-assessment. She relinquishes her teacher 'power', promoting learning as a joint activity between herself and the students. '*What will be a better way of doing it?*' Charts are used on which students write post-it notes about the processes of their learning: What is good? What is not so good? Questions? Things to make it better? Challenges to the usual classroom terminology (for example 'workshops' instead of 'lessons') allow student choice and self-direction. All students understand the importance of respecting learning and the decisions they need to make. As a student puts it, '*If you are not listening you are "off" and then you have to decide to be good…you are back on the "on" list to learn.*'

To summarise thus far, the framework has shown the ways that this particular teacher's pedagogy sends engaging messages to her students. It is a pedagogy where learning connects for students, where they are supported in their learning and have real opportunities for autonomy and choice. When asked about their classroom one Aboriginal student summed up the collective feeling: '*I wouldn't change anything.*'

Nicole

'*Building a dream, keep a goal, something you want. Where do you want to be? What do you want to do? At the start of the year not one student could answer these questions. Now so many kids have aspirations. Part of it is having these conversations about life.*'

Nicole's approaches to teaching resonate strongly with the 'authentic instruction' research of Newmann (1996), the productive pedagogies movement (Hayes et al., 2006). Learning is active, reflective and has high levels of intellectual quality. Aboriginal perspectives are purposefully integrated across the curriculum and an adapted form of Accelerated Literacy (Gray, 2007) is prominent. Student engagement is underpinned by Nicole's belief about high expectations and the need for strong planning and the use of quality literacy texts. Critical reflections are central and bolstered through conversations with students about learning discourses and processes. Authentic, open-ended and culturally relevant experiences support self-regulated students.

Knowledge
Underpinning all learning experiences is Nicole's deep

knowledge about the content and the concepts associated with the learning. There is a strongly embedded technology focus through websites, interactive games, podcasting and animation. There are a variety of tasks characterised by high intellectual quality with embedded opportunities for meta-cognitive reflection. Students are positioned as joint constructors of knowledge through processes of predicting, interpreting and evaluating. *'What information is missing? If we took away a bit of meaning from this sentence, what's lost? Is it possible? Does it always work?'* Activities begin with task positioning, talking, foregrounding content and consolidating prior learning. Lengthy wait times are employed to elicit thoughtful student responses and to allow students to think before answering. Activities connect with students' lives and Nicole explores with students why something is relevant and how language is central to this integration. Learning is related to different audiences and specific purposes. Students are given confidence to take responsibility for their learning: *'Teachers open the door but you must enter by yourself.'* As this student explains, there is an understanding of the importance of learning: *'We don't like free time because we don't learn. It's not enough to just have fun, you need to learn.'*

Ability
There are high expectations that students are capable of completing tasks and this is reinforced through a deliberate pedagogy of differentiation and scaffolding: *'She breaks down everything...if she sees you have been trying she tries to help you get it right.'* Cooperative learning involves group collaboration, priority setting and task delegation. Students confirm the helpful supportive environment. *'Team work, pairing and working together, communicating with people,*

not just friends...She can help all abilities learn together. Sometimes a smart or an older person works with younger people.' Nicole believes students can be supported to believe they can succeed. She uses learning conversations that talk about processes, performance and open-ended tasks. At other times she brings into play explicit instructions and demonstrations followed by practising skills and applying cognitive skills using concrete materials. Nicole avoids unproductive help: *'When we're feeding them answers their brains are dead. They can do the thinking, processing themselves.'* Students have confidence, take risks, complete and reflect on their work. Student interviews revealed how the pedagogy impacted on their view of themselves as learners. *'[She] will keep on doing it with you until you get it right...she speaks to you kindly, she makes you more confident.'*

Control

A recurring theme across case studies in the *Fair Go Project* is that control is achieved through a supportive environment focused on learning. Nicole's classroom exemplifies this approach. Her presence is always calm and positive and it is evident that students do not receive negative criticism (*'She trusts us to stay calm'*). Energy is directed towards discussions about learning and time is freely given in break times for students to catch up on work and improve their skills. Nicole is convinced that *'good planning, organisation and programming will help manage behaviour problems.'* There are frequent opportunities for students to be decision makers, making choices about groups, problem-solving and learning approaches. As Nicole suggests, *'Negotiate with the class, come up with a system, when everyone understands it, hold to it.'* When students are distracted and off task she zeroes in to support them with task completion without mentioning behaviour. As a student explains, '*People can behave. Naughty kids do not have naughty kids to react to.*' Others show they understand how her approaches work positively for them. '*She is very calm, kind to every student. She asks really nicely, encourages people not to do the wrong thing. The people really listen to her.*'

Place

Nicole is a young Aboriginal woman in a school where Aboriginal students are in the minority. Engaging messages about place in Nicole's classroom operate at personal, pedagogical and cultural levels. All students are helped to feel important and looked after and given responsibility to be self-regulated in their learning. Aboriginal students are treated differently as a social justice issue. She considers their background knowledge and ways of knowing and learning and offers support for these. Access to literate discourses through her adapted Accelerated Literacy is paramount for these Aboriginal students. Classroom learning is seen as a long journey that students can drop into without missing out. At a cultural level, Aboriginal perspectives are also seen as an uncompromised social justice issue. Nicole understands the dangers of Aboriginal students becoming 'sidetracked' in cultural activities. She sees culture as a rich source of learning for all of her students and plans hard to explore journeys of cultural discovery with Aboriginal students and their families. Critically, she locates this in the stories of all the students. As she puts it, '*I sell it backward,*' meaning she links cultural narratives and concepts to learning rather than seeing culture as a 'stand alone'. A classroom exchange illustrates how students 'get' this: '[Nicole] *By sharing Aboriginal culture with everyone we...*' [Students] '*learn from each other*', '*are joined together*'. While understanding the timeless continuity of Aboriginal culture, Nicole also believes that, for these urban students, culture also needs to be dynamic, modern, contemporary and hip.

Voice

Students in Nicole's class understand and appreciate that choice and autonomy are integral to their learning. Her classroom is a robust example showing how important conversations about learning can become part of the way students 'see' their education. Learning time, attention and space are shared. There is a carefully planned balance between structure and choice: modelling, scaffolding ('*what's the language of fractions you need to use?*'), guided learning and teacher questioning that deepens intellectual quality and builds student confidence. Problematic knowledge is commonly explored through the recognition and fostering of varied and creative approaches to problem solving: '*There's more than one way to solve a problem.*' Interviews reveal that students have taken this on board. '*There are two or three ways to solve a problem. Ms tells us the easy way but we can go our own way.*' '*Ms checks all the answers* [variations] *but other teachers might only have one answer.*' An emphasis on team work is strengthened through role plays and thoughtful grouping strategies: '*She puts all the shy people in one group so they have to get used to it.*' Frequent hands-on activities are designed to help students become better learners and provide opportunities for choice and self-regulation.

Nicole's case study highlights the ways classroom messages can work to engage students. Her approaches to teaching reflect a thoughtful and carefully crafted pedagogy that is inclusive of all students and particularly sensitive to the needs of Aboriginal students. That these students are the minority highlights a socially just pedagogical standpoint. All students are involved in authentic tasks that connect Aboriginal culture with learning in an environment where classroom discourses encourage the development of a community of autonomous, productive learners. Students' words capture this learning environment. *'The old me used to be a bully. I used to hurt people's feelings but now Ms has taught me not to do that...I used to be really shy but now I'm more confident...I used to get mixed up. Now I have another go...I learnt to be a carer.'*

Conclusion

In the opening lines of this chapter we proposed that productive relationships between Aboriginal students and their teachers are critical for enhanced social and academic outcomes. We also suggested that these relationships are strengthened when they operate constructively at both socio-cultural and pedagogical levels. The argument was, that in Aboriginal education, relationships are complex, culturally situated and institutionally bound. Classroom curriculum is culturally produced, first as Aboriginal students respond to their school and classroom experiences by drawing on local and wider community themes, and then, in turn, by the teachers' pedagogical actions in relation to these responses (Munns, 2005). Within this complexity there is a vital imperative for teachers committed to improved educational success for their Aboriginal students to accept the challenge (Byrne, 2009) of getting both levels of the relationship 'right'.

Two frameworks were then introduced. The REAP framework drew on cultural understandings and research data to illustrate important components of the socio-cultural relationship. The Fair Go engagement framework followed as a way of framing and highlighting the pedagogical relationship developed between two teachers and their Aboriginal students. Taken together, these two frameworks point to directions that teachers might consider as they work on their own contextually-located solutions to the challenges that they face, together with their students, in their schools and classrooms.

11

SEEDING SUCCESS:
GETTING STARTED TEACHING ABORIGINAL STUDIES EFFECTIVELY

Rhonda G. Craven

Aboriginal Charter of Rights

We want hope, not racialism,
Brotherhood, not ostracism,
Black advance, not white ascendance:
Make us equals, not dependants.
We need help, not exploitation,
We want freedom, not frustration;
Not control, but self-reliance,
Independence, not compliance,
Not rebuff, but education,
Self-respect, not resignation.
Free us from a mean subjection,
From a bureaucrat Protection.
Let's forget the old-time slavers:
Give us fellowship, not favours;
Encouragement, not prohibitions,
Homes, not settlements and missions.
We need love, not overlordship,
Grip of hand, not whip-hand wardship;
Opportunity that places
White and black on equal basis.
You dishearten, not defend us,
Circumscribe, who should befriend us.

Give us welcome, not aversion,
Give us choice, not cold coercion,
Status, not discrimination,
Human rights, not segregation.
You the law, like Roman Pontius,
Make us proud, not colour-conscious:
Give the deal you still deny us,
Give goodwill, not bigot bias;
Give ambition, not prevention,
Confidence, not condescension;
Give incentive, not restriction,
Give us Christ, not crucifixion.
Though baptised and blessed and Bibled
We are still tabooed and libelled.
You devout Salvation-sellers,
Make us neighbours, not fringe-dwellers;
Make us mates, not poor relations,
Citizens, not serfs on stations.
Must we native Old Australians
In our land rank as aliens?
Banish bans and conquer caste,
Then we'll win our own at last.

Oodgeroo Noonuccal (2007)

Introduction

Aboriginal Charter of Rights was written by Oodgeroo (also known as the late Kath Walker – one of Australia's leading Aboriginal educators and poets) to present to the 5th Annual General Meeting of the Federal Council for the Advancement of Aborigines and Torres Strait Islanders in Easter, 1962. This seminal poem gave voice to the concerns of Aboriginal Australians and served to help educate other Australians about the dire need for social justice for Aboriginal Australians. It is a poem that all Australians should know and learn from. It provides a series of contrasts of what ought to be and the reality of Aboriginal Australians' rights. In a nation that pays homage to the principle of a 'fair go for all' we can see through Oodgeroo's eyes how this ethos did not extend to Aboriginal Australians. The poem's powerful message still continues to have striking poignancy and relevance over 50 years later as social justice on all socio-economic indicators still remains elusive for Aboriginal Australians.

Much of Oodgeroo's early poems were political works designed to jolt non-Aboriginal Australians into understanding the Aboriginal struggle for justice. Oodgeroo told me that *Aboriginal Charter of Rights* was her most expensive poem as a public reading of it resulted in her home being invaded and her clothes and blankets slashed. This home invasion did not deter Oodgeroo from being a leading spokesperson for her people, an activist for social justice, and a committed educator of Aboriginal Studies. In fact, her life story as one of Australia's human treasures (see Cochrane, 1994; Shoemaker, 1994) is testimony as to why it is a national priority for teachers to be committed to teaching Aboriginal Studies effectively. Oodgeroo recognised that changing the ethos and very frame of reference of Australian society was vital to achieve social justice for her people. To this end, her life's work was dedicated to educating a nation and she proved that one person can make a real difference. Her last wish was to see that every Australian teacher was taught to understand and teach Aboriginal Studies effectively.

> *All Australians, from the oldest to the newest, need to know about Aboriginal Australia – for one simple, fundamental reason – because this is Australia. The nation needs to embrace its truth.*
>
> *Lessons learnt by students percolate into the community. What we have to do is change the frame of reference of mainstream Australia, so that Indigenous people and Indigenous issues are no longer on the margins, or 'out of sight, out of mind', but part of the mainstream agenda, integral and intrinsic to public debate in this country. Teachers have a hugely important role in this. That is why teacher education is so critical. Teachers must be able to lead the way to a new understanding.*
>
> Linda Burney (personal communication)

Teachers have a vital role to play in the struggle for social justice by empowering students to both understand and address Aboriginal issues. It is hoped that this chapter will inspire and empower you to get started toward achieving such an aim. Firstly, to help you develop your own professional rationale for teaching Aboriginal Studies, we will discuss what Aboriginal Studies is and examine some rationales for teaching Aboriginal Studies. Secondly, we will also consider why Aboriginal community partnerships are critical at all phases of the teaching process: development, implementation and evaluation. Finally, some strategies for developing effective teaching units will be outlined. The key purpose of this chapter is to empower you to consider becoming that one person who can stand up to be counted to make a real difference in educating a nation and addressing social justice for Aboriginal Australians.

What is Aboriginal Studies?

Teaching Aboriginal Studies is a policy of the Australian Government in response to the acknowledged inequalities in education experienced by Aboriginal people, and the life-opportunity consequences of these. For example, the Ministerial Council on Education, Employment, Training, and Youth Affairs (MCEETYA, 2008) has developed national goals for schooling that emphasise improving outcomes for Aboriginal students and the need for all students in the primary and second-ary school education sector to understand and respect Aboriginal traditional and contemporary culture. As such, the *Melbourne Declaration on Educational Goals for Young Australians* (MCEETYA, 2008) states that all Australian students should:

> understand and acknowledge the value of Indigenous cultures, and possess the knowledge, skills and understanding to contribute to, and benefit from, rec-onciliation between Indigenous and non-Indigenous Australians (p. 9).

Commonwealth policies provide a framework for teachers that reflect the government's and community's desire for change. Aboriginal Studies policies are often underpinned by a two-fold purpose: (1) Optimising the capacity and capability of Indigenous people and communities; and (2) Educating all Australians to recognise Indigenous cultures and knowledge as being of equal validity to non-Indigenous cultures and to secure Indigenous Australia in the frame of reference of mainstream Australia. For example, the New South Wales Board of Studies (2011) defines the goals of Aboriginal Studies as to:

> explore the cultures, languages and lifestyles of Aboriginal peoples. It emphasises the understanding of issues central to Aboriginal societies and the relevance of these issues to the entire Australian community. It highlights aspects of Australia which all people in the community can learn from Aboriginal people. For Aboriginal students it reaffirms identity, builds pride in cultural heritage and raises self esteem. For all students it provides an understanding of cultural herit-age, and pride in a history of Australian civilisation since the beginning of the Dreaming. The course also assists in the eradication of racism and the develop-ment of a national identity...As students move through Aboriginal Studies K–12 they build from the local emphasis to the national and finally the international context.

Aboriginal Studies also involves teaching all Australian stu-dents about Aboriginal history and culture and how our past has shaped today, and aims to inspire them to develop a commitment to shaping a better future. It is the study of Aboriginal societies past and present, including histories, cultures, values, beliefs, languages, lifestyles and roles, both prior to and following the invasion of Aboriginal Australia. It is the study of Aboriginal people which presents an accurate history of Australia; and is studied in a context which: is central to Aboriginal societies and relevant to all Australians; which acknowledges the sophistication and complexity of Aboriginal culture; and which promotes mutual respect and understanding.

As teachers we can often feel overwhelmed by the breadth and depth of this subject area as described in definitions like those above. However, such feelings diminish when we come to understand the content and recognise that our role is to facilitate learning in this area, as opposed to being experts on all facets of the subject matter.

A simpler way to describe the subject area is that Aboriginal Studies is the study of Aboriginal history, societies, cultures, and current issues. It is designed to focus on understanding today's society, addressing current issues of our time and shaping a better future. History is utilised as a vehicle to critically examine how today's concerns emerged. Obviously, it would not be possible to understand the complexity of today's society without understanding how it was shaped by historical influences. Understanding today's society in light of historical influences provides a basis for empowering children to create and shape preferred futures. That is, this subject area, like other Social Studies areas, empowers children to think about current issues, feel concerned about these issues, recognise Australian achievements and take social action to create a better society. If we teach children to think, feel, and value we have only half done our jobs, as the subject area – like other Social Studies subject areas – should empower children to take social action and there-fore contribute to shaping our society.

It is also important to understand that Aboriginal Studies is both a subject in its own right and also content to be incorpo-rated into all curriculum areas at all levels of education. Many state/territory Social Studies syllabus documents describe the importance of teaching Aboriginal Studies as a key component of this learning area. In addition, such syllabus documents also often stress the importance of including Indigenous perspectives (i.e. Aboriginal Studies content and Indigenous viewpoints) in Social Studies units that do not specifically focus on Aboriginal Studies. For example, a unit of work on conservation could include Indigenous perspectives such as Indigenous world views of the importance of the land and current initiatives which Indigenous people are undertaking to care for their land. It is also important to include Indigenous perspectives in historical studies. There are still too many classrooms today that teach children about Captain Cook and the arrival of the 'First Fleet' without even mentioning Aboriginal Studies content. Such an approach fails to teach Australian history correctly and ignores the catastrophic impact these events had, and continue to have, on Indigenous Australians. In addition, this distortion of his-tory, by omitting Indigenous perspectives, fails to recognise and acknowledge the validity of Indigenous culture and his-tory. Therefore, Aboriginal Studies is not just an isolated Social Studies unit of work but permeates the entire curriculum so that the important contributions of Indigenous people to Australian society are acknowledged and utilised to enrich Australian Studies matter. For example, it would be ludicrous to study

Australian literature without reference to Indigenous writers, poets, and playwrights or Australian art without reference to Aboriginal art.

Some teachers still think the subject is of relevance only to Indigenous children and are reluctant to introduce Aboriginal Studies and perspectives into schools with predominantly non-Indigenous student populations. This is wrong. This subject is of critical interest to all Australian students because Aboriginal Studies is about Australian people, Australian history and critical Australian social justice concerns of our time. In practical terms this means that whether there are none or 30 Indigenous students in a class, all Australian students have the right to be taught Aboriginal Studies as this is an essential part of Australian Studies and every Australian has the right to know our nation has a black history. It is also important to appreciate that 'A policy is just words on paper. It is how these words are translated into action and practices that make the difference...let's work together to effectively implement this policy...so that education continues to not just be a dream to Aboriginal people but a reality' (Berwick, 2008, p. 3).

Why teach Aboriginal Studies?

Ever since I started teaching, I have seen the lack of a decent education for Indigenous Australians as the single biggest education issue in this country.

Brother Paul Hough
Former Principal St Joseph's College
(quoted in Craven, 2011)

No syllabus is 'teacher proof' – the best and most inclusive syllabus can still be taught badly. Ultimately each teacher will develop their own rationale as to why they will or will not teach Aboriginal Studies. Some of the strong teachers of this subject area that I have met, started developing their teaching skills based on the firmly held belief that this was a critical component of the curriculum. This small beginning in recognising the rationale for the subject was the seed that led them to develop themselves as outstanding teachers in the field. Hence early career teachers can take the first step to being excellent Aboriginal Studies teachers simply by developing their own rationale for teaching the subject. There is a wealth of important reasons as to why we as teachers should teach Aboriginal Studies, some of which are discussed in the following sections of this chapter.

Teaching to close the gap

There is a moral imperative also to see that Indigenous studies become one of the foundation stones of Australian learning. Surely our greatest Civil Rights challenge today is Closing the Gap in Indigenous education as this is one of the most important steps to Close the Gap in life expectancy. To create equality in education and health, all Australian children need to understand the paths that brought them together. We must close this space between our children.

Jeff McMullen
(quoted in Craven, 2011)

A key reason for teaching Aboriginal Studies is to address the fact that Indigenous Australians remain the most disadvantaged Australians on all socio-economic indicators (Australian

Bureau of Statistics, 2006e; National Report to Parliament on Indigenous Education and Training, 2006). MCEETYA (2006; p. 4) has lamented that in education:

> despite some gains, Indigenous Australians are yet to achieve equitable outcomes. Many Indigenous students continue to 'drop out' at or before Year 10 and far too few remain at school to complete Year 11 and Year 12, or its vocational equivalent. Of those who do complete Year 12, few obtain the scores needed to gain entry into university. Most Indigenous students, regardless of their completion year, leave school poorly prepared relative to their non-Indigenous counterparts. These outcomes limit the post-school options and life choices of Indigenous students, perpetuating intergenerational cycles of social and economic disadvantage.

The Productivity Commission (2009) has also noted that no significant changes were present for Indigenous students in the national benchmarks for reading, writing, and numeracy between 1999 (2001 for Year 7 students) and 2007 for Indigenous Year 3, 5, and 7 students. Significantly less Aboriginal students compared to other Australian students achieve national benchmark scores for reading (e.g. for Year 5, 63.4 per cent Aboriginal students vs. 92.6 per cent for non-Indigenous students); writing (e.g. for Year 5, 69.7 per cent, Aboriginal students vs. 93.9 per cent for non-Indigenous students); and numeracy (e.g. for Year 5, 69.2 per cent, Aboriginal students vs. 94 per cent for non-Indigenous students). In addition, fewer than half of Indigenous 19 year olds (36 per cent) compared to non-Indigenous 19 year olds (74 per cent) complete Year 12 or equivalent and this gap is widening (COAG, 2009a, p. 16).

Given these alarming statistics, COAG (2009a) has emphasised that:

> Closing the Gap is a great national challenge, but also a great national opportunity to achieve lasting change and ensure that future generations of Indigenous Australians have all the opportunities enjoyed by other Australians to live full, healthy lives and achieve their potential (p. 33).

Similarly, MCEETYA (2008) has emphasised that: 'Australia has failed to improve educational outcomes for many Indigenous Australians and addressing this issue must be a key priority over the next decade' (p. 5). Hence, closing the gap to ensure that Aboriginal children attain commensurate outcomes to their non-Aboriginal peers and therefore enjoy similar life opportunities is a critical social justice issue of our time that teachers can make a real difference to. This will result in Aboriginal children achieving their full potential and stop the sheer wastage of Aboriginal talent – and as such will make an invaluable contribution to enhancing Australia's national well-being.

It will be your job as teachers to create the conditions for our young people to be engaged and unlock their potential. YOU must be there for THEM.

Years ago Aboriginal students in western Sydney said a good teacher is, 'Someone that likes us and is fair'. You need to know your students and like them. And they need to like you. Or they won't achieve. It is that simple.

So much of our young people's talent goes to waste in this country – especially in the backblocks – and especially Indigenous youth. At Croc Festival we saw them do amazing things.

YOUR mission is to unearth that talent and help it bloom. YOU can help make this great country the best it can be. It is YOUR job.

It's that simple.

Peter Sjoquist
(quoted in Craven, 2011)

Teaching to address racism and misconceptions

I bloody love this country and the only way we're ever going to heal in this country is to face up to reality. Face up to the fact that there was a stolen generation...people weren't paid right. My mother was denied an education cos she was black. And I want people to realise that so they understand how to interact with Indigenous people. Cos not many people know how to interact with Indigenous people. And I really want that for the future generation and for my kids to sit in a classroom and do talk about the worries and do talk about the massacres, because we've got to heal, we've got to get over this. We've got to say, 'Hey it's happened, why are we denying it?' And that's what I want.

Enough Rope, ABCTV 27 August 2007
Tania Major

Pedersen and Walker (2000, p. 193; also see Craven, 2011) have identified that racism and misconceptions about Aboriginal people are enduring in Australia and contributing to the educational disadvantage that Aboriginal children suffer. They have suggested that:

> It would appear that the problems faced by Aboriginal children are only likely to be alleviated by structural change, as cultural oppressions are perpetuated by social rules. A good place to start is within the school system itself, which in some respects reflects the societal system at large (p. 195).

Hence, researchers have emphasised the importance of breaking down stereotypes and prejudices to create a more just Australian society. Teachers have an important role to serve in addressing racism and misconceptions (see Craven, 2011). They can teach Aboriginal students effectively; teach the facts about Aboriginal Australia; assist all Australian students to understand and appreciate Aboriginal history and culture; and develop a commitment to walking together to forge better futures for all Australians.

Persistent stereotypes about Aboriginal learning problems are based on erroneous beliefs about Aboriginal kids' capacity, interest and cultural differences. The reality is that lack of achievement for Aboriginal kids has nothing to do with capacity and cultural difference. Aboriginal kids have the same capacity as all kids, and their cultural background can and should be used to facilitate learning.

Dennis McInerney (personal communication)

Relationships with teachers are absolutely fundamental – if our kids don't like the teachers, they won't learn. And it works the other way too – the teachers have to know our kids and like them. Personalised learning means a focus on the students as individuals, getting to know them. And if there's one thing Koori kids are, let me tell you, it's individuals!...High expectations bring better results, better discipline, higher self-esteem and self-confidence, and more satisfaction being at school. That may seem obvious. But think for a moment about what low expectations might therefore be expected to produce – worse results, worse discipline, lower self-esteem, lower self-confidence, no satisfaction being at school. And then think of what generations of our kids have been put through in mainstream education.

We want to get educators to think about what our kids can do if they get a fair go. The world has seen what us blackfellas can do in sports and arts. Let me tell you there is so much more that we can do. Our kids can do anything if we can make education work for them – not against them...When the AECG was involved in the Teaching the Teachers project and we researched Aboriginal pedagogy as part of teaching teachers how to teach Koori kids, we found some experts who said it was hard to tell the difference between Aboriginal teaching styles and best practice!! So maybe we could teach you a thing or two.

Aunty Joyce Woodberry
(quoted in Craven, 2011)

Contributing to social justice

Australian school education is generally very good. It is humane, it has substance, and it is conducted by people who, in the main, believe that their work is full of purpose. Nevertheless, the education of young Indigenous people is the most obvious area of failure, and for many reasons — for the possible futures of those kids, for reasons of professional responsibility, and not least for the quality of our nation — that must be changed. That process begins at the dawning of cross-cultural awareness.

David McRae
(quoted in Craven, 2011)

Teaching Aboriginal Studies is critical to achieving social justice. Many people embark on a teaching career because they are committed to social justice and creating a better nation. That is, they make a difference to the world we live in by helping the next generation shape today's society and create preferred futures. They recognise that education can be a panacea for many of today's social concerns. For such teachers, our appalling record as a nation in relation to Indigenous affairs, endemic racism, and the need for social justice for Indigenous Australians is ample rationale for teaching Aboriginal Studies.

Teaching the truth

Before they even come inside the school gate, teachers of Aboriginal children — and all children — must have a working knowledge of the true history of this country. They must know and appreciate this land is long settled — for tens of thousands of years — occupied very well and in harmony. Teachers need to have a knowledge of the map of Aboriginal Australia — not six states and two territories, but hundreds of countries. They need to appreciate how diverse Aboriginal Australia was, and still is. New teachers, all teachers, need to be able to integrate Aboriginal perspectives in all their teaching. They

> *need to know about the stolen generations and understand how this has affected Aboriginal families down the generations – because, as one woman says in the Bringing Them Home video, 'We're family people. We're family people.'*
>
> Aunty Ruth Simms (personal communication)

Linda Burney says there is an easy answer to the question, 'Why teach Indigenous Australian Studies?', and that is to teach the truth about Australia's history:

> To teach all children, both Aboriginal and non-Aboriginal, about the real history of this country and the role that everyone has had to play in that history is incredibly important so that we don't continue to... pursue the myth that somehow or other Australia started in 1770 (Burney, 1996).

Until recent times, Australian history has been recorded only by non-Indigenous people who have seen events only from their own perspective. Most Australians today are indeed poorer for being ignorant of the greater part of Australia's history. Teaching Aboriginal Studies addresses this widespread ignorance and assists Australians to comprehend and appreciate that 'Australia has a black history'. Aboriginal Studies is not a 'black armband' view of history that is designed to distort history, rather it is about teaching the truth about our historical roots as opposed to 'white washing' history. As Henry Reynolds pointed out, 'History is an important battleground for the soul of Australia; we are up against a way of teaching history and a generation of historians who have put on a white blindfold' (Reynolds, 1997,

p. 6). Teaching history does *not* involve teaching people to feel guilty about the past – we cannot change the past but we can shape the future – rather it is about teaching the true history of this country in a way that all Australians can understand. What Koori historian James Wilson-Miller said years ago is still true:

> Australia's past Indigenous history can be avoided no longer. Both Indigenous and non-Indigenous people today have inherited that history. However it is not up to the present generation of Australians to feel guilty about that history, but more importantly, develop an understanding of, and work to positively address, the many legacies still evident today, which reflect the past treatments of Australia's Indigenous peoples. If we, the present generations of Australians, can do this then we will make this country a great country, not because we avoided the past, but because we confronted it and overcame it (Wilson-Miller, 1997).

Aboriginal Studies is Australian Studies

Nigel Parbury said it is essential to teach Aboriginal Studies in our schools for one simple, fundamental reason:

> and that is because this is Australia. Australia has always been Aboriginal land. The racist lies of terra nullius and White Australia have to be countered by teaching Aboriginal Studies in schools. Teaching Aboriginal Studies is the only way all students can learn the real nature and the real history of this country (Parbury, 1996).

No thinking Australian would argue with the critical need for Australian Studies to be a key component of school curricula. However, rarely have Australians stopped to realise that Aboriginal Studies is Australian Studies. Indigenous people are the first Australians. The greater part of our history is Indigenous history and Indigenous peoples' experiences of our history are our fellow Australians' experiences. Imagine the public outcry if we failed to teach Australians about the First Fleet, the early settlements, the achievements of the pioneers, and the contributions of new Australians – yet the same outcry has not been heard at the omission of our first Australians' history and their achievements. To really teach Australian Studies we must also teach Aboriginal Studies.

Benefits for all children

> Appropriate education will assist in providing young, active, developing minds, Aboriginal and non-Aboriginal, with a basis from which can grow cultural awareness, understanding and respect (New South Wales AECG, pamphlet, 2011).

I make no claim to Aboriginal blood. My ancestors were Scottish highlanders – dispossessed and driven from their homelands. But I know I don't belong in Scotland either. I made it my quest to learn from Aboriginal people in this country so that I can share in a deeper belonging. And by and large that has happened. To me, being indigenous is about that – really belonging to country and being an integral member of a family of living things and objects in that place.

It has more to do with a state of mind and spirit rather than one's ancestry...Aboriginal studies are vitally important.

Neil Murray

Honestly, Aboriginal Studies changed my view on life and Australia forever. It is more than a HSC subject. I can no longer tell you the heating system used in the public baths in Herculaneum and Pompeii, but rest assured I can talk for hours on the lack of Indigenous perspective in the education system; how I can see the crucial understanding many people lack; and most importantly, how the subject should be compulsory, at least for one year in junior school where tie-dyeing an apron and making a barbecue fork are considered more valuable life skills.

Emma Stewart HSC Student, 2009
(quoted in Craven, 2011)

Teaching Aboriginal Studies benefits both non-Indigenous and Indigenous students. Every Australian child has the right to learn about this country's rich cultural heritage and be challenged by the social issues facing all Australians today. Every Australian child also has the right to be empowered to act on social issues in order to create a better society. As Linda Burney has always said, 'Aboriginal education is teaching the truth about this country' (personal communication, 2011).

Teaching students Aboriginal Studies will enhance their understanding and appreciation of Aboriginal cultures and history. Understanding can foster cultural respect, which is an essential value for all Australians, given we are one of the most successful multicultural nations in the world. Cultural respect is also fundamental to the eradication of racism in Australian society and, as such, can lead to a more socially just society for all Australians.

Australia needs informed citizens. Indigenous Studies can help children to understand the truth about Australia's history and how our history still affects Indigenous Australians. It is not a 'guilt trip' – rather it is about comprehending the forces that have shaped Australian society today. The subject allows students access to an accurate knowledge base from which to comprehend the historical causes of Indigenous issues in this country, to appreciate how Indigenous people have helped shape Australia, and to join in current initiatives to address the issues and redress the balance – for a fair Australia. Understanding the full complexity of social issues in terms of their historical causes and consequences for Australians today, enables students to plan and implement strategies for a better future for all Australians.

Learning about Indigenous Studies allows Australian students to acknowledge their – our country's – rich cultural heritage. It helps children to recognise the achievements of Indigenous Australians, both in the past and today, promoting respect and understanding in the wider community. The end result can be a more tolerant and immeasurably richer Australian society in terms of its social capital.

Benefits for Indigenous children

Early on [as Principal at Walgett Public School]…I developed a theory of…'relevance'. Relevance, which is wider than experience, is the key. Relevance can be built into any teaching program – drawing from the psychology of the students, their everyday and extended environments, and the cultural factors in their lives. Linking to these is their acculturated learning modalities. In Walgett at that time most non-Aboriginal students were predominantly aural learners where the Aboriginals were heavily visually oriented...Work at Walgett HS at the same time confirmed a need also with secondary students to make sure the subject material was relevant to the Aboriginal students. Teachers have to engage students, otherwise valuable learning opportunities will be wasted.

Laurie Craddock
(quoted in Craven, 2011)

I trace my achievements to teachers in primary school in the 1940s who took an interest in me. I learnt that education was the key to my future as a young Aboriginal child, growing up in an institution, who could normally only expect to become a domestic for a white family.

A teacher in high school mentored me and consequently I won a scholarship to Business College, thus guaranteeing me another choice in life.

Dr Sue Gordon
(quoted in Craven, 2011)

Teaching Indigenous Australian Studies also has enormous benefits for Indigenous children. For example, some years ago I was assigned to teach a Year 3 class in western Sydney. In my class was an Aboriginal child who various executive staff in the school saw as a difficult pupil – always misbehaving in class and the playground. As a partial intervention for his behaviour, I implemented a unit of work on Aboriginal Studies in consultation with the local Aboriginal community.

Once the unit had begun, the child offered to teach the class how to throw a boomerang. He told me that he was very good at this but some of the children in the class did not think that he could do it because he was not brought up in the bush. He was able to contribute to the unit by inviting some members of the local Aboriginal community to explain aspects of his culture to the class. This improved his self-concept. He became quite popular with his peers over the school year and increased his persistence on academic tasks. This behaviour continued throughout his primary school years. Hence, supporting Aboriginality in the classroom and the school can promote Aboriginal students' sense of identity and pride in their Aboriginality and lead to long-term psycho-social and educational benefits.

> *It was important for Aboriginal students in the schools that we visited to see someone from their heritage represented in the context of people from different walks of life and groups bringing different gifts to Australia with their values. We saw Aboriginal students sitting up straighter and feeling prouder and standing up and speaking about the 'Blackfella's way', so in terms of fostering belonging and reinforcing the idea that we can work together, it was quite effective.*
> Rabbi Zalman Kastel, Together for Humanity
> (Quoted in Craven, 2011)

The most critical issue in Indigenous education is the participation of Indigenous people in education to achieve the same outcomes as their peers. Statistics show that significant proportions of Indigenous Australians do not have access to education and/or do not participate in education commensurate to other Australians (e.g., COAG, 2009a). The development of a culturally relevant curriculum in schools is critical. Teachers cannot expect Indigenous children to actively engage in curricula which do not include their histories, their current concerns and their cultures as part of the nation. Indigenous children should experience an education that is relevant to their needs and their experience. They have the right to be taught how Australia's history has affected Indigenous people. Schools should be places where Indigenous culture is respected and celebrated. For example, one of my local schools has a population of five Indigenous students. The school strives to ensure these children's cultures are respected and celebrated. The school has formed a 'Koori Kids' group (note Koori is a word used by many NSW Aboriginal people to identify themselves) to unite these students. This group has a special role in flag raising ceremonies and often develops cultural presentations for the school (e.g. dance, art, craft, story-telling). These children have told me the best thing they like about their school is being part of the Koori Kids group as it gives them a chance to teach other students about how proud they are to be Indigenous. In other words, this school has ensured they have created a school climate for success for these students. It is also important to note that most Indigenous children experience schooling in low-density settings where they comprise less than 10 per cent of the school population (personal communication with NSW Department of Education and Communities). For example, at my children's primary school there are four Koori students. Catering for these students makes the curriculum relevant for them and importantly also enriches the curriculum for all students.

In the future I hope not to hear teachers saying: 'I don't teach Aboriginal Studies because we don't have any Indigenous children in our school' – clearly Aboriginal Studies is for all Australians – or 'I did Indigenous Studies last term' – Aboriginal Studies needs to permeate Key Learning Areas, and be incorporated to ensure schooling is relevant for our Indigenous students. The new generation of teachers educated in Indigenous Studies will be able to tell their colleagues why teaching Aboriginal Studies to all children is a national priority, what they can do, and why they need to be professionally committed to this goal. Remembering my mentor Oodgeroo, I also hope to see more and more teachers choosing to join the growing movement of Australian teachers committed to closing the gap for Indigenous students and leading the way. The future well being of our nation rests on the quality of our teachers to make a real difference – and I firmly believe that we can do this as we have some of the best teachers in the world.

The essential nature of community partnerships

Because so many teachers know so little about Aboriginal culture and about Aboriginal education history, there is very little understanding of the reasons why Aboriginal people might be reluctant to have much to do with schools, and often even less understanding of what might be the appropriate ways to invite Aboriginal community involvement.

Linda Burney (1991)

Most teachers have never even met or spoken to an Aboriginal person, and that has its own effect, but when an Aboriginal person speaks to them about their history, it ceases to be just a history lesson. People are confronted with a new way of looking at the world, and must decide what they are going to do about that.

Damien Coghlan (1992)

The statements above were made in the 1990s; however, they still resound with relevance over two decades later. While there are a number of universities that have done an outstanding job in delivering high-quality Indigenous Studies teacher education courses, the fact remains that most Australian teacher education institutions do not require student teachers to undertake a mandatory Aboriginal Studies subject that is specifically relevant to teaching. Many of these institutions do not offer Indigenous Studies electives and even if they do, the subjects often are never actually taught but remain on the books, and many say they deliver perspectives across the curriculum but when this is examined more closely really what is delivered is lip service. This is a national disgrace in that research has empirically demonstrated that mandatory teacher education subjects are effective (Craven, et al., 2005a, 2005b, 2005c studies; Mooney, 2011) and all universities have at least some teacher educators who are committed to Aboriginal Studies in teacher education courses, Indigenous Education Centres, and Indigenous academics that could readily deliver appropriate subjects.

The lack of teacher education has also resulted in many teachers being unsure about or even unaware of the fundamental importance of working in a two-way partnership based on mutual respect and understanding with Aboriginal people. While most education systems advocate the involvement of the school's community to enhance the effectiveness of schooling, for Aboriginal Studies programs this is vital to increase Indigenous students' engagement and participation in schooling in that only Aboriginal community members can teach their culture and their experience. Importantly, enabling children to engage with people who have lived our shared history ensures students understand the actual impact of our history on the lives of people from their community. Aboriginal community members may also be able to advise teachers on culturally appropriate pedagogy, resources, and activities for students – and on how Indigenous students can be engaged. It is critically important that partnerships are not a 'rubber stamp' process – rather they must involve genuine partnerships and Aboriginal community member inclusion in all aspects of the teaching process: planning, implementing, and evaluating. As such, Aboriginal Studies is about teaching *with* and learning *from* Indigenous people – in contrast to teaching and learning *about* Indigenous people. Therefore it requires an ongoing school commitment to community partnerships. For example, if an Australian child has never met or listened to or spoken with an Indigenous person, how could it be claimed that they have been taught Aboriginal Studies and perspectives? Yet this is still the case in some schools.

It has been found that students are particularly receptive to, and interested in, Indigenous input and viewpoints, knowledge and experiences. Such input ensures that Aboriginal Studies is taught as a real Social Studies issue that impacts on and is relevant to the lives of Indigenous people today. Understanding the real and ongoing impact of historical events on the lives of Indigenous Australians can be readily brought to life in the classroom by inviting local Indigenous community members to share their life experiences. For example, teaching students about the stolen generations can be enriched by an Indigenous person explaining the impact such government policies have had on their life and those of their family. For example, my daughters' grandmother – Kathleen Miller – was forcibly removed from her mother at the tender age of nine (see Miller, 1985). The history of her life is a very moving and memorable experience that has brought me to tears listening to her tell her history and has made me even more determined as an educator to advocate that all Australians should know about this aspect of our shared history and the enduring impacts thereof on the lives of our first Australians. There is also not an Aboriginal person I have ever met whose lives or those of friends and family have not been adversely affected by the policy of taking Indigenous children away from their parents. Working in partnership with your local school community can help you to identify people that may be willing to share their experiences with students (also see Smith, 2011). For example, recently I was at a school where a young Aboriginal woman shared her story about being taken away from her mother and her subsequent treatment. This experience was so moving that students were in tears – they will never forget what that young woman taught them – the Stolen Generations may have happened years ago but the effects still live on in the lives of Indigenous Australian families today. Working in partnership with Indigenous communities can ensure that key aspects of our shared history are culturally-appropriately and sensitively taught to empower the next generation to make a difference in contributing to the social justice issues that are still to be resolved.

I have often come across teachers who won't teach Aboriginal Studies – not because they cannot see the rationale for the area – but because they fear making mistakes and offending people.

They often hold a view that only Indigenous people can teach Aboriginal Studies. This is simply incorrect – there is a wealth of topics that teachers can and do teach well (e.g. history, current policies and government strategies and contemporary issues). The issue that needs clarification is that only Indigenous people should teach specific aspects of cultural studies (e.g. ceremonial life, information of a secret/sacred nature, information that should only be shared with a specific sex at a specific age). The reason for this is not that mysterious but simple logic. Basically, if you are not part of a culture, it is impossible to teach others about specific aspects of that culture accurately. The many mistakes cultural anthropologists have made over the years are testimony to this fact. This is another reason why genuine community partnerships are so critical.

Approaching the local community

The tips presented below (developed by James Wilson-Miller, one of Australia's leading Koori historians and a former teacher educator), along with common sense, can help you approach your school's Indigenous community to establish genuine partnerships:

- Get to know as much as you can about Indigenous communities and all the positive aspects of them before you go there.
- Get to know and work with your local Indigenous community organisations (e.g. local and regional Aboriginal Education Consultative Groups, local Aboriginal Land Councils, medical services, employment services, legal services and local Indigenous Elder organisations).

- Be aware that all Indigenous communities differ from one another.
- Be aware of the 'differing factions' within Indigenous communities. Keep an impartial position with all of them.
- Greet people with a smile and warm, friendly gestures.
- Never try to impress Indigenous people with your professional level of education. They know you are an educated person or you would not be there. Be aware of the difference between the 'well-educated' and 'wisely educated' person. Both will know the meaning of educational jargon and how to use key educational terms, but a wisely educated person knows when not to use them.
- Become involved in community social events, if invited. These are good ice-breakers.
- Liaise with your Indigenous Education Workers and your principal, remembering that they may know more than you about the community you are in.
- Never assume that Indigenous Education Workers and community members are 'black experts' on all things Indigenous (e.g. history, anthropology, language, social commentators).
- Above all, be approachable, be understanding, be flexible, be empathetic not sympathetic, be *yourself* and be prepared to work in partnership and listen and learn from Indigenous communities. (James Wilson-Miller, personal communication, 2011)

Possible difficulties and possible solutions

At times, difficulties in seeking to consult with the local Indigenous community will arise. These difficulties can be overcome by networking with local, regional, and state/territory sources of advice. Table 11.1 outlines some possible difficulties and proposes some possible solutions.

Table 11.1 – Possible difficulties and solutions when seeking Indigenous input as a teaching resource

Possible difficulty	Possible solutions
No local Indigenous community is available	• Contact regional or State/Territory Indigenous education organisations (e.g. NSW AECG in NSW) • Contact your education systems' Indigenous education personnel (e.g. community liaison officers, regional Indigenous Education consultants)
Members of the local Indigenous community seem reluctant to consult with the school	• Realise that many Indigenous people have historically had negative experiences with schools • Seek assistance from the school's Indigenous staff or relevant counterparts in other systems • Where the school has no Indigenous staff, contact Indigenous organisations or education system personnel (e.g. community liaison officers, Aboriginal Education consultants) to assist • Organise experiences that Indigenous parents may be interested in attending to provide non-threatening opportunities for parents to feel comfortable visiting the school (e.g. cultural day, flag raising ceremony, guest speakers, morning tea)

Only a few Indigenous pupils attend the school and their parents are too busy to assist the school	<ul><li>Seek assistance from local, regional, and state/territory Indigenous Education organisations</li><li>Support children's pride in their Aboriginality in both the classroom and school (e.g. celebrate NAIDOC week, invite guest speakers, form an Indigenous children's group, display Indigenous murals, literature and art around the school)</li><li>Seek assistance from Indigenous Education consultants, Indigenous and community liaison officers to develop Indigenous Studies units and perspectives across the curriculum</li><li>Recognise that Indigenous Education involves the education of all students, both Indigenous and non-Indigenous, about the history, cultures and issues of Australia's Indigenous peoples</li></ul>
A teacher wishes to invite a guest speaker on a specific topic but does not know who to ask or who would be available	<ul><li>Seek advice from your local Indigenous community, Indigenous Education consultants, or local/regional Indigenous organisations</li></ul>
Differing viewpoints on what is to be taught are expressed to the teacher	<ul><li>Hold a community consultation meeting to decide what approaches the community would like to be used. Seek assistance from Indigenous personnel</li><li>Recognise that Indigenous communities are diverse and made up of individuals with different views, hence one person's view should not be taken as constituting community consultation or necessarily representing the views of the community.</li></ul>

Teaching resources

Library research shows that there have always been far more books, references, quotes and images of Aboriginal Australia than most people ever knew about – even in the nineteenth and early twentieth century, what was produced could line the walls of a suburban house. Since Aboriginal people were 'admitted' to Australian society in 1967, and more especially since our education authorities started to take an interest from the 1970s, there has been an upsurge of resource production, growing to a flood in the 'reconciliation decade' of the 1990s, and now increasing exponentially day by day – to the point where a 'definitive' list of Aboriginal Studies resources now could be out of date in a month! There is so much to choose from that there is a real risk of making the wrong choice simply because catalogues cannot tell the whole story on any resource – and remember catalogues are essentially promotions! You will need advice to get started, and both local advice and teacher networks will be critically important.

While there is a wealth of stimulating Aboriginal Studies teaching resources, unfortunately, there are still an alarming number of poor teaching resources – not because they are 'outdated' necessarily, but because of the racist or stereotypical attitudes they convey. It is a mistake to assume that an 'old' resource has less value than a 'new' one – for example, Dame Mary Gilmore's *Old Days, Old Ways* is a valuable seminal primary resource. Some inappropriate resources examine Aboriginal Studies in a superficial manner; some rarely include facts, or if they do, the 'facts' can be presented in a biased way. Others present teaching activities that are based on misconceptions and stereotypes; as such they tend to encourage students to adopt misunderstandings based on stereotypical generalisations. Such materials usually do not acknowledge the diversity of Indigenous Australia and also often focus on a mythical view of past societies rather than dealing with complex contemporary issues.

As noted above, it is impossible to present any complete list here of the best resources to stand the test of time. A further complication is that the best of resources will 'fall off the edge of the earth' once they are no longer in publication. Some of the best teaching resources I have seen are now 'off the radar', gathering dust on shelves or, worse, rotting in dumps because they are no longer produced and/or the people who knew their value have moved on. Updating *Teaching Aboriginal Studies* (Craven, 2011), I was astounded to find how many of the best resources of the 1990s fell into such oblivion in ten years flat! In addition, I was overwhelmed at how much had been produced since and how much the resource landscape had changed – new media, new resource producers, so much more locally focused material, and so many mainstream publishers getting involved. Accordingly, the following is a brief selection of what I regard as some of the best of the past, plus highlights of some new recent resources.

Oldies but goodies

- *1788: The Great South Land* – a school musical and resource kit that may be available in some schools and resource centres; now reissued as *When the Sky Fell Down*. The five-school performance video *Nothing's Going to Stop Our Dream* can be accessed via Google.
- *The Wailing: A National Black Oral History* (1993) Stuart Rintoul. Heinemann – an unrivalled collection of oral history interviews.

- *Beyond A Joke: An Anti-Bicentenary Cartoon Book*, edited by Kaz Cooke; Penguin 1988. Out of print, but invaluable if you can find it; a number of the cartoons are reproduced on Gary Foley's *kooriweb* site.
- *Survival: A History of Aboriginal life in New South Wales*, Nigel Parbury (2005), Ministry of Aboriginal Affairs, Department of Aboriginal Affairs.
- *The Encyclopaedia of Aboriginal Australia* 1994, David Horton AIATSIS, also on DVD.

Recent resources

- *The Little Red Yellow Black Book*, Bruce Pascoe and AIATSIS staff.
- *Emily in Japan: The Making of an Exhibition*, video by Ronin Films with Margo Neale; the story of the biggest exhibition of Australian art ever toured overseas, 2009.
- *Art + Soul*, by Hetti Perkins, book and ABCTV documentary series, 2010.
- *Racial Folly: A twentieth Century Aboriginal Family*, by Gordon Briscoe; can be downloaded from epress at ANU website.
- *Aboriginal Australians* by Richard Broome, 4th edition, Allen & Unwin, 2010.
- *First Australians: The Untold Story of Australia*, TV series and book by Rachel Perkins and Marcia Langton.
- *The Macquarie Atlas of Aboriginal Australia*.
- *The Oxford Companion to Aboriginal Art and Culture*, Margo Neale and Sylvia Kleinert.
- *Yarning Strong*, a range of Aboriginal stories published with Oxford University Press; with teacher notes.

Films

Aboriginal films or films with Aboriginal themes used to be 'box-office poison'. To some extent this is true, but what is changing is more and more award winning films are being made by Aboriginal filmmakers. In current years, check out *Bran Nue Dae* (Rachel Perkins), *Beneath Clouds* and *Toomelah* (Ivan Sen), and *Samson and Delilah* (Warwick Thornton). From the past, largely by other Australian filmmakers: *Backroads*, *The Chant of Jimmie Blacksmith*, *The Fringe Dwellers*, *Australian Rules*, and so many, many more. Of course, this is without even mentioning the huge output of Aboriginal videos and DVDs.

Galleries, museums, keeping places

Don't ever forget what cultural places can do for you! For advice on all this, there is a range of websites, newsletters, catalogues and other publications that offer Aboriginal Studies resources and/or advice on resources for Aboriginal Studies – so many that it can be difficult to know which is most authoritative (even sometimes which to trust). One of the best I have seen is the Creative Spirits site, originated and kept up to date by Jens-Uwe Korff, a German-Australian in Sydney whose own story is an education, who loves Aboriginal Australia and who understands respect. You can find it at www.creativespirits.com.au.

Sources of assistance

Each state/territory has an Aboriginal Education Consultative Group (AECG) or an Indigenous Education Consultative Body (IECB). Indigenous education organisations can provide teachers with guidance on contacting local community members, useful teaching resources, available visiting speakers, curriculum policy,

Indigenous pedagogy and a wealth of other issues. All state/ territory Departments of Education have Indigenous education units and regional Indigenous education resource personnel and consultants to provide advice to teachers in schools. Other systems such as the Catholic Education Commission also employ Indigenous education resource personnel. Increasing numbers of independent schools have scholarships for Indigenous students and some independent school associations provide advice. Indigenous organisations and Indigenous education resource personnel from these organisations can also give guidance to teachers on where to locate appropriate up-to-date material. For example Land Councils often employ education officers who can assist teachers by giving talks to schools and advising teachers of resources they have available.

The Australian Institute of Aboriginal and Torres Strait Islander Studies holds the largest Australian collection of Aboriginal Studies and Torres Strait Islander Studies materials and can provide useful advice to teachers. The Institute also has an Aboriginal education officer. In addition, many museums and art galleries have Aboriginal curators and/or education officers. There are also local resource centres run by Indigenous education officers and local or regional museums. Indigenous book publishers (e.g. Magabala Books) also produce annual catalogues containing popular and recent publications.

Indigenous media can be useful sources of current information. For example *Koori Mail*, *National Indigenous Times*, *Land Rights News* and *Torres News* are Indigenous newspapers that report regularly on current issues in Indigenous Australia. In 2011, they have been joined by *Tracker*, the Indigenous magazine published by the NSW Aboriginal Land Council. For years there have been Indigenous units within ABCTV and SBS. Now they are joined by NITV, National Indigenous Television, based in Alice Springs, funded by the Commonwealth Government, and recently expanding into film production. The Commonwealth Government supports a network of Indigenous community broadcasters across Australia whose programs are disseminated. New media makes it easier and easier to network and share – Facebook can help you!

Recently the Aboriginal Studies Association (ASA) was reformed in New South Wales as a professional association to promote and resource teaching of the NSW HSC Aboriginal Studies syllabus, as well as Aboriginal Studies at all levels of education. As before, the ASA conducts an annual conference and produces regular newsletters. The annual conference includes sessions of interest to novice Aboriginal Studies teachers, as well as 'old hands', and has a focus on resource sharing. ASA membership is open to Indigenous and non-Indigenous educators, and anyone interested in understanding and teaching Aboriginal Studies effectively.

Developing units of work
A theoretical model
In the Aboriginal Studies classroom two key approaches are often used to develop units of work. One approach involves starting with a theme such as Land Rights and exploring contemporary and historical events in relation to this theme. Another approach is developing units of work based on one or more key concepts. For example, focusing on the key concept *caring* could enable students to explore what Indigenous and non-Indigenous people care about today in the light of what people cared about in

the past. Both approaches are worthwhile and can be used as a springboard for developing stimulating activities.

Figure 11.1 is a theoretical model which aims to reflect a holistic approach to developing Indigenous Studies units of work. This model was developed by Craven and Wilson-Miller (see Craven, 2011). Three circle figures are depicted in an interconnected model to demonstrate the interactive nature of subject matter from each of the three circles – past, present, and future perspectives. Futures perspectives are placed at the top of the model to denote the importance of developing teaching activities that will enable children to predict how they can contribute to creating a better future for all Australians. The central arrow demonstrates that all aspects of the model need to be examined in the context of local, state/territory and national perspectives.

The model is designed to work (not in chronological order) by focusing on contemporary society through designing units of work with a present perspective. Each unit of work should then deal with finding out how today's society is affected by past perspectives so that children can understand how society has evolved. This means that knowledge of Australia's past needs to be examined to clarify contemporary issues of concern. Understanding the events and forces that have shaped Aboriginal societies and issues today is the basis for understanding the present and examining future perspectives. Within each circle, examples of content that could be incorporated in a unit of work are listed. The *present perspectives* circle depicts the need for children to appreciate Indigenous culture and issues today. While the content could be ordered in many ways to suit specific regional needs, it is depicted in this order to show the need for teachers to initially devise activities to focus on present perspectives to enable children to:

1. focus on Indigenous culture today and the achievements of Indigenous peoples today, both at the beginning and throughout the unit of work
2. examine any stereotypes or misconceptions they hold about Indigenous societies.

The *past perspectives* circle denotes the importance of integrating historical perspectives stressing pre-invasion as the full range of Indigenous experience in Australia and exploring chronologically, invasion and post-invasion history as the origin of the present. In the past there has been an over emphasis on developing teaching activities that relate to pre-invasion history – as safely remote in time and space, and nothing to do with Indigenous people and issues now – rather than articulating content to also incorporate invasion and post-invasion history so that today's society can be understood in the light of all that has happened in the past. Aspects of history should not be explored in isolation, but related to present and future perspectives as depicted by the overlapping nature of the circles in the model. Past events need to be critically analysed to show their impact on Indigenous societies today. Such knowledge can then be utilised as a basis for shaping preferred futures.

Figure 11.1 – A theoretical model for developing teaching activities

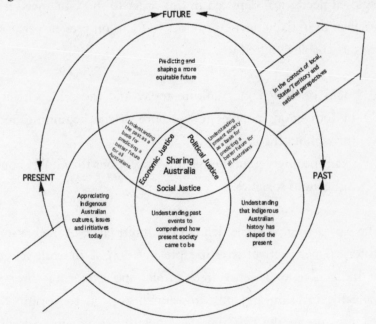

The *futures* perspectives circle advocates teaching activities to enable children to:

- understand the need for reconciliation between Indigenous and non-Indigenous Australians
- understand the importance of Indigenous self-determination – and why it is essential for Reconciliation
- contribute to predicting and thinking about how to create more equitable outcomes in Australian society.

The interaction of all elements of the model – present, past, and future – leads children to understand the importance of all Australians sharing in social, political, and economic justice. The interactive nature of the model emphasises the point that teaching activities need to be developed in tandem in a holistic way to explore present, past and future perspectives rather than to isolate each period. This approach leads to a focus on society today rather than solely a 'content' approach and prepares the foundation for children to be empowered to contribute to create better futures for all Australians.

The model can be used as a basis for developing ideas for a unit of work. It is a helpful tool in assisting teachers to check that units of work contain a balanced approach in relation to the three key perspectives. Both thematic and key-concept approaches can easily be accommodated by the model.

Starting with a theme

There is a wealth of themes that teachers could use as a basis for an Indigenous Studies unit of work (e.g. education, special treatment, land rights, self-determination). One useful way of starting is to:

- choose a theme – where possible in consultation with your local Indigenous community
- write down as many ideas for activities with maximum community involvement using the theoretical model above as a trigger for ideas that relate to:
  - present perspectives
  - past perspectives, making sure pre-invasion, invasion and post-invasion events are presented in a balanced approach
  - futures perspectives
- gather as much multi-media resources as possible that relate to the theme and add to your activities list
- write a summary of the order in which you will develop activities

- write up your unit of work in detail for your teaching program.

Starting with a key concept

Similarly a theme can be developed starting with a key concept (e.g. belonging, caring, respect, tolerance, independence, responsibility, sharing etc.) as the basis for unit development. The concept can be used to link activities together. To do this, it is useful to ask students to define the key concept in the first activity to ensure they understand its meaning. Mentioning the key concept in every activity also helps children to relate each content area to the concept under investigation more fully.

Getting started is just a matter of brainstorming ideas as above but this time the ideas relate to a sequence of key areas to which you will relate the concept.

Checking units

When beginning to develop units of work it is important to check the overall unit structure. Teacher-devised checklists can often be used to achieve this e.g.:

- Is every activity interesting? Would I enjoy doing this task?
- Do I have maximum community involvement in teaching about present, past and future perspectives to ensure students are learning from Indigenous people?
- Do the activities explore the content area in depth?
- Do my activities begin with the present?
- Do my activities teach children about past events and relate them to today's society?

- Do my activities contain a balance of invasion, pre-invasion, and post-invasion activities?
- Do my activities contain a balance of present, past and future perspectives?
- Have I included activities that can help children to create a better future for all Australians?

Summary

As Patrick Dodson has said, we as Australians have, for years, been asked to stand up and be counted. Will you be one person that can make a real difference? Teachers can make such a powerful difference in achieving social justice for Indigenous Australians and all Australians. We can ensure that Indigenous children attain educational outcomes commensurate with those of their non-Indigenous peers and therefore reach their full potential, contributing materially both to national well-being and, immeasurably, to our potential as a nation. We can also ensure that all Australian children have a fair go, the opportunity to learn about the rich cultural heritage and troubled heart of Indigenous Australia, and to celebrate and honour the achievements and contributions of our first Australians, who have always been so much a part of us and we of them. Walking-together in genuine partnerships with Indigenous communities will ensure that together we can't lose.

An appeal

Statesman, who make the nation's laws,
Will power to force unfriendly doors,
Give leadership in this our cause
That leaders owe.

Writers, who have the nation's ear,
Your pen a sword opponents fear,
Speak of our evils loud and clear,
That all may know.

Unions who serve democracy,
Guardians of social liberty,
Warn to the justice of our plea,
And strike your blow.

Churches, who preach the Nazarene,
Be on our side and intervene,
Show us what Christian love can mean
Who need it so.

The Press most powerful of all,
On you the underprivileged call:
Right us a wrong and break the thrall
That keeps us low.

All white well-wishers, in the end
On you our chiefest hopes depend;
Public opinion's our best friend
To beat the foe.

Oodgeroo Noonuccal (2007)

12

BECOMING A CULTURALLY COMPETENT TEACHER: BEGINNING THE JOURNEY

Graeme Gower and Matt Byrne

Introduction

It was a Friday morning and the bell had gone 15 minutes ago and ten year old Crystal turned up at the classroom door. She waited there for a few minutes, then quietly took her seat and began speaking in Aboriginal English to her friend seated next to her about the activity they were doing. The teacher, who had not noticed Crystal walk in, looked over and saw her talking, and addressed the class in a loud tone, 'Look who has turned up late again, and by the way Crystal we speak proper English in this classroom.'

The above scenario happened during a classroom observation for a research project. In looking at the interaction between Crystal and her teacher, how culturally appropriate were the teacher's actions? What impact do you think that this comment had on Crystal? Do you think that this situation could have been handled differently?

This scenario and related questions draw attention to how appropriate the actions of the teacher were. Would this type of interaction lead to the development of a positive teacher–student relationship and engagement in learning for Crystal and the other Aboriginal students in the classroom? In answering this question, one would need to consider Crystal's perspective and the impact this interaction would have on her and her peers and, in doing so, illustrate the importance of being a culturally competent teacher.

This chapter explores how teachers can become culturally competent in their dealings with Aboriginal students and the wider Aboriginal community. It is a new way forward and a different way of thinking in Indigenous education. This chapter is primarily based on research conducted as part of the Universities Australia project on cultural competency (Gower, et al., 2010) and the review of the Aboriginal and Islander Education Officer program (Gower, et al., 2011). In addition, it draws on practical experience in the field over a number of years and extensive involvement in the development of cultural competency training for university staff, teachers, systems and private enterprise

Entering into and empathising with the personal lives of your students and their culture, along with your own values and practices as an aspirant teacher, can help to improve the outcomes of Indigenous students. There are many definitions of cultural competency but for the purpose of this chapter our definition of cultural competency is: to develop an informed position based on an understanding and appreciation of Aboriginal issues, culture and way of life that enables confident and effective interaction with Aboriginal people and the wider society.

An introduction to cultural competency
Background
Gaining Western academic knowledge alone is insufficient if graduates of Australian universities are to be able to operate

effectively in their chosen professions. Effective communication and interaction with persons from different cultural backgrounds is an important factor to be considered as part of university learning. Therefore, in teacher education, Western academic knowledge needs to be coupled with Indigenous studies and practical experience of working with Indigenous people so that students develop appropriate levels of 'cultural competence'.

The cultural competency framework in figure 12.1 below illustrates one way of bringing Indigenous knowledge and Western knowledge together in a meaningful and practical manner in order to bring about better outcomes and services for Indigenous people.

Figure 12.1 – Cultural Competency framework

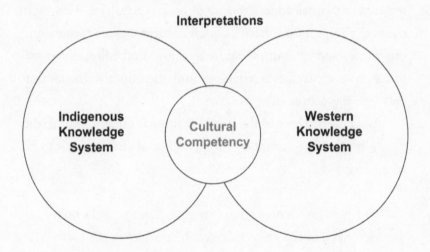

There is strong evidence in the literature to indicate that differences exist between Indigenous knowledge systems and Western knowledge systems (Nakata, 2007; Kelly, et al., 2009, Saunders, et al., 2010; Bedford, et al., 2010). Nakata argued that the differences between Indigenous knowledge systems and Western scientific ones are 'incommensurable' and 'irreconcilable'. Nakata (2007, p. 8) argued further that these differences are such that one knowledge system cannot legitimately verify the 'claims of truth of the other via its own standards and justifications.' The Western knowledge system and the Indigenous knowledge system are grounded in different theories that frame, 'who can be knower', 'what can be known', 'what constitutes knowledge, sources of evidence for constructing knowledge, what constitutes truth, how truth is to be verified, how evidence becomes truth, how valid inferences are to be drawn, the role of belief in evidence and related issues' (Nakata, 2007, p. 8).

This suggests that the values and understandings of one system cannot be superimposed on the other and, that to move forward, a mutual understanding of both is required. This highlights the important role of cultural competency in recognising differences and applying them in a positive and culturally appropriate way to facilitate effective and meaningful interaction between the people of both systems.

As a consequence of the need for mutual understanding, the question of what is meant by Indigenous knowledge needs to be addressed:

Indigenous knowledge maybe very generally described as the knowledge of the peoples of the earth. Indigenous knowledge involves layered understandings that are separate, diverse and individuated yet also related through a focus on ways of being that are in accord with natural systems. As a relational and layered knowledge system Indigenous knowledge also includes highly contextual knowledge that is directly related to specific cultural groups. In this regard, Indigenous knowledge may also be described as the knowledge of the Aboriginal and Torres Strait Islander peoples of Australia (University of Queensland, 2009).

In order to gain a better understanding of Indigenous knowledge, it is helpful to consider the elements from which it is constituted. At least seven interrelated aspects have been identified from an international perspective and these elements have also been highlighted by scholars who represent an Indigenous Australian context.

According to these sources, Indigenous knowledge is:

- locally bound, indigenous to a specific area
- culture and context specific
- non-formal knowledge
- orally transmitted, and generally not documented
- dynamic and adaptive
- holistic in nature
- closely related to survival and subsistence for many people worldwide (Best practices using Indigenous knowledge, 2002, p. 13; Christie, 2006; Nakata, 2007).

In addition, other scholars assert that Indigenous knowledge is:
- governed by ancestral laws of representation (Brady 1997; Christie, 2006, p. 78).
- owned by Aboriginal people (Brady 1997; Christie, 2006; Nakata, 2007).

These key features of Indigenous knowledge can give teachers some insight into other ways of viewing the world when interacting with Indigenous Australians. This view can provide a sound foundation to begin the journey to becoming culturally competent and acquiring a new way of thinking that brings these two systems together. This will enable appropriate and meaningful communication and understandings between members of the two cultures.

Individuals bring their own interpretation of the different knowledge systems and how they can be brought together, and this is why 'interpretations' is a part of the framework. People's interpretations between the two knowledge systems will develop through lifelong experiences and will be at different levels or stages as they engage in the journey of cultural competency. It is important to note that it takes time for these interpretations to manifest to a point where effective interactions are achieved and maintained.

History and development of cultural competency: the story so far

Cultural competence (CC) has its origins in the health sector and is a relatively new concept in education in Australia. As a result, there is a need to create an awareness of its meaning, purpose and value among educational professionals across the various sectors.

The origins of CC emerged from the lack of culturally appropriate health care and social services for Indigenous populations and other minority groups in North America, New Zealand and Australia. This resulted in appalling statistics of the health and general well being of these populations (Grote, 2008). As a result, significant changes in the delivery of health care and social services began to emerge in North America in the 1980s, New Zealand in the late 1980s and in Australia in the late 1990s (Thomson, 2005).

There was increasing recognition among health professionals that, in order to effectively meet the needs of all their patients, they would need to address the socio-cultural factors and related issues that influenced interactions with them, and make appropriate changes to their service delivery. Subsequently, policy development and training programs began to acknowledge this issue in an effort to improve the health and general well-being of Indigenous populations.

Prior to the emergence of CC, cultural awareness was the major focus in training people from the various professions in preparation to work with other cultures. While this was considered to be appropriate at the time, it became apparent that these 'awareness' understandings did not necessarily translate into practice that demonstrated confident and effective interaction with Indigenous Australians and other cultures. Pre-existing thoughts and attitudes would often limit people's capacity to put practices into place that demonstrated cultural competency.

CC has come into prominence in education only within the last decade in Australia. The work of the Indigenous Higher Education Advisory Council (IHEAC) and prior to that the work done in the field of psychology (Ranzijn, et al., 2009) has seen CC gain more prominence across the education sector.

Importance of CC in the workplace

Cultural competency can operate at the individual and organisational levels. For individuals it is a way of demonstrating mutual respect, understanding and empathy towards people from other cultures and confident and effective communication and interaction. For organisations, CC entails implementing effective policy and practices at all levels. These policies and practices will drive organisational behaviour and promote access to, and effective services for, Indigenous communities.

Culturally competent organisations are not merely characterised by the employment of staff who may be representative of the various cultural groups that they serve. It also goes beyond the provision of professional learning to provide cultural understandings to employees. As stated by Olsen, Bhattaccharya & Scharf (2006) culturally competent organisations 'build mechanisms into the daily life of the organisation that foster continual learning, and that help in adapting services on an ongoing basis to be more respectful, effective and appropriate to diverse populations' (p. 3).

At the individual level, culturally competent professionals are in a better position to embrace differences in the knowledge, experiences and understandings of different ethnic groups including Indigenous Australians. This position facilitates effective engagement between both parties who participate equally in achieving positive outcomes in the workplace and the broader community.

In this section we have provided some background to cultural competency and introduced a broad level cultural competency framework. The next section will look more specifically at developing cultural competence in an educational context.

Applying cultural competency in education
Making a Difference framework

It is important to have a framework to base your understandings and practice on when working with Aboriginal students in an educational context. As individuals we tend to interpret things based on our own personal experiences, beliefs and values and beginning teachers will have various levels of cultural understandings and ways of communicating and relating to Indigenous Australians. This framework will help set you upon the journey toward becoming a culturally competent teacher; a journey which can last a lifetime.

A key feature of being culturally competent is the ability to develop strong and genuine relationships with Aboriginal people and other cultural groups. A dominant attribute in achieving this outcome is empathy. Showing empathy in your thoughts, attitudes and behaviour towards Aboriginal people in the community in which you are located is very important because at times you will be challenged by issues such as your beliefs, values and experiences that influence your response to the context.

Empathy

In the context of this chapter, empathy relates to:

- putting yourself in someone else's shoes to try and understand where they are coming from
- going deeper to understand why students/caregivers may behave or respond in the way that they do
- being sincere and genuine in being the catalyst of change
- encouraging your colleagues to join you on the journey towards cultural competency

The learning schema in Figure 12.2 highlights a process of developing cultural competency.

Figure 12.2 – Making a Difference framework

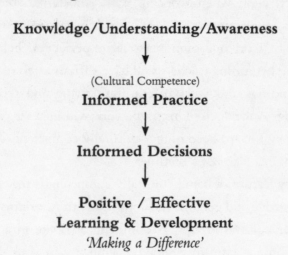

Knowledge/Understanding/Awareness

↓

(Cultural Competence)
Informed Practice

↓

Informed Decisions

↓

**Positive / Effective
Learning & Development**
'Making a Difference'

An important understanding of this learning schema is that having knowledge, understanding and awareness of Indigenous culture alone does not necessary translate into changes in professional practice. The above schema is guided by four key components which make up cultural competency:

- Cultural awareness provides a general understanding of Indigenous culture, society and history. It encourages self-reflection and awareness of personal biases.
- Cultural security addresses changes in actual practice. For example, in the provision of services, cultural rights, values and beliefs will not be compromised in the provision of services.

- Cultural safety focuses on cultural sensitivity and equitable power balance. For example, a practitioner's reflection and recognition of the impact of their own culture when working with people from other cultures.
- Cultural respect is the recognition of, and respect for, the rights and traditions of Indigenous Australians, so that, for example, kinship avoidance rules, sorry business and other ceremonies are recognised and respected (Grote, 2008, pp. 11–12).

These four elements provide a benchmark for students/practitioners to develop appropriate cultural understandings and skills that will lead to effective and confident communication and interaction with Indigenous Australians and other cultural groups. As a consequence of this, informed decisions can be made that can lead to positive and effective learning and development for Aboriginal students.

Cultural competency for teachers: a framework

This Cultural Competency framework highlights the key elements in the journey of becoming effective and culturally competent teachers.

Figure 12.3 – A Cultural Competency framework for teachers

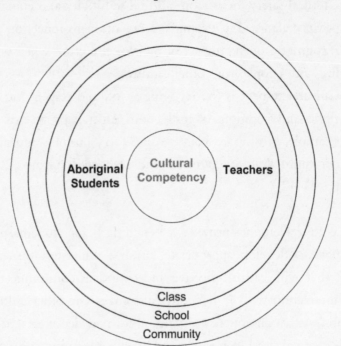

Each part of this framework is closely interrelated with all the other parts – no one part is more important than any other. On the right of the framework are teachers who enter an educational context with their own set of attitudes, beliefs, values, knowledge, background, preconceived ideas and life experiences that have influenced them up to that point in time. These factors will generally play a part in how they will interpret, view and act in an educational setting. Aboriginal students also come into an educational context with their own set of attitudes, beliefs, values, knowledge, background, preconceived ideas and life experiences. These factors play a part in how they will interpret, view and act in an educational setting.

For many teachers and Aboriginal students these factors are very different and this may result in misunderstandings and miscommunication. Rather than view these differences negatively, a culturally competent person will see them as an opportunity for teachers and students alike to embrace the differences and build interactions and relationships that lead to positive consequences.

With this in mind, the starting point for teachers is to get to know the Aboriginal students in their care and the community in which they live. This is important because Indigenous culture is very diverse across Australia and no one educational context is quite the same as another due to differences in language, cultural practices, location, family structure and general life experience. The development of this knowledge will set the foundation for developing strong relationships with students.

To successfully engage with Indigenous students, parents and the community that they come in contact with, teachers need to engage in a two-way cultural exchange that will foreground Indigenous culture in their thoughts, planning and practices.

For cultural competency to be effective in the classroom setting it will require a whole-of-school approach. Policy and planning for the implementation and practice of a cultural competency program should involve school administration staff, teachers and support staff. Importantly, it should incorporate and draw upon the understandings of the local Aboriginal community as active participants in both the planning and practice of cultural competency within the school. Schools should actively source and access professional learning in cultural competency to facilitate the planning, implementation and monitoring of cultural competency. Local school authorities and Indigenous education schools or centres within universities are often a good starting point in accessing cultural competency professional learning.

Culturally competent schools provide ongoing support to staff to reflect on their actions and behaviour when working with Aboriginal students and offer opportunities to network with other teachers and professionals when experiencing difficulties working with Aboriginal students.

Cultural competency and schooling: some examples

A full appreciation of the following five examples that illustrate the application of cultural competency in the school requires an understanding of the key characteristics of school-based cultural competency. These characteristic are as follows:

- Approach the unknown with an open mind and a positive perspective and willingness to embrace new ways of understanding and doing things.
- Things are not always what they seem. Try to dig beneath the surface and interrogate the context to think outside the square before reacting; there are often very valid reasons why things are and have happened the way they have.
- Know when to suspend cultural paradigms. This involves the ability to be able to put aside your own cultural beliefs, values and customs and view a situation from the perspective of another culture.
- Who stands to gain from a particular point of view? This is a question that needs to be asked throughout the cross-cultural interactions, especially when key decisions are being made. Will the process or activity and the outcome

be inclusive and have similar levels of benefits for all key stakeholders including minority groups?

- It's all about relationships, attitude and interaction. The focus should be on the need to build and maintain positive relationships, attitudes and interaction with students and the school community.
- Show genuine interest in students' culture, interests, what they value and their family and community; become familiar with the culture and apply these understandings in your interactions and practices.
- Accept diversity: No one Aboriginal group or community experience is the same because Indigenous communities are diverse across Australia.
- Aboriginal communities (urban, regional, rural and or remote) are dynamic places; the need to be flexible is paramount as situations and plans can change at short notice.

These examples have been drawn largely from personal experience, research into cultural competency in the tertiary sector (Gower, et al., 2010) and a recent review of the role of Aboriginal support staff in schools in Western Australia (Gower, et al., 2010).

Example One: Respecting and acknowledging Indigenous culture

Respecting and acknowledging the beliefs and values of Indigenous culture requires a non-Indigenous person to put their own beliefs and values to one side in order to embrace the differences in understandings between the two cultures.

The following example illustrates knowing when to suspend cultural paradigms and place cultural respect and cultural safety first. The setting is in a primary school in Yamaji country in the mid-west region of Western Australia.

It is a Monday morning and the school principal is greeted by a very excited Yamaji student who is keen to tell him of a major incident that had occurred over the weekend. An earth tremor had shaken the town and nearby mining site. The student asked the principal if he had felt the earth shake. The reply was 'yes' and the student eagerly continued the conversation by saying that the earth tremor was caused by 'Bimarra' (rainbow serpent and creator of fresh water-hole features across the landscape) who was woken up by explosives that were being set off at the mine site. 'Bimarra was not happy by the noise and being woken up, so he shook the earth,' the student explained.

The principal was very interested in all this and asked the student to tell him more about Bimarra. After this, the principal invited the student to retell his story to his class and informed the student that he would be there to listen to the story again. The principal could have chosen to ignore the explanation given by the student and dismiss this for the scientific explanation that the shaking of the ground was caused by two (tectonic) plates rubbing together.

Following the retelling of the story in class, the principal acknowledged and supported the story of Bimarra given by the student. He also explained to the class that there can be other explanations for the cause of the tremor. The principal explained the scientific cause but was quick to point out that the two explanations can exist together.

Example two: Interaction styles in the classroom

The way that people interact is very important to how they develop mutual understanding. Differences in the interaction styles between teachers and students can cause barriers to effective interaction and communication in the classroom (Galloway, 2008). The following practical insights into how many Aboriginal students interact can help teachers better understand how their students communicate. A culturally competent teacher will be able to put their own preferred ways of interacting aside and heed these differences in an effort to facilitate confident and effective communication with their students in the classroom.

- Generally spontaneous and excited: Many Aboriginal students are very tactile in their interaction and will often want to touch you, play with your hair, feel your skin, sit on your lap or rest their head on your shoulder, for example. Aboriginal students have different notions of personal space. It is important for teachers to understand that this is how Aboriginal children connect and to try not to tense up and pull away (because their own notion of personal space may make them feel their space has been invaded) but use their common sense in setting boundaries for their own personal space in a positive fashion.

- Non-response is an option and often a sign of respect: In many instances it is important to ask students for their responses and give permission for them to answer, as students may consider it is acceptable for them to not answer direct teacher questions.

- Looking down is a sign of respect: For many Aboriginal students this is a default setting when interacting with teachers. Rather than looking the teacher in the eye, they may look to the ground. This should not be interpreted as being disrespectful.

- Conversing in community: In many cases, for both adults and children, there are no set rules regarding who speaks to whom and when. This often means there are multiple conversations between a number of people occurring at the same time.
- Listening is an independent choice: For many Aboriginal children the choice not to listen to people is very acceptable. Children are often treated as adults from a young age and when they have heard enough they can choose to leave the conversational setting or no longer participate.

With these points in mind, it is important for teachers to be explicit with their expectations; build on students' initiation of interaction; value students' answers and work to understand meaning in the classroom. Teachers should also avoid shaming students by singling them out or putting them on the spot when questioning the class. Instead, ask for volunteers.

Example 3: The use of humour in connecting with students
Aboriginal children may often poke fun at teachers as a way of connecting. Some teachers get upset and defensive and miss the opportunity that this gives to develop relationships. For example there was a non-Aboriginal teacher who had a receding hair line. The students used to call him 'Big Jungen Banga' (big forehead). They used to make planes with their hands and pretend to land them on his head (like an airstrip) complete with a range of engine noises.

After one such event, the teacher sat the students down and asked if they wanted to hear the story of why he lost his hair on the top of his head. The students were very excited and sat down in anticipation. The teacher said, 'You know cyclone Rosita that came through Broome a while back?' The students nodded. 'Well I was silly enough to stick my head out the window to have a look and all my hair blew off!' The students felt really sorry for the teacher and started apologising, 'Sorry sir.' When the teacher looked at them and said... 'Gotcha!' The students thought it was a great joke.

It is important to note that we are not condoning teasing or bullying in any sense. Rather, this example highlights how humour is used in breaking down barriers and connecting with people.

Example 4: Racism and discrimination

Culturally competent teachers are agents for proactive change when it comes to racism and discrimination in the classroom. The Human Rights & Equal Opportunity Commission (1998) defines racism as, 'an ideology that gives expression to myths about other racial groups and ethnic groups, that devalues and renders inferior those groups, that reflects and is perpetuated by deeply rooted historical, social, cultural and power inequalities in society' (cited at www.racismnoway.com.au/about-racism/understanding/index-what.html). Teachers on the journey of cultural competence will be mindful of any of their own and/or others' practices that would devalue Aboriginal students and their culture.

A researcher, visiting a school, was informed by an Aboriginal support-staff member of an incident involving her and the school principal. She explained that she was coordinating the school activities for the National Aboriginal and Islander Day of Observance Committee (NAIDOC) week. She organised a local Aboriginal dance group to come into the school and work with each class throughout as well as a number of other interactive activities. Having obtained the majority of the funds from external sources she was able to come under budget. The principal inquired about the costs associated with the NAIDOC activities and, in particular, the cost of the dance group.

When told the amount, the principal responded with reference to next year's activities, 'For that amount, if you give me the money I will paint myself black and do the dances myself.' This comment caused a large amount of concern and anger for the Aboriginal staff member and illustrates the extent of racism that continues to exist in schools.

Example 5: The importance of understanding family

On a research fieldtrip a teacher expressed his frustration at not being able to speak with the parents of one of the Aboriginal students in the class. He had arranged a parent-teacher meeting through the Aboriginal education worker, and when the student's grandparents arrived, he refused to meet them, insisting on speaking to the parents.

This incident shows a lack of cultural competency on behalf of the teacher concerned. First, he ignored the advice from the Aboriginal education worker who had explained that the grandparents are at times the primary caregivers. Secondly, extended family ties are very important to Aboriginal people and differ considerably from a Western view of parenting which he did not take into consideration.

Leadership in developing cultural competency

The five examples above clearly illustrate the need for leadership to be demonstrated by the school administration and school staff. For cultural competency to be developed at the school level it is imperative that school leaders are the key drivers in developing and implementing policy and procedures that foster cultural competency practices within the school. In this way all school staff can take ownership of the development of cultural competency throughout the school.

Effective and ineffective practice

This chapter has explored how teachers can become more culturally competent in their dealings with Aboriginal and Torres Strait Islander students and the wider Aboriginal community. To help with your journey to becoming a more culturally competent teacher, table 12.1 below provides a guide for effective practice. It also illustrates a new way of thinking in Indigenous education.

Table 12.1 – Effective vs ineffective practice

Effective practice	Ineffective practice
Approach the unknown with an open mind and a positive perspective and willingness to embrace new ways of understanding and doing things.	Approaching the unknown with a closed mind. Not willing to accept different viewpoints and beliefs resulting in no positive change to practice.
Things are not always what they seem. Try to dig beyond the surface and interrogate the context to think outside the square before reacting. There are often very valid reasons why things are and have happened the way they have.	Reacting negatively to situations without considering reasons why certain things have happened the way they have. Responding to a situation without thinking first of the possible cultural implications and consequences.
Knowing when to suspend cultural paradigms. This involves the ability to be able to put aside your own cultural beliefs, values and customs and view a situation from the perspective of another culture.	No ability or desire to put aside your own cultural beliefs, values, customs and practices when working with Aboriginal people and communities.
Who stands to gain from a particular point of view? This is a question that needs to be asked throughout the cross-cultural interactions, especially when key decisions are being made. Will the process or activity and the outcome be inclusive and have similar benefits for all key stakeholders including minority groups?	Only caring about your own point of view and ignoring other viewpoints for the benefit of self-interest.

Effective practice	Ineffective practice
It's all about relationships, attitude and interaction. The focus should be on the need to build and maintain positive relationships, attitude and interaction with students and the school community.	Not having a relational approach to practice. Not valuing cultural differences when working with Aboriginal people and communities. 'Difference does not equate deficit.' Just because something is different to what you are used to, does not mean that it is a bad thing and not worth considering or doing.
Show genuine interest in students' culture, interests, what they value and their family and community. Become familiar with the culture and apply these understandings in your interactions and practices.	Showing no interest and respect for Aboriginal interests, values, family and culture. Having a self-centred approach and ignoring the inclusion of Aboriginal perspectives.
Accept diversity: No one Aboriginal group or community experience is the same because Indigenous communities are diverse across Australia.	Holding the opinion that all Aboriginal people are the same and share similar viewpoints and then basing interaction with them on this false assumption.
Aboriginal communities (urban, regional, rural and or remote) are dynamic places: The need to be flexible is paramount as situations and plans can change at short notice.	Being inflexible and an unwillingness to adapt to an ever-changing context.

Conclusion

Cultural competence is a relatively new concept and practice in educational settings. This chapter has attempted to introduce cultural competence in a general sense and to illustrate how it can be applied in educational contexts. It is important to note that becoming a culturally competent person/teacher is a lifelong journey. This journey will continually influence your ways of thinking, behaviour and interaction with Indigenous Australians and with people from other cultures.

It is hoped that the development of cultural competence will enable teachers to adopt a more informed position when working with Indigenous students and their families. The underpinnings of cultural competence will help support the teaching and learning practices in schools and classrooms to maximise outcomes for Indigenous students.

13

THE FUTURE:
DIRECTIONS AND BEST PRACTICE

Gary Partington

The effectiveness of schooling for Indigenous students has concerned successive governments at least since the 1970s, when the Interim Schools Committee stated that 'Aboriginal children undoubtedly constitute one of the most educationally disadvantaged groups in Australia' (Interim Committee for the Australian Schools Commission 1973, p. 106). In the past forty years, there have been numerous inquiries, strategies and projects to improve Indigenous students' outcomes and while there has been considerable improvement, they still lag well behind non-Indigenous Australian students on many measures. There are many reasons for the failure of efforts to change this situation and these are grounded in historical, social, health and economic factors. To be effective, the policies and practices have to address a broad array of complex issues confronting Indigenous education. The following list indicates the depth and complexity of the factors inhibiting change:

- Conquest and dispossession dating from the beginning of the European invasion in 1788. The loss of culture and the sense of being one with the land, removal from their traditional homelands and the development of dependence on non-Indigenous people originated with the arrival of the Europeans. The situation of aboriginal populations is repeated in other countries: the Ainu in Japan, the Sami in Sweden, the Inuit in Alaska and the Aborigines of Taiwan, among other nations. For all these people, the consequences have been similar but no less devastating.

- It wasn't just conquest and dispossession, although that would be a sufficient explanation. Subsequent treatment of Indigenous people in Australia has created a history of resistance and alienation: massacres that occurred until the 1930s, removal of children from families until as recently as the 1970s, forced loss of language and culture, and draconian laws regarding residence, work and ownership have resulted in many Indigenous people being downtrodden, dependent and apathetic.

- Initially, dependence developed from being forced to live on reserves and missions, and later due to reliance on welfare benefits to survive in the absence of work – a consequence of the unwillingness of employers to employ Indigenous people. As a result, Indigenous people were forced to rely on welfare for survival, particularly as efforts to make their own way in life were inhibited by legislation and regulations.

- Until the 1950s, most Aboriginal students were not permitted to attend state schools. Those who were fortunate to receive an education before that time did so in mission schools such as the one at Mt Margaret. As a consequence, there is only a recent history of universal participation in schooling.

- The end of missions and reserves coincided with liberalisation of regulations governing the lives of Indigenous people in the late 1960s and early 1970s. While the freedoms were welcomed, there was no effort to prepare Aboriginal communities for the new world. Unlike non-Indigenous people, they did not have a history of generations of children going to school or of being prepared in the preschool years for a literate and numerate society. Neither did parents understand the family structures and processes that contributed to success at school: developing awareness of reading, writing and numbers in the early years, giving priority to homework or using standard Australian English.

- The freedoms acquired in the late 1960s and early 1970s included access to alcohol. Combined with alienation, poverty and a sense of hopelessness among many Indigenous people, excess consumption of alcohol has impaired the functionality of many Indigenous people.

- Poverty accompanied these changes. The granting of equal wages in the 1970s destroyed many occupations previously the province of Indigenous workers, especially in the pastoral industry, where employers chose to employ non-Indigenous workers for the same wages. Poverty resulted in limited access to the resources necessary for the development of a literate life: books, games, appropriate furniture, experiences valued by the school and clothing suitable for attendance.

- Ignorance on the part of the dominant society of the different cultural attributes of Aboriginal people ensured that their children, on entry to school, experienced culture shock resulting in alienation as they endeavoured to work out the rules that applied in the classroom. Nearly all teachers are members of the dominant culture and have limited knowledge and experience of Indigenous ways of life or language.

- In addition, widespread racism in and out of school has a negative impact on Aboriginal students and their families. The effects on self-esteem, affiliation with the school and motivation to succeed can be severely impacted on by racism.
- All of the above contribute to poorer health of Aboriginal children, which has a bearing on their capacity for schooling. More absences, less energy, physical conditions that limit learning such as hearing loss and hepatitis, and lower self-concept reduce their potential for learning.

The above factors also contribute to negative perceptions of schooling on the part of many students. They feel alienated from school, they resist the efforts of teachers to regulate their lives, and they are likely to attend less often. As a consequence, they are perceived as having behavioural problems at school, receive less learning as a consequence of non-attendance and are less likely to conform to teacher expectations.

The chapters of this book provide guidance for teachers to bring about change. The potential for this change, however, depends considerably on the structures and processes put in place by governments to facilitate the work of schools. The most powerful influences are government policies accompanied by strategic initiatives and resources designed to implement them. At present, there is the potential for a coordinated Australia-wide policy-based approach built on four elements:

- a national curriculum
- Australia–wide testing
- the *My School* website
- the promotion of effective interventions.

It must be kept in mind that many Aboriginal students will suffer from none of the above issues. They will go to school, perform tasks diligently, succeed in their studies and graduate from high school ready for entry to university. It is important that teachers do not stereotype all Aboriginal students as requiring special attention. It is equally important, however, that they are able to identify the issues confronting those who are in need and then seek to address those needs quickly and competently.

Given the above factors, it can be seen that many Aboriginal students are confronted by considerable barriers to completing school successfully. To dismantle these barriers, the school not only has to provide instruction in literacy and numeracy but also has to create the climate within which the students will be receptive to learning. This is a complex requirement and can differ from child to child and school to school. On any day, students may enter school feeling tired, weak, hungry, agitated, resistant or angry. They may not be able to hear properly, understand the language of instruction or the expectations of the teacher. They may interpret teacher instructions and comments in ways that are not intended and possibly ignore them or take offence.

In turn, teachers may interpret the behaviours and communication of Aboriginal students as rude or offensive. Such judgments have the potential to put barriers to effective learning and instruction on both sides of teaching and learning.

Willingness to learn is the essential ingredient in successful education. For students who have been socialised to believe in the importance of education and, who are confident in the practices of schooling, willingness is usually inbuilt. This cannot be assumed for Aboriginal students because many have not experienced such socialisation and, to bring about effective learning, schools have to develop the willingness to learn. Teachers have to overcome the barriers that may exist due to the background conditions of the children's lives.

Where to start: policies

There is considerable support for action at many levels to overcome the issues confronting Indigenous students in school. As Nichols (2011) stated:

> The issues of housing, health and employment need to be equal, simultaneous and concurrent foci of government and private attention before education can bring about real and lasting change. These are by no means autonomous fields (Nicholls, 2009).

There are so many factors that contribute to the poor school outcomes of Aboriginal students that setting a starting point for change is difficult. In 2000, the Ministerial Council on Employment, Education, Training and Youth Affairs recommended a multi-faceted approach that entailed cooperative work by providers of education, health, housing, welfare, family services and other government agencies. Unfortunately, except in isolated instances, this never eventuated because of the silo mentality of government departments. Despite this, if change is to come from external inputs, such an approach is the most likely way of succeeding.

The foundation for a new direction in education that would benefit Indigenous students was laid with the *Melbourne Declaration on Educational Goals for Young Australians* (Ministerial Council on Education Employment Training and Youth Affairs, 2008). The declaration identified the education of Indigenous students as a top priority, with two key goals:

- ensure that schools build on local cultural knowledge and experience of Indigenous students as a foundation for learning and work in partnership with local communities on all aspects of the schooling process including to promote high expectations for the learning outcomes of Indigenous students
- ensure that the learning outcomes of Indigenous students improve to match those of other students.

To fulfil the goals specified in the declaration, the joint Commonwealth-State Closing the Gap strategy has been introduced. This strategy depends for its effectiveness on joint actions by all states and territories and agreements for change between Indigenous and non-Indigenous people. The goals of the policy and the areas being targeted were identified in chapter 2. A major focus of the policy is early childhood education and schooling, with the intention of closing the gap between Indigenous and non-Indigenous students in both realms.

The policy follows many previous efforts to improve the educational outcomes of Indigenous students. Nationwide policy initiatives have been proposed since the 1970s, when the Schools

Commission commenced funding for Indigenous education. The successive failure of these initiatives has clearly influenced the structures put in place. For example, for remote areas, a Coordinator General has been appointed to expedite service delivery and achievement of outcomes by cutting through red tape.

The benefit of collaboration between relevant government departments such as those involved in education, health, family services, employment and housing is that they are in a position to coordinate service delivery. For example, collaborating departments could ensure that a family with the following issues:

- receiving unemployment benefits
- children suffering from infections such as conductive hearing loss
- living in overcrowded, substandard accommodation
- living conditions not conducive to effective study, could gain the necessary support from multiple agencies to ensure their children are able to benefit more effectively from schooling.

Previous efforts at service coordination, however, have been difficult to achieve. The territorial protectiveness of government departments inhibits the potential for departmental staff to exchange knowledge and work together for the benefit of the children or their families. The decision to give the Coordinator General the power to cut through red tape may be a solution to departmental resistance to sharing information and coordinating service delivery.

If it were just government departments involved in bringing about change, the potential for success would be limited. However, the principal agent for change is the Council of Australian Governments, the peak intergovernmental body in Australia, which has clearly proposed not just departmental action but also Indigenous community collaboration through agreements:

> Effective engagement with Indigenous communities is critical to ensuring that Indigenous peoples' needs and aspirations are built into the planning and implementation of initiatives agreed by COAG.
>
> Working with Aboriginal and Torres Strait Islander people in the development of implementation plans is critical as their input, ideas and solutions will contribute to the overall success and sustainability of the reforms. Their active participation is integral to the effective design and implementation of the measures.
>
> As bilateral and local implementation plans are developed, it will be important to ensure that appropriate structures are established to facilitate local level community engagement and partnerships, collaborative decision making and ownership of implementation (Council of Australian Governments, 2009c, p. A-30).

The strategy is founded on a number of principles that are intended to ensure quality delivery of services and sustainability of the strategy:

Service delivery principles for services for Indigenous Australians

Priority principle: Programs and services should contribute to closing the gap by meeting the targets endorsed by COAG while being appropriate to local community needs.

Indigenous engagement principle: Engagement with Indigenous men, women, children and communities should be central to the design and delivery of programs and services.

Sustainability principle: Programs and services should be directed and resourced over an adequate period of time to meet the COAG targets.

Access principle: Programs and services should be physically and culturally accessible to Indigenous people recognising the diversity of urban, regional and remote needs.

Integration principle: There should be collaboration between and within governments at all levels and their agencies to effectively coordinate programs and services.

Accountability principle: Programs and services should have regular and transparent performance monitoring, review and evaluation.

(Council of Australian Governments, p. A24)

The purpose of these developments at government level is admirable: across the board improvements in all aspects of the lives of Indigenous people so that the gap between measures of their social situation and the situations of the rest of the Australian population are reduced significantly. This effort is essential and it is supported by a set of innovations described below that increase the potential for success considerably.

A coherent approach to change for Indigenous students in education

In education, three recent developments, when combined with the above policy, will contribute significantly to school efforts to close the gap. These are:

- the introduction of a common curriculum across Australia – the National Curriculum
- the requirement that all students take part in annual NAPLAN testing
- the publication of school performance statistics on the *My School* website.

The potential impact of these three changes on Indigenous education is considerable. The Australian Curriculum will provide a structure that will make it possible to enhance Indigenous students' learning outcomes. The key components that will enable this are:

- School and curriculum authorities can collaborate to ensure high quality teaching and learning materials are available for all schools.
- Greater attention can be devoted to equipping young Australians with those skills, knowledge and capabilities necessary to enable them to effectively engage with and prosper in society, compete in a globalised world and thrive in the information-rich workplaces of the future.
- There will be greater consistency for the country's increasingly mobile student and teacher population (Australian Curriculum Assessment and Reporting Authority, 2011a).

The implementation of these principles depends upon the continuing collaborative effort of the combined federal, state and territory governments. Sustained effort, ongoing provision of human and material resources and maintenance of a focus on the desired outcomes will be needed over the long term. However, the history of policies and practice for Indigenous education, health, welfare and other fields is not a good indicator of success for the present curriculum. Despite this, if the common curriculum is allied with nationwide testing and the evidence available on the My Schools website, there is significant potential for success.

Nationwide testing: NAPLAN

Until recently, there was no regular uniform measure of students' achievement across Australia. The introduction of the National Assessment Program – Literacy and Numeracy (NAPLAN) provides this measure. It is an annual assessment for all students across Australia in Years 3, 5, 7 and 9. The tests are conducted in reading, writing, language conventions (spelling, grammar and punctuation) and numeracy. With the implementation of NAPLAN, schools are accountable for the achievement of all their students, including Indigenous students.

In the past, the poor performance of Indigenous students has been attributed to them and their circumstances rather than the quality of educational provision. A uniform assessment process coupled with a set of curriculum outcomes that all students are expected to achieve will highlight the relative performance of Indigenous students. If it can be shown that students attending one school outperform similar students at other schools, there is a case for focusing on the work performed by the schools.

414

There are risks in implementing NAPLAN. For one thing, even though a broad curriculum may be designated, some teachers will focus on maximising students' scores on the test by concentrating on a narrow range of test-related skills. As a consequence, broader curriculum experiences may be lost. However, this risk has to be weighed against the essential need for Indigenous students to acquire literacy and numeracy skills as the foundation for a complete education. As indicated in chapter 2, their performance to date has been well below the performance of non-Indigenous students at all four levels of testing.

There is a dilemma for governments in obtaining information on students' performance. Schools where students do poorly clearly need more support to raise their performance levels. However, schools that achieve good results need ongoing resources to maintain the level of performance. If the good schools are rewarded for outcomes there will be fewer resources to build the quality of the schools that are performing more poorly.

My School website

The *My School* website came on line at the beginning of 2011. It has a dual purpose: to provide parents and students with information on each school, including school characteristics, policies, staffing, resources, student characteristics and student performance. It is also designed to provide schools and their communities:

with comparisons of their students' performances in literacy and numeracy with those of students in other schools, most importantly those in schools that serve similar students. These comparisons provide information to support improvements in schools. Among schools with similar students, those achieving higher student performances can stimulate others to lift expectations of what they and their students can achieve. The schools with higher performing students can be a source of information for others on the policies and practices that produce those higher performances (*My School*, 2011).

The website provides explicit information on the performance of students on NAPLAN, including improvements in their performance if they have sat two consecutive assessments in the school (such as Year 5 assessment followed two years later by the Year 7 assessment). The school's socioeconomic ranking (the Index of Community Socio-Economic Advantage – ICSEA) is recorded, as is the number of teachers, non-teaching staff and students, and school income. Comparison with schools that have a similar ICSEA, and also with other local schools can be made, so that it is possible to identify the relative performance of each school. This has created considerable debate. For example, the shadow Federal Minister for Education, Christopher Pyne, stated:

We think the *My School* website should provide information to parents but should be matched with new powers of autonomy to principals, so principals can address issues of concern in schools rather than just being shamed or stigmatised by a disadvantage index or ranking of school (C. Pyne, 2011).

For many parents, however, the site has been welcomed as it gives a clear account of their children's school performance for the first time. As one parent stated on the *My School* website:

> I think NAPLAN should go ahead. I think schools, parents and students all need to know how their child(ren) fit into the bigger picture. We should be grateful of such a test. I feel the Government developed this site to keep a more watchful eye on education and identify schools in need. Shouldn't that be celebrated? We can be such a pessimistic society at times and I think it's about time something jolted this country into an Education revolution. I welcome a National Curriculum and anyone who is anti-NAPLAN is selfish. It's for the benefit of the students and their future (Monteith).

The potential to identify schools that are performing below the level of similar schools provides Education Departments with the ability to allocate resources to improve performance. It will be unfortunate if the data are used to penalise those schools rather than to provide support such as professional learning for principals and teachers to improve school outcomes. The diverse social and cultural characteristics of each community in which a school is located cannot be reduced to an ICSEA number and differential characteristics of communities can have a dramatic effect on the performance of students in the school. The data on each school should be used only as a starting point for further investigation rather than a judgment of quality.

For Indigenous students, the combined effects of a common curriculum, NAPLAN testing and the *My School* website are a vehicle for improving the quality of educational provision but also shine a spotlight on the students' application to their schoolwork as well as the contribution of the family and community to students' participation and effort.

However, there is a limitation to the strategy proposed in the Closing the Gap approach: the potential to be assimilationist. With the strong focus on achievement in literacy and numeracy, the importance of maintaining a focus on Indigenous language and culture may be overlooked by schools. The Western Australian Aboriginal Education and Training Council (AETC) stated:

> The Plan is very much an assimilation approach and does not recognise or respect the rich cultural heritage of Aboriginal and Torres Strait Islander Australians nor does it build on their cultural heritage. Whilst Aboriginal Australians want their children to be competent in English literacy and numeracy they also desire that they are literate and fluent speakers in an Aboriginal language as well. The explicit teaching and learning of Aboriginal studies and histories is important for advancing reconciliation for all students but is not included in the Plan and should be (Western Australian Aboriginal Education Training Council, 2010, p. 1).

As one solution to the potentially assimilationist nature of the plan, the AETC advocated 'formalised school and community partnerships where roles, responsibilities, targets and strategies are defined in a concerted effort to significantly improve educational outcomes' (Western Australian Aboriginal Education Training Council, 2010, p. 3). The development of partnerships between schools and communities is a part of ongoing improvement in the quality of schooling for Indigenous students and is promoted in the *What Works* program (www.whatworks.edu.au) and is a key component in Noel Pearson's advocacy for a change in the direction of education (Pearson, 2009b). Both these issues are discussed below.

Support strategies for schools

In recent years a number of productive strategies have commenced that have the potential to provide schools with the professional learning and resources to make changes that will enable them to improve Indigenous students' educational outcomes in line with the expectations of education departments. Two of these strategies have been developed at a national level for principals, on the one hand, and schools generally on the other. *Dare to Lead* and *What Works* have been accepted nationwide as online mentoring programs for schools to change.

Dare to Lead

The Dare to Lead strategy commenced in 2000. It is targeted at school principals to raise the performance of their schools to achieve success for Aboriginal students, particularly in literacy and numeracy. Currently, over half the schools in Australia are affiliated with the strategy. Membership provides access to professional development activities and resources, particularly in relation to intercultural exchange and knowledge and also enables principals to share advice on successful practice (Dare to Lead, 2011a).

Extensive resources are available for schools to draw on to improve the quality of provision for Indigenous students. For example, a checklist to ascertain whether a school is providing a quality program for Indigenous students is available for download (http://www.daretolead.edu.au/DTL08_SchInit_Main). Such resources direct schools towards processes that make the school environment and instruction more amenable for Indigenous students and can improve participation, retention and achievement.

There are many stories from member schools and individuals that describe their innovations, experiences and successes. These are invaluable as tools for professional development for principals, teachers and other staff of schools. One story by an Indigenous researcher described the powerful motivating effect of individuals on her life: a factor that led her, ultimately, to gaining a university degree and becoming a researcher. She identified the following attributes that motivational teachers possessed:

- These people weren't just teachers; they were motivators and inspiring people.
  I grew up in a house with no books, just some magazines. These people introduced me to books.
  They had an interest in what I was doing outside school – I heard you played basketball, how did the team go?'
  They always said I could do better but never put me down.
  They gave us time to think.
  They were great listeners.

- They made learning fun, and took learning outside the classroom.
  They understood your strengths and weaknesses. They understood different students' learning styles.
  They stimulated you with things you could relate to.
  They often wore funky clothes. You'd love to go to their class because you didn't know what they'd be wearing next time.
  They always knew your name and what you were interested in.
  They sat down with students rather than standing in front of you.
  They believed in your ability.
  (http://www.daretolead.edu.au/STORY_What_Makes _A_Difference)

The Dare to Lead strategy is empowering because schools can learn from the experiences of others in similar situations to them through their examples on the web, and they can also make contact with those schools to gain a deeper understanding of the means by which they developed their innovations. Principals also have the opportunity to attend conferences and professional learning activities to enhance their capacity to implement changes consistent with best practice in Indigenous education.

Recently, the Dare to Lead strategy entered a fourth phase of development and this appears to derive from the success of the *Follow the Dream/Partnerships for Success* program as it seeks to embrace a wider range of supporters to bring about change:

In its earlier phases *Dare to Lead* challenged the profession to take action to improve the outcomes of Indigenous students, and to build Reconciliation. It is undeniable that these changes will be achieved and even more strongly when the profession works with partners to build this success. It is partnership which has seen school leaders learning together, school leaders working with community and school leaders working with organisations to create many of the successes to date. In this new phase of *Dare to Lead*, the project will draw further on the cooperative effort of education sectors, professional associations, organisations and the corporate and philanthropic sectors to create sustained, systemic change and improved outcomes, fostered through partnership (*Dare to Lead*, 2011a).

Judging from the examples provided on the *Dare to Lead* website, at present most solutions are being sought either within the school or within the school community. For a more effective resolution of many issues, however, cooperation with other service providers is essential to enable the multi-faceted approach identified earlier. It is to be hoped that the new phase of development of *Dare to Lead* will incorporate this broader service delivery for Indigenous students. According to information in the *What Works* workbook, success for Indigenous students has been elusive. It is stated that:

There were generally no significant changes in Indigenous Year 3, 5 and 7 students' performance against the national benchmarks for reading, writing and numeracy between 1999 (2001 for Year 7 students) and 2007. A substantially lower proportion of Indigenous than non-Indigenous students in all year levels achieved the national minimum standards for reading, writing and numeracy in 2008 (Department of Education Employment and Workplace Relations, 2011b).

The What Works strategy provides another form of support for teachers of Indigenous students, with a web site dedicated to improving the quality of schooling for Indigenous students through promoting effective strategies.

What Works: the works program

The *What Works* program is related to *Dare to Lead* and is another online set of resources for schools to assist them to improve outcomes for Indigenous students. The program is based on the assumption that schools are confronted by a common set of issues that need to be resolved if Indigenous students are to succeed. These issues are student suspensions, literacy, numeracy, engagement (attendance and participation), boarding and health. A more recent innovation than *Dare to Lead*, *What Works* is a school-based program that encourages teachers and administrators to try approaches that have been successful elsewhere. The strategy identifies the following brief for teachers:

The task, for Indigenous students as a group, is to improve levels of literacy and numeracy, increase rates of school completion and successful participation in post-school options while at the same time respecting students' cultures, and maintaining partnerships with carers and community (*What Works*, The Work Program, 2010).

The strategies that are recommended for schools to use in carrying out these tasks are consistent with sound principles and good practice for working with Indigenous students. The approaches are based on local needs so that the issues dealt with are specific to the schools involved. The strategy identifies the formation of relationships as a critical first step towards improved education for Indigenous students, a strategy that is reinforced in Chapter 12 of this book. Three partnerships are noted: between teacher and students, between teacher and Indigenous worker and, as shown below, between teacher and parent or carer:

There can be a partnership between a teacher or teachers and an individual student's parents or carers. These informal partnerships might arise from deliberate efforts by either party, or might develop from informal contacts made outside the school, perhaps at sporting events or shopping centres. Don't ignore these valuable opportunities to begin conversations. Who knows? They may become important partnerships. Remember, though (but don't assume), that Indigenous parents may have had schooling experiences that were negative and relatively brief and their children may be breaking new ground by staying on at school. Be sensitive to this. (*What Works*, The Work Program, 2011)

Data collected by the *What Works* team during work with schools indicate that the approaches are successful (Department of Education Employment and Workplace Relations, 2011b) as student attendance and achievement improve following implementation of changes.

A key issue for schools with the implementation of the Closing the Gap strategy, however, is the maintenance of Indigenous students' language, culture and self-concept in the face of the concerted effort to improve literacy and numeracy. The key to ensuring students are able to retain a balance between the life of the home and that of the school is the development of close links between the school and the community and its families. The initiative for developing these links lies with the schools because they are in a position of power in this situation. They must demonstrate a desire to form relationships with the community if change is to occur.

Many schools already experience the benefits of such links. The *What Works* program promotes the development of school-community relationships and there is ample advice on appropriate steps to this end (*What Works*, The Work Program, 2011). For example, the Mount Lockyer Primary School and its Aboriginal community in Western Australia drew up a school-community partnership agreement which led to an action plan being drawn up each term by a committee of parents and teachers. The consequence of these changes was accompanied by improvements in attendance and performance:

> The agreement has made a difference to attendance, because it's all documented and parents are more aware. We keep them informed about kids whose attendance

is improving and kids who are going down, so it's all recognised. It works because we act on it straight away. It's important that when you bring attendance to parents' attention you have all the documented statistics there. The school–community partnership has definitely helped with that.

Also, since the school–community partnership agreement we now have IEPs [Individual Learning Plans] for every Noongar kid in the school and those Noongar kids who need extra help are picked up in small group work in maths and literacy...The parents know what's happening and know all the processes involved. It's all very clear and I think that's why the community agreement is working here (*What Works*, The Work Program 2011)

Follow the Dream/ Partnerships for Success

One strategy that has relied heavily on engaging with the community is the Follow the Dream/Partnerships for Success strategy (*What Works*, The Work Program, 2006; Partington, Galloway, et al., 2009). This model of intervention has proven to be very effective in guiding Aboriginal students to success in Western Australia and other states. Commenced in 1997 at one regional high school in Karratha, the strategy is now operating in over 25 sites in several states. It has been responsible for hundreds of Aboriginal students completing high school, entering post school educational opportunities and gaining jobs with good career prospects.

The FTD/PFS strategy provides a holistic environment in which successful outcomes are likely to be achieved. The components of this strategy include:

- a coordinator who cares for the students, demands high standards from them and intervenes on their behalf with teachers, parents, educational institutions and employers
- a learning centre where modelling of study practices occurs and where students have a structured, studious environment in which to work
- tutorial assistance that is set within a collaborative setting with other students and tutors that enhances commitment to studies
- enrichment activities such as university visits, employment site visits, camps for personal development, leadership training and the promotion of collegiality
- the deliberate effort to make the students feel special about their participation in the program at their school and so combat other pressures that might drive them away from study: peer pressure, sport commitments and other activities that previously were considered of greater importance
- acknowledgement of the role of parents and caregivers in the education endeavour, so they become partners in the drive for their children to succeed at high school rather than outsiders with limited knowledge and understanding of what is going on
- for many of the students at industry-sponsored sites, the strong motivation that success at school will translate into a well paid occupation with status in the community

- additional resources through the Department of Education and Training, the Department of Education, Employment and Workplace Relations and, for industry sponsored sites, the industry partners, that provide access to the materials and activities that make the strategy possible
- effective training of coordinators and supervision of sites by the Department of Education and Training Central Office staff and The Graham (Polly) Farmer Foundation staff to ensure effective functioning of sites (Partington, Galloway, et al., 2009).

The success of graduates of the program has been a motivating factor for other students to seek entry to it. It is likely that the program will have a significant impact on the lives of Aboriginal people. A key element in the success of the program is the framework of support it provides to the students. The coordinator is central to this framework and manages the allocation of resources, addresses student needs and concerns, and provides advocacy for the student in his or her interactions with teachers and school administration. The coordinator carries out the following roles:

- maintains communication with family and community to inform them of the progress of the student and to keep abreast of issues confronting the student
- ensures students have adequate access to resources at school (and often at home) to do their school work
- monitors and counsels students regarding their performance
- builds group cohesion so that students develop into a peer group seeking success in their schoolwork

- organises events that broaden students' understanding of the world of work and opportunities in higher education, and promotes their self-concept.

The research report on the FTD/PFS strategy concluded that good coordinators demonstrated the following characteristics:

- good relationships with all stakeholders (the 'warmth' component of the warm demander model (Fanshawe, 1989))
- standards and expectations (the 'demander' component of the warm demander model; e.g., Fanshawe, 1999; Scanlon, 2004; Vialle and Quigley, 2002)
- instructional leadership which includes good administrative skills, raising awareness of teachers outside the program about the educational needs of and teaching strategies for Aboriginal students, and raising the profile of the program among stakeholders (Partington, Galloway, et al., 2009, p. 73).

There is a feature of the program that gives it an advantage over many other programs for Indigenous students: it caters for students who are already aspirational. That is, they have a desire to succeed. However, this does not mean they are privileged in other respects when compared with other Aboriginal students. Many, particularly in rural and remote areas, come from severely disadvantaged backgrounds and have few resources within the family or community to complete high school. It is through the support provided by FTD/PFS that they achieve high school graduation and entry to further education or occupations.

The strength of the FTD/PFS program is threefold:

- at the sites at which it has been developed, it has been driven by key staff in the Department of Education and the Polly Farmer Foundation. Program champions in both organisations have ensured the specific school sites focus on the important goals for the program and strive to deliver the outcomes sought
- it develops in the group of students a willingness to strive for achievement so that they resist alternative temptations such as membership of peer groups that are alienated from school and the desire for early school leaving
- it produces successful graduates who will be role models for all Aboriginal students. Their achievement indicates that success is possible, and this has certainly been the case with the program: it has turned out doctors, lawyers, teachers, tradesmen and entrants to a wide range of occupations. Seeing these successes, others are more likely to be motivated to succeed themselves.

The strategy is being extended to other states by the Graham (Polly) Farmer Foundation, who are responsible for securing funding from industry partners and implementing the program in schools. The requirements for a program in a school include a full-time coordinator, tutors (provided by the Aboriginal Tutorial Assistance Scheme, now run by state departments of education), a centre for the after-school enrichment centre and resources for extra curricular enrichment activities. Whether it can be disseminated more broadly depends on the policy directions of the federal and state governments. However, recent changes to *Dare to Lead* indicate that that strategy is incorporating key elements of the FTD/PFS approach.

The greatest threat to the program is the view that resources should be distributed to those with the greatest learning deficits so that they receive the greatest support, while those who demonstrate the capacity to cope with the education system receive less. This view underpinned federal government allocations for ATAS funding in recent years: students who demonstrated success on NAPLAN or equivalent measures of achievement were excluded from receiving ATAS. It should be recognised that many successful students succeed because of the support they receive and without that support they would join the ranks of the failures.

In schooling for the majority of students it is quite common to provide additional resources for the successful. *Gifted and Talented* programs as well as programs in the performing and creative arts have been a feature of the educational landscape for many decades. To provide similar support for motivated and able Indigenous students in the FTD/PFS program would provide a foundation for a culture of success on which other students can model their own school performance.

Accelerated literacy

Literacy is the key to success in all areas of the core curriculum. If students can't read, their failure in school is guaranteed and this is the case for many Indigenous students, as previous chapters have demonstrated. It is essential that effective strategies are employed to develop literacy. A strategy that has the potential to teach reading effectively and make a significant difference to the school outcomes for Indigenous students is based on scaffolded learning (Gray & Cowey 2001). This strategy is gaining acceptance across Australia as a way of overcoming illiteracy. The National Academic Literacy Program (NALP), which teaches this strategy, is now a core part of the What Works program and aims to improve literacy outcomes for students to an age appropriate level. Accelerated literacy is a set of strategies that develop students as literate in the sense that they are able to read and interpret books and also teaches 'how a literate person thinks and acts to be successful at school' (Gray & Cowey, 2005, cited in Cooper, 2008, p. 124):

> In scaffolding interactions teachers manage learning engagement initially through modelling and providing information to learners rather than asking learners to 'discover' or explore using their own learning resources. However, the developing interaction process in the classroom is a highly dynamic one and the roles of teacher and learners shift as interaction progresses over time until the learners can function by themselves without teacher help. This kind of teacher support makes teacher expectations about the ways of learning and thinking necessary for school success clearly visible to learners, especially those who don't have the culturally acquired understandings necessary to 'tune in' to school learning without such explicit help (Gray & Cowey, 2001).

The approach requires teachers to scaffold learning for students. Instead of commencing instruction at the level students are currently at, the teacher works in the *zone of proximal development*, a conceptual region of learning where students are capable of learning *with assistance*, so that their learning is accelerated compared with working without assistance. This is acknowledged in the accelerated literacy program in the first instance by the assessment strategy:

> Assessment in the Accelerated Literacy program regularly takes place at two levels in accord with this understanding. First students are assessed on reading texts they have not seen before to determine what they can read **without support.** This assessment determines their Individual Reading Level (IRL). Secondly they are assessed on the text that has been the focus of an Accelerated Literacy teaching sequence in the classroom: what they can read **with the support of classroom teaching.** This assessment determines their Independent Working Level (IWL) (Gray, et al., 2003, cited in Cowey, 2005, p. 8).

Text selection is important:

- it should be written in literate language – that is, the language of books, not the everyday vernacular or oral language that assumes the speaker and listener share a context
- it should be chosen because it is age-appropriate for the majority of a class, or close to age-appropriate
- it should have the potential to be enjoyed by students, so that they feel motivated to read and can experience the excitement of learning that reading offers (Cowey, 2007).

An overview of the structure of literacy teaching using the method is outlined below. The process begins with low order literate tasks where students gain basic knowledge about the text and acquire the cognitive skills and knowledge to accept and enjoy the text. Then they progress to high order tasks so they can become competent in selecting, analysing and discussing texts. Subsequent stages include transition to spelling and writing.

Overview of teacher tasks in the Accelerated Literacy teaching sequence

1: Low order literate orientation. The teacher...
   a) Summarises text and begins to build shared corpus of knowledge
   b) Interprets illustrations, story and ideology
   c) Poses questions students can answer, having been given information.
2: The teacher reads text passage (while students follow/ read along).
3: High order literate orientation. Using enlarged text, e.g., on OHP, the teacher...
   a) Directs students to locate, recognise and articulate important words and phrases (*preformulation*)
   b) Analyses author's language choices, possible intended meanings and explains author's technique
   c) Guides discussion using planned 'questioning/scaffolding sequence' (Gray,2007, p. 38) to elicit and build on shared knowledge (*reconceptualisation*).

4: Transformations (from readers to writers). The teacher...
   a) guides student groups as they (physically) deconstruct text using cardboard strips of selected passages
   b) directs students' attention to grammatical features, punctuation and author's intended meanings
   c) organises word recognition tasks, leading to spelling (early childhood classes).
5: (or 6) Spelling. The teacher...
   a) analyses structure of key words
   b) guides students to chunk word-letter patterns.
6: (or 5) Writing. The teacher...and students jointly reconstruct text passages
   a) discuss writing techniques previously analysed and students practice
   b) the teacher guides students in their independent writing tasks.

The National Accelerated Literacy Project (AL) has been implemented at many schools across Australia. In Western Australia it has been taught extensively in Aboriginal schools that are a part of the Aboriginal Independent Community Schools (AICS) for over ten years. These schools started using AL in 1999. A 2010 report of the outcomes of student progress in literacy, based on ability to read unseen benchmarked texts, showed a dramatic increase across the schools. In 2001, no junior primary students (Years 1–3, or six–eight year olds) were literate; by 2010, 76 per cent were literate. For Years 4–7, the improvement was from 4 per cent literate in 2001, to 93 per cent literate in 2010 and for Years 8–12, the increase was from 56 per cent to 97 per cent.

The report also showed the students' performance on NAPLAN in 2008 and 2009. There were improvements in all years but not in all areas of literacy. For example, for Year 3 students there was significant improvement in reading and spelling but a slight decline in writing, grammar and punctuation. Similar variable results occurred in Years 5, 7 and 9. However, these are consecutive year results for different cohorts of students (Year 3 students sitting the assessments in 2008 would next sit for the Year 5 assessment two years later). In the schools where the assessments took place, all students, regardless of their time in the school, were included in the testing. Given that most schools would have had a relatively high turnover of students, these results are quite remarkable.

Implementation of Accelerated Literacy at Salisbury North School in South Australia: the Deadly Writin, Readin' and Talkin' Project (DWRAT).

This primary school has a population of around 400 students of whom 16 per cent are Indigenous. The school commenced the scaffolded literacy program in 1998. The following description by Bronwyn Parkin outlines the way the program is used in the classroom (*What Works*, The Work Program, 2006):

> [The program] consists of the careful study of one quality written text per term, using that text as the basis for reading, sight words, spelling and writing. Using functional grammar as a tool, teachers and students pay close attention to the text, and the strategies that writers have used to achieve

their purposes. Gradually, as the students become knowledgeable about the text, they are able to appropriate these strategies, as well as the spelling, and use the original author's resources to produce their own quality texts.

Each DWRAT class has a 50 minute scaffolded literacy lesson four days a week. In addition, the functional grammar teacher gives a focused grammar lesson in some classes once a week. The scaffolded literacy lessons are team taught in various ways, often including Aboriginal Education Workers. There are almost always at least two adults in each classroom, although the older classes have demonstrated that it is possible to teach some aspects of scaffolding effectively without this extra support. There are many other features worthy of note in the pedagogy:

Repetition: The study of one text has typically covered ten weeks of a term. A first reaction by many teachers is that students will get bored. They don't get bored, they become successful.

Choice of texts is crucial to the process. Rich texts with literate, rather than 'spoken', grammatical structures that will assist students in accessing more complex texts are selected at a level of literary complexity commensurate with the child's age.

Language for talking about texts: Functional grammar is used as a rich resource for talking about texts. Comprehensive notes are provided to assist teachers.

Preformulated questions: We try to ensure that all students have the chance to respond successfully to questions. We preface each question with an introduction to the question, a preformulation which tells the students the purpose and scope of the question so that all students know what is in the teacher's head.

Spelling: Words are not taught as spelling words until students are able to read them out of context, and then students are encouraged to use their visual skills to learn groups of letters, rather than only 'sounding it out'. This simple development in teaching spelling has had remarkable results in the DWRAT classrooms for some Aboriginal students and some English as a Second Language [ESL] students who have had little success previously in mastering English spelling.

Potential for critical literacy: The depth at which we study a text provides many opportunities for students and teachers to develop critical analytic skills.

Student behaviour management: Time spent on controlling minor behaviour issues is time not spent on literacy. Therefore we focus on the learning at hand, rather than on minor behavioural issues. We have seen some encouraging changes in student behaviour as students become successful and begin to make sense of their learning. However, behaviour management is sometimes still a struggle in this context.

Committed and skilled teaching teams: While some parts of scaffolding can be taught in a whole class, our experience is that many aspects are best taught in smaller groups, so one extra adult is often needed for literacy lessons. In any case, schools with a high proportion of Aboriginal students will have an Aboriginal Resource Teacher who can assist. Our school has also coordinated the support of the ESL teacher to assist Scaffolded Literacy. This pedagogy is not just for Special Education students. We have been using it successfully in composite classes, with ability skills ranging from Profile level 2 to Profile level 6 in the one class.

One-on-one reading instruction: In addition to scaffolded approaches in the classroom, our Aboriginal Education Workers and School Service Officers have been trained in one-to-one scaffolding in reading. This support supplements the learning in the classroom.

Assessment and monitoring: Of course, assessment is not exclusive to scaffolding. It is, however, fundamental to our project. If we are not sure that our pedagogy is making a difference, there is little point in continuing.
(www.whatworks.edu.au/dbAction.do?cmd
=displaySitePage1&subcmd=select&id=292)

As with any innovation, AL requires support from outside the school so that teachers learn the skills to implement the new strategies required. The program in these schools is dependent on the provision of support funding for professional learning among teachers so they can implement accelerated literacy in their classrooms. This program requires support from the Closing the Gap initiative if it is to succeed and be disseminated across the nation so that Indigenous students throughout the country can close the gap in literacy.

Noel Pearson and Indigenous education

Concern at the failure of schooling to bring about equality of outcomes for Indigenous students led Noel Pearson, an Indigenous leader of communities in the Cape York Peninsula region, to seek solutions elsewhere. Drawing on the *No Excuses* movement in the United States, he has developed a pedagogy based on three elements:

- no excuses for educational failure will be acceptable
- the development of skills, particularly literacy and numeracy, are the key to both self-esteem and success
- instruction based on direct instruction is the ideal pedagogy (Pearson, 2004).

Pearson identified easy access to welfare for Indigenous students once they leave school as a factor in their dependency:

There is no firm bottom-line in the welfare system that young indigenous people enter as they approach adulthood. As long as that system does not say 'there is no alternative to work, education and training', all the youth programs and interventions will come to very little.

There needs to be both help and hassle.

At present the welfare system provides unconditional income support to young people once they leave school. It immediately provides an easy option to young people: you don't have to undertake further education or gain skills or work, because you will receive an income regardless.

This path of least resistance becomes the road well-travelled. Young people have free money to purchase grog, cannabis and other substances. They soon become addicted. Thereafter the welfare system pays for their addiction (Pearson, 2004).

Among the principles underlying his pedagogy, Pearson listed the following:

- Indigenous Australian culture is a culture of responsibility and reciprocity. Ours is a culture of law and learning. Ours is a culture of transmission of knowledge. Our culture is our strength.
- We will take our responsibilities to our children. We will not allow other people to use the fact that our children are Indigenous as an excuse for educational failure.
- Our children have their own culture and languages, other children have other cultures and languages. No culture or language predisposes children for educational failure.
- The fact that some of our children come from disadvantaged,

441

and even dysfunctional, backgrounds, will no longer be an excuse for educational failure.

• We will understand and be sensitive to the difficulties facing our children and we are going to find every support to deal with them, but we will not allow these difficulties to be an excuse for educational failure (Pearson, 2009b).

In Queensland, Pearson's approach to change has resulted in a partnership, Cape York Welfare Reform, between the communities of Aurukun, Coen, Hope Vale and Mossman Gorge, the Australian Government, the Queensland Government and the Cape York Institute for Policy and Leadership to restore social norms and local authority in the face of chronic levels of welfare dependency, social dysfunction and economic exclusion in the Cape York district (Queensland Government, 2010). The partnership is intended to improve educational outcomes, health and employment and reduce violence, welfare dependency and hospital admissions. A particular focus of the reforms is the introduction of alcohol restrictions which are seen as a cause of many of the problems confronting the Cape York communities.

In the 2009–10 report on the partnerships (Queensland Government, 2010) positive change was reported. Violence offences and hospital admissions resulting from harm were reduced and school attendance was improving or was stable in some communities. Unfortunately in others, violence has continue unabated. Employment in community projects has increased and a home building program has improved housing for communities.

NAPLAN results were not available for some of the schools in the area but for those that were, results were varied. For

Hopevale, where Pearson's strategy was principally focused, reading improvement was markedly better than similar schools. This could be due to the use of direct instruction as the preferred method to teach basic skills of literacy and numeracy, an approach that is more effective than student-directed approaches. However, it is doubtful that this strategy will enable students to reach high levels of literacy and numeracy without resorting to alternative instructional strategies, as more conventional methods of instruction would be required for more advanced learners.

Cultural competency training for educators

The success of any teaching method depends very much on the quality of the teachers who work with the students. In the case of Aboriginal students, teachers' ability to work in ways that are culturally appropriate is crucial to being acceptable as mentors and guides. Chapters in this book emphasise the need for teachers to develop an effective relationship with students and instruct them in the most effective ways that are consistent with their backgrounds and needs.

There is a growing awareness in universities of the value of cultural competency training for pre-service teachers so that they enter the school system with the capacity to teach in ways that accommodate the backgrounds of the Indigenous students in their classes.

Cultural competency (CC) has been defined as 'a set of congruent behaviors, attitudes, and policies that come together in a system, agency, or among professionals and enable that system, agency, or those professionals to work effectively in cross-cultural situations' (Cross, Bazron, Dennis & Isaacs, 1999, cited in Grote, 2008, p. 14). Grote reported that there were clear benefits in institutional adoption of CC training:

> The increased numbers of Indigenous people with CC education and training entering the workforce can result in more culturally appropriate services for Indigenous and other clientele. More Indigenous people in the workforce translates into more effective service organisations (Grote, 2008, p. 45).

There are other benefits of CC training:
1. increased sense of empowerment in clientele and greater appreciation for the service providers
2. the reduction in client angst and apprehension about the system
3. an increase in the proportion of community members seeking services and complying with recommendations of service providers
4. higher satisfaction levels among clients
5. enhanced educational experiences of service providers
6. improvements (in health) community-wide
7. a greater valuing and esteem among staff members for one another (Smith, 1998, cited in Grote, 2010, p. 45).

The processes by which pre-service teachers can acquire the skills suitable for teaching within a CC framework are described in detail by Gower and Byrne in Chapter 12. However, CC training is only likely to be widespread in universities if it has the support of university administrators to ensure it is implemented in courses, and the government agencies to ensure no graduate is employed unless they have undergone such training.

Conclusion

Aboriginal education is poised for a dramatic improvement in all outcomes. The persistent efforts of researchers, education institutions and governments to make headway in attendance, participation, achievement and attitudes to school have reached a point where, with suitable coordination of effort and appropriate resources, the gap between non-Aboriginal and Aboriginal students should close. Innovations such as *Follow the Dream/ Partnerships for Success*, accelerated literacy and the approaches employed in *What Works* have been shown to be effective. The dissemination of these innovations more widely is already possible with the structures in place: *What Works* and *Dare to Lead* programs for teachers, NAPLAN to measure outcomes and the *My School* website to moderate the performance of schools and inform the community of school outcomes.

The benefits for Aboriginal students that follow from closing the gap in educational outcomes are considerable: access to further and higher education opportunities, entry to employment, elimination of poverty and freedom from dependence on welfare. However, these goals should cause us to lose sight of other important outcomes, particularly Aboriginal cultural, linguistic and social outcomes that are essential for the maintenance of identity and self-esteem. For educators to attend to these matters, cultural competency is essential and teacher education institutions must incorporate programs in cultural competency in pre-service programs.

BIBLIOGRAPHY

Abjorensen, N. (2009). The history wars. In J. George & K. Huynh (Eds.), *The culture wars: Australian and American politics in the 21st century (pp. 148–56).* South Yarra, VIC: Palgrave Macmillan.

Aboriginal Child Sexual Assault Taskforce. (2006). *Breaking the silence, creating the future: Addressing child sexual assault in Aboriginal communities in NSW.* Sydney: NSW Attorney General's Department.

Aboriginal Education Policy Taskforce. (1988). *Report of the Aboriginal Education Policy Task Force.* Canberra: Department of Employment, Education and Training.

Aboriginal Health Council of South Australia. (1995). *Reclaiming our stories, reclaiming our lives: An initiative of the Aboriginal Health Council of South Australia.* Adelaide: Dulwich Centre Publications.

Aboriginal and Torres Strait Islander Social Justice Commissioner. (1998). *Social Justice Report 1998.* Sydney: Human Rights and Equal Opportunity Commission.

——. (1999a). *Social Justice Report 1999.* Sydney: Human Rights and Equal Opportunity Commission.

——. (1999b). *Submission to the Human Rights and Equal Opportunity Commission: Inquiry into rural and remote education.* Retrieved from http://www.humanrights.gov.au/human_rights/rural_education/index.html

——. (2007). *Social Justice Report 2007.* Canberra: Human Rights and Equal Opportunity Commission.

——. (2008). *Social Justice Report 2008.* Canberra: Human Rights and Equal Opportunity Commission.

——. (2009). *Social Justice Report 2009.* Canberra: Human Rights and Equal Opportunity Commission.

Adams, M., Page, W., & Speare, R. (2003). Strongyloidiasis: an issue in Aboriginal communities [conference report]. *Rural and Remote Health, 3*(152). Retrieved from http://www.rrh.org.au/publishedarticles/article_print_152.pdf

Adermann, J., & Campbell M. A. (2008). *Indigenous youth reaching their potential: Making the connection between anxiety and school attendance and retention rates.* In Proceedings of the Australian Association of Research in Education (AARE) Conference. Brisbane: AARE.

Aithal, S., Yonovitz, A., & Aithal, V. (2008). Perceptual consequences of conductive hearing loss: Speech perception in Indigenous students learning English as a 'school' language. *The Australian and New Zealand Journal of Audiology, 30*(1), 1–18.

Altman, J., & Hinkson, M. (2007). *Coercive Reconcilliation.* Carlton, Victoria: Arena Publications Association.

Al-Yaman, F., Van Doeland, M., & Wallis, M. (2006). *Family violence among Aboriginal and Torres Strait Islander peoples.* Canberra: Australian Institute of Health and Welfare.

Australian Bureau of Statistics. (2002). *Schools Australia, 2002.* Cat. No. 4221.0. Retrieved from http://www.abs.gov.au/AUSSTATS/abs@.nsf/allprimarymainfeatures/6A2BF878DC579A80CA256E43007DDF4C

———. (2004). *Australian Social Trends, 2004.* Cat. No. 4102.0. Retrieved June 6, 2011, from http://www.abs.gov.au/ausstats/abs@.nsf/0/95560b5d7449b135ca256e9e001fd879

———. (2005). *Australian Demographic Statistics, Dec 2005.* Cat. No. 3101.0. Retrieved June 6, 2011, from http://www.abs.gov.au/AUSSTATS/abs@.nsf/0/8486924370CD6CB2CA2571EF007D51B2

———. (2006a). *Australian Social Trends, 2006.* Cat. No. 4102.0. Retrieved May 23, 2011, from http://www.abs.gov.au/ausstats/abs@.nsf/2f762f95845417aeca25706c00834efa/647ed9028f8bfa18ca2571b00014b989

———. (2006b). *Indigenous Statistics for Schools.* Retrieved May 24, 2011, from http://www.abs.gov.au/websitedbs/cashome.nsf/4a256353001af3ed4b2562bb00121564/c733f2f1d1af9dedca25758b00117609

——. (2006c). *National Aboriginal and Torres Strait Islander Health Survey, 2004-05*. Cat. No. 4715.0. Retrieved from http://www.abs.gov.au/AUSSTATS/abs@.nsf/DetailsPage/4715.02004-05

——. (2006d). *Population Characteristics, Aboriginal and Torres Strait Islander Australians, 2006*. Cat. No. 4713.0. Retrieved May 23, 2011, from http://www.abs.gov.au/Ausstats/abs@.nsf/Lookup/2 B3D3A062FF56BC1CA256DCE007FBFFA

——. (2006e). *Self-employed Aboriginal and Torres Strait Islander People, 2006*. Cat. No. 4722.0.55.009. Retrieved from http://www.abs.gov.au/AUSSTATS/abs@.nsf/0/9F82431D52819B C5CA2575EB00155E27

——. (2008). *National Aboriginal and Torres Strait Islander Social Survey, 2008*. Cat. No. 4714.0. Retrieved from http://abs.gov.au/AUSSTATS/abs@.nsf/mf/4714.0/

——. (2009a). *Births Australia, 2008*. Cat. No. 3301.0. Canberra: Australian Bureau of Statistics.

——. (2009b). *Deaths Australia, 2008*. Cat. No. 3302.0. Canberra: Australian Bureau of Statistics.

——. (2009c). *Experimental life tables for Aboriginal and Torres Strait Islander Australians: 2005-2007*. Cat. No. 3302.0.55.003. Canberra: Australian Bureau of Statistics.

——. (2009d). *National Aboriginal and Torres Strait Islander social survey, 2008*. Cat. No. 4714.0. Retrieved April 11, 2011, from http://www.abs.gov.au/ausstats/abs@.nsf/ mf/4714.0?OpenDocument

——. (2010a). *The health and welfare of Australia's Aboriginal and Torres Strait Islander peoples, Oct 2010*. Cat. No. 4704.0. Retrieved from http://www.abs.gov.au/AUSSTATS/abs@.nsf/lookup/4704.0Mai n+Features1Oct+2010

——. (2010b). *Labour force characteristics of Aboriginal and Torres Strait Islander Australians: Estimates from the Labour Force Survey, 2009*. Cat. No. 6287.0. Retrieved from http://www.abs.gov.au/ausstats/abs@.nsf/mf/6287.0

——. (2010c). *Measures of Australia's Progress, 2010*. Cat. No. 1370.0. Retrieved from http://www.abs.gov.au/ausstats/abs@.nsf/Lookup/by%20 Subject/1370.0~2010~Main%20Features~Home%20page%20(1)

——. (2010d). *Schools Australia, 2010*. Cat. No. 4221.0. Retrieved May 23, 2011, from http://www.abs.gov.au/ausstats/abs@.nsf/ lookup/4221.0Main+Features52010

Australian Bureau of Statistics, & Australian Institute of Health and Welfare. (2008). *The health and welfare of Australia's Aboriginal and Torres Strait Islander peoples 2008*. Canberra: Australian Bureau of Statistics and Australian Institute of Health and Welfare.

Australian Centre for Asthma Monitoring. (2008). *Asthma in Australia 2008*. Canberra: Australian Institute of Health and Welfare.

Australian Curriculum Assessment and Reporting Authority (ACARA). (2010a). *National Assessment Program Literacy and Numeracy 2009*. Retrieved August 18, 2010, from http://www. naplan.edu.au/verve/_resources/NAPLAN_2009_National_ Report.pdf

——. (2010b). *National Assessment Program Literacy and Numeracy: National Report for 2010*. Sydney: ACARA.

——. (2011a). *The Australian curriculum*. Canberra: ACARA. Retrieved June 6, 2011, from http://www.australiancurriculum. edu.au

——. (2011b). *NAPLAN*. Retrieved from http://www.nap.edu.au/ NAPLAN/index.html

Australian Education Systems Officials Committee (AESOC) Senior Officials Working Party on Indigenous Education. (2006). *Australian directions in Indigenous education 2005-2008*. Carlton South, VIC: MCEETYA.

Australian Education Union. (2007). *Education is the key: An education future for Indigenous communities in the Northern Territory*. Melbourne: Australian Education Union.

Australian Government. (2010). *Closing the gap – Prime Minister's report 2010*. Canberra: Commonwealth of Australia.

Australian Health Ministers' Advisory Council. (2006). *Aboriginal and Torres Strait Islander health performance framework 2005*. Canberra: AHMAC.

——. (2008). *Aboriginal and Torres Strait Islander health performance framework report 2008*. Canberra: Department of Health and Ageing.

Australian Institute of Health and Welfare. (2008a). *Aboriginal and Torres Strait Islander health performance framework, 2008 report: Detailed analyses.* Canberra: Australian Institute of Health and Welfare.

———. (2008b). *Progress of the Northern Territory Emergency Response Child Health Check Initiative: Preliminary results from the Child Health Check and Follow-up Data Collections.* Canberra: Australian Institute of Health and Welfare.

———. (2009). *A picture of Australia's children 2009.* Canberra: Australian Institute of Health and Welfare.

———. (2010). *Australia's health 2010: the twelfth biennial report of the Australian Institute of Health and Welfare.* Canberra: Australian Institute of Health and Welfare.

———. (2011a). *Australian hospital statistics 2009-10.* Canberra: Australian Institute of Health and Welfare.

———. (2011b). *The health and welfare of Australia's Aboriginal and Torres Strait Islander people: An overview, 2011.* Canberra: Australian Institute of Health and Welfare.

Bateman, F. (1948). *Report of the Survey of Native Affairs.* Perth: Government Printer.

Baugh, J. (1999). Considerations in preparing teachers for linguistic diversity. In C. T. Adger, D. Christian & N. Taylor (Eds.), *Making the connection: Language and academic achievement among African American students: Proceedings of a conference of the Coalition on Language Diversity in Education* (pp. 81–96). McHenry, IL: Center for Applied Linguistics and Delta Systems Co. Inc.

Beazley, K. (1984). *Education in Western Australia. Report of the Commission of Inquiry.* Perth: Government of Western Australia.

Beckenham, P. (1948). *The Education of the Australian Aborigine.* Melbourne: The Australian Council for Educational Research.

Bedford, P., & Casson, S. (2010). Conflicting knowledges: Barriers to language continuation in the Kimberley. *Australian Journal of Indigenous Education, 39,* 76–86.

Behrendt, P. (1996). *Interview: Why teach Aboriginal Studies?* [Film]. Australia: University of New South Wales.

Bell, D. (1985). Topsy Napurrula Nelson: Teacher, Philosopher and Friend. In I. White, D. Barwick & B. Meehan (Eds.), *Fighters and singers: The lives of some Aboriginal women.* Sydney: George Allen and Unwin.

Beresford, Q. (2001). Policy and Performance: Aboriginal education in the 1990s. *Australian Journal of Education, 45*(1), 23–34.

———. (2003). The context of Aboriginal education. In Q. Beresford & G. Partington (Eds.), *Reform and resistance in Aboriginal education* (pp. 10–40). Crawley: University of Western Australia Press.

———. (2004). Indigenous alienation from school and 'the embedded legacy of history': The Australian experience. *International Journal of School Disaffection, 2*(2), 6–13.

———. (2006). *Rob Riley: An Aboriginal leader's quest for justice.* Canberra: Aboriginal Studies Press.

Beresford, Q., & Gray, J. (2006). Models of policy development in Aboriginal education: Issues and discourse. *Australian Journal of Education, 50*(3), 265-280.

Beresford, Q., & Omaji, P. (1996). *Rites of passage: Aboriginal youth, crime and justice.* Fremantle: Fremantle Arts Centre Press.

———. (1998). *Our state of mind: Racial planning and the stolen generations.* Fremantle: Fremantle Arts Centre Press.

Beresford, Q., & Partington, G. (Eds.). (2003). *Reform and resistance in Aboriginal education: The Australian experience.* Crawley, WA: University of Western Australia Press.

Berndt, R. M., & Berndt, C. H. (1977). *The world of the first Australians [2nd Edition].* Dee Why West, NSW: Landsdowne Press.

Bernstein, B. (1996). *Pedagogy, symbolic control and identity: Theory, research, critique.* London: Taylor & Francis.

Berry, R., & Hudson, J. (1997). *Making the jump: A resource book for teachers of Aboriginal students.* Broome, WA: Catholic Education Office, Kimberley Region.

Berwick, C. (2008). Aboriginal Education and Training Policy Launch. *Pemulwuy: Newsletter of the NSW AECG Inc.*, Issue 3, 2008.

Bishop, R., & Kirkwood, C. (2009). Rotavirus diarrhoea and Aboriginal Children. *Microbiology Australia, 30*(5), 205–07.

Blainey, G. (1993, November 10). Land Rights for All. *The Age,* p. 15.

Board of Inquiry into the Protection of Aboriginal Children from Sexual Abuse. (2007). *Report of the Board of Inquiry into the Protection of Aboriginal Children from Sexual Abuse – Little children are sacred.* Darwin: Northern Territory Government.

Boon, H. J. (2008). Risk or resilience? What makes a difference? *Australian Education Researcher 35*(1), 81–102.

Bourke, C., Rigby, K., & Burden, J. (2000). *Better practice in school attendance: Improving the school attendance of Indigenous students.* Canberra: Department of Education, Training and Youth Affairs.

Boven, K., & Morohashi, J. (Eds.). (2002). *Best practices using Indigenous knowledge.* Paris: Nuffic, The Hague & UNESCO/ MOST. Retrieved from

http://www.unesco.org/most/Bpikpub2.pdf

Bower, C. (2006). Primary prevention of neural tube defects with folate in Western Australia: the value of the Western Australian Birth Defects Registry. *Congenital Anomalies, 46,* 118–21.

Boykin, A., & Ellison, C. (1995). The multiple ecologies of black youth socialization: An Afrographic analysis. In R. Taylor (Ed.), *African American youth: Their social and economic status in the United States* (pp. 93–102). Westport: Praeger.

Brady, W. (1997). Indigenous Australian Education and Globalisation. *International Review of Education, 43,* 413–22.

Brewster, D., Nelson, C., & Couzos, S. (2007). Failure to thrive. In S. Couzos & R. Murray (Eds.), *Aboriginal primary health care: An evidence-based approach* (3rd ed., pp. 265–307). South Melbourne: Oxford University Press.

Bridgeman, P., & Davis, G. (2004). *The Australian Policy Handbook.* Sydney: Allen & Unwin.

Brumby, E., & Vaszolyi, E. (Eds.) (1977). *Language problems and Aboriginal education.* Perth: Mount Lawley College of Advanced Education.

Burney, L. (1991). *Keynote address: Aboriginal studies in the 90s: Where to now? Aboriginal Studies Association Inaugural Conference.* Sydney: University of New South Wales.

——. (1996). *Interview: Why teach Aboriginal Studies?* [Film]. Australia: University of New South Wales.

Burns, J., & Thomson, N. (2003). Eye health. In N. Thomson (Ed.), *The health of Indigenous Australians* (pp. 273–89). South Melbourne: Oxford University Press.

Burridge, K., & Mulder, J. (1998). *English in Australia and New Zealand: An introduction to its history, structure and use.* Melbourne: Oxford University Press.

Burrow, S., Galloway, A., & Weissofner, N. (2009). Review of educational and other approaches to hearing loss among Indigenous people. *Australian Indigenous Health Bulletin, 9*(2), 1–37.

Burrow, S., & Thomson, N. (2003). Ear disease and hearing loss. In N. Thomson (Ed.), *The health of Indigenous Australians* (pp. 247–72). Melbourne: Oxford University Press.

Byrne, M. (2009). *An investigation into the challenges teachers face when teaching in a low socio-economic primary school.* Doctoral dissertation, Edith Cowan University, Western Australia. Retrieved from http://library.ecu.edu.au/

Calma, T. (2008a). *Launch of Our Children Our Future Report* [Speech]. Retrieved from http://www.hreoc.gov.au/about/media/speeches/social_justice/2008/20080528_our_children.html

———. (2008b). *Preventing crime and promoting rights for Indigenous young people with cognitive disabilities and mental health issues.* Sydney: Australian Human Rights Commission.

Cappo, D. (2007). *To break the cycle: Prevention and rehabilitation responses to serious and repeat offending by young people.* Retrieved from http://www.socialinclusion.sa.gov.au/files/breakthecycle2007.pdf

Carter, J. (1989). Reflections. In C. Edwards & P. Read (Eds.), *The lost children: Thirteen Australians taken from their Aboriginal families tell of the struggle to find their natural parent* (pp. 95–8). Sydney: Doubleday.

Chang, A. B., & Torzillo, P. J. (2007). Respiratory infection (including Bronchiectasis). In S. Couzos & R. Murray (Eds.), *Aboriginal primary health care: an evidence-based approach* (3rd ed., pp. 355–85). South Melbourne: Oxford University Press.

Christie, M. (1984). The Aboriginal world view: A white person's ideas. *The Aboriginal Child at School, 12*(1), 3–7.

———. (1985). *Aboriginal perspectives on experience and learning: The role of language in Aboriginal education.* Geelong, Australia: Deakin University Press.

———. (1986). *The classroom world of the Aboriginal child.* St. Lucia: University of Queensland Press.

———. (2006). Transdisciplinary research and Aboriginal knowledge. *The Australian Journal of Indigenous Education, 35,* 78–89.

Clark, A. (2002). *First Dymphna Clark Lecture.* Presented at Manning Clark House, 2 March 2002. Unpublished.

Clayton, J. (Compiler) (Ed.) (1996). *Desert schools: An investigation of English language and literacy among young people in seven communities.* Hectorsville, SA: Department of Employment Education Training and Youth Affairs & National Languages and Literacy Institute of Australia.

Clucas, D. B., Carville, K. S., Connors, C., Currie, B., Carapetis, J., & Andrews, R. (2008). Disease burden and health-care clinic attendances for young children in remote Aboriginal communities of northern Australia. *Bulletin of the World Health Organization, 86*(4), 275–81.

Cochrane, K. (1994). *Oodgeroo.* Brisbane: University of Queensland Press.

Coffin, J., Larson, A., & Cross, D. (2010). Bullying in an Aboriginal context. *Australian Journal of Indigenous Education, 39*(1), 77–87.

Coghlan, D. (1992). *Pride and understanding through Aboriginal studies.* Adelaide: Education Department of South Australia.

Collins, R. (1999). *Learning the lessons: An independent review of Indigenous education in the Northern Territory.* Darwin: Northern Territory Department of Education.

Comber, B., & Thomson, P. (2001). *Just new learning environments: New metaphors and practices for learners and teachers in disadvantaged schools.* Keynote Paper in: Department for Education and Skills, Experiencing Change, Exchanging Experience Virtual Conference, June 25–July 13.

Commonwealth of Australia. (2006). *National Report to Parliament on Indigenous Education and Training, 2004.* Canberra: Department of Education Science and Training.

———. (2011). *Closing the gap: Prime Minister's report 2011.* Canberra: Commonwealth of Australia.

Commonwealth Office of the Status of Women. (1999). Partnerships against domestic violence. *Home Front, Jul-Sep 1999*(25), 8-9.

Community Affairs References Committee. (2006). *Beyond petrol sniffing: renewing hope for Indigenous communities.* Canberra: Commonwealth of Australia.

Coombs, H.C., Brandl, M., & Snowdon, W. (1983). *A certain heritage: Programs for and by Aboriginal families in Australia.* Canberra: Centre for Resource and Environmental Studies, Australian National University.

Cooper, J. (2008). Embedding literacy in Indigenous education through assisant teachers: Lessons from the National Accelerated Literacy Program. *The Australian Journal of Indigenous Education, 37,* 120–9.

Coppell, W. (1974). *Education and the Aboriginal child.* Sydney: Macquarie University.

Council of Australian Governments (COAG). (2008). *National integrated strategy for closing the gap in Indigenous disadvantage.* Canberra: Council of Australian Governments. Retrieved August 25, 2011, from http://www.coag.gov.au/coag_meeting_outcomes/2009-07-02/docs/NIS_closing_the_gap.pdf

——. (2009a). *Closing the gap on Indigenous disadvantage: The challenge for Australia.* Canberra: AGPS

——. (2009b). *National Integrated Strategy for Closing the Gap in Indigenous Disadvantage.* Canberra: Council of Australian Governments.

——. (2009c). *National Indigenous Reform Agreement (Closing the Gap).* Canberra: Council of Australian Governments. Retrieved from www.fahcsia.gov.au/sa/indigenous/progserv/ctg/Pages/NIRA.aspx

Couzos, S., Metcalf, S., & Murray, R. B. (2001). *Systematic review of existing evidence and primary care guidelines on the management of Otitis Media in Aboriginal and Torres Strait Islander populations.* Canberra, ACT: Office for Aboriginal and Torres Strait Islander Health, Commonwealth Department of Health and Aged Care. Retrieved from http://www.health.gov.au/internet/main/publishing.nsf/Content/health-oatsih-pubs-Syst+review

——. (2007). Ear health. In S. Couzos & R. Murray (Eds.),

Aboriginal primary health care: an evidence-based approach (3rd ed., pp. 308–54). South Melbourne: Oxford University Press.

Cowey, W. (2005). ACTA Background Paper: A brief description of the National Accelerated Literacy Program. *TESOL in Context, 15*(2), 3–14. Retrieved June 7, 2011, from http://0-search.informit.com.au.library.ecu.edu.au/fullText;dn=149127;res=AEIPT

———. (2007). *Practitioner Guide: The teaching sequence.* Carlton South, VIC: Curriculum Corporation.

Craven, R. G. (1996). *Teaching the teachers Indigenous Australian studies: Framework statement.* Sydney: School of Teacher Education, University of New South Wales in association with the Council for Aboriginal Reconciliation.

———. (1999). *Teaching Aboriginal Studies.* Sydney: Allen and Unwin.

———. (Ed.). (2011). *Teaching Aboriginal Studies: A complete guide to teaching Aboriginal studies in both primary and secondary schools* (2nd ed.). Australia: Allen & Unwin.

Craven, R. G., Halse, C., Marsh, H. W., Mooney, J., & Wilson-Miller, J. (2005a). *Teaching the teachers mandatory Aboriginal Studies: Volume I: Recent successful strategies.* Canberra: Commonwealth of Australia, Department of Education, Science & Training. Retrieved from http://www.dest.gov.au/sectors/higher_education/publications_resources/profiles/teaching_teachers_volume_1.htm#publication

———. (2005b). *Teaching the teachers mandatory Aboriginal Studies: Volume II: Case studies of exemplary practice in pre-service teacher education.* Canberra: Commonwealth of Australia, Department of Education, Science & Training. Retrieved from http://www.dest.gov.au/sectors/higher_education/publications_resources/profiles/teaching_teachers_volume_2.htm#publication

———. (2005c). *Teaching the teachers Aboriginal Studies: impact on teaching [EIP 05/02].* Canberra: Commonwealth of Australia, Department of Education, Science & Training. Retrieved from http://www.dest.gov.au/sectors/higher_education/publications_resources/profiles/teaching_teachers_EIP_report.htm

Craven, R. G., & Miller, J. (1996). *Developing Aboriginal Studies units of work: A new model.* Collected papers of the fifth annual conference of the Aboriginal Studies Association held at Riverview College, Lane Cove, October, 1995.

Cummins, J. (1992). The empowerment of Indian students. In J. Reyhner (Ed.), *Teaching American Indian students* (pp. 3–12). Norman, OK: University of Oklahoma Press.

———. (2001). Empowering minority students: A framework for intervention. *Harvard Educational Review, 71*(4), 649–75.

Cuneen, C. (2006). Racism, discrimination and the over-representation of Indigenous people in the criminal justice system: Some conceptual and explanatory issues. *Current Issues in Criminal Justice, 17*(3), 329–46.

Cunningham, J., Goddard, D., Punch, K., Chaney, F., Simpson, M., Snell, B., et al. (2001). Drivers for success. *Unicorn, 27*(1), 35–40.

d'Abbs, P., & Maclean, S. (2008). *Volatile substance misuse: a review of interventions.* Barton, ACT: Department of Health and Ageing.

Dare to Lead. (2011a). *Dare to Lead: Membership.* Retrieved May 31, 2011, from http://www.daretolead.edu.au/ DTL08_Member_Main

———. (2011b). *Phase Four Dare to Lead: Partnership Builds Success 2009 - 2012.* Retrieved from http://www.daretolead.edu.au/ DTL08_ProjHist_PhaseFour

Deadly Ways to Learn Consortium. (2000). *Deadly yarns.* Perth: Department of Education and Training WA, Catholic Education Office, Association of Independent Schools WA.

Delago, R., & Stefancic, J. (2001). *Critical Race Theory: An introduction.* New York: New York University Press.

Delbridge, A., Bernard, J. R. L., Blair, D., Butler, P., Peters, P., & Yallop, C. (2009). *The Macquarie Dictionary* (5th edn). Sydney: The Macquarie Library Pty. Ltd.

De Maio, J. A., Zubrick, S. R., Silburn, S. R., Lawrence, D. M., Mitrou, F. G., Dalby, R. B., et al. (2005). *The Western Australian Aboriginal Child Health Survey: Measuring the social and emotional wellbeing of Aboriginal children and intergenerational effects of forced separation.* Perth: Curtin University of Technology and Telethon Institute for Child Health Research.

Department of Education. (2010). *Department of Education annual report, 2009–2010.* Perth: The Department of Education.

Retrieved August 30, 2010, from http://www.det.wa.edu.au/
education/AnnualReport/

Department of Education and Children's Services (DECS). (2007).
DECS Countering Racism Policy and Guidelines. Retrieved April
17, 2011, from http://www.decs.sa.gov.au/docs/documents/1/
AntiracismPolicy.pdf

Department of Education and Early Childhood Development.
(2010). *Language support program: Appendix 4 Indigenous students with
language difficulties.* Retrieved April 11, 2011, from
http://www.education.vic.gov.au/studentlearning/programs/lsp/
app-4.htm

Department of Education, Employment & Workplace Relations.
(2008). *National report to Parliament on Indigenous Education and
Training.* Canberra: DEEWR.

———. (2009). *Building the Educational Revolution plan.* Retrieved
August 31, 2011, from http://www.deewr.gov.au/schooling/
Pages/Education_reform_agenda.aspx

———. (2011a). *Indigenous schooling.* Retrieved 18 April, 2011, from
http://www.deewr.gov.au/Indigenous/Schooling/Pages/default.
aspx

———. (2011b). *What Works. The Work Program. Case studies.*
Canberra: National Curriculum Services and the Australian
Curriculum Studies Association. Retrieved from
http://www.whatworks.edu.au/dbAction.do?cmd=displaySitePage
1&subcmd=select&id=34

Department of Education, Science and Training. (2000). *The
National Indigenous English Literacy and Numeracy Strategy.* Canberra:
Commonwealth of Australia.

———. (2004). *Working together for Indigenous youth: A national
framework.* Canberra: Commonwealth of Australia.

Department of Education, Training and Employment. (2000).
*Countering racism – Using a critical approach in teaching and learning
contexts to explore portrayals of Aboriginality.* South Australia: DETE
Publishing.

Department of Education and Training, Western Australia. (2003).
*Indigenous Education Strategic Initiatives Program (IESIP) 2003
performance report.* Perth: Department of Education and Training.

Department of Education, Training and Youth Affairs. (2000). *Better practice in school attendance: Improving the school attendance of Indigenous students.* Retrieved from http://www.dest.gov.au/ sectors/indigenous_education/publications_resources/profiles/ better_practice_school_attendance_improving_indigenous.htm

Department of Education, Training and Youth Affairs. (2001). *Learning for all: Opportunities for Indigenous Australians.* Retrieved May 27, 2011, from http://www.dest.gov.au/archive/iae/analysis/ docs/LEARNING.PDF

Department of Education, Western Australia. (In press). *Tracks to Two-Way Learning: materials to support two-way education for Aboriginal learners.* Department of Education, Western Australia.

Department of Education, Western Australia. (2010a). *Annual Report 2009–2010.* Perth: Department of Education, Western Australia.

———. (2010b). *ESL/ESD information for school personnel 2010.* Retrieved April 13, 2011, from http://www.det.wa.edu.au/curriculumsupport/primary/detcms/ navigation/literacy/esl/#toc1

Department of Employment, Education and Training. (1994). *National review of education for Aboriginal and Torres Strait Islander People: Discussion paper.* Canberra: Australian Government Publishing Service.

Department of Families, Housing, Community Services and Indigenous Affairs (FaHCSIA). (2009). *Closing the gap on Indigenous disadvantage: the challenge for Australia.* Canberra: Commonwealth of Australia.

De Plevitz, L. (2007). Systemic Racism: the hidden barrier to educational success for Indigenous school students. *Australian Journal of Education, 51*(1) 54–71.

Deyhle, D. (1995). Navajo youth and Anglo racism: Cultural integrity and resistance. *Harvard Educational Review, 65*(3), 403–39.

Dockett, S., Perry, B., & Kearney, E. (2010). *School readiness: What does it mean for Indigenous children, families, schools and communities? Closing the Gap Clearinghouse.* Canberra: Australian Government, Australian Institute of Health and Welfare.

Douglas, A. (2009). *Leading Indigenous education in a remote location: Reflections on teaching to be 'Proud and Deadly'.* PhD dissertation,

Queensland University of Technology. Retrieved from http://eprints.qut.edu.au/30275/

Douglas, M. (1974). *Language and the Aborigines*. Sydney: Macquarie University.

Dow, C. (2008). *'Sorry': The unfinished business of the Bringing Them Home Report*. Parliamentary Library Background Note, Parliament of Australia. Retrieved from http://www.aph.gov.au/library/pubs/BN/2007-08/BringingThemHomeReport.htm

Doyle, L., & Hill, R. (2008). *Our children, our future: Achieving improved primary and secondary education outcomes for Indigenous students*. AMP Foundation, effective philanthropy, social ventures Australia.

Dunn, K. (2003). *Racism in Australia: Findings of a survey on racist attitudes and experiences of racism (National Europe Centre Paper No. 77)*. Retrieved from https://digitalcollections.anu.edu.au/handle/1885/41761

Dunne, K., Forrest, J., Burnley, I., & McDonald, A. (2004). Constructing racism in Australia. *Australian Journal of Social Issues, 39*(4), 409–30.

Dunne, R. (1999). *Aboriginal youth and offending*. Retrieved from http://www.aic.gov.au/publications/proceedings/09/dunn

Eades, D. (1982). You gotta know how to talk: information seeking in Southeast Queensland Aboriginal society. *Australian Journal of Linguistics, 2*(1), 61–82.

——. (1988). They don't speak an Aboriginal language, or do they? In I. Keen (Ed.), *Being black: Aboriginal cultures in 'settled' Australia* (pp. 97–115). Canberra: Aboriginal Studies.

——. (2010). Aboriginal English. In S. A. Wurm, P. Mühlhäusler & D. T. Tryon (Eds.), *Atlas of languages of intercultural communication in the Pacific, Asia, and the Americas* (Vol. 2, pp. 133–142). Berlin: De Gruyter Mouton.

Eagleson, R. D., Kaldor, S., & Malcolm, I. G. (1982). *English and the Aboriginal child*. Canberra: Curriculum Development Centre.

Eckermann, A.-K. (1998). The economics of Aboriginal education. *International Journal of Social Economics, 25*(2/3/4), 302–13.

Education Department of The University of Western Australia.

(1975). *The educational status of Aboriginal children in Western Australia*. Unpublished.

Education Queensland. (2000). *Review of education and employment programs for Aboriginal and Torres Strait Islander peoples in Education Queensland*. Brisbane: Education Queensland.

Edwards, V. (2004). *Multilingualism in the English-speaking world: Pedigree of nations*. Carlton, VIC: Blackwell.

Elkin, E. (1937). Education of the Australian Aborigines. *Oceania, 17*(4).

enHealth. (2010). *Environmental health practitioner manual: A resource manual for environmental health practitioners working with Aboriginal and Torres Strait Islander communities*. Canberra: Department of Health, Australia.

Fair Go Team. (2006). *School is for me: Pathways to student engagement*. Sydney: Priority Schools Funding Program, NSW Department of Education and Training.

Fanshawe, J. (1989). Personal characteristics of effective teachers of adolescent Aborigines. *Aboriginal Child at School, 17*(4), 35–47.

Finnegan, W. (1998). *Cold new world: Growing up in a harder country*. New York: Random House.

Fletcher, J. (1989). *Clean, clad and courteous: A history of Aboriginal education in New South Wales*. Marrickville: Southwood Press.

Forde, L. (2000). *Commission of inquiry into abuse of children in Queensland institutions*. Brisbane: Queensland Government

Fredricks, J. A., Blumenfield, P. C., & Paris, A. H. (2004). School engagement: Potential of the concept, state of the evidence. *Review of Educational Research, 76*(1), 59–109.

Fryer-Smith, S. (2002). *AIJA Aboriginal cultural awareness benchbook for Western Australian Courts*. Melbourne: Australian Institute of Judicial Administration Incorporated.

Gale, G., & Brookman, A. (1975). *Race relations in Australia – The Aborigines*. Sydney: McGraw Hill.

Gallaher G., Ziersch A., Baum F., Bentley M., Palmer C., Edmondson W., & Winslow L. (2009). *In our own backyard: Urban health inequalities and Aboriginal experiences of neighbourhood life, social capital and racism*. Adelaide: Flinders University.

Galloway, A. (2008). Indigenous children and conductive hearing loss. In J. Simpson & G. Wigglesworth (Eds.), *Children's language and multiculturalism: Indigenous language use at home and school* (pp. 217–34). London: Continuum International.

Garcia, O., & Menken, K. (2006). The English of Latinos from a pluralingual transcultural angle: Implications for assessment and schools. In S. J. Nero (Ed.), *Dialects, Englishes, creoles, and education* (pp. 167–83). Mahwah, NJ: Lawrence Erlbaum Associates.

Gass, S. M. (1997). *Input, interaction, and the second language learner.* Mahwah, NJ: Lawrence Erlbaum.

Giroux, H. (1992). *Border crossings: Cultural workers and the politics of education.* New York: Routledge.

Godfrey, J., Partington, G., Richer, K., & Harslett, M. (2001). Perceptions of their teachers by Aboriginal students. *Issues in Educational Research, 11*(1), 1–13.

Gollan, M. (2001). The Program. On *Onslaught* [CD]. Adelaide: Skinnyfish Music. Available from http://www.creativespirits.info/resources/music/4real/

Gollan, S., & O'Leary, P. J. (2009). Teaching culturally competent social work practice through black and white pedagogical partnerships. *Social Work Education, 28*(7), 707–21.

Gordon, S. (2002). *Putting the picture together: Inquiry into response by government agencies to complaints of family violence and child abuse in Aboriginal communities.* Perth: State Law Publisher. Retrieved from *http://www.austlii.edu.au/au/journals/AILR/2002/65.html*

Gorman, S. (2006). *Aboriginal students and the Western Australian Literacy and Numeracy Assessment.* Mt Lawley: Centre for Indigenous Australian Knowledges, Edith Cowan University. Retrieved from http://www.aetcwa.org.au/_Documents/Documents/WALNA.pdf

Gottfredson, D. (2001). *Schools and delinquency.* Cambridge: Cambridge University Press.

Gould, J. (2008). Language difference or language disorder: Discourse sampling in speech pathology assessments for Indigenous children. In J. Simpson & G. Wigglesworth (Eds.), *Children's language and multilingualism: Indigenous language use at home and school* (pp. 194–215). London: Continuum International.

Graham, S., Jackson Pulver, L. R., Alex Wang, Y., Kelly, P. M., Laws, P. J., Grayson, N., et al. (2007). The urban–remote divide for Indigenous perinatal outcomes. *Medical Journal of Australia, 186*(10), 509–12.

Gray, B., & Cowey, W. (2001). *Some reflections on the literacy development of children at Amata School, 1998-2000: A case study on an SRP project – 'Scaffolding Literacy with Indigenous Children in School'*. Retrieved October 3, 2008, from http://www.nalp.edu.au/docs/Reflections_Amata_School.pdf

Gray, D., Saggers, S., Atkinson, D., & Wilkes, E. (2007). Substance misuse. In S. Couzos & R. Murray (Eds.), *Aboriginal primary health care: An evidence-based approach* (3rd ed., pp. 755–87). South Melbourne: Oxford University Press.

Gray, D., Stearne, A., Wilson, M., & Doyle, M. (2010). Indigenous-specific alcohol and other drug interventions: Continuities, changes and areas of greatest need. Canberra: Australian National Council on Drugs.

Gray, J. (2000). *The framing of truancy: A study of non-attendance policy as a form of social exclusion in Western Australia*. PhD thesis submitted to Edith Cowan University, Western Australia. Available from http://trove.nla.gov.au/work/153116913

——. (2009a). Staying at school: Reflective narratives of resistance and transition. *Reflective Practice, 10*(5), 645–56.

——. (2009b). *Student engagement research report: Sevenoaks Football Academy*. Unpublished report: Edith Cowan University, Western Australia.

——. (2010). Closing the gap? What chance for an Indigenous child? *The Spray, 2010*(2). Retrieved from http://www.nswteachers.nsw.edu.au/Publications---Research/The-Spray/

Gray, J., & Beresford, Q. (2001). *Alienation from school among Aboriginal students*. Perth: Edith Cowan University.

——. (2002). Aboriginal non-attendance at school: Revisiting the debate. *Australian Educational Researcher, 29*(1), 27–42.

——. (2006). Models of policy development in Aboriginal education. *The Australian Journal of Education, 50*(3), 265–80.

——. (2008). A 'formidable challenge': Australia's quest for equity in Indigenous education. *Australian Journal of Education, 52*(2), 197–223.

Gray, J., & Hackling, M. (2009). Wellbeing and retention: A senior secondary student perspective. *The Australian Educational Researcher, 36*(2), 119-145.

Gray, J., & Partington, G. (2003). Attendance and non-attendance at school. In Q. Beresford & G. Partington (Eds.), *Reform and resistance in Aboriginal education: The Australian experience.* Perth: University of Western Australia Press.

Gray, J., & Sibbel, J. (2009). Students. In G. Partington, A. Galloway, J. Sibbel, G. Gower, J Gray, E. Grote, & K. Goh, (Eds.), *Longitudinal study of student retention and success in high school (Follow the Dream/Partnerships for Success).* Perth, WA: Centre for Indigenous Knowledges.

Green, A. C. (2001). *A handbook of skin conditions in Aboriginal populations of Australia* (pp. 156). Carlton South, Vic: Blackwell Science Asia Pty Ltd.

Grey, A. (1974). Towards an understanding of Aboriginal children. In *Aboriginal children in the classroom: Proceedings of a seminar for teachers of Aboriginal children in the Taree inspectorate.* Taree, NSW: Office of the Inspector of Schools.

Groome, H., & Hamilton, A. (1995). *Meeting the educational needs of Aboriginal adolescents: National Board of Employment Education and Training Commissioned Report No. 35.* Canberra: Australian Government Publishing Service.

Grote, E. (2008). *Principles and practices of cultural competency: A review of the literature* (Paper prepared for the Indigenous Higher Education Advisory Council). Canberra: Department of Employment, Education and Workplace Relations. Retrieved June 10, 2011, from http://www.deewr.gov.au/Indigenous/HigherEducation/Programs/IHEAC/Documents/PrinciplePracCulturalComp.pdf

Grundy, S. (1994). The curriculum and teaching. In E. Hatton (Ed.), *Understanding teaching: Curriculum and the social context of schooling.* Sydney: Harcourt Brace.

Haebich, A. (2000). *Broken circles fragmenting Indigenous families 1800–2000.* Fremantle: Fremantle Arts Centre Press.

Haig, Y., Konigsberg, P., & Collard, G. (2005). *Teaching students who speak Aboriginal English* (Pen 150). Retrieved April 13, 2011, from http://www.elit.edu.au/mediaLibrary/documents/pens/PEN150.pdf

Hall, G. V., Kirk, M. D., Ashbolt, R., Stafford, R., Lalor, K., & OzFoodNet Working Group. (2006). Frequency of infectious gastrointestinal illness in Australia, 2002: Regional, seasonal and demographic variation. *Epidemiology and Infection, 134*(1), 111–8.

Hamilton, A. (1981). *Nature and nurture: Aboriginal childrearing in North-Central Arnhem Land.* Canberra: Australian Institute of Aboriginal Studies.

Harford, J., Spencer, J., & Roberts-Thomson, K. (2003). Oral health. In N. Thomson (Ed.), *The health of Indigenous Australians* (pp. 313–38). South Melbourne: Oxford University Press.

Harkins, J. (1990). Shame and shyness in the aboriginal classroom: A case for 'practical semantics'. *Australian Journal of Linguistics, 10*(2), 293–306.

Harkins, J. (1994). *Bridging two worlds: Aboriginal English and cross-cultural understanding.* St Lucia, Qld: University of Queensland Press.

Harris, P. (1991). *Mathematics in a cultural context: Aboriginal perspectives on space, time and money.* Geelong: Deakin University.

Harris, S. (1980). *Culture and learning: Tradition and education in north-eastern Arnhem Land.* Darwin: Professional Services Branch, Northern Territory Education Department.

——. (1984). Aboriginal learning styles and formal schooling. *The Aboriginal Child at School, 12*(4), 3–23.

——. (1990). *Two-Way Aboriginal schooling: Education and cultural survival.* Canberra: Aboriginal Studies Press.

Harslett, M. (1999). *Relationships, relationships, relationships: That's what sells school to Aboriginal students and parents.* Mt Lawley: Edith Cowan University.

Harslett, M., Harrison, B., Godfrey, J., Partington, G., & Richer, K. (1999). Participation by Indigenous parents in education. *Unicorn, 25*(1), 60–70.

Hayes, D. (2003). Making learning an effect of schooling: Aligning curriculum, assessment and pedagogy. *Discourse: Studies in the cultural politics of education, 24*(2), 225–45.

Hayes, D., Johnston, K., Morris, K., Power, K., & Roberts, D. (2009). Difficult dialogue: Conversations with Aboriginal parents and caregivers. *Australian Journal of Indigenous Education, 38*, 55–64.

Hayes, D., Mills, M., Christie, P., & Lingard, B. (2006). *Teachers and schooling: Making a difference.* Sydney: Allen and Unwin.

Hickling-Hudson, A., & Ahlquist, R. (2003). Contesting the curriculum in the schooling of Indigenous children in Australia and the United States: From ethnocentrism to culturally powerful pedagogies. *Comparative Education Review. 47*(1), 64–89.

Higgins, A. H. (1997). *Addressing the health and educational consequences of otitis media among young rural school-aged children.* Townsville, QLD: University of Otago Press for the Australian Rural Education Research Association.

House of Representatives. (1985). *Report of the Select Committee on Aboriginal Education.* Canberra: Australian Government Printing Service.

House of Representatives Standing Committee on Aboriginal and Torres Strait Islander Peoples. (2001). *We can do it! The needs of urban dwelling Aboriginal and Torres Strait Islander peoples.* Canberra: Parliament of Australia.

House of Representatives Standing Committee on Aboriginal and Torres Strait Islander Affairs. (2011). *Doing Time - Time for Doing: Indigenous youth in the criminal justice system.* Canberra: The Parliament of the Commonwealth of Australia. Retrieved from http://www.aph.gov.au/house/committee/atsia/sentencing/report/fullreport.pdf

House of Representatives Standing Committee on Employment and Training. (1996). *Truancy and exclusion from School.* Canberra: Australian Government Publishing Service.

Human Rights and Equal Opportunity Commission (HREOC). (1991). *Racist violence: Report of the national inquiry into racist violence in Australia.* Canberra: Australian Government Publishing Service.

———. (1997). *Bringing Them Home: Report of the national inquiry into the separation of Aboriginal and Torres Strait Islander children from their families.* Sydney: HREOC. Retrieved from http://www.hreoc.gov.au/social_justice/bth_report/report/index.html

———. (1998). *Race for business: A training resource package.* Sydney: HREOC

——. (1999). *National inquiry into rural and remote education: evidence & submissions.* Sydney: HREOC. Retrieved from http://www.humanrights.gov.au/human_rights/rural_education/index.html

——. (2005). *Voices of Australia: 30 years of the Racial Discrimination Act: 1975–2005.* Sydney: HREOC.

——. (2009). *Social Justice Report 2008.* Canberra: HREOC. Retrieved from http://www.hreoc.gov.au/social_justice/sj_report/sjreport08/index.html

——. (2010). *Social Justice Report 2009.* Sydney: HREOC. Retrieved from http://www.hreoc.gov.au/social_justice/sj_report/sjreport09/index.html

Hunt, J. (2007). Pregnancy care. In S. Couzos & R. Murray (Eds.), *Aboriginal primary health care: An evidence-based approach* (3rd ed., pp. 195–264). South Melbourne: Oxford University Press.

Hymes, D. (1972). Models of the interaction of language and social life. In J. D. Gumperz & D. Hymes (Eds.), *Directions in sociolinguistics* (pp. 35–71). New York: Holt, Rinehard, and Winston.

Iffe, J. (2002). *Community development.* Sydney: Pearson Educational.

Implementation Review of Shared Responsibility Agreements. (2006). Canberra: Department of Families, Housing, Services and Indigenous Affairs.

Indigenous Determinants and Outcomes Unit, & Office for Aboriginal and Torres Strait Islander Health. (2009). *Progress of the Northern Territory Emergency Response Child Health Check Initiative: Update on results from the Child Health Check and follow-up data collections* [Final report]. Canberra: Australian Institute of Health and Welfare and Australian Department of Health and Ageing.

Initial Conference of Commonwealth and State Aboriginal Authorities. (1937). Aboriginal Welfare, Canberra: Commonwealth Government Printer.

Interim Committee for the Australian Schools Commission. (1973). *Schools in Australia: Report of the interim committee for the Australian Schools Commission.* Canberra: Australian Government Publishing Service.

Irvine, J., & Irvine, R. (1995). Black youth in school: Individual achievement and institutional/cultural perspectives. In R. Taylor (Ed.), *African American youth: Their social and economic status in the*

United States (pp. 129–42). Westport: Preager.

Jacoby, P. A., Coates, H. L., Arumugaswamy, A., Elsbury, D., Stokes, A., Monck, R., et al. (2008). The effect of passive smoking on the risk of Otitis Media in Aboriginal and non-Aboriginal children in the Kalgoorlie-Boulder region of Western Australia. *Medical Journal of Australia, 188*(10), 599–603.

Jamieson, L. M., Armfield, J. M., & Roberts-Thomson, K. F. (2007). *Oral health of Aboriginal and Torres Strait Islander children.* Canberra: Australian Research Centre for Population Oral Health (ARCPOH).

Johnston, E. (1991). *Royal Commission into Aboriginal deaths in custody.* Canberra: Australian Government Press.

Johnston, K. (1990). Dealing with difference. *Education Links, 38,* 26–9.

Kelly, J., Shultz, L., Weber-Pillwax, C., & Lang, E. A. (2009). Expanding knowledge systems in teacher education: Introduction. *Journal of Educational Research, 55*(3), 263–8. Retrieved from http://ajer.synergiesprairies.ca/ajer/index.php/ajer/article/view/735

Kelly, K., Dudgeon, P., Gee, G., & Glaskin, B. (2009). *Living on the edge: social and emotional wellbeing and risk and protective factors for serious psychological distress among Aboriginal and Torres Strait Islander people.* Darwin: Cooperative Research Centre for Aboriginal Health.

Kemmis, S. (1999). *Final synthesis report on the 1998 implementation of the Aboriginal education and training strategic plan 1997–1999.* Perth: Western Australian Aboriginal Education and Training Council.

Kendon, A. (2008). Some reflections on the relationship between 'gesture' and sign'. *Gesture, 8*(3), 348–66.

Kickett-Tucker, C. (1999, November). *School sport self-concept of urban Aboriginal school children: Teacher influences.* Paper presented at AARE-NZARE National Conference, Melbourne. Retrieved from http://trove.nla.gov.au/work/153128823

Kidd, R. (1997). *The way we civilise.* St Lucia: University of Queensland Press.

Kilpatrick, P. (1998). Post-registration truancy: The hidden side of truancy. *Youth Studies Australia, 17*(1), 28–33.

Kirov, E., & Thomson, N. (2004). Summary of Indigenous health: respiratory disease. *Aboriginal and Islander Health Worker Journal, 28*(2), 15–18.

Knight, T. (2002). Equity in Victorian Education and 'Deficit' Thinking. *Melbourne Studies in Education, 43*(1), 83–106.

Lambert, W. E. (1981). Bilingualism and language acquisition. *Annals of the New York Academy of Sciences, 379,* 9–22.

Laurie, V. (2010). Life Sentence. *The Monthly, July*(2010), 32–7.

Laws, P., & Sullivan, E. A. (2009). *Australia's mothers and babies 2007.* Sydney: AIHW National Perinatal Statistics Unit.

Legislative Assembly of the Northern Territory. (2004). *Volatile Substance Abuse Prevention Bill 2004* (Serial 270). Darwin: Legislative Assembly of the Northern Territory.

Liberman, K. (1985). *Understanding interaction in central Australia: An ethnomethodological study of Australian Aboriginal People.* Boston: Routledge & Kegan Paul.

Lo Bianco, J. (2008). Language policy and education in Australia. In N. H. Hornberger (Ed.), *Encyclopedia of Language and Education* (Vol. 1, pp. 343–53). New York: Springer.

Long, M. H. (2007). *Problems in SLA.* Mahwah, NJ: L. Erlbaum Associates.

Luke, A., Land, R., Christie, P., Kolatsis, A., & Noblett, G. (2002). *Standard Australian English: Languages for Queensland Aboriginal and Torres Strait Islander students.* Brisbane, QLD: Indigenous Education Consultative Body.

Macklin, J., & Garrett, P. (2009). New National Approach to Preserve Indigenous Languages. Retrieved from http://www.jennymacklin.fahcsia.gov.au/mediareleases/2009/Pages/preserve_indigenous_languages_10aug09.aspx

Maddison, S. (2008). Indigenous autonomy matters: What's wrong with the Australian Government's 'intervention' in Aboriginal communities. *Australian Journal of Human Rights, 14*(1), 41–61.

Makin, C., & Ibbotson, D. (1973). *Survey of education of Aboriginal children in selected Western Australian schools.* Perth: Graylands Teachers College.

Malcolm, I. G. (1993). *Aboriginal English inside and outside the classroom.* Paper presented at the 18th Annual Congress of the Applied

Linguistics Association of Australia. Adelaide. 1993.

——. (1995). *Language and communication enhancement for Two-Way education: Report to the Department of Employment, Education and Training.* Perth: Centre for Applied Language Research, Edith Cowan University.

——. (1998). 'You gotta talk the proper way': Language and education. In G. Partington (Ed.), *Perspectives on Aboriginal and Torres Strait Islander education* (pp. 117–46). Katoomba: Social Science Press.

Malcolm, I. G., & Grote, E. (2007). Aboriginal English: Restructured variety for cultural maintenance. In G. Leitner & I. G. Malcolm (Eds.), *The habitat of Australia's Aboriginal languages: Past, present and future* (pp. 153–79). Berlin: Mouton de Gruyter.

Malcolm, I. G., & Königsberg, P. (2007). Bridging the language gap in education. In G. Leitner & I. Malcolm (Eds.), *The habitat of Australia's Aboriginal languages: Past, present and future* (pp. 267–97). Berlin: Mouton de Gruyter.

Malcolm, I. G., Haig, Y., Königsberg, P., Rochecouste, J., Collard, G., Hill, A., et al. (1999a). *Towards more user-friendly education for speakers of Aboriginal English.* Perth: Centre for Applied Language and Literacy Research, Edith Cowan University and Education Department of Western Australia.

——. (1999b). *Two-Way English.* Perth: Centre for Applied Language and Literacy Research, Edith Cowan University and Education Department of Western Australia.

Malcolm, I. G., & Koscielecki, M. M. (1997). *Aboriginality and English: Report to the Australian Research Council.* Mount Lawley, WA: Centre for Applied Language Research, Edith Cowan University.

Malcolm, I. G., & Rochecouste, J. (2000). Event and story schemas in Australian Aboriginal English discourse. *English World-Wide, 21*(2), 261–89.

Malin, M. (1989). *Invisibility in success, visibility in transgression for the Aboriginal child in the urban classroom: Case studies at home and at school in Adelaide.* Unpublished PhD dissertation, University of Minnesota, Minneapolis.

——. (1990). Why is life so hard for Aboriginal students in urban classrooms? *The Aboriginal Child at School, 18*(1), 9–30.

———. (1998). They listen and they've got respect: Culture and pedagogy. In G. Partington (Ed.), *Perspectives on Aboriginal and Torres Strait Islander education* (pp. 245–73). Katoomba: Social Science Press.

———. (2003). *Is schooling good for Aboriginal children's health?* Canberra: Cooperative Research Centre for Aboriginal Health.

Malin, M., Campbell, K., & Agius, L. (1996). Raising children in the Nunga-Aboriginal way. *Family Matters, 43*, 43–7.

Malin, M., & Maidment, D. (2003). Education, Indigenous survival and well-being: emerging ideas and programs. *Australian Journal of Indigenous Education, 32*, 85–100.

Malin, M., Mitchell, A., Graham, A., Hammond, B., Aston, E., Carter, B., Coleman, N., et al. (2010, September). Racism in Australia is alive and kicking. Poster presentation at the Public Health Association of Australia 40th Annual Conference, Adelaide.

Manne, R. (2001). *The Australian Quarterly Essay – In denial: The stolen generations and the right* (Vol. 1). Melbourne: Schwartz Publishing.

Mansouri, F., Jenkins, L., Morgan, L., & Taouk, M. (2009). *The Impact of racism on the health and wellbeing of young Australians.* Melbourne: The Foundation for Young Australians.

Martin, D. (2001). *Is welfare dependency 'welfare poison'? An assessment of Noel Pearson's proposals for Aboriginal welfare reform* (CAEPR Discussion Paper 213/2001). Canberra: Centre for Aboriginal Policy Research, Australian National University.

Masters, G. (2010). NAPLAN and My School: Shedding light on a work in progress. *Teacher, 2010*(213), 22–5.

McCarthy, J. S. (2009). Control of intestinal helminths in Indigenous communities. *Microbiology Australia, 30*(5), 200–201.

McConnochie, K. (1982). Aborigines and Australian education: Historical perspectives. In J. Sherwood (Ed.), *Aboriginal education issues and innovations.* Perth: Creative Research.

McDonald, E. L., Bailie, R. S., Brewster, D., & Morris, P. S. (2008). Are hygiene and public health interventions likely to improve outcomes for Australian Aboriginal children living in remote communities? A systematic review of the literature. *BMC*

Public Health, 8(2), Article 153. Retrieved from http://www.
biomedcentral.com/1471-2458/8/153

McDonald, E. L., Bailie, R. S., Rumbold, A. R., Morris, P. S.,
& Paterson, B. A. (2008). Preventing growth faltering among
Australian Indigenous children: Implications for policy and
practice. *Medical Journal of Australia, 188*(Supplement 8), S84–S86.

McFadden, M., & Munns, G. (2002). Student engagement and the
social relations of pedagogy. *British Journal of Sociology of Education,
23*(3), 357–66.

McGregor, R. (1997). *Imagined destinies: Australian Aborigines and
the Doomed Race Theory, 1880–1939.* Melbourne: Melbourne
University Press.

McKeich, R. (1969). Part-Aboriginal education. In R. Berndt
(Ed.), *Thinking about Aboriginal welfare.* Nedlands: Department of
Anthropology, University of Western Australia Press.

McKenry, R. (1996). *Deadly eh, Cuz!: Teaching speakers of Koorie
English.* Melbourne, VIC: Language Australia.

McLaren, P. (1998). *Life in schools: An introduction to pedagogy in the
foundations of education.* New York: Longmans.

McMeekin, G. (1969). Race relations in Aboriginal education. In
T. Roper (Ed.), *Aboriginal education the teacher's role.* Canberra:
National Union of Australian University Students.

McNamara, L. (2000). Tackling racial hatred: Conciliation,
reconciliation and football. *Australian Journal of Human Rights,
6*(2), 5. Retrieved from www.austlii.edu.au/au/journals/
AJHR/2000/18.html

Miller, J. (1985). *Koori: A will to win-the heroic resistance: Survival and
triumph of black Australia.* Sydney: Angus & Robertson.

Mills, C., & Gale, T. (2002). Schooling and the production of social
inequalities: What can and should we be doing? *Melbourne Studies
in Education, 43*(1), 107–25.

Milnes, P. (1985). *A history of Aboriginal education in Western Australia
with particular reference to the Goldfields District since 1927.* PhD thesis,
University of New England, NSW.

MindMatters. (2010). *Community matters draft manuscript.* Retrieved
from http://www.mindmatters.edu.au/whole_school_approach/
community_matters_draft.html

Minister for Education Training and Youth Affairs. (2005). *Minister archive: 'Mutual Obligation' Questions and Answers* [Media release]. Retrieved from http://www.dest.gov.au/archive/ministers/kemp/kqa_mo.htm

Ministerial Council for Education, Early Childhood Development and Youth Affairs (MCEECDYA). (2008). *Statements of learning.* Retrieved form http://www.mceetya.edu.au/mceecdya/statements_of_learning,22835.html

———. (2010). *Aboriginal and Torres Strait Islander Education and Action Plan 2010-2014.* Canberra: MCEECDYA.

———. (2000). *Report of MCEETYA taskforce on Indigenous education.* Canberra: MCEETYA.

———. (2006). *Australian directions in Indigenous education 2005-2008.* MCEETYA Australian Education Systems Officials Committee, Senior Officials Working Party on Indigenous Education. Carlton South, VIC: MCEETYA. Retrieved from http://www.mceecdya.edu.au/mceecdya/publications,11582.html

———. (2008). *Melbourne declaration on educational goals for young Australians.* Melbourne: MCEETYA. Retrieved June 6, 2011, from http://www.mceetya.edu.au/mceecdya/melbourne_declaration,25979.html

Monteith, S. (2010, 14 April). *Re: NAPLAN Results - What is the problem* [My School Forum Comment]. Retrieved September 4, 2011, from http://www.myschool.com.au/forum/topics/naplan-results-what-is-the?commentId=2031059%3AComment%3A27334

Mooney, J. (2011). *Teaching Aboriginal studies: A critical analysis of core Aboriginal studies teacher education courses and their impact on schooling.* Unpublished PhD thesis, University of Western Sydney, Australia.

Morris, P. S., Leach, A. J., Silberberg, P., Mellon, G., Wilson, C., Hamilton, E., et al. (2005). Otitis media in young Aboriginal children from remote communities in Northern and Central Australia: A cross-sectional survey. *BMC Pediatrics, 5*(1), 1–10.

Moses, K., & Yallop, C. (2008). Questions about questions. In J. Simpson & G. Wigglesworth (Eds.), *Children's language and multilingualism: Indigenous language use at home and school* (pp. 113–28). New York: Continuum International Publishing Group.

Munns, G. (2005). School as a cubbyhouse: Tensions between intent and practice in classroom curriculum. *Curriculum Perspectives, 25*(1), 1–12.

———. (2007). A sense of wonder: Student engagement in low SES school communities. *International Journal of Inclusive Education, 11,* 301–15.

Munns, G., Martin, A., & Craven, R. (2008). To free the spirit? Motivation and engagement of Indigenous students. *Australian Journal of Indigenous Education, 37,* 98–107.

Munns, G., & McFadden, M. G. (2000). First chance, second chance or last chance? Resistance and response to education. *British Journal of Sociology of Education, 21,* 59–76.

Mushin, I., & Gardner, R. (2009). Silence is talk: conversational silence in Australian Aboriginal talk-in-interaction. *Journal of Pragmatics, 41*(10), 2033–52.

My School website. (2011). http://www.myschool.edu.au

Nakata, M. (1999). History, cultural diversity, and English language teaching. In P. Wignell (Ed.), *Double power: English literacy and Indigenous education* (pp. 5–22). Melbourne: Language Australia.

Nakata, M. (2007). The cultural interface. *The Australian Journal of Indigenous Education, 36,* 7–14.

National Aboriginal Community Controlled Health Organisation. (2005). *National guide to a preventive health assessment in Aboriginal and Torres Strait Islander peoples.* Melbourne: Royal Australian College of General Practitioners.

National Organisation for Fetal Alcohol Syndrome and Related Disorders. (2009). Submission to the House of Representatives Standing Committee on Aboriginal and Torres Strait Islander Affairs: Inquiry into the High Level of Involvement of Indigenous Juveniles and young Adults into the Criminal Justice System. Retrieved from http://202.14.81.34/house/committee/atsia/sentencing/subs/Sub073.pdf

National Tertiary Education Union (2003, October 29). *Federal Government withholds ABSTUDY review.* Retrieved from http://www.nteu.org.au/getinvolved/equal/indige nous/news/2003/7926

Nero, S. J. (Ed.). (2006). *Dialects, Englishes, creoles, and education.* Mahwah, NJ: Lawrence Erlbaum Associates.

Neville, A. (1947). *Australia's coloured minority.* Sydney: Currawong Publishing.

Newmann, F., & Associates. (1996). *Authentic achievement: Restructuring schools for intellectual quality.* San Francisco: Josey Bass.

New South Wales Board of Studies. (2000). *Evaluative Research into the Office of the Board of Studies', Aboriginal Careers Aspiration Program for Aboriginal Students in NSW High Schools.* Retrieved from http://ab-ed.boardofstudies.nsw.edu.au/go/resources/aboriginal-career-aspirations-program-acap

———. (2008). *Working with Aboriginal Communities: A Guide to Community Consultation and Protocols* (Revised Edition). Sydney: Board of Studies, NSW

———. (2011). *Aboriginal studies.* Retrieved May 28, 2011, http://www.schools.nsw.edu.au/learning/yr07_10/hsie/aboriginal/index.php

New South Wales Government. (2010). Submission to the House of Representatives Standing Committee on Aboriginal and Torres Strait Islander Affairs Inquiry into the High Level of Involvement of Indigenous Juveniles and young Adults into the Criminal Justice System.

Nicholls, C. (2009). Radical hope: Correspondence. *Quarterly Essay, 36*(2009), 93–102. Retrieved September 1, 2011, from http://search.informit.com.au/fullText;dn=327928328977217;res=IELHSS

Noonuccal, O. (2007). *Father Sky and Mother Earth.* Melbourne: John Wiley and Sons.

Norris, R. (2001). Australian Indigenous employment disadvantage: What, why and where to from here? *Journal of Economic and Social Policy, 5*(2). Retrieved form http://epubs.scu.edu.au/jesp/vol5/iss2/2

Northern Territory Department of Education. (2000). *Aboriginal and Islander Tertiary Aspirations Program.* Retrieved from http://www.mceecdya.edu.au/mceecdya/stepping/projects/17/rec17-nt.htm

Northern Territory Emergency Response Review Board. (2008). *Report of the NTER Board.* Canberra: Attorney General's Department. Retrieved from http://www.nterreview.gov.au/docs/report_nter_review.PDF

Nyquist, G. (n.d.). *Elitism good and bad.* Retrieved from

http://homepage.mac.com/machiavel/Text/elitism.html

Ogbu, J. (1978). *Minority education and caste: The American system in cross-cultural perspective.* New York: Academic Press.

O'Grady, K.-A. F., & Chang, A. B. (2010). Lower respiratory infections in Australian Indigenous children. *Journal of Paediatrics and Child Health, 46*(9), 461–5.

Oliver, R. (2009). How young is too young? Investigating negotiation of meaning and feedback in children aged five to seven years. In A. Mackey & C. Polio (Eds.), *Multiple perspective on interaction: Second language research in honor of Susan M. Gass* (pp. 135–56). NY: Routledge.

Olsen, L., Bhattacharya, J., & Scharf, A. (2006). *Cultural competency: What it is and why it matters.* Emeryville, California: California Tomorrow. Retrieved from http://www.californiatomorrow.org/

Paradies, Y., & Cunningham, J. (2009). Experiences of racism among urban Indigenous Australians: Findings from the DRUID study. *Ethnic and Racial Studies, 32*(3), 548–73.

Parbury, N. (1996). *Interview: Why teach Aboriginal Studies?* [Film]. Sydney: University of New South Wales.

Parliament of Victoria & Drugs and Crime Prevention Committee. (2002). *Inquiry into the inhalation of volatile substances: Final report.* Melbourne: Drugs and Crime Prevention Committee.

Partington, G. (Ed.). (1998). *Perspectives on Aboriginal and Torres Strait Islander education.* Katoomba: Social Science Press.

——. (2004). *Report on the Attendance Grants Program: An evaluation for the Aboriginal Education Directorate of the Department of Education and Training of the projects conducted in 2003.* Mt. Lawley, Perth: Edith Cowan University, Centre for Indigenous Australian Knowledges.

Partington, G., & Galloway, A. (2005). Effective practices in teaching Indigenous students with conductive hearing loss. *Childhood Education, 82*, 101-6.

Partington, G., Galloway, A., Byrne, M., Anderson, K., Ferguson, N., et al. (2011). *The Happy Kids program.* Mt Lawley, WA: Edith Cowan University.

Partington, G., Galloway, A., Sibbel, J., Gower, G., Gray, J., Grote, E., & Goh, K. (2009). *Longitudinal study of student retention and*

success in high school (Follow The Dream/Partnerships For Success).
Mt Lawley, Perth: Centre for Indigenous Australian Knowledges,
Edith Cowan University.

Partington, G., Godfrey, J., & Richer, K. (2001). 'The principal
is hopeless. She needs a good boot in the read end': Cultural
diversity and conflicting school agendas. Paper presented at the
Australian Association for Research in Education Conference.
Fremantle, December 2001. Available at: http://www.aare.edu.
au/01pap/par01107.htm.

Partington, G., & Gray, J. (2003). Classroom management and
Aboriginal students. In Q. Beresford & G. Partington, (Eds.),
Reform and resistance in Aboriginal education: The Australian experience.
Perth: University of Western Australia Press.

Partington, G., & McCudden, V. (1992). *Ethnicity and education.*
Wentworth Falls: Social Science Press.

——. (1990). Classroom interaction: some qualitative and
quantitative differences in a mixed ethnicity classroom. *Australian
Journal of Teacher Education, 15* (2), Article 4. Available at:
http://ro.ecu.edu.au/ajte/vol15/iss2/4.

Partington, G., Kickett-Tucker, C., & Mack, L. (1999). *Barrumundi
school: Alternative educational program.* Mt Lawley, Perth:
Kurongkurl Katitjin, Edith Cowan University. Unpublished
report.

Peach, I. (2004). *Managing complexity: The lessons of horizontal policy-
making in the provinces.* Canada: University of Regina.

Pearson, N. (2003). *Our right to take responsibility.* Victoria: The
Institute of Public Administration Australia. Retrieved from
http://www.vic.ipaa.org.au/document/item/106

Pearson, N. (2004, April 24). When welfare is a curse.
The Age. Retrieved from http://www.theage.com.au/
articles/2004/04/22/1082616260495.html

Pearson, N. (2007, December 1) 'Sorry we require a synthesis'. *The
Australian.*

——. (2009a) *Up from the Mission: Selected writings.* Melbourne: Black
Inc.

——. (2009b) Radical hope: education and equality in Australia.
Quarterly Essay, 35(2009), 1–106. Retrieved from

http://search.informit.com.au/fullText;dn=144579891796529;res =IELHSS

Pedersen, A., & Walker, I. (2000). Urban Aboriginal-Australian and Anglo-Australian children: In-group preference, self-concept, and teachers' academic evaluations. *Journal of Community & Applied Social Psychology, 10*(3), 183–97.

Peters, P. (2007). *The Cambridge guide to Australian English usage.* Cambridge, UK: Cambridge University Press.

Pinar, W. (1981). Whole, bright, deep with understanding': Issues in qualitative research and autobiographical method. *Journal of Curriculum Studies, 3*(3), 173–88.

Plevitz, L. (2007). Systemic racism: the hidden barrier to educational success for Indigenous school students. *Australian Journal of Education, 51*(1), 54–71.

Preston, G. (1994). Hearing health needs for Aboriginal and Torres Strait Islander people. *Australian Family Physician, 23*(1), 51–3.

Prime Minister's Youth Pathways Action Plan Taskforce. (2001). *Footprints to the future.* Canberra: Department of Prime Minister and Cabinet.

Productivity Commission. (2009). *Overcoming Indigenous disadvantage: Key indicators 2009.* Canberra: AGPS.

Purdie, N., & Buckley, S. (2010). *School attendance and retention of Indigenous Australian students.* Canberra: Australian Institute of Health and Welfare/Australian Institute of Family Studies.

Purdie, N., Dudgeon, P. & Walker, R. (Eds.). (2010). *Working together: Aboriginal and Torres Strait Islander mental health and wellbeing principles and practice.* Canberra: Australian Government Department of Health and Ageing.

Purdie, N., Frigo, T., Ozolins, C., Noblett, C. G., Thieberger, N., Sharp, J. (2008). *Indigenous languages programmes in Australian schools: A way forward.* Canberra: Department of Employment, Education and Workplace Relations.

Purdie, N., Tripcony, P., Boulton-Lewis, G., Fanshawe, J., & Gunstone, A. (2000). *Positive self-identity for Indigenous students and its relationship to school outcomes.* Canberra: Department of Education, Training and Youth Affairs.

Pyne, C. (2011). SA: Oppn says school website will highlight, not solve, problems. *The Australian Teacher.* Retrieved 7 November 2011 from http://www.ozteacher.com.au.

Queensland Department of Education. (2000). *Enhancing career opportunities: 1999 performance report on the Aboriginal and Torres Strait Islander Career Aspirations Pathways Program (AICAPP).* Brisbane: Queensland Government.

Queensland Government. (2010). *Annual highlights report for Queensland's discrete Indigenous communities July 2009 – June 2010.* Brisbane: Queensland Government. Retrieved September 1, 2011, from www. parliament.queensland.gov.au

Quitadamo, T. C. (2009, May). Beyond post-sorry: A letter to child carers. *SNAICC News*, pp. 19. Retrieved from http://www. snaicc.asn.au/_uploads/rsfil/02538.pdf

Ranzijn, R., McConnochie, K., & Nolan, W. (2009). *Psychology and Indigenous Australians: Foundations of cultural competence.* South Yarra, VIC: Palgrave Macmillan.

Ravichandran, L. (2008, 5 May 2011). *School problems and the family physician: School attendance problems.* Retrieved from http://www.medindia.net/education/familymedicine/ schoolproblems-attendance.htm

Reconciliation Australia. (2011). Available from http://www. reconciliation.org.au

Reconciliation Network. (2007). *Stolen generations fact sheet.* Retrieved April 14, 2011, from http://reconciliaction.org.au/nsw/ education-kit/stolen-generations/

Reeders, E. (2008). The collaborative construction of knowledge in a traditional context. In J. Simpson & G. Wigglesworth (Eds.), *Children's language and multilingualism: Indigenous language use at home and school.* (pp. 113–28). New York: Continuum International Publishing Group.

Reynolds, H. (1994, August). Invasion versus settlement debate wears on. *The Weekend Australian,* pp. 13–14.

——. (1997). Presentation at the seminar 'A view from the other side of the hill' held at the State Library of NSW, May 24. Quoted in Australians for Reconciliation. (1997). *Footsteps, 3,* 6.

Richards, K. (2007). *Juveniles' contact with the criminal justice system.* Canberra: Australian Institute of Criminology.

Rigney, L. I. (2010). Closing the gap? Let's start by closing the gap in strategy. *The Spray 2010*(2). NSW Institute of Teachers: ACER Press.

Rittle, H., & Webber, M. (1973). Dilemmas in a general theory of planning. *Policy Sciences, 4*, 155–64.

Robinson, C., & Bamblett, L. (1998). *Making a difference: The impact of Australia's Indigenous Education and Training policy.* Leabrook, SA: National Centre for Vocational Educational Research Limited.

Ross, S. (2009). *Youth transitions: Re-entry into second chance education.* Unpublished master's thesis, Edith Cowan University, Western Australia.

Ross, S., & Gray, J. (2005). Transitions and re-engagement through second chance education. *Australian Educational Researcher, 32*(3), 103–40.

Rowe, K. (2003). *The importance of teacher quality as a key determinant of students' experiences and outcomes of schooling.* Background paper to keynote address presented at ACER Research Conference, 'Building teacher quality: What does the research tell us?', 19–21 October 2003, Melbourne.

Royal Commission into Aboriginal Deaths in Custody (Commissioner Elliott Johnston). (1991). *National Report* (Vol. 2). Canberra: Australian Government Publishing Service.

Royal Commission into the Treatment and Conditions of Aborigines. (1934). *National Report: Votes and Proceedings* (Vol. 1). Western Australian Parliament.

Rudd, K. (2008). *Apology to Australia's Indigenous peoples.* Retrieved from http://australia.gov.au/about-australia/our-country/our-people/apology-to-australias-indigenous-peoples

Russell, D. (2007). *What educators can do to help Aboriginal students stay at school and succeed* (Online Refereed Article No. 48). Retrieved April 18, 2011, from http://www.pipalya.com/rlt/ascs/What_Educators_Can_Do.pdf

Rutter, M., & Madge, N. (1976). *Cycles of disadvantage: A review of the research.* London: Heinemann.

Sarra, C. (2005). Strong and smart: The way forward for Indigenous boys. *Boys in Schools Bulletin, 8*(2), 4–9. Retrieved from http://www.newcastle.edu.au/Resources/Research%20Centres/Family%20Action%20Centre/downloads/bis-bulletin/

BISB-2005-Vol8-No2.pdf

Saunders, V., West, R., & Usher, K. (2010). Applying Indigenist research methodologies in health research: Experiences in the borderlands. Australian *Journal of Indigenous Education, 39,* 1–7.

Schapper, H. (1969). Present needs of Aborigines. In D. Hutchinson (Ed.), *Aboriginal progress: A new era?* Nedlands: University of Western Australia Press.

Schmidt, R. (1990). The role of consciousness in second language learning. *Applied Linguistics, 11*(2), 129–58.

Seagrim, G. (1974). *Cognitive development of the Aborigines.* Sydney: Macquarie University Press.

Secretariat of National Aboriginal and Islander Child Care (SNAICC). (2011). *Growing up our way: Aboriginal and Torres Strait Islander child rearing practices matrix.* North Fitzroy: SNAICC.

Senate Community Affairs References Committee. (2010). *Hear us: Inquiry into hearing health in Australia.* Canberra: Parliament of Australia: Senate.

Senate Employment, Workplace Relations, Small Business and Educational References Committee. (2000). *Katu Kalpa: Report on the inquiry into the effectiveness of education and training programs for Indigenous Australians.* Canberra: Senate Printing Unit.

Senate Select Committee on Regional and Remote Indigenous Communities. (2010). *Fourth report, 2010.* Canberra: Department of the Senate.

Senior Secondary Assessment Board of South Australia (SSABSA). (2001). *SSABSA annual report.* Retrieved August 30, 2011, from http://www.sace.sa.edu.au/c/document_library/get_file?p_l_id= 10423&folderId=111074&name=DLFE-6406.pdf

Seth, S. P. (1994). Australia's Aboriginal problem. *Economic and Political Weekly, 29*(41), 2661.

Sharifian, F. (2001). Schema-based processing in Australian speakers of Aboriginal English. *Language and Intercultural Communication 1*(2), 120–34.

——. (2003). On cultural conceptualisations. *Journal of Cognition and Culture 3*(3), 187–207.

——. (2005). Cultural conceptualizations on English words: A study of Aboriginal children in Perth. *Language and Education 19*(1), 74–88.

481

——. (2006). The cultural-conceptual approach and world Englishes: The case of Aboriginal English. *World Englishes, 25*(1), 11–22.

——. (2008): Aboriginal English in the classroom: An asset or a liability? *Language Awareness, 17*(2), 131–8.

——. (2009). On collective cognition and language. In H. Pishwa (Ed.), *Language and social cognition: Expression of social mind.* Berlin/New York: Mouton de Gruyter.

Sharifian, F., Rochecouste, J., & Malcolm, I. G. (2004). 'But it was all a bit confusing…': Comprehending Aboriginal English texts. *Language, Culture, and Curriculum, 17*(3), 203–28.

Shoemaker, A. (Ed.). (1994). *Oodgeroo: A tribute.* Australia: University of Queensland Press.

Siegel, J. (2010). *Second dialect acquisition.* Cambridge: University of Cambridge Press.

Sims, M., O'Connor, M., & Forrest, M. (2003). Aboriginal families and the school system. In Q. Beresford & G. Partington (Eds.), *Reform and resistance in Aboriginal education.* Perth: University of Western Australia.

Smith, B. (2011). Community involvement. In R. Craven (Ed.), *Teaching Aboriginal studies: A complete guide to teaching Aboriginal studies in both primary and secondary schools* (2nd ed., pp. 194–209). Australia: Allen & Unwin.

Social Inclusion Board. (2007). *Supporting young people's success - Forging the links: Learning from the School Retention Action Plan.* Adelaide, SA: Department of the Premier and Cabinet.

Steering Committee for the Review of Government Service Provision. (2005). *Overcoming Indigenous disadvantage: Key indicators 2005.* Melbourne: Productivity Commission.

——. (2009). *Overcoming Indigenous disadvantage: Key indicators 2009.* Canberra: Productivity Commission.

Strakosch, E. (2009). A reconsideration of the Political Significance of Shared Responsibility Agreements. *Australian Journal of Politics and History, 55*(1), 80–96.

Stringer, R. (2007). A Nightmare of the neocolonial kind: Politics of suffering in Howard's Northern Territory Intervention. *Borderlands e-journal, 6*(2). Retrieved from http://www.borderlands. net.au/vol6no2_2007/stringer_intervention.htm

Taft, R., Damson, J., & Beazley, P. (1970). *Aborigines in Australian society: Attitudes and conditions.* Canberra: ANU Press.

Tatz, C. (1999). *Aboriginal suicide is different: Aboriginal youth suicide in New South Wales, the Australian Capital Territory and New Zealand - Towards a model of explanation and alleviation: Report to the Criminology Research Council* (CRC Project 25/96-7: 164). Sydney: Criminology Research Council.

Taylor, R. (Ed.). (1995). *African American youth: Their social and economic status in the United States.* Westport: Praeger.

Taylor, H. R., & National Indigenous Eye Health Survey Team. (2009). *National Indigenous eye health survey: Minum barreng (tracking eyes)* [full report]. Melbourne: Indigenous Eye Health Unit, The University of Melbourne.

The Australian Teacher. (2011) SA: Oppn says school website will highlight, not solve, problems. *The Australian Teacher.* Retrieved 1 September 2011 from http://ozteacher.com.au/html/index.php?searchword=oppn+says+school+web&ordering=&searchphrase=all&Itemid=173&option=com_search

Thomson, N. (2003). The impact of health on the education of Aboriginal children. In Q. Beresford & G. Partington (Eds.), *Reform and resistance in Aboriginal education: The Australian experience* (pp. 110–32). Crawley, WA: The University of Western Australia Press.

Thomson, N. (2005). Cultural respect and related concepts: a brief summary of the literature. *Australian Indigenous Health Bulletin, 5*(4), 1–11. Retrieved from http://www.uq.edu.au/hupp/index.html?page=50247&pid=25173

Tilbrook, L. (1977). *Moora: Aboriginal children in a wheatbelt town.* Perth: Mt Lawley College of Advanced Education.

Turner, M. K. (2010). *Iwenhe Tyerrtye – What it means to be an Aboriginal person.* Alice Springs: IAD Press.

University of Queensland (2009). Aboriginal and Torres Strait Islander Employment Policy. Available at http://www.uq.edu.au/hupp/index.html?page=50247.

Vinson, A. (2002). *Inquiry into public education in New South Wales.* Sydney: NSW Public Education Enquiry NSW. Retrieved from http://www.pub-ed-inquiry.org

Walker, J. C. (1992). Education for democracy: The representation/ participation dualism. *Educational Theory, 42*(3), 315–30.

Walker, K. (1969). Aborigines: Assets or Liabilities? In S. S. Dunn & C. M. Tatz (Eds.), *Aborigines and Education* (pp. 104–12). Melbourne: Sun Books.

Walker, N., & Wigglesworth, G. (2001). The effect of conductive hearing loss on phonological awareness, reading and spelling of urban Aboriginal students. *The Australian and New Zealand Journal of Audiology, 23*(1), 37–51.

Walker, Y. (1993, August). Aboriginal family issues. *Family Matters, 35*, 51–3.

Walsh, M. (1991). Conversational styles and intercultural communication: An example from northern Australia. *Australian Journal of Communication, 18*(1), 1–12.

Watson, D. (2002). *Recollections of a Bleeding Heart: A Portrait of Paul Keating PM.* Sydney: Knoff.

Watts, B. (1978). *Aboriginal futures: Review of research and developments and related policies in the education of Aborigines.* Draft Confidential Report. Available May O'Brien Collection, Edith Cowan University.

Watts, B., & Henry, M. (1978). *Focus on parent/child: Extending the teaching competence of urban Aboriginal mothers.* Canberra: Australian Government Publishing Service.

Welch, A. (1996). *Australian education: Reform or crisis?* St Leonards, NSW: Allen & Unwin.

Western Australian Aboriginal Education and Training Council. (2010). Western Australian Aboriginal Education and Training Council submission to the 2010 Indigenous Education Action Plan. Retrieved June 10, 2011, from http://www.mceecdya.edu. au/verve/_resources/IEAP2010Sub-WA_Aboriginal_Ed_and_ Training_Council.doc

Western Australian Aboriginal Legal Service [WAALS]. (2009). *Inquiry into the high level of involvement of Indigenous juveniles and young adults in the criminal justice system.* Submission to the House of Representatives Standing Committee on Aboriginal and Torres Strait Islander Affairs.

Western Australian Department of Health. (2000). *Western Australian Aboriginal Health Strategy: A strategic approach to improving the health of Aboriginal people in Western Australia.* Western Australian Joint Planning Forum on Aboriginal Health. Perth: Western Australian Department of Health. Retrieved from http://www.aboriginal. health.wa.gov.au/docs/waahs.pdf

Westley, I. (1984). *Irregular attendance: Education and treatment.* A Report of the Education Department of South Australia and Flinders University.

What Works: The Work Program. (2006). *Improving outcomes for Indigenous students: Successful practice* (2nd, revised edition). Retrieved from http://www.whatworks.edu.au/ upload/1251417159008_file_SuccessPrac.pdf

———. (2010). *The Workbook and guide for school educators.* Abbotsford, VIC: National Curriculum Services Pty Ltd and the Australian Curriculum Studies Association. Retrieved August 25, 2011, from http://www.whatworks.edu.au/upload/1269678468869_file_ WorkbookEd3.pdf

———. (2011). *Improving outcomes for Indigenous students: Successful practice.* Retrieved June 10, 2011, from http://www.whatworks. edu.au/dbAction.do?cmd=displaySitePage1&subcmd=select &id=353

White, R. (2009). Indigenous youth and gangs as family. *Youth Studies Australia, 28*(3), 47–56.

Wieviorka, M. (1995). *The Arena of Racism.* London: Sage.

Wild, R., & Anderson, P. (2007). *Ampe Akelyernemane Meke Mekarle: 'Little Children are Sacred Report': Report of the Northern Territory Board of Inquiry into the Protection of Aboriginal Children from Sexual Abuse.* Darwin: Northern Territory Government. Retrieved from http://www.inquirysaac.nt.gov.au/

Wilkinson, R., & Marmot, M. (2003). *Social determinants of health: The solid facts.* Denmark: World Health Organisation.

Williamson, I., & Cullingford, C. (1997). The uses and misuses of 'alienation' in the social sciences and education. *British Journal of Education studies, 45*(3), 263–75.

Wills, R.-A., & Coory, M. D. (2008). Effect of smoking among

Indigenous and non-Indigenous mothers on preterm birth and full-term low birthweight. *Medical Journal of Australia, 189*(9), 490–4.

Wilson-Miller, J. (1997). *Annual Lecture: History Council of NSW.* Sydney: Government House.

Wilson, J. (1995). *Social work practice and Indigenous Australians.* Sydney: Federation Press.

World Health Organization. (2004). *Chronic suppurative Otitis Media: Burden of illness and management options.* Geneva: World Health Organization.

Zhang, Q., & Zhu, W. (2008). Exploring emotion in teaching: Emotional labor, burnout, and satisfaction in Chinese higher education. *Communication Education, 57*(1), 105–22.

Zubrick, S. R., Lawrence, D. M., Silburn, S. R., Blair, E. M., Milroy, H., Wilkes, T., et al. (2004). *The Western Australian Aboriginal child health survey [Volume 1]: The health of Aboriginal children and young people.* Perth: Telethon Institute for Child Health Research.

Zubrick, S. R., Silburn, S. R., Lawrence, D. M., Mitrou, F. G., Dalby, R. B., Blair, E. M., et al. (2005). *The Western Australian Aboriginal child health survey [Volume 2]: The social and emotional wellbeing of Aboriginal children and young people.* Perth: Curtin University of Technology and Telethon Institute for Child Health Research

Zubrick, S. R., Silburn, S. R., De Maio, J. A., Shepherd, C., Griffin, J. A., Dalby, R. B., et al. (2006). *The Western Australian Aboriginal child health survey [Volume 3]: Improving the educational experiences of Aboriginal children and young people.* Perth: Curtin University of Technology and Telethon Institute for Child Health Research.

CONTRIBUTORS

Quentin Beresford

Professor Quentin Beresford has taught politics and public policy at Edith Cowan University for over 20 years. He is the author/co-author of ten books including several on Aboriginal affairs. These include *Rites of Passage: Aboriginal Youth Crime and Justice* (1996); *Our State of Mind: Racial Planning and the Stolen Generations* (1998) and the multi-award winning biography of Aboriginal leader Rob Riley: *Rob Riley: An Aboriginal Leader's Quest for Justice* (2006).

Jane Burns

Jane Burns is a Senior Research Officer with the Australian Indigenous Health*InfoNet*, based at Edith Cowan University (ECU) in Perth. She joined the Health*InfoNet* more than ten years ago after completing an honours degree in health science from ECU. Jane also works as a volunteer at a women's health centre where she sits on the board of management. Jane has contributed to a number of reviews about Indigenous health and chapters in *The Health of Indigenous Australians*.

Matt Byrne

Dr Matt Byrne is a lecturer in the School of Education at Edith Cowan University. Matt is an experienced teacher and teacher educator. He is involved in Aboriginal education and research and undergraduate and postgraduate teaching. He is actively involved in the development and delivery of courses within and outside the university sector on developing the cultural competence of non-Indigenous undergraduates and professionals so that they are able to work respectfully in partnership to improve outcomes for Indigenous people.

Rhonda Craven

Professor Rhonda Craven is Head of the Educational Excellence and Equity Research Program, Centre for Educational Research, University of Western Sydney. She is a highly accomplished researcher having successfully completed numerous nationally funded research projects in Australia. She is an expert in self-concept, key psycho-social drivers of potential, Indigenous education, and interventions that make a tangible difference in educational settings. Her publications include: eight authored books, 35 book chapters, 61 refereed journal articles and 157 refereed conference papers.

Sharon Gollan

Sharon Gollan is a descendent of the Ngarrindjeri nation of South Australia, with cultural connections to many communities within and beyond South Australia. Sharon has worked professionally and academically in a range of human services fields in Australia. Sharon has over 30 years of experience in the health, youth, children and community services sector with a primary focus on creating better services for Aboriginal people.

Graeme Gower

Graeme Gower is a Senior Lecturer in Kurongkurl Katitjin, the Centre for Indigenous Education & Research at Edith Cowan University. He is a descendant of the Yawuru people of Broome and has been involved in Indigenous education for 32 years, eight years as a primary school teacher and 24 years in higher education. He is actively involved in the development and delivery of courses both in and outside the university sector to equip future Indigenous leaders and to develop the cultural competence of non-Indigenous undergraduates and professionals so that they are able to work respectfully in partnership to improve outcomes for Indigenous people. He is also actively involved in research in Aboriginal education.

Jan Gray

Dr Jan Gray is an Associate Professor of Education at Edith Cowan University. She has a strong theoretical and practical understanding of two key areas: The factors impacting on development of a school culture conducive to student engagement; and the framework within which school leaders can implement changes in policies and practices to support the sustained development of such a school culture. Her recent research outcomes include 38 international and national publications.

Dr Ellen Grote

Dr Ellen Grote has a background in applied linguistics and consults for various government departments and university research centres. Her research interests include Aboriginal English and cross-cultural communication in education, vocational education training, legal and justice contexts; and Aboriginal education more generally. Her publications include Two-Way bi-dialectal education professional development materials; journal articles/book chapters on Aboriginal English and second language acquisition and proficiency.

Merridy Malin

Dr Merridy Malin teaches research methods to Aboriginal researchers at the Aboriginal Health Council of South Australia. She has long-term experience in, and commitment to, research and education in Aboriginal communities. She has published in the areas of Aboriginal education, childrearing and the social determinants of health.

Helen McCarthy

Dr Helen McCarthy is coordinator of Fairway UWA – an alternative entry pathway to The University of Western Australia. She has more than thirty years experience working with primary, secondary and tertiary Aboriginal students. She has worked extensively in regional and remote communities in Arnhem Land in the Northern Territory and in Western Australia. Her interest is in two-way bi-dialectal approaches in the development of holistic emergent curriculum frameworks which venerate Indigenous epistemologies. Her critical auto/ethnographic PhD study investigated the struggle for culturally-sensitive educational pathways for at-risk adolescent Aboriginal girls.

Naoibh McLoughlin

Naoibh McLoughlin is an Information Officer within the Australian Indigenous Health*InfoNet*, based at Edith Cowan

University in Perth. Since graduating with an honours degree in science from the University of Western Australia several years ago, she has worked in several fields, including alcohol and other drug research at UWA. She joined the Health*InfoNet* in January 2011.

Geoff Munns

Associate Professor Geoff Munns (University of Western Sydney) researches ways to improve social and academic outcomes for educationally disadvantaged students, including those from Indigenous backgrounds. As a researcher, he has a valuable and rare combination of classroom experiences as a teacher of students in poverty, long standing relationships with, and commitment to, poor Australian communities, and these have formed the focus of his academic pursuits and publications.

Gary Partington

Professor Gary Partington has been working in the field of Aboriginal education for over 25 years. He has conducted extensive research in teaching practices in relation to Aboriginal students, most recently completing two major projects funded by the Australian Research Council and the National Health and Medical Research Council. He has edited, authored and co-authored numerous publications in the field, including many research reports and two previous books on Aboriginal education, *Ethnicity and Education* (1992) and *Perspectives on Aboriginal and Torres Strait Islander Education* (1998).

Dr Judith Rochecouste

Dr Judith Rochecouset is adjunct Senior Lecturer at Monash

University. Her discipline homes are linguistics and applied linguistics and her research interests include international students' experiences, tertiary student learning, enquiry-based learning, academic/tertiary literacy, Aboriginal education, language variation and creole languages. Judith has published widely on Aboriginal English and its implications for the educational success of students across all levels of education, as well as on academic literacy and international student experience.

Neil Thomson

Professor Neil Thomson is Director of the Australian Indigenous HealthInfoNet at Edith Cowan University in Perth, WA and the University's Professor of Indigenous Health. His long-term involvement in Indigenous health is based on tertiary training in medicine, public health, mathematics and anthropology. After five years of clinical medical practice, including positions in the Kimberley region of WA, he has had more than 30 years experience in Indigenous health, where his special interests have been in the translation of research and other information to inform policy-making, planning and service delivery. In 1997, Neil established the Internet-based Australian Indigenous Health*InfoNet* (http://www.healthinfonet.ecu.edu.au/), an innovative way of contributing to 'closing the gap' in health between Indigenous and other Australians by developing and maintaining the evidence base to inform practice and policy in the area of Indigenous health. The Health*InfoNet* also supports the sharing of knowledge and experiences among people working in Indigenous health.

INDEX